ANARCHIST PORTRAITS

Anarchist Portraits

PAUL AVRICH

PRINCETON UNIVERSITY PRESS

This book has been composed in Linotron Sabon type

Clothbound editions of Princeton University Press books are printed
on acid-free paper, and binding materials are chosen for strength
and durability. Paperbacks, although satisfactory for personal
collections, are not usually suitable for library rebinding

Printed in the United States of America by Princeton
University Press, Princeton, New Jersey

Library of Congress Cataloging-in-Publication Data
Avrich, Paul.
Anarchist portraits.
Includes index.
1. Anarchists—Biography. I. Title.
HX830.A96 1988 335'.83'0922 [B] 88–9889
ISBN 0–691–04753–7 (alk. paper)

"V. M. Eikhenbaum (Volin): Portrait of a Russian Anarchist" appears
in *Imperial Russia, 1700–1917: State, Society, Opposition,*
edited by Ezra Mendelsohn and Marshall S. Shatz. © 1988 by
Northern Illinois University Press. Used by
permission of the publisher.

In Memory of Ahrne Thorne
1904–1985

Contents

CONTENTS

PART III : EUROPE AND THE WORLD

Illustrations

Ricardo and Enrique Flores Magón (International Institute of Social History, Amsterdam)

Mollie Steimer, around 1918 (courtesy of Hilda Adel)

Nestor Makhno and Alexander Berkman, Paris, around 1927 (International Institute of Social History, Amsterdam)

Gustav Landauer, around 1917 (Library of Congress)

The Frayhayt Group, New York, 1918; includes Hyman Lachowsky (seated, third from left), Jacob Schwartz (standing, top, second from left), and Jacob Abrams (seated, right of center, mouth and chin obscured) (courtesy of Hilda Adel, in picture, seated, third from right, behind newspaper)

Senya Fleshin, Volin, and Mollie Steimer, Paris, around 1926 (International Institute of Social History, Amsterdam)

Preface

"THE NEW LEFT today," proclaimed a libertarian broadsheet in 1970, "comes upon Anarchy like Schliemann uncovering Troy." Until the Vietnam War, anarchism had seemed a moribund and half-forgotten movement. Since the defeat of the Spanish Revolution of the 1930s, its groups had been scattered and ineffectual, its membership shrinking, its literature drying up. Some historians, indeed, had begun to write the movement's epitaph, when the social ferment of the 1960s and 1970s saw it gain a new lease on life. Anarchist groups revived and multiplied, their adherents taking part in many forms of social activity, from the campaigns for racial equality and nuclear disarmament to resistance to the draft and the war. New anarchist journals made their appearance, as well as pamphlets, books, and manifestoes, which provided a fundamental criticism of state power and questioned the premises of virtually all other schools of political thought.

In the wake of this activity came a spate of scholarly works on anarchist themes—histories, biographies, anthologies, bibliographies—of which the essays in the present volume form a part. Written over a twenty-year period, they focus chiefly on Russia and the United States, my primary areas of specialization, although, anarchism being an international movement with contacts all over the globe, other countries are also included, ranging from Germany and France to Australia and Brazil. One of the longest essays ("Jewish Anarchism in the United States") was written specifically for this collection. The rest have been revised, expanded, and brought up to date, so extensively in some cases as to constitute new texts.

As in my previous writing on anarchist history, my approach has been largely biographical, seeking to evoke the flavor of the movement through the lives of selected participants. Some of the subjects (Bakunin and Kropotkin, for instance) are known to the wider world; most are not. All, however, led interesting lives and were endowed with remarkable human qualities that I have endeavored to convey in brief compass, without ignoring their faults and inconsistencies. Examining the careers of these anarchists, both well known and obscure, one is struck above all by their passionate hatred of injustice, of tyranny in all its forms, and by the perceptiveness of their warnings against the dangers of concentrated power, economic and political alike. They were among the earliest and most consistent opponents of totalitarianism, both of the left and of the right, marked by the growth of a police state, the subjugation of the individual, the dehumanization of labor, and the debasement of language and culture—in short, by what Herbert Spencer described a century ago as "The Coming Slavery."

What Spencer foresaw regarding centralized authority in general and state socialism in particular has been amply borne out in our time. Under modern dictatorships, the values of truth and justice, of decency and honor, of freedom and equality, have been trampled underfoot. One is reminded, when pondering the anarchist criticisms of concentrated power, of George Orwell's characterization of totalitarianism as "a boot stamping on a human face—for ever." One is reminded, too, of the warning of both Proudhon and Bakunin that socialism without liberty would be the worst form of slavery.

OVER THE SPAN of a quarter century I have visited and revisited numerous libraries and archives in quest of material on anarchism. The following are the most important: the International Institute of Social History in Amsterdam, the Labadie Collection of the University of Michigan, the Tamiment Library of New York University, the New York Public Library, the Library of Congress, and the libraries of Harvard and Columbia universities. My thanks are due to the staffs of these institutions for their courteous and efficient assistance. I am grateful, moreover, to Gail Ullman and Elizabeth Gretz of Princeton University Press, who read the manuscript with care and offered their expert advice. I should also like to thank the following publishers and journals for permission to reprint material in this volume: Penguin Books (London), *Black Rose* (Boston), Dover Publications (New York), *Freedom* (London), the *International Review of Social History* (Amsterdam), Charles H. Kerr Publishing Company (Chicago), *The Match!* (Tucson), *The Nation* (New York), *The New Republic* (Washington), and *The Russian Review* (Cambridge, Massachusetts).

My greatest debt, however, is to the late Ahrne Thorne, to whom this volume is dedicated. Ahrne was born on December 26, 1904, of a Hasidic family in Łódź, Poland. In his teens he broke with tradition and worked his way to Paris, where he was converted to anarchism during protests for Sacco and Vanzetti. He emigrated to Toronto in 1930, became an associate of Emma Goldman, and began to write for the *Fraye Arbeter Shtime* (Free Voice of Labor), a Jewish anarchist journal in New York. From 1940, when Ahrne moved to New York, he worked as a printer for Yiddish publications before assuming the editorship of the *Fraye Arbeter Shtime*. Under his supervision, the paper occupied a distinctive niche in the Yiddish intellectual and cultural world. It closed its doors in 1977, after eighty-seven years of publication. Ahrne himself passed away on December 13, 1985, in his eighty-first year.

For more than twenty years I enjoyed the pleasure of Ahrne's acquaintance. He was at all times a genial companion, an interested advisor, and a devoted friend. His was a liberal and humane mind, endlessly curious and inquiring, and there was so much sanity and decency in everything he said and wrote. Those of us who knew him will always be conscious of our debt. Particularly when we need wise counsel and a sympathetic ear will his absence be acutely felt.

New York City   P.H.A.
December 1987

ANARCHIST PORTRAITS

Part I : Russia

CHAPTER ONE

The Legacy of Bakunin

A CENTURY AGO anarchism was a major force within the European
revolutionary movement, and the name of Michael Bakunin, its foremost champion and prophet, was as well known among the workers
and radical intellectuals of Europe as that of Karl Marx, with whom
he was competing for leadership of the First International. In contrast
to Marx, however, Bakunin had won his reputation chiefly as an activist rather than as a theorist of rebellion. He was not one to sit in libraries, studying and writing about predetermined revolutions. Impatient for action, he threw himself into the uprisings of 1848 with
irrepressible exuberance, a Promethean figure moving with the tide of
revolt from Paris to the barricades of Austria and Germany. Men like
Bakunin, a contemporary remarked, "grow in a hurricane and ripen
better in stormy weather than in sunshine."[1]

Bakunin's arrest during the Dresden insurrection of 1849 cut short
his revolutionary activity. He spent the next eight years in prison, six
of them in the dungeons of tsarist Russia. When he finally emerged, his
sentence commuted to a life term in Siberian exile, he was toothless
from scurvy and his health had been seriously impaired. In 1861, however, he escaped his warders and embarked on a sensational odyssey
that circled the globe and made his name a legend and an object of
worship in radical groups all over Europe.

As a romantic rebel and an active force in history, Bakunin exerted
an attraction that Marx could never rival. "Everything about him was
colossal," recalled the composer Richard Wagner, a fellow participant
in the Dresden uprising, "and he was full of a primitive exuberance
and strength."[2] In his *Confession* of 1851, Bakunin himself speaks of

5

his love for "the fantastic, for unusual, unheard-of adventures," opening "vast horizons, the end of which cannot be foreseen."[3] This inspired extravagant dreams in others, and by the time of his death in 1876 he had won a unique place among the adventurers and martyrs of the revolutionary tradition. "This man," said Alexander Herzen, "was born not under an ordinary star but under a comet."[4] His broad magnanimity and childlike enthusiasm, his burning passion for liberty and equality, and his volcanic onslaughts against privilege and injustice all gave him enormous appeal in the libertarian circles of his day.

But Bakunin, as his critics never tire of pointing out, was not a systematic thinker. Nor did he claim to be. For he considered himself a revolutionist of the deed, "not a philosopher and not an inventor of systems like Marx."[5] He refused to recognize any preordained laws of history. He rejected the view that social change depends on the gradual unfolding of "objective" historical conditions. He believed, on the contrary, that individuals shape their own destinies, that their lives cannot be squeezed into a Procrustean bed of abstract sociological formulas. "No theory, no ready-made system, no book that has ever been written will save the world," Bakunin declared. "I cleave to no system. I am a true seeker."[6] By teaching the workers theories, he said, Marx would only succeed in stifling the revolutionary fervor that humans already possess—"the impulse to liberty, the passion for equality, the holy instinct for revolt." Unlike Marx's "scientific socialism," his own socialism, Bakunin asserted, was "purely instinctive."[7]

Bakunin's influence, as Peter Kropotkin remarked, was primarily that of a "moral personality" rather than of an intellectual authority.[8] Although he wrote prodigiously, he did not leave a single book to posterity. He was forever starting new works that, owing to his turbulent existence, were broken off in mid-course and never completed. His literary output, in Thomas Masaryk's description, was a "patchwork of fragments."[9]

And yet his writings, however erratic and unmethodical, abound in flashes of insight that illuminate some of the most important questions of modern times. Kropotkin speaks of the "sometimes unarranged but always brilliant generalizations" of Bakunin's written legacy. In truth, Bakunin has been underestimated both as a thinker and as a stylist, for his literary gifts were of a high order, distinguished by a remarkable clarity and vigor of expression. More than that, in *God and the State* and other works he put forward a coherent social philosophy and theory of revolution, condemning all forms of tyranny and exploitation, religious as well as secular, economic as well as political. His ideas, no less than his personality, have exerted a lasting influence, an influence that was particularly noticeable during the 1960s and 1970s. If ever the spirit of Bakunin spoke, it was in the student quarter of Paris in May 1968, where the black flag of anarchism was prominently displayed and where, among the graffiti inscribed on the walls of the Sorbonne, Bakuninist phrases ("The urge to destroy is a creative urge") occupied a conspicuous place. In our own country the black militants Eldridge Cleaver and George Jackson expressed their indebtedness to Bakunin and Nechaev's *Catechism of a Revolutionary*, which, in 1969, was published in pamphlet form by the Black Panther organization in Berkeley, California. The sociologist Lewis Coser detected a neo-Bakuninist streak in Régis Debray, whom he dubbed "Nechaev in the Andes," after Bakunin's fanatical young disciple.[10] And Frantz Fanon's influential book, *The Wretched of the Earth*, with its Manichaean vision of the despised and rejected rising from the depths to exterminate their colonial oppressors, reads as though lifted out of Bakunin's collected works.

What then are Bakunin's central ideas? Above all, he foresaw the nature of modern revolution more clearly than any of his contemporaries, Marx not excepted. For Marx, the socialist revolution required the emergence of an organized and class-conscious proletariat, something to be expected in highly industrialized countries like Germany or England. Marx regarded the peasantry as the social class least capable of constructive revolutionary action: together with the *Lumpenproletariat* of the urban slums, the peasants were benighted barbarians, the bulwark of counterrevolution. For Bakunin, by contrast, the peasantry and Lumpenproletariat, having been least exposed to the corrupting influences of bourgeois civilization, retained their primitive vigor and turbulent instinct for revolt. The real proletariat, he said, did not consist in the skilled artisans and organized factory workers, tainted by the pretensions and aspirations of the middle classes, but in the "uncivilized, disinherited, and illiterate" millions who truly had nothing to lose but their chains. Accordingly, while Marx believed in a revolution led by a trained and disciplined working class, Bakunin set his hopes on a peasant jacquerie combined with a spontaneous rising of the infuriated urban mobs, driven by an instinctive passion for justice and by an unquenchable thirst for revenge. Bakunin's model had been set by the great rebellions of Stenka Razin and Emelian Pugachev in the seventeenth and eighteenth centuries. His vision was of an all-embracing upheaval, a true "revolt of the masses," including, in addition to the working class, the darkest elements of society—the Lumpenproletariat, the peasantry, the unemployed, the outlaws—pitted against those who thrived on their enslavement.

7

Subsequent events have, to a remarkable extent, confirmed the accuracy of Bakunin's vision. It is small wonder that contemporary historians have shown a new appreciation of the role of "primitive" movements in shaping history. For modern revolutions, like those of the past, have been largely unplanned and spontaneous, driven by throngs of urban and rural laborers, and in spirit predominantly anarchistic. No longer can these largely unorganized groups be written off as fringe elements to be ignored by the historian. They lie, rather, at the very root of social change.

Bakunin foresaw that the great revolutions of our time would emerge from the "lower depths" of comparatively undeveloped countries. He saw decadence in advanced civilization and vitality in backward nations. He insisted that the revolutionary impulse was strongest where men had no property, no regular employment, no stake in things as they were; and this meant that the universal upheaval of his dreams would start in the south and east of Europe rather than in such prosperous and stable countries as England or Germany.

These revolutionary visions were closely related to Bakunin's early pan-Slavism. In 1848 he spoke of the decadence of western Europe and saw hope in the more primitive, less industrialized Slavs for the regeneration of the Continent. Convinced that an essential condition for a European revolution was the breakup of the Austrian Empire, he called for its replacement by independent Slavic republics, a dream realized seventy years later. He correctly anticipated the future importance of Slavic nationalism, and he saw, too, that a revolution of Slavs would precipitate the social transformation of Europe. He prophesied, in particular, a messianic role for his native Russia akin to that of the Third Rome of the past and the Third International of the future. "The star of revolution," he wrote in 1848, "will rise high above Moscow from a sea of blood and fire, and will turn into the lodestar to lead a liberated humanity."[11]

We can see then why Bakunin, rather than Marx, can claim to be the true prophet of modern revolution. The three greatest revolutions of the twentieth century—in Russia, Spain, and China—have all occurred in relatively backward countries and have largely been "peasant wars" linked with outbursts of the urban poor, as Bakunin predicted. The peasantry and the unskilled workers, groups for whom Marx expressed disdain, have become the mass base of twentieth-century social upheavals—upheavals which, though often labeled "Marxist," are more accurately described as "Bakuninist." Bakunin's visions, moreover, have anticipated the social ferment within the Third World, the

8

modern counterpart on a global scale of Bakunin's backward, peripheral Europe.

It is hardly surprising, therefore, that the spirit of Bakunin should pervade the writings of Fanon and Debray and, to a lesser degree, of Cleaver and Herbert Marcuse. Fanon, no less than Bakunin, was convinced that the more advanced workers in underdeveloped countries, corrupted by middle-class values, had lost their revolutionary fervor. The great mistake, he wrote, had been "to approach in the first place those elements which are the most politically conscious: the working classes in the towns, the skilled workers and the civil servants—that is to say, a tiny portion of the population, which hardly represents more than one percent."[12] Fanon, like Bakunin, pinned his hopes on the mass of unprivileged and un-Europeanized village laborers and Lumpenproletariat from the shanty towns, uprooted, impoverished, starving, and with nothing to lose. For Fanon, as for Bakunin, the more primitive the man, the purer his revolutionary spirit. When Fanon refers to "the hopeless dregs of humanity" as natural rebels, he is speaking the language of Bakunin. With Bakunin, moreover, he shares not only a faith in the revolutionary potential of the underworld but also a thoroughgoing rejection of European civilization as decadent and repressive—in place of which, he says, the Third World must begin "a new history of man." The Black Panthers, in turn, appropriated many of Fanon's ideas, and Cleaver, Jackson, and Huey Newton freely acknowledged their debt to him—and indirectly to Bakunin—when describing the blacks in America as an oppressed colony held in check by an occupation army of white policemen and exploited by white businessmen and politicians.

In a similar vein, Marcuse wrote in *One-Dimensional Man* that the greatest hope of revolutionary change lies in "the substratum of the outcasts and outsiders, the exploited and persecuted of other races and other colors, the unemployed and the unemployables." If these groups, he added, should ally themselves with the radical intellectuals, there might occur an uprising of "the most advanced consciousness of humanity and its most exploited forces."[13] Here again it is Bakunin rather than Marx whose influence is apparent. For Bakunin set great store by the disaffected students and intellectuals and assigned them a key role in the impending world revolution. Bakunin's prophetic vision of an all-encompassing class war, in contrast to Marx's more narrowly conceived struggle between proletariat and bourgeoisie, made room for this additional element of society for which Marx had small regard. In Marx's view, rootless intellectuals did not comprise a class of their own, nor were they an integral component of the bourgeoisie. They were merely "the dregs" of the middle class—lawyers without clients, doctors without patients, petty journalists, impecunious students—with little role in the process of class conflict.[14] For Bakunin, on the other hand, the intellectuals were a valuable revolutionary force, "fervent, energetic youths, totally *déclassé*, with no career or way out."[15] The déclassés, Bakunin pointed out, like the jobless Lumpenproletariat and the landless peasantry, had no stake whatever in things as they were and no prospect for improvement except through an immediate revolution that would demolish the existing order.

In general, then, Bakunin found the greatest revolutionary potential in uprooted, alienated social elements, elements either left behind by or refusing to fit into modern society. In this also he was a truer prophet than his contemporaries. For the alliance of estranged intellectuals with the dispossessed masses in guerrilla-style warfare has been a central feature of modern revolutions. Debray, in *Revolution in the Revolution?*, another influential manual of modern rebellion, carried this idea to its ultimate conclusion. People who have jobs, he says, who lead more or less normal working lives, are, however poor and oppressed, essentially bourgeois because they have something to lose—their work, their homes, their sustenance. For Debray only the rootless guerrilla, with nothing to lose but his life, is the true proletarian, and the revolutionary struggle, if it is to be successful, must be conducted by bands of professional guerrillas—i.e., *déclassé* intellectuals—who, in Debray's words, would "initiate the highest forms of class struggle."[16]

BAKUNIN differed with Marx on still another point that is relevant for the present and recent past. Bakunin was a firm believer in immediate revolution. He rejected the view that revolutionary forces will emerge gradually, in the fullness of time. What he demanded, in effect, was "freedom now." He would countenance no temporizing with the existing system. The old order was rotten, he argued, and salvation could be achieved only by destroying it root and branch. Gradualism and reformism were futile, palliatives and compromises of no use. Bakunin's was a dream of immediate and universal destruction, the leveling of all existing values and institutions, and the creation of a libertarian society on their ashes. In his view, parliamentary democracy was a shameless fiction so long as men and women were subjected to economic exploitation. Even in the freest of states, he declared, such as Switzerland and the United States, the civilization of the few is founded on the degradation of the many. "I do not believe in constitutions and laws," he said. "The best constitution in the world would not be able to satisfy me. We need something different: inspiration, life, a new lawless and therefore free world."[17]

In rejecting the claim of parliamentary democracy to represent the people, Bakunin, as his biographer E. H. Carr noted, "spoke a language which has become more familiar in the twentieth century than it was in the nineteenth."[18] Sounding still another modern note, Bakunin saw the ideal moment for popular revolution in time of war— and ultimately during a world war. In 1870 he regarded the Franco-Prussian War as the harbinger of an anarchist revolution in which the state would be smashed and a free federation of communes arise on its ruins. The one thing that could save France, he wrote in his *Letter to a Frenchman*, was "a spontaneous, formidable, passionate, energetic, anarchic, destructive, and savage uprising of the popular masses,"[19] a view with which Daniel Cohn-Bendit and his fellow Paris rebels of May 1968 enthusiastically agreed. Bakunin believed, like Lenin after him, that national war must be converted into social rebellion. He dreamt of a general European war, which he thought to be imminent and would destroy the bourgeois world. His timing, of course, was faulty. As Herzen once remarked, Bakunin habitually mistook "the second month of pregnancy for the ninth." But his vision was at length fulfilled when the First World War brought about the collapse of the old order and released revolutionary forces that have yet to play themselves out.

Let us focus for a moment on the Russian Revolution, the prototype of twentieth-century social upheavals. Here, in essence, was the "revolt of the masses" that Bakunin had foreseen some fifty years before. In 1917 Russia experienced a virtual breakdown of political authority, and councils of workers and peasants sprang up that might form the basis of libertarian communes. Lenin, like Bakunin before him, encouraged the untutored elements of Russian society to sweep away what remained of the old regime. Bakunin and Lenin, for all their differences of temperament and doctrine, were similar in their refusal to collaborate with the liberals or moderate socialists, whom they regarded as incurably counterrevolutionary. Both men were antibourgeois and antiliberal to the roots. Like Bakunin, Lenin called for instantaneous socialism, without any prolonged capitalist phase of development. He too believed that the global revolution might be centered on backward peasant Russia. In his *April Theses*, moreover, he put forward a number of specifically Bakuninist propositions: the transformation of the world war into a revolutionary struggle against the capitalist system; the renunciation of parliamentary government in favor of a regime of soviets patterned after the Paris Commune; the abolition of the police, the army, and the bureaucracy; and the leveling of incomes. Lenin's appeal for "a breakup and a revolution a thousand times more powerful than that of February" had a distinctly Bakuninist ring—so much so that one anarchist leader in Petrograd was convinced that Lenin intended to "wither away the state" the moment he got hold of it.[20]

And, indeed, Lenin's greatest achievement was to return to the anarcho-populist roots of the Russian revolutionary tradition, to adapt his Marxist theories to suit the conditions of a relatively backward country in which a proletarian revolution made little sense. While the Marxist in Lenin told him to be patient, to let Russia evolve in accordance with the laws of historical materialism, the Bakuninist in him insisted that the revolution must be made at once, by fusing the proletarian revolution with the revolutions of a land-hungry peasantry and a militant elite of *déclassé* intellectuals, social elements for which Marx, as we have seen, expressed contempt. Small wonder that Lenin's orthodox Marxist colleagues accused him of becoming an anarchist and "the heir to the throne of Bakunin."[21] Small wonder, too, that several years later a leading Bolshevik historian could write that Bakunin was "the founder not only of European anarchism but also of Russian populist insurrectionism and therefore of Russian Social Democracy from which the Communist party emerged," and that Bakunin's methods "in many respects anticipated the emergence of Soviet power and forecast, in general outline, the course of the great October Revolution of 1917."[22]

But if Bakunin foresaw the anarchistic nature of the Russian Revolution, he also foresaw its authoritarian consequences. If 1917 began, as Bakunin had hoped, with a spontaneous mass revolt, it ended, as Bakunin had feared, with the dictatorship of a new ruling elite. Long before Wacław Machajski or Milovan Djilas, Bakunin warned that a "new class" of intellectuals and semi-intellectuals might seek to replace the landlords and capitalists and deny the people their freedom. In 1873 he prophesied with startling accuracy that under a so-called dictatorship of the proletariat "the leaders of the Communist party, namely Mr. Marx and his followers, will proceed to liberate humanity in their own way. They will concentrate the reins of government in a strong hand. . . . They will establish a single state bank, concentrating in its hands all commercial, industrial, agricultural, and even scientific production, and then divide the masses into two armies—industrial and agricultural—under the direct command of state engineers, who will constitute a new privileged scientific and political class."[23]

And yet, for all his assaults on revolutionary dictatorship, Bakunin was determined to create his own secret society of conspirators, subject to "a strict hierarchy and to unconditional obedience." This clandestine organization, moreover, would remain intact even after the revolution had been accomplished, in order to forestall the establishment of any "official dictatorship."[24] Thus Bakunin committed the very sin he so bitterly denounced. He himself was one of the originators of the idea of a closely knit revolutionary party bound together by implicit obedience to a revolutionary dictator, a party that he likened at one point to the Jesuit order. Although he recognized the intimate connection between means and ends and saw that the methods used to make the revolution must affect the nature of society *after* the revolution, he nonetheless resorted to methods that contradicted his libertarian principles. His ends pointed towards freedom, but his means—the clandestine party—pointed towards dictatorship.

More than that, on the question of revolutionary morality Bakunin, under the influence of his disciple Nechaev, preached in effect that the ends justify the means. In the *Catechism of a Revolutionary*, written with Nechaev more than a century ago,[25] the revolutionist is portrayed as a complete immoralist, bound to commit any crime, any treachery, to bring about the destruction of the prevailing order. Eldridge Cleaver tells us in *Soul on Ice* that he "fell in love" with the *Catechism of a Revolutionary* and took it as a revolutionary bible, incorporating its principles into his everyday life by employing "tactics of ruthlessness in my dealings with everyone with whom I came into contact."[26] (The *Catechism*, as mentioned above, was reprinted by Cleaver's Black Panthers.)

Here again, as in his belief in a clandestine organization of revolutionaries as well as a "temporary" revolutionary dictatorship, Bakunin was a forebear of Lenin. This makes it easier to understand how it was possible for many anarchists in 1917 to collaborate with their Bolshevik rivals to overthrow the Kerensky government. After the October Revolution, in fact, one anarchist leader even tried to work out an "anarchist theory of the dictatorship of the proletariat."[27] There is tragic irony in the fact that, as in Spain twenty years later, the anarchists helped to smother the fragile embryo of democracy, thus preparing the way for a new tyranny that was to be the author of their downfall. For once in power the Bolsheviks proceeded to suppress their libertarian allies, and the revolution turned into the opposite of all Bakunin's hopes. Among the few anarchist groups allowed to remain in existence was one that vowed to launch the stateless society "in interplanetary space but not upon Soviet territory."[28] For most anarchists, however, there remained only the melancholy consolation that their mentor Bakunin had predicted it all nearly fifty years before.

BAKUNIN'S LEGACY, then, has been an ambivalent one. This was because Bakunin himself was a man of paradox, possessed of an ambivalent nature. A nobleman who yearned for a peasant revolt, a libertarian with an urge to dominate others, an intellectual with a powerful anti-intellectual streak, he could preach unrestrained liberty while fabricating a network of secret organizations and demanding from his followers unconditional obedience to his will. In his *Confession* to the tsar, he was capable of appealing to Nicholas I to carry the banner of Slavdom into western Europe and do away with the effete parliamentary system. His pan-Slavism and anti-intellectualism, his hatred of Germans and Jews (Marx, of course, being both), his cult of violence and revolutionary immoralism, his hatred of liberalism and reformism, his faith in the peasantry and Lumpenproletariat—all this brought him uncomfortably close to later authoritarian movements of both the left and the right, movements from which Bakunin himself would have recoiled in horror had he lived to see their mercurial rise.

Yet, for all his ambivalence, Bakunin remains an influential figure. Herzen once called him "a Columbus without an America, and even without a ship."[29] But recent revolutionary movements owe him a good deal of their energy, audacity, and tempestuousness. His youthful exuberance, his contempt for middle-class conventions, and his emphasis on deeds rather than theories have exerted considerable appeal among the rebellious youth of the late twentieth century, for whom Bakunin has provided an example of anarchism in action, of revolution as a way of life. His ideas, too, continue to be relevant—in some ways more relevant than ever. Whatever his defects as a scholar, especially when he is compared with Marx, they are more than outweighed by his revolutionary vision and intuition. Bakunin was a prophet of primitive rebellion, of the conspiratorial revolutionary party, of terrorist amoralism, of guerrilla insurrectionism, of revolutionary dictatorship, and of the emergence of a new class that would impose its will on the people and rob them of their freedom. He was the first Russian rebel to preach social revolution in cosmic terms and on an international scale. His formulas of self-determination and direct action have exercised a continuing appeal, while his chief *bête noire*, the centralized bureaucratic state, continues to fulfill his most despairing predictions. Of particular note, after the lessons of Russia, Spain, and China, is Bakunin's message that social emancipation must be attained by libertarian rather than dictatorial means. At a time when workers' control is being discussed, it is well to remember that Bakunin, perhaps

even more than Proudhon, was a prophet of revolutionary syndicalism, who believed that a free federation of trade unions would be the
"living germs of the new social order which is to replace the bourgeois
world."[30]

But above all Bakunin remains attractive to radicals and intellectuals
because his libertarian brand of socialism provides an alternative vision to the bankrupt authoritarian socialism of the twentieth century.
His dream of a decentralized society of autonomous communes and
labor federations appeals to those who are seeking to escape from a
conformist and artificial world. "I am a human being: do not fold,
spindle, or mutilate" has a distinctive Bakuninist flavor. Student rebels
since the 1960s, even when professed Marxists, have often been closer
in spirit to Bakunin. Their stress on the natural, the spontaneous, the
unsystematic, their urge towards a simpler way of life, their distrust of
bureaucracy and centralized authority, their belief that men and
women should take part in decisions affecting their lives—all this has
been in harmony with Bakunin's vision. Even the ambivalence among
rebels of the sixties and seventies, who combined the antithetical methods of libertarian anarchism and authoritarian socialism, reflected the
ambivalence within Bakunin's own revolutionary philosophy and personal makeup.

Finally, Bakunin has found an echo wherever young dissidents have
questioned uncritical faith in self-glorifying scientific progress. More
than a hundred years ago Bakunin warned that scientists and technical
experts might use their knowledge to dominate others and that one day
ordinary citizens would awake to find that they had become "the
slaves, the playthings, and the victims of a new group of ambitious
men."[31] Bakunin therefore preached a "revolt of life against science, or
rather, against the rule of science." Not that he rejected the validity of
scientific knowledge. He recognized its dangers, however. He saw that
life cannot be reduced to laboratory formulas and that efforts in this
direction might lead to tyranny. In a letter written barely a year before
his death, he spoke of the "development of the principle of evil"
throughout the world and warned of what has come to be called the
military-industrial complex. "Sooner or later," he wrote, "these enormous military states will have to destroy and devour each other. But
what a prospect!"[32]

How justified were his fears can be appreciated in an age of nuclear
and biological weapons of mass destruction. At a time when modern
technology threatens Western civilization with extinction, Bakunin
clearly merits a reappraisal. As Max Nettlau, the foremost historian of
anarchism, remarked, Bakunin's ideas "remain fresh and will live forever."[33]

CHAPTER TWO

Bakunin and the United States

"MIKHAIL ALEKSANDROVICH BAKUNIN is in San Francisco," announced the front page of Herzen's *Kolokol* in November 1861. "HE IS FREE! Bakunin left Siberia via Japan and is on his way to England. We joyfully bring this news to all Bakunin's friends."[1] Arrested in Chemnitz in May 1849, Bakunin had been extradited to Russia in 1851 and, after six years in the Peter-Paul and Schlüsselburg fortresses, condemned to perpetual banishment in Siberia. On June 17, 1861, however, he began his dramatic escape. Setting out from Irkutsk, he sailed down the Amur to Nikolaevsk, where he boarded a government vessel plying the Siberian coast. Once at sea, he transferred to an American sailing ship, the *Vickery*, which was trading in Japanese ports, and reached Japan on August 16. A month later, on September 17, he sailed from Yokohama on another American vessel, the *Carrington*, bound for San Francisco.[2] He arrived four weeks later, completing, in Herzen's description, "the very longest escape in a geographical sense."[3]

Bakunin was forty-seven years old. He had spent the past twelve years in prison and exile, and only fourteen years of life—extremely active life, to be sure—lay before him. He had returned like a ghost from the past, "risen from the dead," as he wrote to Herzen and Ogarev from San Francisco.[4] His sojourn in America, one of the least well known episodes of his career, lasted two months, from October 15, when he landed in San Francisco, to December 14, when he left New York for London. As far as the sources permit, the present chapter will describe this interlude—the places he visited, the people he met, the impression he made on them. It will also explore his attitude to-

16

wards the United States, both during and after his visit, and trace his influence on the American anarchist movement over the last hundred years.

When Bakunin reached San Francisco, he wrote immediately to Herzen and Ogarev in London. First and foremost, he asked that $500 be sent to New York to enable him to proceed to England. For his passage to New York he had already borrowed $250 from F. P. Koe, a young English clergyman whom he had met on the *Carrington*. His own funds, he wrote, were exhausted, and he had "no acquaintances, let alone friends," in San Francisco, so that "had I not found a kind person who gave me a 250 dollar loan to New York, I should have been in great difficulty."[5] Bakunin begged Herzen and Ogarev to get word of his escape to his family in Tver province. Expecting his wife to join him when she heard the news, he asked his friends to find them an "inexpensive nook" in their neighborhood.[6]

It was Bakunin's intention, on reaching London, to resume his revolutionary activities. Like a man awakened from a trance, as E. H. Carr noted, Bakunin was determined to take up life again at the point where he had laid it down a dozen years before. As Herzen put it, "the fantasies and ideals with which he was imprisoned in Königstein in 1849 he had preserved complete and carried across Japan and California."[7] Above all, he would devote himself to the liberation of the Slavic peoples. "Friends," he wrote to Herzen and Ogarev, "I long to come to you with all my being, and as soon as I arrive, I will set to work. I will assist you on the Polish and Slavic question, which has been my *idée fixe* since 1846 and was my special sphere of activity in 1848 and 1849. The destruction—the total destruction—of the Austrian empire will be my last word, not to say deed—that would be too ambitious. To serve this great cause I am ready to become a drummer-boy or even a scoundrel, and if I succeed in advancing it even by a hair's-breadth, I shall be satisfied. And after that will come the glorious free Slavic federation, the one way out for Russia, the Ukraine, Poland, and Slavic peoples in general."[8]

On October 21, after six days in San Francisco, Bakunin left for New York by way of Panama on the steamship *Orizaba*. The next day, some 400 miles from the Isthmus, he wrote again to Herzen and Ogarev, repeating his request for money (to be sent to the banking house of Ballin & Sanders in New York) and inquiring after his family in Russia. The *Orizaba* docked in Panama on October 24. On November 6, after a delay of two weeks, Bakunin embarked on the *Champion* bound for New York.[9] His fellow passengers included the commander in chief of the Union army in California, General Sumner, with 430 regulars under Colonel C. S. Merchant. Also on board were three Confederate sympathizers, ex-Senator William M. Gwin of California, Calhoun Benham, a former state attorney at San Francisco, and Captain J. Brant, the former commander of a revenue cutter. One day out of Panama, General Sumner placed the three under arrest as secessionists conducting business for the South.[10]

Bakunin arrived in New York on the morning of November 15[11] and registered at Howard House on lower Broadway at Cortlandt Street. Among the people he called on were two old German comrades, Reinhold Solger and Friedrich Kapp, both well-known Forty-Eighters. Solger had been educated at Halle and Greifswald, where he received the Ph.D. in 1842, intending to pursue an academic career in history and philosophy. A Left Hegelian, he was a friend of Arnold Ruge, Ludwig Feuerbach, and Georg Herwegh. Solger and Bakunin first met in Zurich in 1843, after which they corresponded for several years, meeting again in Paris in 1847, together with Herzen and Herwegh.[12] In 1848 Solger joined the revolutionary army in Baden, serving as adjutant to General Mieroslawski, commander of the insurgent forces. When the rising was suppressed, he fled to Switzerland "with a price on his head," emigrating to America in 1853 and becoming a citizen six years later. A gifted speaker and writer, Solger was twice invited to give the Lowell Institute Lectures in Boston (1857 and 1859) and won two literary prizes, in 1859 for a poem on the centennial of Schiller and in 1862 for a novel on German-American life. An abolitionist and radical Republican, he applied his verbal talents as a campaigner for Abraham Lincoln, who rewarded him with a post in the Treasury Department. He ended his days as a bank director, dying in January 1866 at the age of forty-eight.[13]

Like Solger, Friedrich Kapp had known both Bakunin and Herzen in Europe during the 1840s (for a time he was tutor to Herzen's son)[14] and had been a participant in the 1848 Revolution. Compelled to flee to Geneva, he emigrated to America in 1850, becoming a successful lawyer in New York as well as a prominent historian and journalist who aroused public opinion against the mistreatment and exploitation of immigrants. Kapp, again like Solger, became active in the radical wing of the Republican party, winning the support of German-Americans for the Union cause.[15]

On November 21 or 22, Bakunin interrupted his stay in New York to visit Boston, where he remained a little over a week. It proved to be the high point of his sojourn in America. Armed with letters of introduction from Solger and Kapp, he called on a number of influential figures, among them the governor of Massachusetts, John Andrew, a friend of Solger's and a radical Republican who had spoken out against slavery and raised funds for the defense of John Brown. Bakunin also carried letters to General George B. McClellan, commander in chief of the Union army, who had visited Russia in 1855-1856 as an observer of the Crimean War, and to both Massachusetts senators, Charles Sumner and Henry Wilson, radical Republicans and abolitionists like Governor Andrew. A few years later, Bakunin was to praise Sumner, "the eminent Boston senator," for espousing a form of "socialism" by favoring the distribution of land among the freed slaves of the South.[16]

Sumner's colleague, Henry Wilson, was a former shoemaker who had risen to the position of senator and, a decade later, vice president of the United States under Ulysses S. Grant. A labor reformer as well as an abolitionist, his sympathies were always with the workingmen from whose ranks he had sprung (in 1858 he addressed the Senate on the question, "Are Working-Men 'Slaves'?"). He was best known, however, for his championship of the antislavery cause, speaking before the Senate on "Aggressions of the Slave Power" and "The Death of Slavery Is the Life of the Nation" and publishing some years later his three-volume *History of the Rise and Fall of the Slave Power in America*.[17] Bakunin also called on George H. Snelling, a Boston reformer who, like Bakunin himself, was an avid partisan of Polish emancipation and the translator of a history of the Polish insurrection of 1830-1831. Bakunin thus took special pleasure in making his acquaintance, and "at their first meeting he embraced him with much warmth," a contemporary recalls.[18]

Bakunin, in short, mingled with the leading lights of progressive Boston society. Politicians and generals, businessmen and writers, they were men of liberal temperament and advanced social and political views who favored the growth of democracy and national independence in Europe. As abolitionists and reformers, they could see the parallel between the freeing of the serfs in Russia and their own antislavery crusade, and among them Bakunin found a great sympathy for the Russian people in their continuing struggle against autocracy.

One such reformer was Martin P. Kennard, an abolitionist and partner in a Boston jewelry firm, to whom Solger had given Bakunin a letter of introduction.[19] Bakunin dined twice at Kennard's home in Brookline and visited his office in Boston. Kennard describes his guest as "a large heavily framed yet well proportioned man, more than six feet in height, in bearing noble, in personage genial and attractive, and well-nigh entirely enveloped in a rubber Mackintosh." Bakunin, who amusingly called himself a "Russian bear," found in Kennard a sympathetic listener. As Oscar Handlin notes, Kennard's progressive convictions, which had drawn him into societies to protect runaway slaves, reflected a broader concern for human freedom, in Europe as well as America. At their first meeting, Bakunin told Kennard "of the struggle for the life of Poland, the unification of Germany, and of the republican movement throughout Europe, and of its temporary failure." As Bakunin spoke, it was clear to his host that "his courage was still undaunted, and his ardor in no wise abated."[20]

Like Kennard and his other hosts, Bakunin was firmly opposed to Negro slavery, indeed to slavery in all its manifestations. Throughout his sojourn in America, he moved in abolitionist circles, defended the antislavery movement, and, unlike the French anarchist Proudhon, supported the Union in the struggle between the states. The Civil War "interests me in the highest degree," he wrote to Herzen and Ogarev from San Francisco. "My sympathies are all with the North."[21] So strong were his feelings on the slavery issue that, had circumstances permitted, according to Kennard, "he would have cast his future fortune with Americans and heartily joined in the events of the War."[22] In later years he condemned the Northern apologists of slavery, along with "the ferocious oligarchy" of Southern planters, as being "demagogues without faith or conscience, capable of sacrificing everything to their greed, to their malignant ambition." Such men, he said, had "greatly contributed to the corruption of political morality in North America."[23]

Not that the South was totally devoid of merit. No less than Proudhon, Bakunin distrusted the growing centralization of Union power and cherished the waning agrarian virtues of the Confederacy, whose political structure he considered in some ways freer and more democratic than that of the North. In reaching this conclusion, we learn from Kennard, Bakunin was probably influenced by Senator Gwin, "whose acquaintance he had made on his voyage from San Francisco via Panama, and who has sometimes been mentioned in the newspapers as 'Duke Gwin.' "[24] Southern federalism, however, Bakunin was quick to point out, had been tarnished by the "black spot" of slavery, with the result that the Confederate states had "drawn upon themselves the condemnation of all friends of freedom and humanity." Moreover, with "the iniquitous and dishonorable war which they fomented against the republican states of the North, they nearly overthrew and destroyed the finest political organization that ever existed in history."[25]

Soon after arriving in Boston, Bakunin went to Cambridge to visit his "old friend" Louis Agassiz,[26] the famous Swiss naturalist, whom he had met at Neuchâtel in 1843. Agassiz had emigrated to the United States in 1846 and was now Professor of Zoology at Harvard and a friend of Henry Wadsworth Longfellow, to whom he gave Bakunin a letter of introduction. Longfellow, a man of abolitionist sympathies, was well known, apart from his other writings, for his *Poems of Slavery*; and when Bakunin dined at Craigie House, Longfellow's Cambridge home, George Sumner, a brother of the abolitionist senator, was also invited. The date was November 27, and, according to Van Wyck Brooks, Bakunin arrived at noon and stayed until almost midnight.[27] Longfellow recorded the occasion in his diary: "George Sumner and Mr. Bakounin to dinner. Mr. B. is a Russian gentleman of education and ability—a giant of a man, with a most ardent, seething temperament. He was in the Revolution of Forty-eight; has seen the inside of prisons—of Olmütz, even, where he had Lafayette's room. Was afterwards four years in Siberia; whence he escaped in June last, down the Amoor, and then in an American vessel by way of Japan to California, and across the isthmus, hitherward. An interesting man."[28]

Bakunin had read some American literature—including the works of James Fenimore Cooper in German translation—and had studied English while in prison, so that he could speak it, says Kennard, "with fair facility."[29] Despite his years of confinement, he still possessed much of his old vitality and exuberance. He had aged, to be sure, had lost his teeth from scurvy and grown quite fat. But the grey-blue eyes retained their penetrating brilliance; and his voice, eloquence, and physical bulk combined to make him the center of attention. He was, moreover, a nobleman as well as a rebel, endowed, as Carr noted, with the kind of aristocratic temperament that dissolved all barriers of class and enabled him to move with ease among men of different social and national background. "Without the least reserve," writes Kennard in this connection, "my new acquaintance made himself at once on good terms, and in a free and easy manner rendered himself agreeable, with a cosmopolitan complaisance that bespoke an intelligent and affable gentleman, and energetic man of affairs."[30]

Wherever he went Bakunin exercised a powerful fascination, making a favorable impression on nearly everyone he met. In after years, says Kennard, Longellow "regularly enquired for the latest news of his radical guest, and of whom he related to me some amusing incidents." The sole dissenter, it seems, was Longfellow's youngest daughter Annie, the "laughing Allegra" of *The Children's Hour*, who left an amusing memoir of Bakunin's visit. When she came down to dinner she saw an "ogre" in her customary seat beside her father, a "big creature with a big head, wild bushy hair, big eyes, big mouth, a big voice and still bigger laugh." She had not been brought up on *Grimm's Fairy Tales* for nothing, she writes. "No entreaties or persuasion could induce me to cross the threshold of that door. I stood petrified and while I resented his having my place at table, what was dinner to me as long as he didn't make his dinner off me. So I vanished dinnerless."[31]

At the beginning of December, Bakunin returned from Boston to New York. With letters of recommendation obtained in these cities, he had intended to go on to Washington, as he told Herzen and Ogarev, and possibly "learn something" there.[32] Carr writes that it is not known whether he made the trip. From Kennard, however, we learn that he did not, owing to "a constant anxiety and characteristic impatience to depart to London, where it has been arranged he should rendesvous to meet his wife, of whom he often spoke with the tenderest affection."[33] Thus, when money arrived from England, Bakunin booked passage on the next available ship, the *City of Baltimore*, which sailed for Liverpool on December 14. Arriving on December 27, he went directly to London where, greeted by Herzen and Ogarev "as a brother," he rejoined the revolutionary movement.[34]

WHAT IMPRESSION of the United States did Bakunin carry away with him? On the whole it was a favorable one, but with reservations concerning the nation's political and social character. "I spent over a month in America and learned a great deal," he wrote to a Russian friend in February 1862. "I saw how the country has been brought by demagogy to the same miserable results which we have achieved by despotism. Between America and Russia, in fact, there is much in common. But most important to me, I found in America such universal and unconditional sympathy for Russia and faith in the future of the Russian people that, in spite of all that I saw and heard there, I left America a strong partisan of the United States."[35]

Beyond this sympathy for Russia, what impressed Bakunin most about America was its history of political liberty and its federalist system of government. Extolling the American Revolution as "the cause of liberty against despotism," he was "very anxious to possess, as a souvenir of his visit to America, an autograph of Washington," with which Martin Kennard was able to present him as a parting token.[36] In his future writings, he would characterize the United States as "the classic land of political liberty," the freest country in the world, endowed with "the most democratic institutions." American federalism left a particularly deep impression, enriching his own ideas on the subject. To European progressives he warmly recommended "the great and salutary *principle of federalism*" as embodied in the United States. "We must reject the politics of the State," he told the League of Peace and Freedom in 1868, "and adopt resolutely the politics of liberty of the North Americans."[37]

In spite of his anarchist doctrines, which matured over the next few years, Bakunin did not lump all governments together as equally wicked and oppressive. From his personal experience in America, and afterwards in England and Switzerland, he was convinced that "the most imperfect republic is a thousand times better than the most enlightened monarchy." The United States and Britain, he remarked, were "the only two great countries" where the people possessed genuine "liberty and political power," and where even "the most disinherited and miserable foreigners" enjoyed civil rights "as fully as the richest and most influential citizens."[38] In both these countries, of course, he himself had found political asylum; moreover, the United States government, during his visit, had refused to extradite him, which convinced the Russian ambassador, Baron Stoeckel, that the American republic would never cease "to protect revolutionists."[39] While in Boston, interestingly enough, Bakunin made a primary declaration of American citizenship, the equivalent of taking out his "first papers." "He probably never entertained a serious thought of ever becoming an American citizen," noted Kennard, "and yet, with some vague idea of such a possibility or of some remote advantage to himself, he made and duly recorded in Boston his primary declaration of such intention." And in the last years of his life, while living in Switzerland, he again spoke of emigrating to America and becoming naturalized there.[40]

Looking back to his American sojourn, Bakunin recalled a society in which workers never starved and were "better paid" than their European counterparts. "Class antagonism," he wrote, "hardly yet exists," for "all workers are citizens," part of a "single body politic," and education is "widespread among the masses." These benefits, he said, were rooted in the "traditional spirit of liberty" that the first colonists had imported from England and, along with the principle of "individual independence and communal and provincial *selfgovernment*," had transplanted into a wilderness that was free from "the obsessions of the past." In less than a century, therefore, America had been able "to equal and even surpass the civilization of Europe" and to offer "a freedom which does not exist anywhere else."[41]

According to Bakunin, America owed its "marvelous progress" and "enviable prosperity" to its "immense reaches of fertile land," its "great territorial wealth." Because of this abundance, he said, hundreds of thousands of settlers were being absorbed every year, and an unemployed or ill-paid worker could, as a last resort, "always migrate to the *far west*" and set about clearing a stretch of land for cultivation.[42] To some extent, perhaps, Bakunin's image of the American wilderness was shaped by the stories of Fenimore Cooper; and there were moments, particularly in prison, when he himself longed for the life of a western mountaineer. His *Confession* to Nicholas I, written in the Peter-Paul fortress in 1851, contains a striking passage to this effect: "In my nature there has always been a basic flaw: a love for the fantastic, for unusual, unheard-of adventures, for undertakings that open up vast horizons, the end of which cannot be foreseen. Most men seek tranquillity, which they consider the highest blessing. In me, however, it produces only despair. My spirit is in constant turmoil, demanding action, movement, and life. I should have been born somewhere in the American forests, among the settlers of the West, where civilization has hardly begun to blossom and where life is an endless struggle against untamed people, against untamed nature—and not in an organized civic society. And if fate had in my youth made me a sailor, I would probably now be a respectable person, without any thought of politics and seeking no other adventures and storms but those of the sea."[43]

Bakunin, however, was not without criticism of America. On the day of his arrival in San Francisco, he complained to Herzen and Ogarev of the "banality of soulless material prosperity" and the "infantile national vanity" that he found in the United States. The Civil War, he thought, might save America and restore its "lost soul."[44] "He used to assert," writes Kennard, "that after the War, America would become a great power, more individualized, so to speak, and better poised in her social life, and that her great trial could bring out great men, indeed greater than she had ever known."[45]

Yet America's favored position was only temporary, Bakunin believed. For recent years had seen the crowding together in such cities as New York, Philadelphia, and Boston of "masses of proletarian workers" who were beginning to find themselves in a condition "analogous to that of workers in the great manufacturing states of Europe." As a result, "we see in fact the social question confronting the Northern states just as it confronted us much earlier."[46] Before long, the American laborer would be no better off than his European counterpart, the victim of rapacious capitalism and of centralized political power. No state, Bakunin insisted, however democratic, could get along without "the forced labor of the masses." Wage slavery, rather, was an "indispensable necessity for the leisure, liberty, and civilization of the political classes—the citizens. On this point, not even the United States of North America can as yet form an exception."[47]

Although Bakunin continued to prefer the democratic system of the United States, England, and Switzerland to the despotism of most other countries, his criticism of government in general mounted as the years advanced. "What do we really see in all states, past and present, even those endowed with the most democratic institutions, such as the United States of North America and Switzerland?" he asked in 1867. "The self-government of the masses, despite the pretense that the people hold all the power, remains a fiction most of the time." Representative government, he added, benefits only the wealthy classes, and universal suffrage is merely a tool of the bourgeoisie; the masses are "sovereign in law, not in fact." For "ambitious minorities," the "seekers of political power," attain predominance "by wooing the people, by pandering to their fickle passions, which at times can be quite evil, and, in most cases, by deceiving them." While preferring a republic, therefore, "we must nevertheless recognize and proclaim that whatever the form of government may be, so long as human society continues to be divided into different classes as a result of *hereditary* inequality of occupation, wealth, education, and rights, there will always be a class-restricted government and the inevitable exploitation of the majority by the minority."[48]

These themes are often repeated in Bakunin's subsequent writings. In *God and the State*, drafted in 1871, he stresses that even parliamentary regimes elected by universal suffrage quickly degenerate into "a sort of political aristocracy or oligarchy. Witness the United States of America and Switzerland."[49] In *The Knouto-Germanic Empire and the Social Revolution*, an unfinished work of which *God and the State* is a fragment, he reemphasizes that even "in the most democratic lands, such as the United States of America and Switzerland," the state represents an instrument of "minority privilege and the practical subjugation of the vast majority." And again in *Statehood and Anarchy*, published in 1873, he writes that the United States "is run by a special, thoroughly bourgeois class of so-called politicians or political dealers, while the masses of workers live under conditions just as cramped and wretched as in monarchic states."[50]

During the last years of his life, Bakunin despaired of any immediate improvement. To Elisée Reclus, the French geographer and anarchist, he wrote in 1875 that "evil has triumphed" everywhere, what with the restoration of the Spanish monarchy, Bismarck at the helm of a rising German state, the Catholic church still rich and powerful over a vast part of the world, England faltering, Europe as a whole degenerating, "and farther away the model republic of the United States of America coquetting already with military dictatorship. Poor humanity!"[51]

DURING his brief visit to the United States, Bakunin left no discernible imprint on the revolutionary and working-class movements, then in an embryonic phase of development. The International Working Men's Association, for example, was not founded until 1864, and its first American section was formed only in 1867. Bakunin himself did not become a member of the International until 1868, after which, however, his influence spread rapidly. By the early 1870s, at the height of his conflict with Marx, he could count on substantial support within the American branch of the International, which was far from being an exclusively Marxist organization, as historians sometimes portray it.

Between 1870 and 1872, federalist sections of the International were established in New York, Boston, and other American cities. In New York, for example, Sections 9 and 12 were organized by such prominent libertarians as William West, Victoria Woodhull, her sister Tennessee Claflin, and Stephen Pearl Andrews, who hailed Bakunin as "a profound thinker, an original genius, a scholar and a philosopher."[52] William B. Greene, the leading American disciple of Proudhon, helped start a libertarian section of the International in Boston; his colleague Ezra Heywood addressed Internationalist meetings in New York and other cities. In 1872, Heywood launched a monthly magazine, *The Word*, in Princeton, Massachusetts, one of the first American journals to publish Bakunin's writings.[53] Together with *Woodhull & Claflin's Weekly* in New York, *The Word* became the unofficial organ of the International's libertarian wing in the United States, defending the principles of decentralist socialism and criticizing the Marxist-controlled General Council for its authoritarian orientation. "It is not pleasant to see Dr. Marx and other leaders of this great and growing fraternity lean so strongly towards compulsory politics," declared *The Word* in May 1872. "Let us be governed by the laws of nature until we can make better. If the International would succeed it must be true to its bottom idea—voluntary association in behalf of our common humanity."

In addition to the native American groups, a number of foreign-language (principally French) sections of the International in America adhered to the Bakuninist rather than the Marxist wing. These included Section 2 of New York (composed in part of refugees from the Paris Commune), Section 29 of Hoboken, New Jersey, and Section 42 of Paterson, New Jersey, a city soon to emerge as a major anarchist stronghold. Bakunin found additional adherents within the Icarian community at Corning, Iowa, where his portrait decorated the common room.[54]

In spite of Bakunin's expulsion from the International in 1872, his influence continued to grow on both sides of the Atlantic. Nor did it decline after his death in 1876. During the 1880s, on the contrary, his writings began to be published in the United States, making a powerful impression on the emerging anarchist and socialist movements.

It was a young New England anarchist named Benjamin R. Tucker who did the most to publicize Bakunin's ideas in North America. In 1872 Tucker, an eighteen-year-old student at the Massachusetts Institute of Technology, attended his first anarchist meeting in Boston. There he met Ezra Heywood, William Greene, and Josiah Warren (the "father" of American anarchism), who impressed him so favorably that he became a lifelong convert to their cause. After serving as associate editor of *The Word* during the mid-1870s, Tucker founded his own journal, *Liberty*, which ran from 1881 to 1908, superseding *The Word* as the principal organ of individualist anarchism in the United States.

Like Bakunin's Boston hosts of twenty years before, Tucker had great sympathy for the Russian people and the Russian revolutionary movement. In the first issue of *Liberty* (August 8, 1881) page one displayed a portrait of Sophia Perovskaya, who earlier that year had been hanged for her part in the assassination of Alexander II. Beneath the portrait was a moving poem by Joaquin Miller, "Sophie Perovskaya, Liberty's Martyred Heroine, Hanged April 15, 1881, For Helping to Rid the World of a Tyrant." In the same number, Tucker hailed Perovskaya's associate Lev Hartmann, who had come to America as an envoy of the People's Will, as "a fine writer, an heroic worker, a grand man."

Succeeding issues of *Liberty* contained news of Russian revolutionists exiled in western Europe or banished to Siberia by Alexander III. In addition to Perovskaya, Tucker praised such "remarkable types of Nihilist women" as Vera Zasulich, Vera Figner, and Sophia Bardina. In January 1882 he printed an appeal of the Red Cross Society of the People's Will, signed by Zasulich and Peter Lavrov, who, said Tucker, "speak authoritatively for the best elements of Russian life."[55] He himself became the Society's American representative and took up a collection in *Liberty*, forwarding the proceeds to Nicholas Chaikovsky in London.

Apart from Bakunin, Tucker published such well-known Populists and revolutionaries as Chernyshevsky and Tolstoy, Kropotkin and

Stepniak, Korolenko and Gorky.[56] It was Tucker who (working from a French edition because he lacked any knowledge of Russian) produced the first English translation of Chernyshevsky's *What Is to Be Done?*, calling the author a "martyr-hero of the modern Revolution."[57] In 1890 Tucker published *The Kreutzer Sonata* by Tolstoy, which he again translated from the French, as well as a review of the book by N. K. Mikhailovsky, translated from the Russian by Victor S. Yarros (Yaroslavsky), a former Narodnik from Kiev who was *Liberty*'s associate editor.[58]

The first mention of Bakunin in *Liberty*'s columns occurred on November 12, 1881, when Tucker announced that he had obtained a photograph of "the great revolutionist," which he offered for sale at fifty cents a copy. Two weeks later, an engraving of the picture appeared on the front page of *Liberty*, captioned "Michael Bakounine: Russian Revolutionist, Father of Nihilism, and Apostle of Anarchy." This was accompanied by a biographical sketch of Bakunin compiled by Tucker from French and German sources.[59] Of Bakunin Tucker wrote: "We are willing to hazard the judgment that coming history will yet place him in the very front ranks of the world's great social saviours. The grand head and face speak for themselves regarding the immense energy, lofty character, and innate nobility of the man. We should have esteemed it among the chief honors of our life to have known him personally, and should account it a great piece of good fortune to talk with one who was personally intimate with him and the essence and full meaning of his thought and aspiration."[60]

Tucker's greatest contribution towards familiarizing the American reading public with Bakunin was his translation of *God and the State*, Bakunin's most famous work. The original French edition appeared in 1882, with a preface by two of Bakunin's most devoted disciples, Carlo Cafiero and Elisée Reclus. Tucker began selling it (at twenty cents a copy) as soon as he received a shipment from Geneva. Scarcely a year later, in September 1883, he published his English translation, including the Cafiero and Reclus preface. The booklet had an excellent sale and went through at least ten printings, becoming the most widely read and frequently quoted of all Bakunin's works, a distinction which, a century later, it still enjoys.[61] Tucker, furthermore, published another important work of Bakunin's, *The Political Theology of Mazzini and the International*, translated from the French by Sarah E. Holmes and serialized in *Liberty* in 1886 and 1887.[62]

That an individualist and "philosophical" anarchist like Tucker should have been the chief American expositor of Bakunin, himself an apostle of collectivism and revolution, may seem odd. It stems from their common devotion to freedom and rejection of coercive authority, whether religious or secular, economic or political. Not surprisingly, however, Bakunin won his principal following in America among those who, unlike the Tuckerite school, shared his revolutionary and communalist convictions. An example was the group around *The Anarchist*, a "Socialistic Revolutionary Review" published by Edward Nathan Ganz in Boston in 1881, of which only two issues were printed, the second being suppressed by the police.

Another case in point was the San Francisco *Truth* ("A Journal for the Poor"), organ of the International Workmen's Association founded by Burnette G. Haskell. Even more, the spirit of Bakunin pervaded the Chicago *Alarm*, with its special concern for the disinherited and unemployed. Edited by Albert R. Parsons, the Haymarket martyr, *The Alarm* sold copies of *God and the State* (and of Stepniak's *Underground Russia*) and printed extracts from Bakunin and Nechaev's *Catechism of a Revolutionary*.[63] Still another militant journal with a strong Bakuninist flavor was the New York *Solidarity*, which appeared in the 1890s. Its editor, John H. Edelmann, an architect by profession and host to Kropotkin during his 1897 visit to America, had become an anarchist after studying Bakunin, "whose memory he revered."[64]

With the influx of immigrants during the late nineteenth and early twentieth centuries, the revolutionary anarchist movement received a fresh supply of recruits. Beginning in the 1880s, Bakunin's writings were translated into a number of European languages—German, Czech, Russian, Yiddish, Italian, Spanish—by newly formed anarchist groups. Here, again, *God and the State* was his most popular and widely distributed work. A German translation, by Moritz A. Bachmann, appeared in Philadelphia in 1884, barely a year after Tucker's English version, and was afterwards serialized in Johann Most's *Freiheit*, together with a long biographical article on Bakunin.[65] In due time, Czech, Russian, and Yiddish editions made their appearance.[66] Other writings by Bakunin cropped up in a whole range of anarchist journals in different languages and locations.[67]

Bakunin, it goes without saying, exerted a particularly strong influence on the Russian anarchist movement that emerged in North America after the turn of the century. Speakers for the Anarchist Red Cross and the Union of Russian Workers in the United States and Canada were active in spreading Bakunin's doctrines, while selections from his writings appeared in *Golos Truda* (The Voice of Labor), the organ of the Union of Russian Workers, and in its successor, *Khleb i Volia* (Bread and Freedom), whose masthead displayed his famous dictum, "The passion for destruction is also a creative passion."[68] After the

First World War, Bakunin's works were collected for publication in book form, but during the "Red Scare" hysteria of 1919-1920 the Russian anarchist movement was broken up and its leaders imprisoned or deported, so that only the first of several projected volumes found its way into print.[69]

The years of the war and the decade preceding it constituted the last period for nearly half a century that Bakunin enjoyed a significant following in America. In that age of industrial ferment, Bakunin's notion that a free federation of trade unions would form the "living germs"[70] of a new social order made a deep impression on the anarcho-syndicalists and the Industrial Workers of the World, founded in 1905 in Chicago. Inspired by similar ideas, a Bakunin Institute was established in 1913 near Oakland, California, by the Indian revolutionary Har Dayal.[71] And in May 1914 the hundredth anniversary of Bakunin's birth was celebrated in Webster Hall in New York, where an audience of two thousand heard eulogies by Alexander Berkman, Harry Kelly, and Hippolyte Havel in English, Bill Shatoff in Russian, and Saul Yanovsky in Yiddish.[72]

But the antiradical repressions during and after the war inflicted a blow from which the anarchists never recovered. Languishing in prison, a celebrated victim of the Red Scare, Bartolomeo Vanzetti, pondered the similar fate of Bakunin: "Bakounin, a healthy giant such as he was—died at 62 years—killed by the prisons, the exile, and the struggle."[73] During the interwar decades Bakunin's influence rapidly declined. Although excerpts from his writings continued to appear in anarchist publications—for instance, in *The Road to Freedom* and *Vanguard* of New York and in *Man!* of San Francisco—his books and pamphlets went out of print and became increasingly hard to find. Gregory Maximoff, a refugee from the Bolshevik dictatorship, did more than anyone else to keep Bakunin's ideas alive, especially in *Delo Truda* (The Cause of Labor) and *Delo Truda—Probuzhdenie* (The Cause of Labor—The Awakening), which he edited in Chicago and New York until his death in 1950.

With the upsurge of the New Left in the 1960s, Bakunin had a conspicuous revival. Previously, American readers had had to content themselves with Maximoff's posthumous compendium, *The Political Philosophy of Bakunin*, and Eugene Pyziur's *The Doctrine of Anarchism of Michael A. Bakunin*.[74] Now, however, fresh anthologies and biographies appeared in print,[75] and in campus demonstrations from Berkeley to Columbia the black flag of anarchy, inscribed with Bakuninist slogans, was once again unfurled. To the young radicals of the Vietnam era the "warfare state" seemed to be fulfilling Bakunin's most despairing predictions, while his formulas of self-determination and direct action exercised a growing appeal. Of particular relevance, after the lessons of Russia, Spain, and China, was his message that social emancipation must be attained by libertarian rather than authoritarian methods—that socialism without liberty, as he put it, is the worst form of tyranny.

In 1976, America's bicentennial year, anarchists in New York commemorated the hundredth anniversary of Bakunin's death, proclaiming the virtues of workers' self-management, sexual liberation, equality of education and income, and the dispersal of state power.[76] Similar gatherings took place in Zurich, Vienna, and other cities around the world. To a new generation of rebels, a century after Bakunin's passing, his vision was as vital as ever.

CHAPTER THREE

Bakunin and Nechaev

THE NECHAEV PERIOD of Bakunin's career (1869-1872) was relatively brief. Yet, apart from presenting a fascinating psychological drama, it forms an important chapter in the history of the Russian revolutionary movement, posing fundamental questions of revolutionary tactics and morality with which radicals have continued to grapple to this day. Bakunin's relationship with Nechaev was also a contributing factor in his conflict with Marx and his expulsion (in 1872) from the First International. And it led him to a reexamination of his revolutionary doctrines and to a reassertion of his libertarian principles against what he called the "Jesuitism" and "Machiavellianism" of his young disciple.[1]

Sergei Gennadievich Nechaev was born on September 20, 1847, at Ivanovo, a growing textile town northeast of Moscow that was beginning to acquire the reputation of a "Russian Manchester." His father was a sign painter, his mother a seamstress, and both were of serf origin, so that Nechaev was one of the first prominent Russian radicals with a thoroughly plebeian background. He was "not a product of our world," wrote Vera Zasulich in her memoirs, but was "a stranger among us."[2] As a son of the people, however, he was all the more impressive in the eyes of his fellow revolutionists, repentant noblemen who yearned to repay their debt to the lower elements. An acquaintance called Nechaev "a real revolutionist, a peasant who has preserved all the serf's hatred against his masters,"[3] a hatred that was to be turned even against his own comrades, with their aristocratic birth and education.

In April 1866, at the age of eighteen, Nechaev left Ivanovo for St. Petersburg, where he taught in a parochial school. In the fall of 1868 he enrolled in the university as a nonmatriculating student, and he joined a group of young revolutionaries that included such future anarchists as Z. K. Ralli, V. N. Cherkezov, and F. V. Volkhovsky, as well as such near anarchists or libertarian socialists as Mark Natanson, German Lopatin, and L. B. Goldenberg. Though Nechaev as yet knew no French, he attended discussions of Buonarroti's history of Babeuf's Conspiracy of Equals,[4] a book that helped shape a whole generation of Russian rebels, and his dreams were soon dominated by secret societies and the conspiratorial life. He found himself irresistibly drawn to Jacobinism and Blanquism; and when he later visited Ralli in Switzerland, he was carrying books by Rousseau and Robespierre, and his authoritarian tendencies, his pretense of knowing "the general will" and of "forcing the people to be free," were already well developed.

Nechaev was also attracted by the Jacobin tradition within the Russian revolutionary movement itself, a tradition dating back to the Decembrist leader Pavel Pestel in the 1820s and to Nicholas Speshnev in the 1840s, who emphasized the need for conspiratorial tactics and a revolutionary dictatorship based, as he put it, on the "Jesuit" model—a suggestion that led the Fourierist Michael Petrashevsky to declare: "I would be the first to raise my hand against the dictator."[5] In 1862, four years before Nechaev's arrival in St. Petersburg, a clandestine leaflet called *Young Russia* was issued by Peter Zaichnevsky, a leading Russian Jacobin who was influenced by Robespierre and Babeuf and by Mazzini and the Italian Carbonari (the title of his leaflet is derived from Young Italy) with their methods of revolutionary conspiracy. His ultimate goal, however, a federation of self-governing communes, was inspired by the decentralist socialism of Proudhon, and when the police came to arrest him they found an unfinished Russian translation of *What Is Property?*, Proudhon's first anarchist book, among his papers.

In *Young Russia* Zaichnevsky called for a "bloody and pitiless" revolution, on the model of Razin and Pugachev, and for the merciless annihilation of the tsarist family and its supporters: "We will cry 'To your axes' and then we will strike the imperial party without sparing our blows, just as they do not spare theirs against us. We will destroy them in the squares, if the cowardly swine dare to go there. We will destroy them in their houses, in the narrow streets of the towns, in the broad avenues of the capital, and in the villages. Remember that, when this happens, anyone who is not with us is against us, and an enemy, and that every method is used to destroy an enemy." Herzen was repelled by the ruthlessness and crude immoralism of the leaflet, and even Bakunin condemned its author for his "mad and really doctrinaire scorn for the people."[6] Yet *Young Russia* exerted a powerful influence among the youth of Nechaev's generation, the "men of the sixties," who were inspired by its defiant and uncompromising rhetoric.

Another source of inspiration was the character of Rakhmetov in Chernyshevsky's novel *What Is to Be Done?*, which appeared in 1864. Rakhmetov was the literary prototype of the new revolutionary, a man possessed and living a pure ascetic life, subjecting himself to intense physical privation in preparation for his revolutionary role. To harden himself, he eats raw meat and sleeps on a bed of nails. He has no personal life, no wife, no friends, no family ties that might deflect him from his purpose. He adopts a deliberately brusque manner of conversation and behavior both to cut himself off from conventional society and to avoid wasting time on empty words and formalities. He uses his money not for personal needs but to help impoverished students and the revolutionary cause.

The figure of Rakhmetov gripped the imagination of young revolutionaries for decades to come (in 1892 Alexander Berkman used "Rakhmetov" as his cover name when he went to shoot Henry Clay Frick). During the mid-1860s Rakhmetov served as a model for the Ishutin circle, whose members (including Kropotkin's future comrade, Varlaam Cherkezov, and Dmitri Karakozov, whose attempt on the tsar in 1866 was hailed by Nechaev as "the beginning of our sacred cause") renounced all personal pleasures and led rigorously ascetic lives, sleeping on floors, giving all their money to the cause, and devoting all their energies to the liberation of the people. They also exhibited a strong anti-intellectual bias, scorning the university for training "generals of culture" rather than helpers of the workers and peasants. Some even abandoned their studies and organized cooperatives. As one member remarked, "the masses are uneducated; therefore we have no right to an education. You don't need much learning to explain to the people that they are being cheated and robbed."[7] Like Zaichnevsky, they rejected reforms or palliatives and despised the older generation of radicals, the "men of the forties" exemplified by Herzen and his circle, as impotent intellectuals who, for all their erudition and revolutionary phrases, were powerless to break with the old order or with their own aristocratic roots. They called, again like Zaichnevsky, for the extermination of the tsarist family in order to spark off a social upheaval, a Pugachev revolt that would bring the existing order to dust.

To carry out this task a small group called "Hell" was organized within the Ishutin circle, an ascetic cadre of terrorists shrouded in secrecy and leading an anonymous underground existence. Every member of Hell considered himself a doomed man, cut off from normal society and dedicated entirely to the revolution. He must give up his

friends, his family, his personal life, even his name in total self-efface-
ment for the cause. In Ishutin's words (later to be echoed by Nechaev)
he must "live with one single exclusive aim,"[8] the emancipation of the
lower classes.

To accomplish this end every means was permitted, including theft,
blackmail, even murder, not to speak of fraud, deception, the denunciation of innocent people, or the infiltration of rival secret societies to
gain control over them—all under strict revolutionary discipline, the
violation of which carried a penalty of death. One member even considered poisoning his own father and giving his inheritance to the
cause; and plans were made for armed robberies—later to be called
"expropriations"—of commercial and governmental establishments.
The main object, however, was the assassination of the tsar and his
officials. The deed once done, the terrorist must carry out the ultimate
gesture of self-annihilation by squeezing a pellet of fulminate of mer-
cury between his teeth—Berkman tried to do this after his attempt on
Frick—so that the police would never know his true identity. Ishutin,
who was inspired by Orsini's attempt on Napoleon III, spread it about
that Hell was merely the Russian section of a European-wide revolutionary organization whose purpose was to eliminate monarchs everywhere, thus pioneering a technique of mystification that Nechaev
would develop into a fine art.

Still another link in the chain of Russian Jacobinism, a chain that
extended from Pestel to Lenin, was Peter Tkachev, who maintained
that a successful revolution could be brought about only by a closely
knit elite that "must have intellectual and moral power over the majority" and whose organization demanded "centralization, strict discipline, speed, decisiveness, and coordination of activities." Zaichnevsky, it is worth noting, became one of Tkachev's most steadfast
supporters, remaining faithful to his Jacobin principles to the end of
his life; and in 1869 Nechaev collaborated with Tkachev in drafting *A
Program of Revolutionary Action* that called for an organization of
"revolutionary prototypes" who would operate, like the Ishutin circle,
according to the principle that the revolutionary end justifies any and
all means. "Those who join the organization," they wrote, "must give
up every possession, occupation, or family tie, because families and
occupations might distract members from their activities."[9] Again like
Ishutin, they envisioned a union of European revolutionary organizations, with a center in the West, and it was perhaps with this in mind
that Nechaev, in 1869, went to Switzerland, where he first met Michael Bakunin.

BEFORE LEAVING Russia, Nechaev began his career of mystification and deception. In March 1869 Vera Zasulich received an anonymous letter with the following words: "When walking today on the Vasilevsky Island, I saw a carriage conveying prisoners. A hand reached out of the window and dropped a note. At the same time I heard the following words: 'If you are a student, deliver this to the indicated address.' I am a student and consider it my duty to comply with the request. Destroy the letter."[10] The accompanying note, in Nechaev's hand, informed his friends that he had been arrested and was being taken to the Peter-Paul fortress. Soon after this, a rumor was circulated that he had escaped from the fortress—an unprecedented feat—and was on his way to the West. Yet in fact there had been no escape, nor even an arrest. It was all a fabrication, the first of a series of escapades invented by Nechaev to build himself up as a hero, to surround himself with an aura of mystery, and to cast himself in the role of the "revolutionary prototype" of his and Tkachev's *Program of Revolutionary Action.*

Nechaev crossed the Russian frontier on March 4, 1869. When he reached Geneva, he immediately called on Bakunin, claiming to represent a powerful revolutionary organization within the tsarist empire. Bakunin was infatuated with this "young savage," this "tiger cub," as he called Nechaev. "I have here with me," he wrote to James Guillaume on April 13, 1869, "one of those young fanatics who know no doubts, who fear nothing, and who realize that many of them will perish at the hands of the government but who nevertheless have decided that they will not relent until the people rise. They are magnificent, these young fanatics, believers without God, heroes without rhetoric."[11] He saw in Nechaev the ideal revolutionary conspirator, the herald of a new generation whose energy, determination, and intransigence would overthrow the imperial order. Nechaev's arrival in Switzerland, as E. H. Carr observed, gave the aging Bakunin a new lease on life, a rebirth of revolutionary hope, and a breath of his native land, which he would never see again. For Bakunin, as Michael Confino puts it, "Nechaev was Russian youth, revolutionary Russia, Russia itself."[12]

During the spring and summer of 1869, Bakunin and Nechaev issued a series of pamphlets and manifestoes calling for a social upheaval in Russia. In *Some Words to Our Young Brothers in Russia* Bakunin exhorted the revolutionary youth to "go to the people" with a message of rebellion, to rouse them to a life-and-death struggle against the state and the privileged classes, following the model set by Stenka Razin two centuries before. "Young men of education must become not the people's benefactors, not its dictators and guides, but merely a lever for the people to free itself, the unifier of the people's own energies and forces," Bakunin declared. "Take notice of learning, in whose name men try to shackle you and strip you of your power. Learning of this kind must die together with the world of which it is an expression."

A similar proclamation, *To the Students of the University, the Academy, and the Technical Institute*, was drafted by Nechaev, and another called *Russian Students* by Nicholas Ogarev, an associate of Herzen and Bakunin. The rest—*How the Revolutionary Question Presents Itself, Principles of Revolution*, and *Publications of the Society of "The People's Justice," No. 1* (consisting of two articles dated Summer 1869)—were all unsigned and their authorship has not been conclusively determined. Extolling indiscriminate destruction in the name of the revolution, they preached the justification of every means by the revolutionary end. *How the Revolution Presents Itself* is noteworthy for its eulogy of banditry in distinctively Bakuninist terms: "The brigand in Russia is the only true revolutionary—the revolutionary without phrase-making, without bookish rhetoric, the irreconcilable, indefatigable, indomitable revolutionary of the deed. . . . The anniversaries of Stenka Razin and Pugachev are approaching; let us prepare for the feast."

The authorship of *Principles of Revolution* (which seems to be the work of Nechaev) is especially important because of its strong stylistic resemblance to the *Catechism of a Revolutionary*: "We recognize no other activity but the work of extermination, but we admit that the forms which this activity will take will be extremely varied—poison, the knife, the rope, etc. In this struggle the revolution sanctifies everything alike." *The People's Justice No. 1*, with its appeals for peasant rebellion à la Razin and Pugachev and criticisms of the "unasked-for teachers" whose learning has sapped them of their life-giving "popular juices," bears the earmarks of both Bakunin and Nechaev, though its appeal to the example of Ishutin sounds more like the "young savage" ("Ishutin has taken the initiative; and now it is time for us to begin, before his hot tracks have cooled").

It was during this period, between April and August 1869, that the notorious *Catechism of a Revolutionary* was written, the object of heated controversy ever since. Foreshadowed by earlier documents of the European revolutionary movement, it expresses ideas and sentiments that had already been propounded by Zaichnevsky and Ishutin in Russia and by the Carbonari and Young Italy in the West. Yet, by carrying to an extreme the ruthlessness and immorality of its predecessors, it constitutes the fullest statement of a creed that has occupied a prominent place in revolutionary history for more than a century. In the *Catechism* the revolutionary is depicted as a complete immoralist, bound to commit any crime, any treachery, any baseness or deception to bring about the destruction of the existing order. Because of this, Nicolas Walter has described it as a "revolting rather than revolutionary document," the expression of "pure, total, fanatical, destructive, nihilistic, self-defeating revolutionism."[13]

The *Catechism* is divided into two parts: (1) General Rules of the Organization, consisting of twenty-two numbered paragraphs, and (2) Rules of Conduct of Revolutionaries, with twenty-six paragraphs under three headings: The Attitude of the Revolutionary towards Himself, The Attitude of the Revolutionary towards His Revolutionary Comrades, and The Attitude of the Revolutionary towards Society. The original version of the *Catechism*, written in cipher, was taken back to Russia by Nechaev in August 1869. It was found by the police during a roundup of Nechaev's followers three months later and was used as evidence against them at their trial. The original manuscript, first published in *Pravitel'stvennyi Vestnik* (Government Herald) in July 1871, was lost in a fire in the Ministry of Justice in 1917; but the text was reprinted in 1924 in the journal *Bor'ba Klassov* (Class Struggle) from a copy found in the archives of the tsarist secret police.

Part Two of the *Catechism* was published in French by the Marxists in 1873, during their campaign against Bakunin in the First International. The first English translation was published in 1939 in Max Nomad's *Apostles of Revolution*, and another appeared in 1957 in Robert Payne's *The Terrorists* (reprinted in 1967 in an expanded version of the book called *The Fortress*). There are extensive excerpts in Franco Venturi's *Roots of Revolution* (1960); and between 1969 and 1971 at least three editions appeared in pamphlet form, the first (as noted in Chapter 1) issued by the Black Panther party in Berkeley, the second by Kropotkin Lighthouse Publications in London with a foreword by Nicolas Walter (both reproducing the Nomad translation), and in a new translation as Red Pamphlet No. 01 with an unsigned preface and no place of publication indicated.

"The revolutionary is a doomed man," begins Part Two of the *Catechism*, in language reminiscent of Ishutin. "He has no personal interests, no affairs, no sentiments, attachments, property, not even a name of his own. Everything in him is absorbed by one exclusive interest, one thought, one passion—the revolution" (Paragraph 1). He studies chemistry and other sciences for the purpose of destroying his enemies (Paragraph 3). He has severed all connections with the social order, with the world of education, and with conventional morality: "whatever aids the triumph of the revolution is ethical; all that hinders it is unethical and criminal" (Paragraph 4). "All tender, softening sentiments of kinship, friendship, love, gratitude, and even honor itself must be snuffed out in him by the one cold passion of the revolutionary cause. For him there is only one satisfaction, consolation, and delight—the success of the revolution. Day and night he must have one thought, one aim—inexorable destruction. Striving coldly and unfalteringly towards this aim, he must be ready to perish himself and to destroy with his own hands everything that hinders its realization" (Paragraph 6).

The revolutionary organization must draw up a list of persons to be exterminated (Paragraph 15), and "those men must be destroyed who are particularly harmful to the revolutionary organization" (Paragraph 16). The revolutionary must trap those with money or influence, the *Catechism* continues, and "turn them into one's slave" (Paragraph 18). As for liberals, "one should take hold of them, get possession of all their secrets, compromise them to the utmost, so that no avenue of escape may be left to them" (Paragraph 19). The final paragraph repeats the incendiary message of *Some Words to Our Young Brothers, How the Revolutionary Question Presents Itself*, and *Principles of Revolution*: "Our business is destruction, terrible, complete, universal, and merciless" (Paragraph 24). "Let us join hands with the bold world of bandits—the only genuine revolutionists in Russia" (Paragraph 25).

The authorship of the *Catechism* has been a subject of prolonged and bitter dispute. In the absence of conclusive evidence, scholars hostile to the anarchists have usually attributed it to Bakunin, while others have attributed it to Nechaev, and still others to both men as a product of their collaboration during 1869. Thus the Kropotkin Lighthouse edition gives Nechaev as the author, but both the Black Panther and Red Pamphlet editions list Bakunin, the anonymous editor of the latter insisting that "the myth that Nechaev wrote it was invented by petty bourgeois pseudo-'anarchists' who were revisionists from Bakunin."

Such eminent scholars as Max Nettlau, E. H. Carr, and Franco Venturi in the West and B. P. Kozmin in the Soviet Union have attributed the *Catechism* to Bakunin, as have Bakunin's own associates Ralli and Michael Sazhin ("Armand Ross"), who claimed to have seen a copy of the manuscript in Bakunin's handwriting. Some, including Carr, have argued that the *Catechism* carries echoes of Bakunin's style and that the catechism was one of Bakunin's favorite forms of composition (he had published a *Revolutionary Catechism* in 1866). On the other hand, the catechism as a literary form was widely used by revolutionaries in both Russia and the West throughout the nineteenth century.

Michael Confino, moreover, maintains that a comparison of the *Catechism of a Revolutionary* with Bakunin's earlier *Revolutionary Catechism* shows that they are "radically dissimilar" in style and terminology.[14] In both language and content, rather, the former seems to have emerged from the milieu of student revolutionism inside Russia during the 1860s—a milieu in which Bakunin, unlike Nechaev, played no part—rather than from among the older generation of exiles in Switzerland.

Striking new evidence on this question is contained in a letter from Bakunin to Nechaev of June 2, 1870, buried for many years in the Natalie Herzen Archives of the Bibliothèque Nationale in Paris and first published by Confino in 1966 in the *Cahiers du Monde Russe et Soviétique*. It is the longest and most interesting letter that Bakunin ever wrote, requiring eight days to complete and occupying more than thirty pages of closely printed text. It forms the centerpiece of both Confino's and Arthur Lehning's volumes on Bakunin and Nechaev, and we shall have more to say about it later.

In his letter Bakunin explicitly repudiates what he calls "your catechism," along with Nechaev's whole "Jesuitical system." On the basis of this statement the *Catechism* must now be attributed primarily to Nechaev, although it is by no means certain that Bakunin had no role in its composition or revision. For it was written during a period of intimate cooperation between the two men, and even if the burden of authorship was Nechaev's, Bakunin may have helped with the writing or editing. This, indeed, would account for the occasional Bakuninist phraseology as well as for the alleged existence of a copy in Bakunin's handwriting. Bakunin's letter to Nechaev of June 2, 1870, acknowledges that he was familiar with it at the time of its composition—a time when he was extremely susceptible to Nechaev's influence—and, significantly, he raised no known protest against it until his falling out with Nechaev a year later.

BEFORE Nechaev returned to Russia with the manuscript of the *Catechism*, he had already begun to carry out its provisions. Having already deceived his revolutionary comrades with the fake story of his arrest and escape, he now sent incriminating letters and revolutionary literature to his more moderate acquaintances in Russia in order to compromise them with the authorities and (in accordance with paragraphs 18 and 19 of the *Catechism*) to involve them more deeply in radical activity. Between March and August 1869 some 560 items involving 387 persons were intercepted in St. Petersburg alone. Following the same principle, Nechaev would later steal private letters and papers from Bakunin and his circle in order to exert pressure on them and would even carry out murder so as to bind his accomplices to his will. All this was part of a system of total disregard for decency and fairness that has gone down in revolutionary history under the name of "Nechaevism."

Meanwhile, Bakunin had indulged in a bit of mystification of his own. In May 1869 he issued Nechaev with a certificate designating him as "one of the accredited representatives of the Russian Section of the World Revolutionary Alliance, No. 2771." Signed by Bakunin, it bore the seal of the "European Revolutionary Alliance, Central Committee," a mere invention—similar to that already used by Ishutin and Nechaev—designed to create the impression of a worldwide network of revolutionaries. "Thus did Nechaev, the self-styled representative of a probably non-existent Russian revolutionary committee, receive from Bakunin authority to act in Russia as the representative of a nonexistent European Revolutionary Alliance," Carr wryly comments. "It was a delicious situation which can have few parallels either in comedy or in history."[15] To add further to Nechaev's prestige, Bakunin persuaded Ogarev to dedicate a poem, written for a student who had died a martyr's death in Siberia, to his "young friend Nechaev." The poem was printed as a leaflet, and in the fall of 1869 it was circulated in Russia, where it helped to build up the Nechaev legend.

At the end of August 1869 Nechaev returned to Russia armed with the poem, the *Catechism*, and the blessings of Bakunin and Ogarev. Arriving in Moscow he proceeded to organize a revolutionary society called The People's Justice—the same name as the brochure published in Geneva—on lines prescribed in the *Catechism*. It was a secret, disciplined association organized in groups of "revolutionary fives," as in Ishutin's Hell and the first Land and Freedom organization of the 1860s, as well as in secret societies throughout western Europe, with each member owing implicit obedience to a leader, who in turn took his orders from a central committee. Its chief aim was to unleash a popular upheaval on February 19, 1870, the ninth anniversary of the emancipation of the serfs, and its official seal was an axe with the words "Committee of the People's Justice of February 19, 1870." The organization was dominated by the person of Nechaev, who, all sources agree, demanded unquestioning obedience from his comrades, to whom he issued orders in the name of a nonexistent central committee. Nechaev set the members spying on one another and encouraged the use of extortion and blackmail to obtain money for the cause.

Such methods apparently proved repugnant to one of the ablest members of the organization, a student at the Petrovsk Agricultural

Academy with the improbable name of Ivan Ivanovich Ivanov. Ivanov seems to have been an honorable and intelligent member of the circle at the Academy. He was active in student cooperatives, spent time teaching children of peasants, and exercised considerable influence among his revolutionary comrades. At some point he evidently objected to Nechaev's orders, questioned the existence of the central committee in whose name Nechaev claimed to speak, and may even have threatened to form a new revolutionary group on more democratic lines, something that Nechaev would hardly tolerate. In any event, Nechaev managed to convince some of his followers that Ivanov was planning to inform on them, and that, in accordance with Paragraph 16 of the *Catechism* ("those men must be destroyed who are particularly harmful to the revolutionary organization"), it was necessary to do away with him.

On the night of November 21, 1869, Ivanov was lured to a grotto in the park of the Agricultural Academy on the pretext of unearthing a clandestine printing press. There he was set upon and beaten by Nechaev and four accomplices. Nechaev tried to strangle him but was bitten severely on the hand, whereupon he drew a pistol and shot Ivanov in the head. The body was weighted down with stones and dumped through an ice hole in a nearby pond. In this way Nechaev removed a potential adversary, while at the same time incriminating his comrades to ensure their obedience to his authority. It was an extreme example of his technique of gaining compliance through involving his comrades in crime. Their victim, however, was not an agent of the autocracy but one of their own number who had aroused the leader's antagonism.

The murder of Ivanov created a sensation. Dostoevsky used the incident in the plot for his novel *The Possessed*, with Verkhovensky representing Nechaev and Shatov, Ivanov. The discovery of Ivanov's body four days after the murder led to the arrest of some three hundred revolutionaries and to the trial of eighty-four *Nechaevtsy* in the summer of 1871. One of the condemned was Peter Lavrov's son-in-law Michael Negreskul, who had previously opposed Nechaev's tactics in St. Petersburg and who was among those whom Nechaev had sought to compromise by sending revolutionary proclamations from Switzerland. Imprisoned in the Peter-Paul fortress, Negreskul fell ill with consumption and died under house arrest in February 1870. Nechaev, meanwhile, had slipped out of Moscow for St. Petersburg, where he obtained a false passport and succeeded in crossing the border in December 1869, leaving his comrades behind to take the rap.

ON JANUARY 12, 1870, Bakunin, who was then living in Locarno, received a letter from Ogarev announcing that Nechaev had arrived in Geneva. Bakunin jumped for joy so violently that he "nearly smashed the ceiling with my old head."[16] A short while later Nechaev came to Locarno and the two men resumed their collaboration, issuing two manifestoes to the Russian nobility, the first probably written by Bakunin and the second by Nechaev. Nechaev also published a second number of *The People's Justice* (dated Winter 1870), as well as six issues of *The Bell* in April and May 1870.

To finance these ventures Nechaev used money from the so-called Bakhmetiev fund, left to Alexander Herzen by a young Russian nobleman who in 1858 went to the South Pacific to found a utopian community. When Herzen met Nechaev in Geneva in 1869 he instinctively disliked him. But under pressure from Bakunin and Ogarev, he relinquished to them half of the fund, a good part of which passed to Nechaev, who used it to finance his revolutionary activities when he returned to Russia. When Herzen died in January 1870, Bakunin urged Ogarev to claim the balance of the fund from Herzen's family. Herzen's son handed it over, and from Ogarev nearly all of it went to Nechaev, who refused to sign a receipt but accepted it in the name of his nonexistent central committee.

About the same time, Bakunin was having financial troubles of his own. He had accepted a commission from a Russian publisher named Poliakov to translate Marx's *Kapital* and had been paid an advance of 300 rubles. But he was unable to make any headway with the project. On February 17, 1870, Nechaev wrote a threatening letter to a Russian student named Liubavin, who had acted as an intermediary between Bakunin and Poliakov, in which he demanded that Bakunin be left alone and be released from all claims upon him. The letter, written on stationery of the Central Committee of the People's Justice adorned with an axe, a dagger, and a pistol, was later used by Marx to discredit Bakunin and have him expelled from the International.

Before long, however, relations between Bakunin and Nechaev began to deteriorate. The ensuing rift, as Lehning and Confino show, was a complicated affair involving psychological, financial, moral, and ideological considerations. During his second sojourn in Switzerland, Nechaev's attitude towards Bakunin was not the same as it had been a year earlier. According to Ralli, he no longer showed any deference to his mentor. On the contrary, he demanded that notice be taken of him as the only person with a serious revolutionary organization. He dealt more and more brusquely with Bakunin, even denying him money from the Bakhmetiev fund for his day-to-day needs. He complained to

Sazhin that Bakunin no longer had "the level of energy and self-abnegation"[17] required of a true revolutionary, a reflection of the conflict of generations—of the "men of the sixties" against the "men of the forties"—within the populist movement. He began, indeed, to treat Bakunin as the *Catechism* said liberals ought to be treated after one had gotten out of them all that one could. He sought to impose on Bakunin and his friends his own authoritarian methods, going so far as to steal their private papers in order to blackmail or manipulate them in the future ("one should take hold of them, get possession of all their secrets, compromise them to the utmost, so that no avenue of escape may be left to them"—Paragraph 19 of the *Catechism*).

Bakunin's disillusionment was shattering. His pride had suffered dearly for his infatuation with the "Boy." "If you introduce him to a friend, he will immediately proceed to sow dissension, scandal, and intrigue between you and your friend and make you quarrel," Bakunin wrote. "If your friend has a wife or a daughter, he will try to seduce her and get her with child in order to snatch her from the power of conventional morality and plunge her despite herself into revolutionary protest against society."[18] (This was precisely Nechaev's behavior towards Natalie Herzen, as described in her diary.) Meanwhile, German Lopatin had arrived from Russia and was telling the truth about Ivanov's murder, explaining that the scars on Nechaev's finger were the death marks of his victim. Lopatin also exposed the fiction of Nechaev's central committee and of his boasted escape from the fortress.

The climax of the dispute came with the letter from Bakunin to Nechaev of June 2, 1870, an English translation of which (by Lydia Bott) was published in *Encounter* magazine in July and August 1972 with a note by Michael Confino. Confino is justified in calling it one of the most extraordinary documents in the history of the nineteenth-century revolutionary movement. For it not only throws light on the authorship of the famous *Catechism* but also clarifies the reasons for Bakunin's break with Nechaev, helps us to understand their differing views on secret organizations, and, above all, illuminates the question of revolutionary ethics—of the relationship between means and ends—which revolutionists everywhere have continued to face.[19]

Bakunin, expressing his disappointment and almost unbearable humiliation, writes with great feeling and power. He complains to Nechaev of having had "complete faith in you, while you duped me. I turned out to be a complete fool. This is painful and shameful for a man of my experience and age. Worse than this, I spoilt my situation with regard to the Russian and International causes." On the question of revolution Bakunin firmly rejects Nechaev's Jacobinism and Blanquism—his belief in the seizure of power by a revolutionary minority and the establishment of a revolutionary dictatorship—calling instead for a spontaneous mass upheaval by the people themselves: "I am deeply convinced that any other revolution is dishonest, harmful, and spells death to liberty and the people."

What, then, is the role of the revolutionary organization? Nechaev's conception is false, preparing new "exploiters of the people," killing "all feeling of personal fairness," and "educating them in lying, suspicion, spying, and denunciation." The true revolutionary organization, says Bakunin, "does not foist upon the people any new regulations, orders, styles of life, but merely unleashes their will and gives wide scope to their self-determination and their economic and social organization, which must be created by themselves from below and not from above." The revolutionary organization must "make impossible after the popular victory the establishment of any state power over the people—even the most revolutionary, even your power—because any power, whatever it calls itself, would inevitably subject the people to old slavery in new form." "I loved you deeply and still love you," Bakunin writes, but you must repudiate your "false Jesuit system," your "system of deceit, which is increasingly becoming your sole system, your main weapon and means, and is fatal to the cause itself."

Such was Bakunin's plea to his wayward disciple. Yet his own rejection of "Nechaevism" was far from complete. For all his disillusionment, his attitude towards Nechaev was ambivalent. Nechaev, in his eyes, remained a devoted revolutionary who acted while others merely talked, and whose energy, perseverance, audacity, and willpower still exerted a powerful appeal. "You are a passionate and dedicated man," writes Bakunin to Nechaev. "This is your strength, your valor, and your justification." If you alter your methods, he adds, "I would wish not only to remain allied with you, but to make this union even closer and firmer." Bakunin sent a similar message to Ogarev and his associates: "The main thing for the moment is to save our erring and confused friend. In spite of all, he remains a valuable man, and there are few valuable men in the world. . . . We love him, we believe in him, we foresee that his future activity will be of immense benefit to the people. That is why we must divert him from his false and disastrous path."

Thus, for all his wounded pride, for all his disapproval of Nechaev's principles and tactics, so strong was Bakunin's affection for his "tiger cub" that he was unable to break decisively with him—notwithstanding the lies and humiliations, the unbridled immorality of the *Catechism*, and even the murder of Ivanov. Then, too, there remained much common ground between them. Their programs, admitted Bakunin, had been "truly identical." It was only after Nechaev had begun to employ his devious methods against Bakunin himself that he expressed his revulsion against them.

Bakunin, no less than Nechaev, had a passion for conspiracies and secret organizations. For all his assaults on revolutionary dictatorship, he was himself, as has been noted, a tireless advocate of a close-knit revolutionary association bound together by implicit obedience to a revolutionary leader. Bakunin's uncritical admirers are unconvincing when they maintain that his references to "iron discipline" and to an "invisible dictatorship" are isolated and uncharacteristic, either antedating the period when his anarchist theories were fully developed or being expressed while he was under Nechaev's pernicious influence. On the contrary, conspiracy was a central thread in his entire revolutionary career. Not for nothing did he praise Buonarroti as "the greatest conspirator of his age."[20]

Throughout his adult life, from the 1840s until the 1870s, Bakunin sought to create clandestine societies modeled on those in the West. In 1845 he became a Freemason. And in 1848 he called for a secret organization of three- to five-man groups that would be "subject to a strict hierarchy and unconditional obedience to a central control." Nor did he abandon this goal in subsequent years. During the 1860s he founded a whole series of secret societies—the Florentine Brotherhood (1864), the International Brotherhood (1866), the International Alliance of Social Democracy (1868)—and elaborated rules governing their memberships' behavior. The organization was to act as "a sort of general staff," working "invisibly on the masses" and remaining intact even after the revolution had been accomplished, in order to forestall the establishment of any "official dictatorship." It would itself exercise a "collective dictatorship," a dictatorship "without any badge, without title, without official right, and the more powerful because it lacks the appearance of power." Its members, declared Bakunin in language reminiscent of the *Catechism*, must submit to "strict discipline," breaches of which were to be considered a "crime" punishable by "expulsion combined with delivery to the vengeance of all members." As late as 1872 he could still write: "Our goal is the creation of a powerful but always invisible organization, which must prepare the revolution and lead it."[21]

The same position is taken in his letter to Nechaev. The popular revolution, he repeats, must be "invisibly led, not by an official dictatorship, but by a nameless and collective one, composed of those in favor of total people's liberation from all oppression, firmly united in a secret society and always and everywhere acting in support of a common aim and in accordance with a common program." He calls the revolutionary organization "the staff of the people's army" and adds, again in the language of the *Catechism*, that it must be composed of persons "who are passionately and undeviatingly devoted, who have, as far as possible, renounced all personal interests and have renounced once and for all, for life or for death itself, all that attracts people, all material comforts and delights, all satisfaction of ambition, status, and fame. . . . They must be totally and wholly absorbed by one passion, the people's liberation."

The organization, moreover, must have an executive committee and require strict discipline of its members. Paradoxically, it must be a morally pure vanguard, yet in certain cases—here again we have the language of the *Catechism*—engage in lying and deception, particularly against rival revolutionary groups: "Societies whose aims are near to ours must be forced to merge with our Society or, at least, must be subordinated to it without their knowledge. . . . All this cannot be achieved only by propagating the truth; cunning, diplomacy, deceit are necessary. Jesuit methods or even entanglements can be used for this. . . . Thus this simple law must be the basis of our activity: truth, honesty, mutual trust between all Brothers and towards any man who is capable of becoming a Brother—lies, cunning, entanglement, and, if necessary, violence towards enemies." Bakunin's methods, then, are not so far removed from Nechaev's. The chief difference, perhaps, is that Nechaev actually put them into practice—including blackmail and murder, directed against friends and enemies alike—while Bakunin limited himself to mere words or to such relatively harmless mystifications as the worldwide revolutionary alliance in whose name he pretended to speak.

AFTER their falling out in the summer of 1870, Bakunin and Nechaev never saw each other again. Nechaev went to London, where he published a new journal called *Obshchina* (The Commune), in which he demanded from Bakunin and Ogarev the remainder of the Bakhmetiev fund. After visiting Paris on the eve of the Commune, he returned to London, then went again to Switzerland, where he eked out a precarious existence by his father's old trade of sign painting and where he was sheltered for a time by Italian disciples of Mazzini. The tsarist government, however, was determined to get him, spending more money and effort on his pursuit than on that of any other nineteenth-century revolutionary. Bakunin sent Nechaev a warning that the authorities were on his trail, but Nechaev ignored it, convinced that his

47

old mentor was merely "trying to draw [me] away from Zurich." Finally, on August 14, 1872, Nechaev was betrayed to the Swiss police by Adolph Stempkowski, a former Polish revolutionary who had become a Russian spy. Soon afterwards he was extradited to Russia as a common murderer, in spite of protests by his fellow expatriates (Bakunin among them) that he was in fact a political refugee.

On November 2, 1872, Bakunin expressed his sympathy for Nechaev in a remarkable letter to Ogarev, which deserves to be quoted at length: "I pity him deeply. No one ever did me, and intentionally, as much harm as he did, but I pity him all the same. He was a man of rare energy, and when we met there burned in him a very ardent and pure flame for our poor, oppressed people; our historical and current national misery caused him real suffering. At that time his external behavior was unsavory enough, but his inner self had not been soiled. It was his authoritarianism and his unbridled willfulness which, very regrettably and through his ignorance together with his Machiavellianism and Jesuitical methods, finally plunged him irretrievably into the mire. . . . However, an inner voice tells me that Nechaev, who is lost forever and certainly knows that he is lost, will now call forth from the depths of his being, warped and soiled but far from being base or common, all his primitive energy and courage. He will perish like a hero and this time he will betray nothing and no one. Such is my belief. We shall see if I am right."[22]

The rest of Nechaev's story can be briefly told. When tried in Moscow in January 1873, he bore himself with unbending defiance. "I refuse to be a slave of your tyrannical government," he declared. "I do not recognize the Emperor and the laws of this country." He would not answer any questions and was finally dragged from the dock shouting "Down with despotism!" After being sentenced to twenty years at hard labor, he declared himself "a son of the people" and invoked Razin and Pugachev "who strung up the nobles as in France they sent them to the guillotine." At the ceremony of "civil execution" following his trial he shouted: "Down with the tsar! Long live freedom! Long live the Russian people."[23]

The last ten years of Nechaev's life were spent in solitary confinement in the Peter-Paul fortress, the prison from which he had falsely claimed to have escaped in 1869. His behavior behind bars, as Max Nomad remarked, was "one of the great episodes of revolutionary history."[24] When General Potapov of the secret police visited his cell and offered him leniency if he would serve as a spy, Nechaev struck him across the face, drawing blood. For the next two years his hands and feet remained in chains until the flesh began to rot.

48

Yet Nechaev's spirit was unbroken. Indeed, even in prison he was able to exert his charismatic power, winning over his own guards, who began to call him their "eagle." He got them to read the illegal journal of the People's Will group and even taught them how to write letters in code. With their help, in fact, he was able to communicate with his fellow prisoners and eventually with the outside world, including the central committee of the People's Will on the eve of their assassination of Alexander II. Vera Figner tells in her memoirs of their excitement when they leaned that Nechaev was still alive and in the nearby Peter-Paul fortress rather than in Siberia, to which he had been condemned. Their plans to free him were deferred, however, in order to concentrate their energies against the tsar. After the assassination, the People's Will was suppressed and Nechaev's relationship with his guards was discovered, owing to the treachery of a fellow inmate. As a result, more than sixty prison employees were arrested and tried, while Nechaev himself was subjected to a murderous regimen which before long broke down his health. He died of consumption and scurvy on November 21, 1882, at the age of thirty-five, perishing "like a hero" as Bakunin had predicted.

WHAT THEN may we conclude about Nechaev? Was he an unmitigated scoundrel without redeeming qualities, or a devoted revolutionary who has been unjustly maligned by his detractors? To some extent, of course, he remains an enigma. Yet the biography by Philip Pomper sheds valuable light on his character and motives, so that a number of judgments can be made. On the positive side, Nechaev's courage and dedication cannot be denied. He was endowed, according to Sazhin, with "colossal energy, fanatical devotion to the revolution, a character of steel, and an indefatigable capacity for work."[25] He lived a life of poverty and self-denial. Of the money that he obtained from the Bakhmetiev fund he did not spend a penny on himself. Nor can the genuineness of his revolutionary fervor or his hatred of privilege and exploitation be doubted. He paid for it by being shut up in a dungeon for nearly a third of his life, a fate that he bore with an endurance unsurpassed in the annals of revolutionary martyrdom.

But his selfless dedication carried a harsh and ruthless stamp. It was untempered by the warmth and human compassion that Bakunin possessed in such abundance. Nechaev won his influence, rather, by his fierce energy, his calculated immoralism, and his boundless hatred of the establishment and of all whom he considered his enemies. His chief faults, wrote Lev Deutsch, were "an infinite confidence in his own infallibility, a total scorn of human beings, and a systematic application of the principle that the end justifies the means."[26] He regarded all men and women as mere tools in the revolutionary struggle, thereby stripping them of their personal dignity, indeed of their very identity. From the beginning of his career, wrote Albert Camus in *The Rebel*, Nechaev "never ceased to suborn the students around him, Bakunin himself, the revolutionary refugees, and finally the guards in his prison." He thought nothing of bringing less uncompromising radicals under police suspicion in order to involve them more deeply in his own conspiratorial activities. He raised revolutionary expediency to an absolute good, before which all accepted morality must retreat. In the interests of the revolution, of which he himself was to be the sole judge, every action was justified, every crime was legitimate, however repugnant it might be. He himself practiced the theft, blackmail, and murder that he preached to his fellow conspirators. He practiced them, moreover, on friends as well as enemies. "He deceived everyone he met," as Carr observed, "and when he was no longer able to deceive them, his power was gone." His originality, as Camus pointed out, lay in "justifying the violence done to one's brother."[27] Thus he ultimately foreshadows, on however small a scale, the mass murders of Stalin in the name of revolutionary necessity.

In short, while Bakunin, whatever his failings, was essentially a libertarian, Nechaev, whatever his virtues, was essentially an authoritarian. His real mentors were not Fourier, Proudhon, and Bakunin, but Robespierre, Babeuf, and Tkachev, whose Jacobin principles he pushed to their ultimate extent. Far from being an anarchist, he was an apostle of political expediency, concerned with the means of conspiracy and with centralized organization rather than with the goal of a stateless society. His Jacobinism and Machiavellianism clashed fundamentally with the libertarian spirit, surrounding anarchism with an aura of brutality and ruthlessness that was foreign to its basic humanity. In Nechaev's hands, anarchism, the ideal of human freedom and dignity, was soiled, debased, and finally distorted beyond recognition.

Yet Nechaev had a profound influence upon the revolutionary movement, among anarchists and nonanarchists alike. Though revealed as a murderer of a fellow revolutionary, not to say a thief and a blackmailer, his misdeeds were held by some to be offset by his zeal and self-sacrifice. Thus the People's Will raised his courage and dedication above the darker aspects of his career; and Lenin, who admired his organizational talents and selfless devotion to the cause, praised him as a "revolutionary titan." During the revolutions of 1905 and 1917 the image of Nechaev gripped more than a few young militants of the extreme left, who, in their passion for revolutionary conspiracy, their terrorist methods, and their extreme hostility towards intellectuals, bore their mentor's peculiar stamp.

More recently, groups like the Black Panthers, the Red Brigades, the Weather Underground, and the Symbionese Liberation Army have employed the methods of Nechaev—including indiscriminate terror and the subordination of means to ends—in the name of the revolutionary cause. Eldridge Cleaver, as has been noted, took the *Catechism of a Revolutionary* as his revolutionary bible.[28] The Symbionese Liberation Army was charged with the assassination (using cyanide-tipped bullets) of the superintendent of schools in Oakland, California, and some members broke with the organization because of its "devotion to violence and its 'egotistical' leadership's insistence on making secret decisions."[29] Even the murder of Ivanov, strangely enough, has had its modern counterparts in the slaying of an alleged informer by the Black Panther group in New Haven in 1969 and in the massacre in 1972 by the leader of the United Red Army in Japan of fourteen members of his group for violations of "revolutionary discipline."

But the tactics of "Nechaevism" have also provoked widespread revulsion within the revolutionary movement. In his own circle in St. Petersburg at the end of the 1860s Nechaev already found opponents in such libertarian socialists as Mark Natanson, Felix Volkhovsky, German Lopatin, and Michael Negreskul. The Chaikovsky circle of the 1870s—including Kropotkin and Stepniak as well as Natanson, Volkhovsky, and Lopatin—also recoiled from Nechaev's Jacobin methods, his cynical immoralism, and his dictatorial party organization. In contrast to his People's Justice, they sought to create an atmosphere of confidence and trust and to found an organization based on mutual aid and respect among its members. Repelled by Nechaev's Machiavellianism, they argued that no end, however noble, could fail to be corrupted by such monstrous means; and they asked, like Bakunin, whether the training of revolutionary groups along the lines proposed by Nechaev might not create an arrogant elite of power seekers who would give the people what they *ought* to want, whether they in fact did so or not. Thus they ranged themselves with the libertarian socialism of Herzen, Bakunin, and Lavrov against the authoritarian revolutionism of Ishutin, Tkachev, and Nechaev, who, they felt, could not inspire a true socialist revolution because they lacked a true socialist morality.

The identical criticism was later leveled against the Bolsheviks by Peter Kropotkin, on whose lips, said Maria Goldsmith, "the word 'Nechaevism' was always a strong rebuke." As a member of the Chaikovsky circle, Kropotkin decried all self-contained associations of "professional revolutionaries," with their subordination of means to ends. He insisted that "a morally developed individuality must be the foundation of every organization."[30] For Kropotkin the ends and means were inseparable, and he was inflexible in his opposition to all tactics that conflicted with his principles and goals. Nor would Bakunin, in his more farsighted moments, have disagreed. As he wrote to Sazhin less than two years before his death: "Realize, after all, that nothing living and firm can be built upon Jesuitical trickery, that revolutionary activity aiming to succeed must not seek its support in base and petty passions, and that no revolution can achieve victory without lofty, humane, and well-considered ideas."[31]

CHAPTER FOUR

Kropotkin's Ethical Anarchism

IN THE LIVES and writings of Michael Bakunin and Peter Kropotkin, Russia contributed more than any other country to the creation of a worldwide anarchist movement. Though different in many respects, the two men had much in common. Born into the landed nobility, both abandoned their heritage for the career of a professional revolutionist. Both made dramatic escapes from tsarist confinement that gave their names the aura of legend, Kropotkin fleeing in 1876, the year of Bakunin's death. Both called for a social revolution of workers and peasants and rejected any intervening dictatorship in favor of the immediate realization of the stateless millennium. Both were international figures who spent a major part of their lives in the West and played a decisive role in shaping anarchist movements in many countries. And both, with their vision of a decentralized libertarian society, left a legacy to inspire succeeding generations of rebels.

Kropotkin, more than a century ago, sounded a modern note when he called on the young to join the struggle for social justice. A young man who has studied a trade or profession, he wrote, "has not done this in order that he should make use of his acquirements as instruments of plunder for his own gain, and he must be depraved indeed and utterly cankered by vice, who has not dreamed that one day he would apply his intelligence, his abilities, his knowledge to help on the enfranchisement of those who today grovel in misery and ignorance." How apropos this sounded during the 1960s and 1970s, when high-minded students in many countries, sick of war and oppression, yearned to use their talents for the benefit of mankind. For such young people Kropotkin's advice seemed as pertinent as when he offered it:

Join the cause of humanity, "the never-ceasing struggle for truth, justice, and equality among the people, whose gratitude you will earn—what nobler career can the youth of all nations desire than this?"[1]

A scion of the old aristocracy whose ancestors had been princes in medieval Russia, Kropotkin had himself taken the course which he was now prescribing to others. In 1871 he was offered the coveted post of secretary of the Imperial Geographical Society in St. Petersburg. Though not yet thirty (he was born in Moscow in 1842), he richly deserved the honor and only a few years earlier would eagerly have accepted it. During his military service in Siberia in the 1860s, he had explored vast stretches of uncharted territory and, on the basis of his observations, elaborated a theory that revised the cartography of eastern Asia. The structural lines of Asia, he saw, did not run north and south or east and west, as Humboldt and others had represented them, but from northeast to southwest. In his memoirs Kropotkin describes the immense pleasure he felt at the moment of scientific discovery, when all the data fell into place. "There are not many joys in human life," he wrote, "equal to the joy of the sudden birth of a generalization, illuminating the mind after a long period of patient research. What has seemed for years so chaotic, so contradictory, and so problematic takes at once its proper position within an harmonious whole."[2]

His reports on the topography of Siberia won Kropotkin immediate recognition and opened the way to a distinguished academic career. Had he continued his scientific work, one can only surmise what further discoveries he might have made and what honors he might have won. When the offer from the Geographical Society reached him, he was studying glacial deposits in Finland, about which he made a host of valuable observations that enhanced his scientific reputation. By this time, however, Kropotkin was undergoing a crisis that was to change the direction of his life. No longer could he find peace in the work to which he had brought such gifts of observation and insight. He was deeply troubled by the fact that, while he had been privileged to attain intellectual distinction, the mass of people lived in poverty and ignorance. "What right had I to these higher joys," he asked, "when all around me was nothing but misery and struggle for a mouldy bit of bread; when whatsoever I should spend to enable me to live in that world of higher emotions must needs be taken from the very mouths of those who grew the wheat and had not bread enough for their children?"[3]

Kropotkin's course was settled. Deeply as he cherished his scientific pursuits, to continue them seemed self-indulgent when there was so much suffering and injustice in the world. A higher calling beckoned, and wherever it might lead, whatever sacrifices it might require, he was prepared to follow. Indeed, as a comrade remarked, it was with an "ecstasy of expiation" that he dedicated his life to oppose that very injustice of which fate had made him the involuntary beneficiary.[4] Accordingly, he declined the offer of the Geographical Society and, renouncing his aristocratic birthright, embarked on a future of prison and exile that was to last nearly half a century.

His refusal of the secretaryship was not the first time that Kropotkin, to the consternation of his family, had rejected the path of personal advancement. In 1862, when he was graduated from the exclusive Corps of Pages in St. Petersburg, he could have made a brilliant career at court, but he applied instead for a commission in the unfashionable Cossack regiment of the Amur in eastern Siberia. Whatever others might have thought, it was a decision he himself was never to regret. For it was in Siberia that his libertarian philosophy first began to take shape. Here he first read Proudhon, the father of French anarchism, and learned of the exploits of Bakunin, who barely a year before had escaped down the Amur and around the world to western Europe, where he founded an anarchist movement among workers, artisans, and intellectuals. Most important of all, in Siberia he shed his hopes that the state could act as a vehicle of social progress. Soon after his arrival, he drafted, at the request of his superiors, elaborate plans for municipal self-government and for the reform of the penal system (a subject that was to interest him for the rest of his life), only to see them vanish in an impenetrable bureaucratic maze. And towards the end of his tour, in 1866, the authorities put down with great brutality a revolt of Polish exiles near Lake Baikal, an incident that shattered whatever remained of Kropotkin's faith in the virtues of government.

At the same time, however, he was favorably impressed by the small, autonomous communities that flourished in the Siberian wilderness. The successful cooperation that he observed among the Russian peasants—especially the Dukhobor religious sectarians—and native tribesmen illuminated his subsequent thinking. "I began to appreciate the difference between acting on the principle of command and discipline and acting on the principle of common understanding," he later recalled. "Although I did not then formulate my observations in terms borrowed from party struggles, I may say now that I lost in Siberia whatever faith in state discipline I had cherished before. I was prepared to become an anarchist."[5]

A few years later, Kropotkin's favorable impressions of uncorrupted communal life were reinforced when he visited the watchmaking communities of the Jura mountains in Switzerland. He was drawn at once to their voluntary associations of mutual support and to the absence among them of political ambition or of any distinction between leaders and subordinates. Their mixture of manual and mental labor as well as the integration in their mountain villages of domestic manufacture and agricultural work won his admiration and helped shape his vision of the ideal society of the future. After Siberia, his experience in Switzerland confirmed Kropotkin in his new libertarian creed, "and when I came away from the mountains, after a week's stay with the watchmakers, my views upon socialism were settled. I was an anarchist."[6]

Siberia, then, marked an important turning point in Kropotkin's life. It was there that he began to develop his celebrated theory of mutual aid, which was to occupy a central place in his philosophy. He had left for the Far East in 1862, deeply impressed by Darwin's *Origin of Species* (published three years before) and eager to discover new evidence of the "struggle for existence" that most Darwinists considered the main factor in the evolution of species. What he observed, however, quite astonished him and led him to conclude that the theory of evolution, then the talk of intellectual Europe, had been seriously distorted by Darwin's followers. Kropotkin's observations of animal and human life revealed few instances of internecine struggle among members of the same species. Far from ruthless competition, what he found was mutual aid "carried on to an extent which made me suspect in it a feature of the greatest importance for the maintenance of life, the preservation of each species, and its further evolution."[7]

The theory of mutual aid had thus begun to take shape. But fully two decades were to elapse before Kropotkin could find the occasion to elaborate it. In the meantime, he threw himself into revolutionary activity that made his name an object of admiration in radical groups all over Europe. In 1872, on his return from the Jura, he joined the Chaikovsky circle, an organization of young populists who were spreading revolutionary propaganda among the workers and peasants of Moscow and St. Petersburg. Caught in a police dragnet, he was imprisoned in 1874, but made a dramatic escape two years later, fleeing to western Europe where he became the foremost theorist and leader of the anarchist movement. The next few years were spent mostly in Switzerland, until, at the demand of the Russian government, he was expelled after the assassination of Alexander II in 1881. He moved to France but was arrested in December 1882 and locked up for three years in Clairvaux prison on trumped-up charges of sedition. Here his theory of mutual aid was carried a further step.

During the first year of his confinement, Kropotkin chanced to read a lecture "On the Law of Mutual Aid," delivered in 1880 by Professor Karl Kessler, a respected Russian zoologist and the dean of St. Petersburg University. Kessler's thesis was that cooperation rather than conflict was the chief factor in the process of evolution. Besides the "law of mutual struggle," he argued, there existed a "law of mutual aid" that was far more important for the survival and evolution of species. In particular, Kessler emphasized that the desire to protect their offspring brought animals together, and that "the more individuals keep together, the more they mutually support each other, and the more are the chances of the species for surviving, as well as for making further progress in its intellectual development." All classes of animals practice mutual aid, said Kessler, who provided examples from the behavior of beetles, birds, and mammals.

Kessler's lecture had a great impact on Kropotkin's thinking. It struck him, he wrote, "as throwing a new light on the whole subject" of evolution.[8] Not only did it corroborate his own observations in Siberia, as well as among the Swiss watchmakers of the Jura mountains, but it suited the libertarian social philosophy that he was then evolving. Indeed, Kessler's thesis seemed to Kropotkin so correct and so important that he began at once to collect new data to develop it as far as he could. He soon found, to his great interest, that other writers had been making similar observations. In a doctoral dissertation published in 1877, for instance, Alfred Espinas, a French philosopher, had stressed the importance of social behavior among animals for the preservation of species. The idea, as Kropotkin noted, was "in the air."[9]

To concede this, however, is not to minimize Kropotkin's own achievement. Kessler himself had presented his views only in a cursory sketch, which his death in 1881—scarcely a year after delivering his lecture—prevented him from developing. Nor had anyone else, before Kropotkin, given the theory of mutual aid coherent and systematic expression. It was left to the anarchist prince to elaborate it and buttress it with a wealth of evidence derived both from first-hand observation and from extensive study of the works of anthropologists and field naturalists, to which his copious reference notes in *Mutual Aid* bear witness.

By the time Kropotkin began to publish his findings, he had been released from Clairvaux prison and had settled in England, where he was to remain for the next thirty years, until the Russian Revolution allowed him to return to his native country. The impetus to make his theory known came in 1888 when T. H. Huxley, one of Darwin's leading disciples, published an influential essay on "The Struggle for Existence" in the widely read London periodical *The Nineteenth Century*.

The burden of Huxley's argument was that life is a "continuous free fight," and that competition among individuals of the same species is not merely a law of nature but the driving force of progress. "From the point of view of the moralist," he wrote in a famous passage, "the animal world is on about the same level as a gladiators' show. The creatures are fairly well treated and set to fight; whereby the strongest, the swiftest, and the cunningest live to fight another day. The spectator has no need to turn his thumbs down, as no quarter is given."[10]

To Kropotkin, Huxley's essay seemed a conspicuous—indeed a grotesque—example of how Darwin's theories were being distorted by his followers. Kropotkin had no quarrel with Darwin himself. On the contrary, he had profound respect for Darwin's discoveries and regarded the theory of natural selection as perhaps the most brilliant scientific generalization of the century. Nor did he deny that the "struggle for existence" played an important role in the evolution of species. In *Mutual Aid* he declares unequivocally that "life *is* struggle; and in that struggle the fittest survive."[11] But who were the fittest to survive? What Kropotkin could not accept was the single-minded emphasis placed by Huxley and others on competition and conflict in the evolutionary process. There was no infamy in the relations of the whites towards other races or of the strong towards the weak, he wrote, that would not have found its excuse in Huxley's formula of unmitigated conflict. In addition, Huxley's picture of the natural world as a savage jungle, red in tooth and claw, contrasted sharply with his own findings, which indicated that, in the process of natural selection, spontaneous cooperation among animals was more important than ferocious competition, and that "those animals which acquire habits of mutual aid are undoubtedly the fittest" to survive.[12] Kropotkin, moreover, hastened to point out that Darwin himself, in *The Descent of Man*, acknowledged the importance of mutual cooperation in the struggle for existence, though Darwin never developed this idea in any serious way.

Kropotkin replied to Huxley in a series of articles that appeared in *The Nineteenth Century* between 1890 and 1896 and were brought together in his famous book, *Mutual Aid*, in 1902. Here he documents his theory of mutual aid with abundant illustrations from animal and human life. Among animals he shows how mutual cooperation is practiced in hunting, in migration, and in the propagation of species. He draws examples from the elaborate social behavior of ants and bees, from wild horses that form a ring when attacked by wolves, from the wolves themselves that form a pack for hunting, from migrating deer that, scattered over a wide territory, come together in herds to cross a river. From these and many similar illustrations Kropotkin demonstrates that sociability is a prevalent feature at every level of the animal world. Moreover, he finds that among humans too mutual aid has been the rule rather than the exception. With a wealth of data he traces the evolution of voluntary cooperation from the primitive tribe, peasant village, and medieval commune to a variety of modern associations that have continued to practice mutual support despite the rise of the coercive bureaucratic state. His thesis, in short, is a refutation of the doctrine that competition and brute force are the sole—or even the principal—determinants of social progress. For Kropotkin mutual aid has played a far greater role—indeed, it has been "the chief factor of progressive evolution."[13]

Mutual Aid has become a classic. With the exception of his memoirs, it is Kropotkin's best-known work and is widely regarded as his masterpiece. It has been translated into many languages, Asian as well as European, and has gone through numerous printings. The reasons are not hard to find. *Mutual Aid* is more than a contribution to the theory of evolution. It forms the very cornerstone of Kropotkin's anarchist philosophy. In the first place, it was his most successful attempt to provide anarchist theory with a scientific foundation. Deploying his extensive knowledge of zoology, anthropology, and history, he could show, as no one had shown before, the importance of solidarity and cooperation in the evolutionary process. But even more, mutual aid was for Kropotkin the basis of ethical principles. Morality, he argues, has evolved from the instinct of human sociability, the unconscious recognition of "the close dependency of every one's happiness upon the happiness of all; and of the sense of justice, or equity, which brings the individual to consider the right of every other individual as equal to his own."[14]

Not that there was no negative side to human behavior. While man's natural instincts were by and large cooperative, competitiveness and self-assertion were by no means absent, Kropotkin admitted. As a self-proclaimed Darwinist, he was hardly blind to the existence of conflict in the human as in the animal world. But the task, as he saw it, was to discourage those feelings which "induce man to subdue other men in order to utilize them for his individual ends" and to foster those which "induce human beings to unite for attaining common ends by common effort: the first answering that fundamental need of human nature—struggle, and the second representing another equally fundamental tendency—the desire for unity and mutual sympathy."[15]

This brings us to the place of mutual aid in Kropotkin's social thought. Here again, as in virtually every area on which he turned his scholarly gaze, its role was of critical importance. Throughout the

past, he maintained, humans had displayed a propensity to work together in a spirit of solidarity and fellowship. Mutual aid among human beings had been a far more potent force than the egoistic will to
dominate others. Mankind, in fact, owed its very survival to mutual
assistance. The theories of Hegel, Marx, and Darwin notwithstanding,
Kropotkin held that cooperation rather than conflict lay at the root of
the historical process. Furthermore, he refuted Hobbes's conception of
man's natural condition as a war of each against all. In every period of
history, he declared, mutual-aid associations of diverse kinds had
sprung into existence, reaching a high point in the guilds and communes of medieval Europe. The rise of centralized states from the six-
teenth through the nineteenth centuries was for Kropotkin merely an
aberration from the normal pattern of Western civilization. In spite of
the state's emergence, voluntary associations had continued to play a
central role in human affairs, and the spirit of mutual support was
reasserting itself "even in our modern society, and claims its right to
be, as it has always been, the chief leader towards further progress."[16]
The dominant trends of modern history were pointing back towards
decentralized, nonpolitical cooperative societies in which men could
develop their creative faculties, without the machinations of rulers,
priests, or soldiers. Everywhere, said Kropotkin, the artificial state was
abdicating its "holy functions" in favor of natural voluntary groups.

BUT HOW must society be constructed in order to stimulate rather
than repress voluntary cooperation? Kropotkin seeks to answer this
question in *The Conquest of Bread*. If *Mutual Aid* is widely regarded
as Kropotkin's scientific masterpiece, *The Conquest of Bread* is perhaps the clearest statement of his anarchist social doctrines. Written
for the ordinary worker, it possesses a lucidity of style not often found
in books on social themes: when it first appeared Emile Zola acclaimed
it as a "true poem." In Kropotkin's succinct description, the book is "a
study of the needs of humanity, and of the economic means to satisfy
them." Taking the Paris Commune for its model, its aim is to show
how a social revolution can be made and how a new society, organized
on libertarian lines, can then be built upon the ruins of the old. Kropotkin, however, made no attempt to construct a future utopia in every
detail. On the contrary, he refused to force the natural evolution of
society into any preconceived mold but was content merely to sketch
its general outline.

The Conquest of Bread was first published in French as a series of
articles in the journals *Le Révolté* and *La Révolte*, of which Kropotkin
was an editor, and was brought out as a book in Paris in 1892 with a

preface by the noted anarchist geographer Elisée Reclus, who also suggested the title. Its underlying theme is that both the instruments and the fruits of production, now unjustly appropriated by the few, are the collective achievement of humanity as a whole. "All belongs to all," writes Kropotkin. "All things are for all men, since all men have need of them, since all men have worked in the measure of their strength to produce them, and since it is not possible to evaluate every one's part in the production of the world's wealth."[17] On this point Kropotkin was emphatic. It was impossible to assess each person's contribution to the production of social wealth because millions of human beings had toiled to create the present riches of the world. Every acre of soil had been watered with the sweat of generations, every mile of railroad had received its share of human blood. Indeed, there was not a thought or an invention that was not the common inheritance of all mankind. "Each discovery, each advance, each increase in the sum of human riches, owes its being to the physical and mental travail of the past and the present," Kropotkin insists. "By what right then can anyone whatever appropriate the least morsel of this immense whole and say—This is mine, not yours?"[18]

Starting from this premise, Kropotkin argues that the wage system, which presumes to measure the work of each individual, must be abolished in favor of a system of equal rewards for all. This was a major step in the evolution of anarchist economic thought. From Max Stirner's individualism, Proudhon's mutualism, and Bakunin's collectivism, Kropotkin proceeded to the principle of "anarchist communism," by which private property and inequality of income would give place to the free distribution of goods and services. Even under Bakunin's collectivism the criterion for distribution was, as under the proletarian dictatorship of the Marxists, performance rather than need. Kropotkin, by contrast, regarded any system of rewards based on an individual's capacity to produce as merely another form of wage slavery. By drawing a distinction between what is mine and what is yours, a collectivist economy rendered itself incompatible with the ideals of pure anarchism. Collectivism, moreover, necessitated some authority within the producers' associations to measure individual performance and to supervise the distribution of goods and services accordingly. Thus the collectivist order contained the seeds of inequality and domination.

Kropotkin considered his own theory of anarchist communism the antithesis of the wage system in all its forms. He himself, however, had not been the first to conceive the idea. Like his theory of mutual aid, anarchist communism was already "in the air," awaiting a thinker of his talents to give it systematic expression. In this he was notably successful, winning an impressive number of workers, as well as intellectuals, to the anarchist cause. The appeal of his theory is obvious. For the principle of wages he substituted the principle of needs: persons would be the judge of their own requirements and would take from the common storehouse whatever they deemed necessary, whether or not they contributed a share of the labor. Kropotkin's benign optimism led him to assume that once political and economic exploitation had been eliminated, all—or very nearly all—would work of their own free will, without any compulsion whatever, and take from the communal warehouse no more than they required for a comfortable existence. Anarchist communism would put an end, at long last, to every manner of coercion and privilege and usher in a golden age of liberty, equality, and brotherhood.

Kropotkin was convinced that, throughout the Western world, anarchist communism was everywhere on the rise, manifesting itself "in the thousand developments of modern life."[19] Roads and bridges were free to all; streets paved and lighted for everyone's use; water supplied to every house; parks, museums, libraries, and schools open to all. In every case, said Kropotkin, such arrangements were founded on the principle of need, so that when you go to a public library, for instance, the librarian does not ask you what services you have rendered to society before giving you the books you require. Kropotkin was greatly encouraged by these developments. Little by little, he believed, the government principle was yielding before the principle of voluntary cooperation. In every sphere of life voluntary associations—trade unions, learned societies, the Red Cross—were binding together men and women with common interests and aspirations and were preparing the way for a future society of free communes existing side by side in harmonious cooperation.

At bottom, what Kropotkin yearned for was the decentralized society of medieval Europe, with a few up-to-date trappings. His study of history, together with his firsthand experiences in Siberia and among the Jura watchmakers, nourished his deeply rooted conviction that people were happiest in communities small enough to permit the natural instincts of solidarity and mutual aid to flourish. His nostalgic desire for a simpler but richer life led him to idealize the autonomous social units of a bygone age. Faced with the growing concentration of economic and political power in nineteenth-century Europe, he looked backward to a world as yet undefiled by the intrusion of capitalism and the modern state. What he envisioned in *The Conquest of Bread* was a new decentralized society in which men and women, joined by

62

the natural bonds of cooperative effort, would be rid of the artificiality of bureaucratic states and massive industrial complexes.

Not that he had any aversion to modern technology in itself. For all his medieval yearnings, he never succumbed to the pastoral visions of a Tolstoy or a Gandhi. He criticized the English socialist William Morris for his antipathy to the machine and shared William Godwin's belief that mechanization would relieve individuals of drudgery and fatigue and hasten the distribution of interesting work for all. He was delighted when a Mrs. Cochrane in Illinois invented a washing machine that would lighten the burden of domestic labor. "I fully understand," he remarks in his memoirs, "the pleasure that man can derive from the might of his machine, the intelligent character of its work, the gracefulness of its movements, and the correctness of what it is doing."[20] Placed in small voluntary workshops, machinery would rescue human beings from the monotony and toil of large-scale capitalist enterprise, allow time for leisure and cultural pursuits, and remove forever the stamp of inferiority traditionally borne by manual labor.

What disturbed Kropotkin about the emergence of modern technology, however, was the division of labor that accompanied it. The division of labor was, in his view, destructive of the human spirit. It meant "labeling and stamping men" and took no account of the "social value of the human being." Minute specialization in industry benefited only the employer, while "the worker, who is doomed for life to making the eighteenth part of a pin, grows stupid and sinks into poverty."[21] A related evil was the disagreeable and often oppressive character of factory work, which, together with the division of labor, diminished the productive capacity of the workers while promoting their boredom and frustration. Such conditions, argued Kropotkin, were neither necessary nor excusable. They stemmed, rather, from the greed of the manufacturers, who had little concern for the welfare and happiness of their hired hands. Spacious and well-ventilated factories were not only possible, he maintained, but could be "as healthy and magnificient as the finest laboratories in modern universities, and the better the organization the more will man's labor produce."[22]

In a similar vein, Kropotkin sought an end to the invidious separation between manual and brain work and between work in the field and in the factory. What he envisioned, by contrast, was an integrated society "where each individual is a producer of both manual and intellectual work; where each able-bodied human being is a worker, and where each worker works both in the field and the industrial workshop." In such circumstances work would no longer appear "a curse of fate" but would become "what it should be—the free exercise of *all* the faculties of man."[23] Human happiness, according to Kropotkin, required a variety of occupations, on the land as in the factory. Men will gladly labor in the fields, he wrote, echoing a theme of Fourier and Owen, when it is "no longer a slavish drudgery, but has become a pleasure, a festival, a renewal of health and joy."[24]

What the foregoing implies is a system of regional self-sufficiency, of which Kropotkin was an articulate advocate. He argued that the use of electric power, distributed among small units of production, would permit a reduction of the size of industrial enterprises, so that the manufacture of goods could be shifted to the countryside without the sacrifice of up-to-date technology. In this way the main burden of production could be left to workshops in which labor was more efficient as well as more agreeable from the standpoint of human happiness. At the same time, he believed, methods of intensive farming would increase the production of food to the point where even countries as populous as Britain might feed their inhabitants in abundance without relying on imports from abroad. Thus Kropotkin, as Lewis Mumford has noted, foresaw in advance of future proponents of the "garden city" that the use of electricity, together with the techniques of market gardening, might lay the foundation for a decentralized society combining the advantages of urban and rural life while allowing full scope for the development of the human personality.[25]

For Kropotkin, then, as for so many of his contemporaries, the most pressing social problems were the organization of production and the distribution of wealth. If production were better organized, he was convinced, a modest amount of pleasant work would provide a comfortable living for all. By better organization he meant, as we have seen, "industry combined with agriculture and brain work with manual work," to quote the subtitle of *Fields, Factories and Workshops* (1899), the sequel to *The Conquest of Bread*. But he meant, too, that materials and labor must no longer be squandered on military weapons, government bureaucracies, or private luxuries "destined only to satisfy the dull vanity of the rich."[26] When a woman spends a hundred pounds for a dress, he wrote, a juster system might have provided a hundred women with attractive dresses. Overproduction is only a myth: the real problem, rather, is underconsumption. When the tools of production are placed at the service of all, when workers are liberated from wage slavery and can perform their jobs in agreeable surroundings, when the production of armaments and luxuries is abandoned for socially useful tasks, says Kropotkin, the needs of all will be fulfilled. Members of the community would work from their twenties to their forties, four or five hours of labor a day sufficing for a comfortable life. The division of labor, including the pernicious separation between mental and manual tasks, would yield to a variety of pleasant jobs, resulting in the sort of organic existence that had prevailed in the medieval city.

In such a community, Kropotkin insisted, although no one would be compelled to work, nearly everyone would prefer work to idleness. For work is "a psychological necessity, a necessity of spending accumulated body energy, a necessity which is health and life itself. If so many branches of useful work are reluctantly done now, it is merely because they mean overwork or they are improperly organized."[27] The truly lazy individual is extremely rare, says Kropotkin. The so-called idler is often only a person to whom it is repugnant to spend life making the hundredth part of a watch while in possession of exuberant energy to expend elsewhere. Once work no longer means drudgery or involves excessive specialization, once it becomes, rather, a series of agreeable tasks for a few hours a day, giving the worker a feeling of useful achievement, idleness and malingering will disappear.[28]

Yet, for all the value he attached to work, Kropotkin was no advocate of spartan austerity. Adequate leisure was no less vital for the human spirit. "After bread has been secured," he writes, "leisure is the supreme aim." In the stateless society of the future thousands of associations would spring up "to gratify every taste and every possible fancy," and what was once the privilege of a small minority would become available to all.[29] Kropotkin, moreover, recognized that a measure of privacy was yet another essential need. "Isolation," he says, "alternating with time spent in society, is the normal desire of human nature."[30]

To prepare men for this happier life Kropotkin pinned his hopes on the education of the young. His vision of the new society presupposed a thorough overhaul of the existing educational system. The present school was a "university of laziness," he complained. "Superficiality, parrot-like repetition, slavishness and inertia of mind are the results of our method of education. We do not teach our children to learn."[31] What then was to be done? To achieve an integrated society Kropotkin called for an "integral education" that would cultivate both mental and manual skills. Due emphasis was to be placed on the humanities and on the basic principles of mathematics and science. But instead of being taught from books alone, children would receive an active outdoor education and learn by doing and observing at first hand, a recommendation that has been widely endorsed by modern educational theorists.

Kropotkin also advocated a thorough modification of the penal system. His own experience of prison life had intensified his belief in penal reform; and in *In Russian and French Prisons* (1887) he shows from firsthand knowledge the immense suffering caused by incarceration—how it degrades and humiliates the prisoner, how it perverts his character and robs him of his dignity, how his whole life is subjected to a deadly mechanical routine, how everything is done to break his spirit, to kill his inner strength, to make him a docile tool in the hands of those who control him. Prisons, moreover, punish the innocent—the family who depends on the convict's earnings experiences hardships and humiliations often worse than those to which the prisoner is subjected.

And all for nothing, says Kropotkin. Abundant data prove the utter futility of prisons as a means of deterring crime. Indeed, far from reforming the offender, they kill the qualities that might adapt him to community life. They are "schools of crime," subjecting him to brutalizing punishments, teaching him to lie and cheat, and generally hardening him in his criminal ways, so that when he emerges from behind bars he is condemned to repeat his transgressions. Kropotkin concluded that prisons are worthless, that the millions allotted each year for so-called rehabilitation are spent to no purpose. Prisons neither improve the prisoners nor prevent crime; they achieve none of the ends for which they are designed.[32] The solution, ultimately, was a total reorganization of society on libertarian lines. In the coming anarchist world, where work would be a joy and rewards distributed on an equal basis, antisocial behavior would be rare and would be dealt with not by laws but by human understanding and the moral pressure of the community.

SUCH, in broad outline, was Kropotkin's vision of the future. From the rubble of the old order, he believed, would emerge a golden age without government, without property, without hunger or want, a shining era of freedom in which men would live in harmony and direct their affairs without interference from any authority. But how was this dream to be realized? Kropotkin's answer, in a word, was "expropriation." For all his mild benevolence, he did not shrink from the necessity of revolution, because he did not expect the propertied classes to give up their privileges and possessions without a fight. Yet he wished it to be as humane a revolution as possible, with the "smallest number of victims, and a minimum of mutual embitterment."[33] Furthermore, it was to be a *social* revolution, carried out by the masses themselves rather than by any political party or group. Political revolutions, he warned, merely exchange one set of rulers for another without altering the essence of tyranny. He deplored, in particular, the use of putschist revolutionary tactics. As a member of the Chaikovsky circle during the 1870s, he decried the shadowy intrigues of Nechaev, whose mania for secret organizations exceeded even that of Bakunin. Kropotkin had little use for secret organizations of "professional revolutionists," with their clandestine schemes, ruling committees, and iron discipline. The proper function of the intellectuals, he believed, was to disseminate propaganda among the people in order to hasten their own spontaneous rising. All self-contained conspiratorial groups, divorced from the workers and peasants, carried the germ of authoritarianism. Still less could he accept the notion of a revolutionary dictatorship. Again and again he warned that political power is evil, that it corrupts all who wield it, that governments of any kind stifle the libertarian instincts of the people and rob them of their freedom.

Kropotkin realized—perhaps better than any of his predecessors—that the methods which were used to make the revolution would affect the nature of society after the revolution. For this reason he rejected Bakunin's idea of a secret revolutionary party bound together by implicit obedience to a revolutionary dictator. He insisted that social emancipation must be attained by libertarian rather than dictatorial means. His conception of the revolutionist, moreover, was a far cry from Bakunin and Nechaev's fanatical immoralist, bound to commit any crime and any treachery to bring about the destruction of the existing order. For Kropotkin the ends and the means were inseparable. He was inflexible in his opposition to all tactics that conflicted with his lofty principles. Just as he himself would not purchase release from prison by lies or false confessions, he would not have the anarchist cause perverted by the immorality of others. Indeed, he went so far as to condemn his comrades who jumped bail, both because of the breach of faith involved and because of the practical effect on securing bail in other political cases.[34]

At the same time, however, he condoned the use of violence in the struggle for freedom and equality. In fact, during his early years as an anarchist militant, he was among the most vigorous exponents of "propaganda by the deed" to supplement oral and written propaganda in awakening the rebellious instincts of the people. "One courageous act has sufficed to upset in a few days the entire governmental machinery, to make the colossus tremble," he wrote in 1880. "The government resists; it is savage in its repressions. But, though formerly persecution killed the energy of the oppressed, now, in periods of excitement, it produces the opposite result. It provokes new acts of revolt, individual and collective; it drives the rebels to heroism; and in rapid succession these acts spread, become general, develop."[35]

Kropotkin refused to accept the Tolstoyan doctrine of nonresistance to evil, since there were times, he felt, when acts of violence became the only means of protesting against tyranny and exploitation. He upheld, for example, the assassination of despots—a rash of which occurred during the late nineteenth century—if the assassins were impelled by noble motives, though his acceptance of bloodshed in such cases was inspired by compassion for the oppressed rather than by hatred for the victims. He would not sit in judgment over terrorists driven by desperation to retaliate against the authors of popular misery. Such acts of violence, in his view, were replies to the much greater violence—war, torture, execution—perpetrated by the state against the people.

But as time wore on Kropotkin put less and less faith in violence as a means of relieving oppression. During the Russian Revolution of 1905 he repeatedly expressed his opposition to organized campaigns of terrorism waged by small conspiratorial bands in isolation from the masses. Random murders and holdups, he insisted, could effect no more change in the existing social order than could the mere seizure of political power. Individual "expropriations" had no place in a full-scale revolt of the masses, the aim of which was not the transfer of wealth from one group to another but the elimination of private property itself. For Kropotkin, indiscriminate terrorism had become a grotesque caricature of anarchist doctrine, demoralizing the movement's true adherents and discrediting anarchism in the eyes of the general public. But his criticisms were unavailing. By the time of the First World War, though terrorism occupied a relatively small place in the movement, anarchism had acquired a reputation of violence for its own sake which the ensuing decades have failed to alter.

THE PERIOD from 1886, when Kropotkin settled down in England (residing in turn in Harrow, Acton, Bromley, Highgate, and finally, when his health demanded it, Brighton) until the First World War was the most fruitful in his career as a writer and propagandist. During this time both *Mutual Aid* and *The Conquest of Bread*, as well as a host of other books and articles on history, geography, and social questions, saw their way into print. In 1886 he helped found the London *Freedom*, which remains, a century later, the leading anarchist journal in England. Beyond this, he took part in launching a number of Russian expatriate periodicals and contributed regularly to many libertarian publications in a variety of languages. More than any other individual,

Kropotkin was responsible for spreading the ideas of anarchism and, in the face of serious obstacles, keeping the anarchist movement alive throughout the world.

But the outbreak of the war created a rift between Kropotkin and many of his closest comrades. The dispute began when he unequivocally blamed Germany for the war and came out strongly in support of the Entente. His action was prompted mainly by the fear that German militarism and authoritarianism might prove fatal to social progress in France, the revered land of the great revolution and the Paris Commune. Germany, with its political and economic centralization and its Junker spirit of regimentation, epitomized everything Kropotkin detested. As the bulwark of statism, it blocked Europe's path to the libertarian society of his dreams. He was unshakably convinced that the kaiser had launched the war with the aim of dominating the continent, a view which has been buttressed by the investigations of Fritz Fischer.[36] Accordingly, he urged everyone "who cherishes the ideals of human progress" to help stop the Prussian onslaught.[37] Kropotkin's stand, however, touched off bitter polemics that sapped the strength of the movement for which he had labored nearly half a century. In contrast to their teacher, the majority of anarchists remained faithful to their antimilitarist heritage. This break with his comrades was one of the darkest moments in Kropotkin's career.

Events, however, took a brighter turn with the outbreak of the Russian Revolution. Kropotkin, now in his seventy-fifth year, hastened to return to his homeland. Despite his unpopular stand on the war, when he arrived in Petrograd in June 1917 after forty years in exile, he was greeted warmly by a crowd of sixty thousand, while a band played the "Marseillaise," a hymn of revolutionists everywhere and the anthem of the great French revolution so close to Kropotkin's heart. Kerensky offered him a cabinet post as minister of education as well as a state pension, both of which the venerable anarchist declined. He had become an isolated figure. Alienated from the government by his anarchist convictions and from the revolutionary left by his support of the war, he was, as a contemporary described him, an "icon of the Russian Revolution."[38] Yet his hopes for a libertarian future were never brighter, for 1917 saw the spontaneous appearance of communes and soviets that might form the basis of a stateless society. The February Revolution, indeed, seemed the very model of the bloodless overturn he had envisioned in *The Conquest of Bread*.

With the Bolshevik seizure of power, however, his enthusiasm turned to disappointment. "This buries the revolution," he remarked to a friend. How disheartening it must have been to see his dream of a free society trampled underfoot in the name of the very ideals for which he had struggled all his life. There was only the feeble consolation that his repeated warnings against conspiratorial parties and revolutionary dictatorships had been vindicated. The Bolsheviks, he said, had shown how the revolution was *not* to be made. Russia had become "a Soviet Republic only in name," he wrote to Lenin in March 1920. "At present it is not the soviets which rule in Russia but party committees," and if the situation should be allowed to continue, "the very word 'socialism' will become a curse, as happened in France with the idea of equality for forty years after the rule of the Jacobins."[39]

Perhaps another consolation for Kropotkin was that the Bolshevik coup reunited him with his estranged comrades. Together they clung to the hope that workers' committees and peasants' cooperatives might yet restore the revolution to its true path. But Kropotkin's health was failing. In January 1921, in his seventy-ninth year, he fell mortally ill with pneumonia. A few weeks later, on February 8, he died. His funeral was the last occasion when the black flag of anarchy was paraded through Moscow. Tens of thousands, braving the bitter cold, marched in Kropotkin's cortege to the Novodevichi monastery, the burial place of his ancestors. A chorus chanted "Eternal Memory," and as the procession passed the Butyrki prison the inmates shook the bars on their windows and sang an anarchist hymn to the dead. In a eulogy to his fallen teacher, a disciple vowed "to cry relentless protests against the new despotism: the butchers at work in their cellars, the dishonor shed upon socialism, the official violence that was trampling the Revolution underfoot."[40]

Kropotkin's passing sounded the death knell of Russian anarchism. His birthplace, however, a large house in the old aristocratic quarter of the capital, was turned over to his comrades to be used as a museum for his books, papers, and personal belongings. It was maintained by contributions from admirers throughout the world, until closed after his widow's death in 1938.

NEARLY seventy years have passed since Kropotkin's death, and it is time for a new assessment of his work. His libertarian dream, to be sure, has not been realized, nor is there any prospect that it will be in the foreseeable future. Yet we must not judge Kropotkin a failure. On the contrary, he was an immense success. His whole life exemplified the high ethical standard and the combination of thought and action that he preached throughout his writings. He achieved renown in a number of disparate areas, ranging from geography and geology to sociology and history. At the same time, he shunned material success for the life of a hunted revolutionist. He did not impose sacrifices on others, an acquaintance remarked, but made them himself.[41] He endured long years in prison and exile, yet, even under the most trying circumstances, his optimism and integrity remained intact. He displayed none of the egotism or lust for power that marred the image of so many other revolutionaries. Because of this, he was admired not only by his own comrades but by many for whom the label of anarchist meant little more than the dagger and the bomb. Romain Rolland said that Kropotkin lived what Tolstoy only advocated. And Oscar Wilde called him one of the two really happy men he had known (the other being the poet Verlaine).

Kropotkin became the soul of the anarchist movement and its leading theorist. Though he adopted many of the ideas of Proudhon and Bakunin, from the moment he took up the torch of anarchism it burned with a gentler flame. His personal nature was generally mild and benevolent. He lacked Bakunin's violent temperament, titanic urge to destroy, and irrespressible will to dominate, nor did he possess his forebear's anti-Semitic streak or display the hints of fantasy that crop up in Bakunin's words and actions. With his courtly manner and qualities of character and intellect, Kropotkin seemed the picture of reasonableness; and his scientific training and optimistic outlook gave anarchist theory a constructive aspect that stood in sharp contrast to the spirit of negation that permeated Bakunin's works.

Kropotkin's personal qualities exerted a strong appeal and did much to win sympathy for his cause. His writings, too, with their orderly and elegant presentation, drew additional adherents to the movement. In such classics as *Mutual Aid* and *The Conquest of Bread* he brought all his talents to the task of lucid exposition, and they possess a consistency and a persuasiveness that are not always evident in the works of Bakunin and Proudhon. Kropotkin's aim, as he often remarked, was to put anarchism on a scientific basis by studying the dominant trends of society that might indicate its further evolution. An eminent geographer and naturalist, he believed, no less than Marx, that his social theories rested on a scientific foundation. There was no important area that escaped his scholarly attention—industry and agriculture, housing and education, law and government—and though he abandoned his scientific career at an early age, he retained a firm grasp of scientific method that gave anarchism a coherence it might otherwise have never attained.

Yet, for all his scientific gifts, Kropotkin was at bottom a moralist, whose techniques of scientific investigation served to buttress his ethical teachings. That he came closer than anyone else to placing anarchism on a scientific footing is beyond dispute. But one may doubt whether any social philosophy, anarchism not excepted, can be genuinely scientific. What dominates Kropotkin's writings, rather, is a great ethical vision—the vision of a new order based on mutual support in which no man is the master of another. Near the end of his life he was convinced that Bolshevism, because it lacked a guiding moral ideal, would be powerless to create a new social system on the principles of justice and equality. And it is characteristic that his last work, which he did not live to complete, was a study of ethical doctrines.[42]

It was primarily as an ethical thinker that Kropotkin was disturbed by the dehumanization caused by large-scale production and the division of labor. He feared that, for all the benefits of modern technology, the worker might be trapped in the gears of a centralized industrial apparatus. And it was to forestall this danger that he advanced the idea of an integrated community where manual and mental work were combined and where industry and agriculture went hand in hand. By doing so, he sought to preserve the advantage of machinery within the context of a small society. He foresaw, as Lewis Mumford has pointed out, what many large corporations were to discover only during the Second World War: that the farming out of specialized industrial operations was often more efficient and economical than large-scale organization, and that the finer the technique the greater the need for the kind of human initiative and skill that is preserved only in the small workshop. Kropotkin realized, moreover, that new means of rapid communication, together with the introduction of electrical power in rural districts, would raise the technological level of the small community to that of the large city. The invention of the automobile, radio, motion picture, and television has further substantiated his diagnosis by equalizing the advantages between the metropolitan center and the once peripheral and dependent rural community.[43]

In his suggestions for integrating urban and rural life, Kropotkin anticipated the remarkable movement pioneered by Ebenezer Howard (originator of the "garden city") and developed by such men as Patrick Geddes, Lewis Mumford, and Percival and Paul Goodman. In our present age of overcongested cities, Kropotkin's recommendations have become more appealing than ever. What is more, his ideas on intensive cultivation take on new significance in a world desperately seeking solutions to the "population explosion." At the same time, one may be sure that Kropotkin, were he alive today, would be standing in the forefront of the ecological struggle to restore a healthy balance between people and their environment.

Kropotkin's ideas, in short, are relevant to those very social problems with which the modern world is most severely afflicted. His chapter on "Dwellings" in *The Conquest of Bread*, where he complains that "whole generations perish in crowded slums, starving for air and sunlight,"[44] sounds especially up to date in view of the squatters' movement in Holland and Britain and the acute housing crisis in American cities. Similarly, his suggestions for prison reform have been embraced by a number of subsequent penologists and today are by no means out of date. Furthermore, his idea of an "integral education" in both mental and physical skills has become a popular theme among contemporary educators, and his appeal for the simultaneous study of science and the humanities has been echoed by C. P. Snow, among others, whose warnings about a widening gulf between the "two cultures" have provoked discussion within intellectual circles.

To call Kropotkin a moral thinker, however, is by no means to imply that he was not an active revolutionist. On the contrary, as we have seen, he combined the qualities of the moralist and scientist with those of the revolutionary organizer and propagandist. His biographers skate lightly over the fact that he was one of the earliest exponents of "propaganda by the deed," endorsing the use of "dagger, gun, and dynamite" to awaken the spirit of revolt.[45] Yet Kropotkin felt no embarrassment over this episode in his career. He would have resented being called a mere philosophical anarchist, content to sit at his writing table and elaborate theories about a remote and unattainable utopia. And his resentment would have been justified. For throughout most of his adult life he was a devoted anarchist militant: his participation in the Chaikovsky circle, his imprisonment in the Peter-Paul fortress, his term at the Clairvaux prison, his tireless activity in exile, and his unflinching opposition to the Bolsheviks all bear testimony to this fact.

As an activist, Kropotkin was a principal founder of both the English and the Russian anarchist movements, to say nothing of his influence on the movements in France, Belgium, and Switzerland. Addressing meetings, founding periodicals, and spreading the doctrines of his creed, he did more than any other figure to further the libertarian cause in Europe and around the world. As far afield as Japan his works were published by the anarchist martyr Kotoku; in India they influenced Gandhi and his followers. In China, too, Kropotkin opened new vistas to students and intellectuals. One impressionable boy, while reading the *Appeal to the Young*, felt at once that he was one of those with "warm hearts and noble natures" to whom Kropotkin's words were addressed, and, adopting the pen name of Pa Chin (a contraction of Bakunin and Kropotkin), dedicated himself to transmitting the message to others.[46]

Today, when opposition to heavy-handed bureaucratism is once again widespread, Kropotkin's appeal seems as timely as ever. His theory of mutual aid retains its attraction, while the centralized state continues to justify some of his worst apprehensions. Witness, for example, his belief that the existence of coercive governments implies the existence of wars: "wars for the possession of the East, wars for the empire of the sea, wars to impose duties on imports and to dictate conditions to neighboring states, wars against those 'blacks' who revolt! The roar of cannon never ceases in the world, whole races are massacred, the states of Europe spend a third of their budgets on armaments; and we know how heavily these taxes fall on the workers."[47] If these phrases have a familiar ring, it is because they anticipate criticisms of the military-industrial complex and the "warfare state." Student attacks during the 1960s and 1970s on the military draft, on academic participation in military research, on the use of the "multiversity" to provide specialists for government and industry resounded with the echoes of Kropotkin, whose moral position is similar to that of many young militants of that day. "Struggle," he declared, "so that all may live this rich, overflowing life. And be sure that in this struggle you will find a joy greater than anything else can give."[48]

Such was his advice to the young. And, twenty years ago, it found an eager response. The student movement in Berkeley and Columbia owed to Kropotkin more than a little of its idealism and humanity, and it is not surprising to find a "Kropotkin House" among the radical communes that sprang up throughout America during those years.[49] Kropotkin's dream of a federation of autonomous communes appealed to those who were seeking an alternative to a centralized and artificial world. Student rebels, even when professed Marxists, were often closer in spirit to Kropotkin and Bakunin.

Kropotkin's writings, finally, provide much more than a critique of the capitalist system: his warnings against the centralized state cut across political lines, offering a prophetic analysis of twentieth-century communism, especially as it evolved in Maoist China and in the Soviet Union under Bolshevik rule. He has been attractive to young dissidents because his libertarian brand of socialism, elaborated in *The Conquest of Bread* and other works, provides an alternative to the authoritarian socialism that has triumphed in so many countries throughout the world. With Kropotkin, militants have demanded a totally reconstructed society in which compulsion will give place to cooperation, and the bureaucratic state, whether capitalist or communist, will be shorn of its arbitrary power.

BUT KROPOTKIN, for all his contemporary appeal, is by no means immune from criticism. Despite his reputation for tolerance, he was a rigid, at times dogmatic thinker, who, in the words of the Italian anarchist Errico Malatesta, "always felt sure that right was on his side, and could not calmly bear to be contradicted." His Russian collaborators Cherkezov and Stepniak spoke of his "inflexible principles" and determination to "make certain ideas prevail at all cost"; Max Nettlau, the Austrian historian of anarchism, found him "unalterable" in his adherence to his theories and totally disinclined to reexamine them. "I should have wished," wrote Nettlau, "to see his ideas thrown into the crucible of general scientific discussion to a much greater extent than they were, modified by criticism, augmented by the efforts of many others."⁵⁰

For the most part these criticisms were justified. Kropotkin's optimistic view of human nature, his faith in mutual aid as opposed to Darwinian competition, his belief that the centralized state had reached its apogee in his own time—these have scarcely been borne out in our century of world wars and large-scale government. His theory of mutual aid was, to be sure, a valuable corrective to the extreme pessimism, verging on outright cynicism, of Huxley and the Social Darwinists. But Kropotkin erred in the opposite direction. He took insufficient account of the naked violence that dominates the life of most animals, from insects and fish to reptiles and mammals. He underestimated the widespread brutality in nature, the persecution of the weak by the strong, among humans as well as among animals. Until the end of his life he retained his faith in the innate goodness of mankind, in the ties uniting people of different classes and nations in defiance of state barriers.

One wonders whether he would have altered his views had he lived to see the rise of totalitarianism, the Second World War, and the invention of nuclear and biological weapons of mass destruction. Probably not. His optimism, despite his own life of hard experience, was seemingly inexhaustible. And because of this he exaggerated the extent of human solidarity in the world and emphasized the bonds rather than the hatreds and divisions. He remained convinced that humans, if unperverted by political and social authority, are inherently virtuous and thus capable of living in harmony. At times he seemed quite unaware that men and women have been driven to irrational acts by personal neuroses and social myths, that they have always been prone to delusions and to urges of self-destruction, so that now, in the nuclear age, they are threatened at last with extinction. Moreover, he underrated the urge to power in many and the willingness of the mass of people to follow charismatic leaders. Even the Dukhobor sectarians, whom Kropotkin so keenly admired, put their faith in a series of autocratic messiahs to whom they swore unquestioning allegiance. It is doubtful, in short, whether our aggressive, authoritarian, and acquisitive impulses are merely the product of a degenerate social system and whether, even with a radical change in that system, governments, laws, police, and courts will ever become superfluous. Conflict and oppression, after all, existed long before the emergence of capitalism or of the modern centralized state; and, barring a transformation of human nature itself, they will continue to exist in the future.

It has been said of Kropotkin that if all were like him anarchism would be the only possible system, since government and restraint would be unnecessary.[51] But few of his character have graced the pages of history, a fact that he himself, for all his study of the past, failed to recognize. What is more, he never explained why the coercive state had come to dominate the world when man's natural inclination towards mutual aid should have led him along quite the opposite path. Governments and laws, he noted at one point, arose from the "desire of the ruling class to give permanence to customs imposed by themselves for their own advantage."[52] But beyond this he did not venture. Nor did he explain in any convincing way how the impulse to dominate was to be eliminated. His assertion that the centralized state is only a temporary aberration has not been confirmed by subsequent events. Despite his belief that the tendency of mankind was to "reduce government to zero," this has scarcely been a hallmark of the modern age. On the contrary, the growth of state power is visible everywhere. And, for all Kropotkin's predictions to the contrary, this growth has been due largely to technological changes in the direction of greater rather than less specialization in the productive process. However many contracts have been farmed out to smaller firms, this has done little to reduce the division of labor, and in some cases has even increased it.

The weakness of Kropotkin's analysis stems, at least in part, from his misleading definition of government. The state, as he saw it, was a comparatively recent phenomenon in the history of Western civilization. It was the bureaucratic nation-state of modern times that he so vehemently opposed, as distinguished from the local city-state, of which he was a more or less uncritical admirer. He associated tyranny and oppression primarily with centralized governments as opposed to the decentralized regimes that had flourished in ancient Greece or medieval Europe. He was not, it is true, completely blind to the negative aspects of medieval society. "It will be said, no doubt, that I forgot the conflicts and the internal struggles with which the history of the communes is filled: the embitterment and battles with the nobles . . . the bloodshed and the reprisals which always occurred during these struggles," he wrote in his *Words of a Rebel*. "No, I forgot nothing. . . . I hold that these struggles were in themselves proof of the freedom of life in the free cities."[53] Yet rejoinders of this sort do not alter the fact that he minimized the darker side of medieval life. In particular, he failed to emphasize that during the Middle Ages the great mass of peasants lived in poverty and bondage and that serfdom was eliminated only when the state increased its power at the expense of the feudal nobility.

More important, Kropotkin, because of his narrow definition of government, tended to ignore the problem of coercion within small communities in general. He believed, for instance, that primitive tribes were not subjected to state compulsion, although in fact within primitive societies compulsion rooted in custom and ritual, if not in a bureaucratic apparatus, was commonplace. Nor was the situation much different in his vaunted medieval commune, where breaches of habit drew severe punishments, including maiming and death. Ignoring the tyranny of custom, Kropotkin invoked community opinion as a means of restraining antisocial behavior in his projected libertarian utopia. By doing so, however, he accepted a form of compulsion that is scarcely less oppressive than that imposed by centralized authority. The warning of John Stuart Mill on this point is worth recalling: "The question is, whether there would be any asylum left for individuality of character; whether public opinion would not be a tyrannical yoke, whether the absolute dependence of each on all, and the surveillance of each by all, would not grind all down into a tame uniformity of thoughts, feelings, and actions."[54] Thus the perennial question of the relationship between the individual and society, far from being solved in Kropotkin's anarchist millennium, remains as thorny as ever.

Yet, whatever his failings as a prophet, Kropotkin has exerted a lasting influence. "In these times," noted the sociologist Pitirim Sorokin, "when state totalitarianism menaces to turn human beings into enslaved puppets, and free human creativeness into a coercive, soulless drudgery, the warnings and teachings of this great man are especially timely and significant."[55] For voluntary cooperation, Kropotkin insisted, is the only hope for man's survival. "We all know," he wrote in *The Conquest of Bread*, "that without uprightness, without self-respect, without sympathy and mutual aid, human kind must perish, as perish the few races of animals living by rapine, or the slave-keeping ants."[56] Even those for whom Kropotkin's stateless vision is an unattainable utopia can appreciate the wisdom of these words. And if governments will not wither away overnight, perhaps they can shed their more oppressive functions while a greater measure of autonomy filters down to local voluntary organizations. For all who share such hopes, Kropotkin, who achieved in his life what Albert Camus said was the most difficult of modern tasks—to become a saint without God—remains a source of inspiration.

"Kropotkins never die!" proclaimed one of the telegrams received by his widow after his passing in 1921. Today admirers throughout the world continue to cherish his ideals. Even in the Soviet Union he is honored as a scientist and a humanist, if not for his libertarian teachings or his criticisms of the centralized state. In 1961 a new Soviet book appeared on his explorations of Siberia, in 1966 a scholarly edition of his classic memoirs, in 1972 a sympathetic biography.[57] A Moscow metro station is named after him, as well as a square and two streets, including the one in which he was born. In 1967 my wife and I visited Kropotkin's birthplace in the old nobles' quarter of Moscow. The museum is gone, its contents long since dispersed among the archives of the Soviet government. The house now serves as a school for children of British and American embassy personnel. There is a playground in the garden, and children's art decorates the classrooms inside. Kropotkin would have been pleased.

CHAPTER FIVE

Kropotkin in America

IT IS A well-established fact that foreign immigrants and visitors played a major role in the emergence of American anarchism. During the nineteenth and twentieth centuries, European-born artisans and peasants—Germans and Czechs, Italians and Spaniards, Russians and Jews—constituted the mass base of the movement, while its intellectual leadership included well-known speakers and writers from diverse countries, who came either as permanent settlers or on extended lecture tours.

Among the Russians, as has been seen, Bakunin spent nearly two months in the United States after his flight from Siberia in 1861. Stepniak (S. M. Kravchinsky) came to lecture in 1891, N. V. Chaikovsky to join a utopian community and again to raise funds for the Russian revolutionary movement. The flood of Russian immigrants before and during the First World War included V. M. Eikhenbaum ("Volin"), Efim Yarchuk, Aaron and Fanny Baron, Boris Yelensky, and William Shatoff, not to mention Emma Goldman and Alexander Berkman, who had arrived in the 1880s. After the Bolshevik consolidation of power came such figures as Gregory Maximoff, Abba Gordin, and Mark Mratchny, who died in New York in 1975, the last of the Russian anarchists with an international reputation.

Of all the Russian visitors, however, it was Kropotkin who made the greatest impression. Kropotkin, as David Hecht has noted, had an "active and abiding interest in the United States" which, strengthened by his knowledge of English, extended over a forty-year period.[1] Like Bakunin before him, he was an admirer of American federalism, extolling the American Revolution and Declaration of Independence as land-

79

marks in the struggle for human freedom.[2] He was well versed in American literature and praised the poetry of Longfellow and the prose of Bret Harte, as well as Harriet Beecher Stowe's *Uncle Tom's Cabin* for its role in the emancipation of the slaves.[3] Emerson, Thoreau, and Whitman were other writers he held in esteem; and in calling for the expropriation of land he was indebted to Henry George's *Progress and Poverty*, which provoked an "outburst of socialist feeling in England."[4] Abreast of American scholarship in both the natural and social sciences, Kropotkin invoked the anthropologist Lewis H. Morgan and the sociologist Franklin H. Giddings in support of his theory of "mutual aid."[5] And in *The Conquest of Bread* and *Fields, Factories and Workshops* he paid tribute to American economic progress, citing advances in agriculture and especially industry, "aided as it is by a wonderful development of technical skill, by excellent schools, a scientific education which goes hand in hand with technical education, and a spirit of enterprise which is unrivalled in Europe."[6]

Yet Kropotkin was not blind to the defects of American society. On the contrary, he was sharply critical of the capitalist system and of government abuses of power. He condemned the persistence of child labor and the "travesty" of American democracy, which he claimed was in fact a "plutocracy." He hailed the railroad strike of 1877 as a sign of rising revolutionary consciousness among the workers. "Its spontaneity," he wrote, "its simultaneity at distant points connected only by telegraph, the aid given by workers of different trades, the resolute character of the rising since its outbreak, the happy idea of striking the owners at their most sensitive nerve—their property—arouses all our sympathies, excites our admiration, and awakens our hopes."[7] Nearly twenty years later, when Eugene Victor Debs was jailed during the Pullman strike, Kropotkin sent him an inscribed volume of his writings as a token of solidarity and support.[8]

Kropotkin, moreover, took an active part in protests against the trial of the Haymarket anarchists in 1886. Describing the Chicago affair as "a retaliation upon prisoners taken in the virtual civil war that was going on between the two classes," he wrote a letter to the American press objecting to the death sentences imposed on the defendants and, together with Stepniak, William Morris, and George Bernard Shaw, addressed a mass rally in London against their impending execution. A year after the hangings he declared that "the commemoration of the Chicago martyrs has almost acquired the same importance as the commemoration of the Paris Commune." The integrity and courage of the hanged men, he said a decade later, "remain a lesson for the old, an inspiration for the young."[9]

Michael Bakunin

Peter Kropotkin

William B. Greene

Anatoli Zhelezniakov, around 1917

НЕСТОР МАХНО

Nestor Makhno, around 1920

Benjamin R. Tucker, Boston, around 1887

Benjamin R. Tucker, Pearl Johnson Tucker, and Oriole Tucker, Monaco, June 1, 1914

Luigi Galleani

Sixtieth anniversary banquet of *Fraye Arbeter Shtime*, New York, 1950

Jewish anarchists: M. Spanier and S. Yanovsky, 1910

Alexander Berkman addressing May First rally, Union Square, New York, 1908

Upper right, Emma Goldman delivering eulogy at funeral of Peter Kropotkin, Moscow, February 13, 1921; Berkman, in white scarf and glasses, is standing in front of her

Lower right, Alexander Berkman in Paris, around 1927, photograph by Senya Fleshin; note picture of Emma Goldman on wall

Ricardo and Enrique Flores Magón

Mollie Steimer, around 1918·

Nestor Makhno and Alexander Berkman, Paris, around 1927

Gustav Landauer, around 1917

The Frayhayt Group, New York, 1918; includes Hyman Lachowsky (seated, third from left), Jacob Schwartz (standing, top, second from left), and Jacob Abrams (seated, right of center, mouth and chin obscured)

Senya Fleshin, Volin, and Mollie Steimer, Paris, around 1926

Deeply moved by the Haymarket tragedy, Kropotkin followed the development of American anarchism with special interest. Long before his visits, he corresponded with American anarchists, read their books and journals, and sent them messages of support. He was familiar with the writings of both the individualist and collectivist schools, mentioning Josiah Warren, Lysander Spooner, and Benjamin Tucker, together with Albert Parsons, August Spies, and Johann Most, in his well-known *Encyclopaedia Britannica* article on "Anarchism."

For his own part, Kropotkin exerted an increasing influence on American anarchists, as well as on socialists, single taxers, and other reformers. During the 1880s and 1890s, his articles appeared in all the leading anarchist journals, including Tucker's *Liberty*, Parsons's *Alarm*, and Most's *Freiheit*. Tucker, in spite of their philosophical differences, counted Kropotkin "among the most prominent anarchists in Europe" and praised his paper, *Le Révolté*, as "the most scholarly anarchist journal in existence." Apart from translating Kropotkin's "Order and Anarchy" and "Law and Authority" for *Liberty*, Tucker published news of Kropotkin's activities in Europe, including his expulsion from Switzerland in 1881 and his trial at Lyons in 1883 (lamenting "the cruel fate of Kropotkine and his comrades," sentenced to long terms in prison). Tucker also published Sophia Kropotkin's story, "The Wife of Number 4,237," based on her own experience with her husband at Clairvaux prison.[10]

Of all Kropotkin's early writings, however, it was *An Appeal to the Young* that had the greatest impact, making numerous converts in America as in other parts of the world. "Thousands and hundreds of thousands had read that pamphlet," remarked Anna Strunsky Walling, "and had responded to it as to nothing else in the literature of revolutionary Socialism." For Elizabeth Gurley Flynn, this work "struck home to me personally, as if he were speaking to us there in our shabby poverty-stricken Bronx flat: 'Must you drag on the same weary existence as your father and mother for thirty or forty years? Must you toil your life long to procure for others all the pleasures of well-being, of knowledge, of art, and keep for yourself only the eternal anxiety as to whether you can get a bit of bread?' "[11]

By the 1890s the anarchist movement in America had become predominantly anarchist-communist in orientation, owing to Kropotkin's influence. "He was a prominent figure in the realm of learning," wrote Emma Goldman in her memoirs, "recognized as such by the foremost men of the world. But to us he meant much more than that. We saw in him the father of modern anarchism, its revolutionary spokesman and brilliant exponent of its relation to science, philosophy, and progres-

sive thought."[12] No wonder that she and her comrades should have
repeatedly urged him to visit America. As early as 1891, he was invited
by both the Autonomie group and the Pioneers of Liberty, German and
Jewish anarchists in New York; but though he had long wanted to tour
the New World, he was forced to decline because of poor health, impaired by five years in Russian and French prisons, and because of a
conflict then raging within the immigrant wing of the movement, between the Autonomists (followers of Josef Peukert) and the Mostians.[13] In 1893 and in 1896 it was reported in the anarchist press that
Kropotkin was preparing to voyage to America, but once again ill
health and divisions within the movement, compounded by the controversy over Alexander Berkman's *attentat* of 1892 (which the Autonomists defended and the Mostians condemned), caused Kropotkin to
delay his trip.[14]

IT WAS as a delegate to the British Association for the Advancement of
Science, holding its 1897 meeting at Toronto, that Kropotkin finally
came to North America. In fragile health when he received an invitation from the organizing committee, he was reluctant to accept it. But
his friend James Mavor, whom he had known since settling in England
in 1886, induced him to participate. A former member of William
Morris's Socialist League, Mavor was now professor of political economy at the University of Toronto and an authority on both Russia and
Canada. (His two-volume economic history of Russia, published in
1914, remains a standard work on the subject.)[15]

For Mavor it was a "great pleasure" to have Kropotkin as his guest
when the conference convened in the latter part of August. Kropotkin
delivered two papers, "On the Åsar of Finland" and "On the Direction
of Lines of Structure in Eurasia".[16] After the conference, an excursion
to the Pacific Coast was arranged by the Canadian Pacific Railway,
and Kropotkin took this opportunity to see the country. He recorded
his impressions in a still unpublished diary and in an interesting article
for the well-known London magazine, *The Nineteenth Century*, to
which he was a frequent contributor.[17]

On the journey to the coast, which led him over the Rockies to Van-
couver, Kropotkin observed many "striking analogies between the
structure and the geological growth" of North America and Eurasia.[18]
The trip was "thoroughly beautiful," he wrote to his friend Patrick
Geddes, the Scottish biologist and social thinker. The prairies and forests and rugged mountains reminded him of Siberia, where he had
served as an officer in his youth.[19] Kropotkin again recalled Siberia
while crossing the plains of Manitoba on the way back to Toronto.

Visiting the Mennonite settlers, who had left Russia to avoid military service and other encroachments of the tsarist state, "one is at once transported to Russia," he wrote, noting that the name of Tolstoy was "a subject of deep reverence."[20]

When Kropotkin's description of Canada appeared in *The Nineteenth Century*, it was read by a member of the Tolstoyan Committee, who, moved by the sympathetic account of the Mennonites, suggested to Kropotkin that the Canadian prairie might provide a haven for the Dukhobors as well. Kropotkin agreed. When he had encountered the Dukhobors on the Amur some thirty years before, he had been struck by their integrity and spirit of mutual aid, and now he was anxious to help them. In August 1898 he wrote to Mavor suggesting that the Canadian government be approached in their behalf. In due course an agreement was reached, and thousands of Dukhobors left Russia and Cyprus and settled in western Canada, where many of their descendants still live.[21]

Kropotkin was greatly impressed by the agricultural abundance throughout the Canadian Northwest, and especially by the experimental farms in the area, which he visited with their director, Dr. William Saunders. "How rich mankind could be," he mused, "if social obstacles did not stand everywhere in the way of utilising the gifts of nature." At the same time, he feared that Canada was "making rapid strides towards the building up of the same land monopolies which now drive the European peasants out of Europe."[22]

Returning to Toronto, Kropotkin was met at the railroad station by a student sent by Mavor. On the way to Mavor's home, they discussed the merits of communal land ownership, which the student, a staunch individualist and future Conservative member of the Canadian parliament, vigorously opposed; and while he respected Kropotkin's knowledge and decency, his national pride was stung when Kropotkin referred to western Canada as "a little Siberia."[23] Kropotkin spent three weeks with Mavor, during which he wrote his article for *The Nineteenth Century*. To supplement his personal observations, he made use of Mavor's excellent library, which "contains everything about Canada," he told Patrick Geddes. He drew, moreover, on Mavor himself, "a living encyclopedia of Canadian economics."[24]

Kropotkin thoroughly enjoyed his ten-week sojourn in Canada. Though ill when he departed from England, he wrote that the trip across the continent had raised his spirits and "given me a new lease on life." Wherever he went he had received "the most friendly welcome" and was treated "with the utmost cordiality and hospitality." Struck by the degree of freedom enjoyed by Canadian citizens, especially as compared with that of his own countrymen, he concluded that "the only possible solution for Russia would be frankly to acknowledge the Federalist principle, and to adopt a system of several autonomous Parliaments, as we see it in Canada, instead of trying to imitate the centralized system of Great Britain, France, and Germany."[25]

In the middle of October Kropotkin left Toronto for the United States. Crossing the border at Niagara Falls, he traveled to Buffalo to call on Johann Most, the German anarchist firebrand, who had taken up temporary residence there following years of persecution in New York City. By making a special detour to see Most, Kropotkin gave the lie to stories that the two anarchist leaders were sworn antagonists, representing irreconcilable schools of thought. "With a few more Mosts," Kropotkin afterwards remarked, "our movement would be much stronger." Most, for his part, writing of the visit in his journal *Freiheit*, called Kropotkin the "celebrated philosopher of modern anarchism" and "one of the greatest scientists of this century." It was a pleasure, added Most, "to look into his eyes and shake his hand."[26]

From Buffalo Kropotkin went to Detroit to attend the annual meeting of the American Association for the Advancement of Science. What he witnessed at the meeting so stirred his enthusiasm that he predicted the United States would soon surpass Europe in scientific discoveries. He was equally impressed by American economic and technical advances. "America," he told a reporter, "possesses all the possibilities for happiness. Its agriculture is admirably developed, and agriculture is the foundation of all well being. It is bound, too, to become a great manufacturing country."[27] Before leaving Detroit, Kropotkin called on Joseph A. Labadie, the well-known American anarchist who later founded the Labadie Collection of radical literature at the University of Michigan. A member of the Detroit Water Board, Labadie conducted his visitor—"a small man with a large head, bushy hair and whiskers," as he describes him—through the engineering room of the city water works, in which Kropotkin took a lively interest. Kropotkin, according to Labadie, "talked English very well, and his movements were quick, as tho surprised."[28]

Kropotkin journeyed next to Washington, D.C., where he addressed a conference of the National Geographic Society on October 22. From Edward Singleton Holden, the noted American astronomer and a delegate to the conference, he had "the pleasure of hearing an appreciative estimate" of the research performed by his brother Alexander while a political exile in Siberia. During his stay in the American capital, Kropotkin, like many another sightseer, visited the Smithsonian Institution, rode to the top of the Washington Monument, and looked at the outside of the White House (but did not go in). After a busy but pleasant visit, he departed by train for New York on the morning of October 23.[29]

That afternoon Kropotkin's train was met in Jersey City by two of his American comrades, Harry Kelly, who had called on him in London in 1895, and John H. Edelmann, a respected architect and frequent contributor to anarchist journals. Also awaiting his arrival was a group of newspaper reporters, who asked Kropotkin for a statement. "I am an anarchist," he told them, "and am trying to work out the ideal society, which I believe will be communistic in economics, but will leave full and free scope for the development of the individual. As to its organization, I believe in the formation of federated groups for production and consumption." Kropotkin distinguished the anarchist position from that of the social democrats: "The social democrats are endeavoring to attain the same end, but the difference is that they start from the centre—the State—and work toward the circumference, while we endeavor to work out the ideal society from the simple elements to the complex." Finally, as in Canada, he praised the federalist system. "I am a strong federalist," he declared, "and I think that even under the present conditions the functions of government could be with great advantage decentralized territorially. Your theory of home rule in America I consider a distinct step in advance of the European centralized state, and it ought to continue in all directions."[30]

The reporters were favorably impressed. For in appearance and behavior Kropotkin belied the newspaper stereotype of the wild-eyed, depraved anarchist. "Prince Krapotkine," wrote one, "is anything but the typical anarchist. In appearance he is patriarchal, and while his dress is careless it is the carelessness of the man who is engrossed in science rather than that of the man who is in revolt against the usages of society. His manners are those of the polished gentleman, and he has none of the bitterness and dogmatism of the anarchist whom we are accustomed to see here."[31]

As soon as Kelly and Edelmann could get Kropotkin away from the reporters, they conducted him to Edelmann's apartment on Ninety-Sixth Street and Madison Avenue, where he was to stay during his New York visit. There, Kelly tells us, they spent a long evening talking of mutual acquaintances and of events in America and Europe. No doubt they also discussed the lecture on "Socialism and Its Modern Development" that Kropotkin was slated to deliver the following evening. While still in Toronto, Kropotkin had written to Kelly and his comrades about a speaking engagement in New York. To work out the necessary arrangements, a meeting had been held in Justus Schwab's saloon on East First Street, where anarchists and other radicals congregated. In advance of Kropotkin's arrival, tickets were put on sale (at twenty-five cents a piece) at Schwab's and other locations around the city.

The lecture was held at Chickering Hall, a fashionable auditorium on lower Fifth Avenue, which seated about two thousand. A steady rain fell all day. Kropotkin, accompanied by Kelly and Edelmann, took the Third Avenue Elevated to Fourteenth Street, "the heavy drops pelting against the car windows." The hall was filled to capacity and the lecture well received, but Kropotkin was disturbed because the entrance fee made it too expensive for poorer workers to attend. To Harry Kelly it seemed that a large proportion of the audience, prosperous in appearance, had come "to *see* the Prince rather than to *hear* the Anarchist." At all events, noted a reporter, "every seat was filled, there was not a foot of standing room to spare and hundreds were turned away because there was no room for them."[32] Elegantly dressed listeners rubbed shoulders with workers and immigrants for whom the price of admission was "a real sacrifice." Three women wearing red shirts and neckties and one in a red sweater occupied seats in the front row. At opposite ends of the platform sat Justus Schwab and Edward Brady (Emma Goldman's then companion), both powerfully built and dressed in grey with red carnations in their lapels.

Presiding was John Swinton, the veteran labor reformer who, in the opinion of Benjamin Tucker, was "the best after-dinner speaker in the city of New York." Though Swinton was nearly seventy, his voice was still strong and carried to every corner of the hall. Swinton introduced Kropotkin, who was "loudly applauded" and addressed the "enthusiastic house" on the lessons of the Paris Commune, the evils of prison, and the dangers of state socialism. As one reporter described him, "he wore a patriarchal beard and beamed on his audience from behind a pair of spectacles like an old fashioned clergyman looking over a familiar congregation."[33]

From all accounts Kropotkin was not a dynamic speaker. He was not of the flamboyant school of orators, of whom Most was a leading example, who overwhelm their listeners with tirades of venom and irony. He spoke, rather, in a quiet voice with a heavy Russian accent. His words, thought one reporter, came "tumbling out in any order," and yet "his evident sincerity and his kindliness hold the attention of his audience and gain its sympathy." Steadily building his argument, he was an intense figure on the platform. As his friend Stepniak once noted: "He trembles with emotion; his voice vibrates with that accent of profound conviction, not to be mistaken or counterfeited, and only heard when it is not merely the mouth which speaks, but the innermost heart. His speeches, although he cannot be called an orator of the first rank, produce an immense impression; for when feeling is so intense it is communicative, and electrifies an audience."[34]

Such was the effect of Kropotkin on his Chickering Hall listeners. The meeting, according to one member of the audience, was "a great success in every way." Returning from a visit to Europe a few days later, Voltairine de Cleyre, the American anarchist poet, found her New York comrades "jubilant" over the lecture, which had given their movement a badly needed lift.[35]

Kropotkin, however, did not remain long in New York. On October 25 he left for Philadelphia to address a meeting in Odd Fellows' Temple sponsored by the Jewish anarchists of that city. As in New York, the house was packed and the lecture, followed by a reception for the speaker, a great success. Some two thousand people attended, one of whom, many years later, told Kropotkin's biographers that "the audience was extremely attentive and sympathetic." With the exception of one or two "yellow journals," as Voltairine de Cleyre remarked, the press was "fair to our gentle revolutionist," particularly the staid old *Philadelphia Ledger*, which gave "an excellent and uncolored report" of the meeting.[36]

The decade of the 1890s was a period of bitter industrial strife in America, and Kropotkin's indignation was aroused by a recent massacre of workers at Hazleton, Pennsylvania. It occurred on September 10, six weeks before his visit to Philadelphia, when a column of protesting strikers, Slovak and Polish miners, was fired on by a detachment of police led by the local sheriff. Twenty-one were killed and forty wounded. Outraged by the unprovoked slaughter, Kropotkin dispatched an article to the leading French anarchist journal, *Les Temps Nouveaux*, alerting his European associates to the labor struggles in America. "Nothing, nothing but war, war without mercy, will lead to any solution in the United States," he concluded. "And the war will be terrible, for the limit of the workers' patience has long since been surpassed."[37]

From Philadelphia Kropotkin proceeded to Boston, where he stayed about two weeks and delivered seven or eight lectures, two of them ("Savages and Barbarism" and "The Medieval City") at the famous Lowell Institute, to which he was to return in 1901. His opening lecture, however, was sponsored by the Workingmen's Educational Club and took place before a large audience in the Columbia Theatre, the subject, as in New York, being "Socialism and Its Modern Development." The progress of mankind, he told his listeners, "points in the direction of less government of man by man, of more liberty for the individual, of freer scope for the development of all individual faculties, for the greatest development of the initiative of the individual, for home rule for every separate unit, and for decentralization of power."[38]

Kropotkin also spoke before the Woman's Industrial Club of Cambridge on "Siberia, the Land of Exile," and before the Prospect Union of Cambridge, an organization of Harvard students and local workers, on "The Socialist Movement in Europe." Two more lectures, on "Christianity" and "Morality," were delivered in churches where Kropotkin had been invited to speak. Although the audiences were large and enthusiastic, and Kropotkin was satisfied with the meetings from the standpoint of propaganda, they brought little money into the anarchist coffers. Fortunately, Kropotkin wrote to Geddes, the lectures at the Lowell Institute and Harvard were "very well paid," for the rest "barely covered expenses."[39]

There were, however, other compensations. For one, Kropotkin was impressed by a cooperative dining room organized by less affluent Harvard students. He saw this as an example of "mutual aid," the theme of his Lowell Institute lectures and of his celebrated book of that title.[40] He had the pleasure, moreover, of making a wide circle of new acquaintances, including a number of Harvard professors who were to invite him to return on his next visit. Among them was the literary scholar, Charles Eliot Norton, who was quite charmed by Kropotkin, "the mildest and gentlest of anarchists," as he described him in a letter to a friend. Norton was especially delighted by a remark of Kropotkin's regarding metaphysics: "Yes, your metaphysician is a blind man hunting in a dark room for a black hat which does not exist."[41]

In the middle of November, Kropotkin returned to New York for a final round of lectures before departing for England. Staying again with John Edelmann, he received a steady stream of visitors, among them Saul Yanovsky, editor of the *Fraye Arbeter Shtime*, and Benjamin Tucker.[42] Some of Kropotkin's callers, however, were not as welcome as Yanovsky and Tucker. One afternoon, a prominent New York banker stopped by to invite the Russian prince to dinner. Edelmann told him that Kropotkin had not been feeling well and had gone to Central Park for some air. Just as the banker left, two anarchist workmen arrived to pay their respects to their teacher. Kropotkin emerged from an adjacent room and warmly embraced them, explaining that he did not care to receive bankers but was delighted to see his young comrades, with whom he spent a few hours conversing in their native Yiddish.[43]

To publicize Kropotkin's forthcoming lectures, Edelmann, at Yanovsky's suggestion, arranged a press conference in his apartment. Kropotkin, who had always been reluctant to grant interviews because of the distortions that invariably resulted, was nevertheless pleased by the session. "But his joy was short-lived," recalls Yanovsky. "That same afternoon there appeared in the 'Evening Journal' the news that Prince Kropotkin ran along the street asking for a cigarette. I laughed at this idiotic anecdote which was printed. But I never saw Kropotkin so wrought up and irritated as then. 'How can one be such a liar?' This roused him to such a pitch that he and Edelmann went to the office of the 'Evening Journal' and they succeeded in getting a denial of this idiotic incident in the following morning, but hidden in an obscure corner and printed in their very smallest type."[44]

Meanwhile, Chickering Hall was again chosen as the site of Kropotkin's next lecture, arranged for Friday evening, November 19, by the American Friends of Russian Freedom, a group of influential liberals and reformers including clergymen and jurists as well as labor leaders and scholars, Professors Robert Erskine Ely and Franklin Giddings among them. Presiding was Ernest Howard Crosby, a former judge on the International Court and now Tolstoy's leading American disciple, who gave his impressions of Russia as he had seen it a few years before. Then, for more than hour, Kropotkin spoke on "The Struggle for Freedom in Russia," with an "earnestness and conviction" that won him an enthusiastic reception. Yet Kropotkin, who always preferred the company of ordinary workers to that of the upper classes into which he himself had been born, thought the meeting a "complete fiasco," with its "chic-très" well-to-do sponsors.[45]

The next day he found himself in happier surroundings when, at the request of his anarchist comrades, he delivered a lecture in Russian on "The Philosophic and Scientific Bases of Anarchism." Admission was fifteen cents and, after expenses were paid, a balance of $125 was forwarded to a Russian group in Switzerland for the publication of anarchist literature.[46] The following afternoon Kropotkin attended a private gathering at the home of Hillel Solotaroff, a leading Jewish anarchist and physician, where the Dreyfus case and other important questions of the day were discussed. In the evening he attended a banquet in his honor arranged by the Russian Students' Club and was drawn into a debate by Doctors Hourwich and Ingerman, socialist intellectuals whose knowledge, he felt, was limited "to what Karl Marx has uttered."[47]

In spite of his crowded schedule, Kropotkin found time to cross the Hudson and lecture to his comrades of Paterson, New Jersey, a militant anarchist center with an immigrant working-class population. On November 22, the eve of his departure for Europe, he delivered his final address in New York on "The Great Social Problems of Our Century." To his comrades who arranged the farewell gathering he had insisted on a low admission fee, "so that ordinary workers would be able to attend." Accordingly, only five cents was charged, and the Great Hall of Cooper Union, where Abraham Lincoln had spoken, was filled to capacity. It was probably the largest meeting Kropotkin ever addressed, with more than five thousand people in attendance, according to one estimate. Trade unionists had been invited, and workers of all nationalities were present, as well as such men of letters as Professor Ely of the Friends of Russian Freedom and Walter Hines Page, editor of the *Atlantic Monthly*. Ernest Howard Crosby was again in the chair. According to Harry Kelly, the meeting was a magnificent demonstration of "love and appreciation for a great man and a great revolutionist."[48]

The following day Kropotkin left for England on the RMS *Majestic*. His trip to North America, lasting nearly four months, had been a resounding success. He had traversed the Canadian continent, making valuable observations of its geographic and agricultural features. He had attended three scientific conferences (in Toronto, Detroit, and Washington), addressing two of them and exchanging ideas and information with his colleagues. He had visited other American cities, including New York, Buffalo, Paterson, Boston, and Philadelphia. Far from leaving him exhausted, his travels had revived his spirits. Moreover, his physical health had improved. That in itself, noted the London *Freedom*, "is an immense gain."[49]

Looking back at his American journey, Kropotkin recalled with pleasure the warmth with which he had everywhere been received. On board the *Majestic* he wrote of "the fine impression of this beautiful continent" and of the people he had encountered. In both Canada and the United States he had made many friends and met anarchists of diverse national backgrounds and economic persuasions, including Johann Most and Benjamin Tucker, the leading spokesmen of the collectivist and individualist wings of the movement. In general he had found the Americans "very sympathetic" and regretted not being able to visit the western states, whose inhabitants, he said, constituted "a different race from the New Englanders." Indeed, had it been possible to do so, he would have liked to spend a whole year in America, traveling from place to place, recording his impressions, and conducting anarchist propaganda.[50]

While particularly impressed by the economic and scientific progress of North America, Kropotkin had also had an opportunity to study the federalist system at first hand, acclaiming it as a model for Russia and Europe to follow. At the same time, however, he was disturbed by the political atmosphere in the United States. He found it, despite the advantages of representative democracy, "corrupting and enervating." As he told an American reporter: "Men who are elected to office to do the fighting for the masses against the rule of the few are every time, or with insignificantly few exceptions, bought over by the enemy, so that to secure full liberty by the people for the people the American nation is beginning to realize that the traditional forms of government are entirely inadequate." Kropotkin took comfort in the emerging labor movement, citing the large number of strikes in America as a sign of growing resistance to exploitation. "The Socialist sentiment in the United States was never in a more flourishing condition than it is today," he declared. "The growth of the feeling is steadily on the increase, and particularly in such cities as New York and Chicago."[51]

To guide this sentiment into libertarian channels was one of the chief objects of Kropotkin's visit. And, to some extent at least, his efforts were not wasted. Financially, Kropotkin admitted, the voyage had been a "complete fiasco," for the money taken in at most of his lectures had barely covered expenses. Yet the two big meetings, in New York— at Chickering Hall in October and Cooper Union in November—had netted a handsome $500. The greater part of this sum Kropotkin handed over to John Edelmann to revive his journal *Solidarity*, which had suspended publication in 1895 for lack of funds.[52] Moreover, the lectures had "left a most gratifying impression," injecting "new life into our movement," noted Emma Goldman. In Boston and New York, as the London *Freedom* observed, "the meetings were especially large, enthusiastic, and in every way successful, the farewell meeting in the Cooper Hall being the finest he ever addressed." *Freedom* predicted that Kropotkin's tour "will give an immense impetus to the Anarchist movement in the States. The demand for Anarchist literature from America during the past months goes to prove the truth of this."[53]

In the wake of Kropotkin's visit, a flood of his speeches and essays appeared in the American anarchist press. One journal, *Free Society* of San Francisco, whose editor, Abe Isaak, was a Russian Mennonite turned anarchist, printed such important works as "Law and Authority," "Anarchist Morality," "Revolutionary Government," "The Wage-System," and "Anarchism: Its Philosophy and Ideal." *Free Society* had been launched in November 1897, and Kropotkin read the first issue while lecturing in New York. Favorably impressed, he had but one serious criticism, which he expressed in a letter to the editor after returning to England. "I should advise you," he wrote, "to leave alone the sexual question, which the *Firebrand* [*Free Society*'s predecessor] devoted so much attention to. Free men and women will better find the ways for arranging their mutual relations than we can even foresee now. This is to be a result of the free work of an evolution of free life, in which any newspaper guidance is as illusory as it is in most cases wrong."[54]

Two years later, when Emma Goldman visited Kropotkin in the company of Mary Isaak, the wife of *Free Society*'s editor, he once again broached the subject. "The paper is doing splendid work," he said, "but it would do more if it would not waste so much space discussing sex." Goldman emphatically disagreed, and a heated argument ensued. According to her account, she and Kropotkin "paced the room in growing agitation, each strenuously upholding his side of the question. At last I paused with the remark: 'All right, dear comrade, when I have reached your age [she was then thirty, Kropotkin fifty-seven], the sex question may no longer be of importance to me. But it is *now*, and it is a tremendous factor for thousands, millions even, of young people.' Peter stopped short, an amused smile lighting up his kindly face. 'Fancy, I didn't think of that,' he replied. 'Perhaps you are right after all.' He beamed affectionately upon me, with a humorous twinkle in his eye."[55]

Among the most important results of Kropotkin's trip to America was the publication of his autobiography, which in a short time became a classic. According to James Mavor, it was he who induced Kropotkin to undertake the task. Through Robert Erskine Ely, who was a friend of Mavor's, arrangements were made for publication in the *Atlantic Monthly*, whose editor, Walter Hines Page, persuaded the reluctant board of managers to go along.[56] Written in elegant English, Kropotkin's reminiscences appeared as a series of articles from September 1898 to September 1899, prefaced with an introduction by Ely, who called Kropotkin "one of the most remarkable men of this generation."[57]

When the first installment reached him at Bromley, Kropotkin was greatly displeased by the title, "The Autobiography of a Revolutionist," assigned by the magazine's editors. He at once dispatched a telegram asking them to change it in subsequent issues to "Around One's Life," but his request went unheeded. An expanded version of the articles was published in book form by Houghton Mifflin of Boston in 1899, under the title *Memoirs of a Revolutionist*, which equally displeased the author.[58] The introduction this time was by the Danish critic Georg Brandes, a friend of Kropotkin's since 1895. According to

Mavor, who took "great satisfaction" in the book's appearance, there did not exist "a more charming series of autobiographical sketches or any more vivid account of the social movement of the latter half of the nineteenth century."[59]

KROPOTKIN'S second visit to the United States took place in 1901. The previous fall he had been invited by the Lowell Institute, where he had spoken in 1897, to deliver a series of lectures on Russian literature. He accepted the invitation and, towards the end of February, made his second crossing of the Atlantic. Docking at Boston, he remained in Massachusetts for more than a month, staying at the Colonial Club in Cambridge and renewing many friendships of his earlier visit.[60]

Kropotkin labored long and hard over his Lowell lectures, correcting and revising them up to the last minute. "To tell the truth," he wrote to Professor Norton of his opening speech, "I feel nervous for it. Such as I wrote it, it is too long, and so long as it is not done, I feel quite nervous. So I sit now, and write, and will work till late at night." His fears, however, proved groundless. For the series, as Harry Kelly noted, was an "unqualified success."[61] Roger Baldwin tells us that the audiences were "large and alert, plying him with questions at the close of each address. He spoke from notes in an English strongly accented, in a professorial but very earnest style." There were eight lectures in all, which Kropotkin afterwards expanded and published in book form.[62]

During his prolonged stay in Boston, Kropotkin delivered a number of other lectures. He spoke, for example, at Wellesley College and also at Harvard, where, in addition to Norton, he was warmly received by two pioneers of Slavic studies in the United States, Professor Leo Weiner, whose *Anthology of Russian Literature*, published the following year, Kropotkin considered an "excellent" work, and Professor Archibald Cary Coolidge, for whom the history of Russia was his "first love" and who put at Kropotkin's disposal a "valuable collection" of materials that Kropotkin used in preparing his Lowell lectures.[63] Beyond this, the Reverend Edward Everett Hale invited Kropotkin to speak in his church, but though Kropotkin had addressed Boston church groups in 1897, he declined, says Roger Baldwin, because of his antipathy to organized religion, though he was finally persuaded to speak in the church's lecture room.[64]

Kropotkin's largest meeting took place, appropriately enough, in Paine Hall, the home of Boston's freethinking community. Organized by the Boston Anarchist Group, the meeting was opened by A. H. Simpson, a British-born follower of Benjamin Tucker. The chairman,

Edwin D. Mead, a member of the American Friends of Russian Freedom and a cousin of William and Henry James, introduced Kropotkin as "the most valiant, courageous, and noble champion of freedom in our time." The audience, noted a Boston reporter, presented "a most cosmopolitan, picturesque and enthusiastic gathering," with many women present, all demonstrating their affection for the "grand old man" of their movement. When Kropotkin entered the hall, another reporter observed, "a storm of applause broke out. The chorus of Italian 'comrades' sang the 'Marseillaise,' the audience applauded again and Kropotkin smiled, shook hands with the people who flocked about him and seemed happy." From their seats members of the audience called out greetings in Russian, French, German, and Italian, and Kropotkin answered each in the appropriate language.[65]

Kropotkin spoke on "Anarchism: Its Philosophy and Ideal," severely criticizing state socialism, which, he argued, would entail unprecedented concentration of power and lead inevitably to slavery. He called instead for a free, voluntary, spontaneous, and decentralized society, with "absolute home rule and the highest individual freedom." He then launched into what one reporter called "a learned yet lucid and impressive enunciation of anarchism, its literature, its philosophy and ideal." He spoke of the growth of the anarchist movement all over the world. Twenty years earlier, he noted, only a handful of anarchist journals were being published, but now there was an immense literature—books, pamphlets, periodicals—in all languages. Ten years before, he added, such a meeting as he was now addressing could not have been possible, for the mere word "anarchism" would have been enough to keep people away. At the close of his speech Kropotkin defended those anarchists who used violence against coercive authority, citing "the countless cruelties and brutalities of kings, rulers, and all governments, practiced upon the poor, oppressed, starving, defenseless people." He spoke of government persecutions that he himself had experienced and related how the Spanish anarchists had been tortured, then said: "It is we who have the right to speak of violence, not they."[66]

During the course of his "fervid" speech, as the *Boston Post* described it, Kropotkin was repeatedly applauded and was "listened to with the greatest attention by all present." His manner on the platform was striking and intense. "Here was no longer Kropotkin, the lecturer on Russian literature before the Lowell Institute, where he does quite well but is not at home—for literature is not his forte; here was Kropotkin, the enthused and enthusing agitator; the stirring, inspiring champion of his cause, the idolized leader of his movement, who feels and lives every word he utters."[67]

94

This was Kropotkin's last major appearance in Boston. He left for New York on March 29. On the eve of his departure, a farewell gathering was held at Phoenix Hall on Washington Street. He was given a warm send-off, proving, said Harry Kelly, that "the spirit of Emerson, Phillips, and Garrison is not dead but has been sleeping—may this visit help to awaken it."[68]

When Kropotkin arrived in New York, he spoke to a group of reporters at the Hotel Gerard, where he was staying. The conversation turned to his native country, whose secret police, the Okhrana, kept track of him throughout his tour. He spoke of the disturbances in Russia's universities, calling the tsar, Nicholas II, "an irresponsible, not very clever, young man." He was convinced, however, that Russia had entered on the path of constitutional reform, which he hoped would give it a federalist government on American lines.[69]

A full schedule of lectures had been arranged for Kropotkin, by Emma Goldman on behalf of the anarchists and by Robert Erskine Ely, who had been so helpful to Kropotkin on his previous trip.[70] In a single week Kropotkin lectured half a dozen times, on Russian literature and on anarchism, as in Boston. His first appearance, on March 30, was before the Educational League for the Study of Political Economy, a middle-class organization of which Professor Ely was chairman. Of Ely, however, Goldman had a low opinion. "An extremely timid man, he seemed forever in fear that his connexion with anarchists might ruin his standing with the backers of the League for Political Economy," was her uncharitable judgment. "I felt that to Ely the *prince* was the most important feature about Kropotkin. The British have royalty and love it, but some Americans love it because they would like to have it. It did not matter to them that Kropotkin had discarded his title in joining the revolutionary ranks."[71]

The lecture, at all events, was a great success. Kropotkin was greeted with enthusiasm, recalls a member of the audience that crammed the Berkeley Lyceum. According to the *New York Times*, "every seat was filled, extra chairs brought in, and people stood in the rear of the theatre, upstairs and down." "Turgenev and Tolstoy" was Kropotkin's topic. "He spoke an hour and a half," noted the *Times*, "easily and pleasantly, but with an accent which at times made it difficult for those who were out of range of his voice to understand." An anarchist who was present encountered no such difficulty: "To hear an old teacher talk of his countrymen, was a never-to-be-forgotten treat, especially so when telling us of the manner in which the populace greeted Tolstoy, by patting him on the back and accosting him with endearing terms of affection and fraternal love."[72]

The following afternoon, a Sunday, Kropotkin addressed a mass meeting arranged by his anarchist comrades at the Grand Central Palace, one of the largest auditoriums in the city. This, says Harry Kelly, was the biggest and most successful anarchist meeting ever held in New York, apart from Kropotkin's address at Cooper Union three and a half years before. People came from all parts of town, in spite of the high admission fee of twenty-five cents, and the hall, with a seating capacity of four thousand, was "packed to the doors." The anarchist bookseller, Max Maisel, set up a stand in the vestibule and displayed his wares, aided by the pioneer libertarian educator Alexis C. Ferm.[73]

In the chair was Dr. George D. Herron, the well-known Christian Socialist, who had met Kropotkin four years earlier as a student at the London School of Economics. "He did not at all approve of my way of looking at things at that time, either sociologically or religiously," Herron remembered, "but he was always so kindly and so reasonable in his admonitions and arguments, that I found him a vastly better teacher than the Fabian professors of political economy who constituted the faculty of the School of Economics." Now Herron felt honored to be chairing the immense gathering. He had presided at many meetings, he told the audience, but would always look back to this one as the happiest of his life because the speaker was "like unto a host in the cause of human freedom." Herron added that he considered Kropotkin's writings "a veritable bible," and that he was "immensely indebted to him for the light he had shed on the social darkness prevalent up to this time."[74]

Kropotkin spoke on "Anarchism: Its Philosophy and Ideal," the subject of his Paine Hall lecture in Boston. Again the reporter from the *Times* had trouble making out his words ("he spoke so rapidly and with such a patois that it was almost impossible to understand him"), while the anarchists hailed the address as a model of eloquence and clarity. "Comrades," wrote one, "it was truly glorious! I have been to many meetings, have spoken at some myself . . . but I never witnessed in all my life so impressive a reception as the one accorded to the grand man of the Socialist movement."[75]

Over the next few days Kropotkin delivered a number of additional lectures. One evening he spoke in Russian to a Russian audience at "the famous and notorious Tammany Hall."[76] He also spoke at several colleges in the city on "Work As It Should Be." All told, some $750 was collected at these meetings, over and above expenses, and sent to the London *Freedom*, to *Les Temps Nouveaux* in Paris, and to *Free Society*, now located in Chicago.

In between lecture engagements, Kropotkin received a host of visitors and himself called on old and new acquaintances. A day or two after his arrival, he met with Johann Most, whom he had visited during his previous trip. Their meeting took place at the Hotel Gerard, after Kropotkin, through some misunderstanding, had gone looking for Most at the offices of *Freiheit* on Gold Street. When Most finally caught up with Kropotkin at his hotel, the men embraced very warmly and talked for an hour over tea, mainly about the anarchist movement in Europe and America.[77]

On another occasion, strange to relate, Robert Ely took Kropotkin to call on the widow of Jefferson Davis, president of the Confederacy during the Civil War. During the interview, which Mrs. Davis had requested, Booker T. Washington, who was in search of Ely, was announced as being in the lobby, and Mrs. Davis expressed a desire to meet him. Thus Kropotkin, as Roger Baldwin observed, was the unwitting means of bringing together two persons as little likely to meet as any in the country, and the anarchist prince, the black educator, and the widow of the slave-owning president "sat politely and conversed as if it were a most ordinary occasion."[78]

Apart from his lectures and visits, Kropotkin spent much time at private gatherings with anarchist and liberal friends. After the Grand Central Palace meeting, for instance, a small group of anarchists, Emma Goldman among them, dined with "our beloved teacher."[79] The following evening, April 1, a large reception was held for him at the Labor Lyceum, featuring refreshments, entertainment, and discussion. Kropotkin, who stayed and chatted till nearly midnight, was greeted with a warmth and respect that bordered on veneration. "To see his beaming, kindly face, aglow with true benevolence, his intellectual brow, and, most remarkable of all—for one who has passed through so much and has lived so strenuous a life—his mild, soft eyes, is an inspiration and a tonic," wrote an anarchist who attended the reception. "No wonder that men and women spontaneously embraced him with brimming eyes and high-beating hearts." Though deeply touched by their affection, Kropotkin tried to discourage such adulation on the part of his followers. Thus when the *Fraye Arbeter Shtime*, the principal Jewish anarchist paper in America, made plans to publish a group of Kropotkin photographs as a supplement, he put a stop to it, refusing, he told the editor, to be made into "an icon."[80]

The last such gathering took place on Saturday evening, April 6, when a small dinner was arranged on Henry Street on the Lower East Side. That afternoon, the *Weekly People*, organ of the Socialist Labor party, had published a sneering report of Kropotkin's Grand Central Palace meeting. Written by the editor, Daniel De Leon, who detested anarchists even more than capitalists, it displayed sharper hostility than accounts in the regular press, which was generally fair in its treatment of Kropotkin. With withering contempt De Leon derided the "Prince's retinue," among whom he named "Do-Unto-Others Herron," "poor old John Swinton," and Emma Goldman, "with her severe little pug face and glistening spectacles." Kropotkin himself, wrote De Leon, had "a mental apparatus that is a prize collection of intellectual junk. His English is very poor. As to ideas or information he had nothing new to say—the same long, disjointed, incoherent anarchistic ramble, touching about everything under the sun, except the working class and the capitalist class."[81]

Kropotkin, for all his reputation for benign saintliness, was capable of great fits of wrath and moral outrage. At such moments, his features would grow tense, his eyes flash with indignation, his face grow flush and angry. Such was the case at the Henry Street dinner when Jacob Gordin, the famous Jewish playwright, happened to mention De Leon's article. Kropotkin began to tremble, so violently that the table shook (Yanovsky, sitting next to him, could feel the vibrations), and, interrupting Gordin, would not allow him to spoil the dinner with "such filth."[82]

Both emotionally and physically, Kropotkin's crowded schedule proved too much of a strain on his fragile constitution. Exhausted by the excitement and by the endless speeches and receptions, he came down with influenza, which kept him in bed for over a week. By the middle of April, however, he had recovered sufficiently to leave for the Midwest, where a further series of lectures had been arranged, primarily in Chicago.

On the way to Chicago, Kropotkin made a special stop at Pittsburgh to visit Alexander Berkman, the Russian-born anarchist who was serving a twenty-two-year prison sentence for his attempt on the life of Henry Clay Frick, manager of the Carnegie Steel Company. Having himself spent five years in prison, Kropotkin felt a special sympathy for Berkman, whose act he had defended in 1892. "Berkman," he had written, "has done more to spread the anarchist idea among the masses than the reading of any journal or newspaper. . . . He has shown that our Chicago martyrs were not the last Mohicans of the anarchist movement in America."[83] Three years later, when Goldman visited Kropotkin in London, he had asked her about Berkman. "He had followed the latter's case," she writes, "and he knew every phase of it, expressing great regard and concern for Sasha." And when Kropotkin came to New York in 1897, he had declined an invitation from Andrew Carnegie to visit his mansion on Fifth Avenue. "Because of your power and influence," he had written, "my comrade Alexander Berkman received twenty-two years of prison for an act that the state of Pennsylvania punishes with a maximum of seven years. I cannot accept the hospitality of a man who assists in condemning another man to twenty-two years."[84]

When Kropotkin arrived in Pittsburgh, Berkman was being held in solitary confinement after an unsuccessful attempt to tunnel his way to freedom, and Kropotkin was refused permission to see him. A few days later Berkman received a letter from Kropotkin, who had written on the envelope, beneath Berkman's name, "Political Prisoner." The warden was furious. "We have no political prisoners in a free country," he shouted at Berkman, tearing up the envelope. "But you have political grafters," Berkman retorted. "We argued the matter heartily," Berkman told a friend, "and I demanded the envelope. The Warden insisted that I apologize. Of course I refused, and I had to spend three days in the dungeon."[85]

Thwarted in his efforts to see Berkman, Kropotkin went on to Chicago, his principal midwestern destination. At Englewood, two stations from Chicago, he was met by the Isaaks, Abe, Mary, and their son Abe Jr., publishers of *Free Society*, who wanted to greet him and talk to him "before he was swamped by an admiring crowd in the city." Also waiting were a reporter and a newspaper artist, "but the newspapermen were kindly invited to call at another time, while he received the comrades. The Anarchist movement and the comrades are always his first consideration."[86]

On reaching Chicago, Kropotkin was taken in charge by Jane Addams, a disciple of Tolstoy who was also influenced by Kropotkin's social and ethical teachings. Addams took Kropotkin to her famous social settlement, Hull House, where he stayed during his week-long visit. For the occasion, says Emma Goldman, the rooms were decorated with Russian folk art, and Addams and her staff wore Russian peasant costumes. Of all her Russian guests, and there were many, Addams considered Kropotkin "the most distinguished."[87] According to Dr. Alice Hamilton, who was living at Hull House at the time, "we all came to love him," as did the Russian refugees who flocked to the settlement to see him. "No matter how down-and-out, how squalid even, a caller would be, Prince Kropotkin would give him a joyful welcome and kiss him on both cheeks."[88]

On his first evening at Hull House Kropotkin agreed to meet with the Chicago press, whose writers, said Abe Isaak, Jr., were "pretty fair, as compared with their usual misrepresentations of Anarchists." After the reporters had left, Kropotkin spoke privately with the elder Abe

Isaak on the state of the anarchist movement in Europe. Though especially pleased with the progress of libertarian ideas within the labor unions of Spain, Italy, and France, Kropotkin was also much interested in the trade-union movement in America and "urged that Anarchists join and agitate more among them."[89]

It was at Hull House, on April 17, that Kropotkin delivered the first of his five lectures in Chicago. Speaking before the Arts and Crafts Society, he presented a digest of his "remarkable book" (as Jane Addams called it) *Fields, Factories and Workshops*, stressing the value of work as a form of art and the importance of practical learning to supplement education from books. On April 18 and 19 he addressed the Twentieth Century Club on "Medieval Cities" and the High School Teachers' Club on "The Law of Mutual Aid and the Struggle for Existence," drawing on both occasions from his forthcoming book, *Mutual Aid*.

On the afternoon of April 20, a Saturday, Kropotkin, accompanied by a group of Chicago anarchists, visited the Waldheim Cemetery and placed flowers at the tomb of the Haymarket martyrs, Parsons, Spies, Lingg, Fischer, and Engel, whose cause he had championed from the time of their arrest in 1886. The same morning a group of society women, led by Mrs. Potter Palmer, had invited him to lunch. Mrs. Palmer, the wife of one of Chicago's "richest and 'hardest' businessmen," was a financial supporter of Hull House. "You will come, Prince, will you not?" she pleaded. "I am sorry, ladies, but I have a previous engagement with my comrades," Kropotkin excused himself. "Oh, no, Prince; you *must* come with us!" Mrs. Palmer insisted. "Madame," Kropotkin replied, "you may have the Prince, and I will go with my comrades."[90]

Kropotkin, however, could not escape the attention of Chicago high society any more than in Boston or New York. As a Russian nobleman from a distinguished family and a scientist of international renown, he was tirelessly pursued by America's upper crust. One time, expecting to meet his anarchist comrades, he accepted an invitation to a social gathering, only to find himself among "vulgar bourgeois women who pestered him for his autograph," writes Emma Goldman's associate, Hippolyte Havel. "The irony of it! The man who gave up gladly his position at the Russian court to go to the people being entertained by the porkocracy of Chicago!"[91]

Yet there were some prominent Chicagoans whom Kropotkin was more than happy to meet, above all John Peter Altgeld, the former Illinois governor who had pardoned the Haymarket anarchists in 1893. The meeting was arranged by Graham Taylor, founder of the

Chicago Commons settlement house, who was present at the occasion. The conversation turned to Russia, where student disorders and government repressions had culminated in the assassination of the minister of education. "When asked by me whether nothing short of violence could deliver the Russian people from oppression," Taylor recalls, Kropotkin replied that "the despotic bureaucrats could be overcome only by being blown off the face of the earth." Altgeld, for his part, "filed exceptions to any justifications for such conclusions in America."[92]

On the evening of April 20, following his pilgrimage to Waldheim Cemetery, Kropotkin met with students and professors of the University of Chicago, where he spoke on "Science and the Social Question" and started a movement to protest the treatment of Russian students by the tsar. To arouse American opinion against the Russian government, Kropotkin published articles in two leading periodicals, *The Outlook* and *The North American Review*, blaming the disturbances on the repressive policies of the authorities and on the general atmosphere of reaction in which all efforts to achieve greater liberty were ruthlessly crushed.[93] Kropotkin cited a protest of Harvard students, during his recent stay at Cambridge, against the "mutton monotony" of their dining-room food. "What," he asked, "would the Americans say if President McKinley had ordered the Harvard students . . . to be sent to the Philippines? The country would certainly rise in indignation; that is what happened in Russia." Arguing that Russia had outgrown its autocratic government, Kropotkin once again called for a parliamentary system on decentralist and federalist lines. Nicholas II, he wrote, "will soon be brought to realize that he is bound to take steps for meeting the wishes of the country. Let us hope that he will understand the proper sense of the lesson which he has received during the past two months."[94]

Kropotkin's article in *The North American Review* brought a rejoinder from Konstantin Pobedonostsev, procurator of the Holy Synod and chief advisor to the tsar, whose name was synonymous with reaction. Calling Kropotkin "a professional apostle of anarchy and socialism," Pobedonostsev defended the Russian political and educational systems. Kropotkin, he declared, "does not know Russia, and is incapable of understanding his country; for the soul of the Russian people is a closed book to him which he has never opened." And even if we were to admit that autocracy is outmoded, "God forbid we should seek for the amelioration of this form of government in the remedy proposed by Kropotkin."[95]

Kropotkin replied, in what was the last article in the series, praising the efforts of Russian liberals to achieve a constitution. Not that he had abandoned his antistatist views. "If I speak of the coming Constitution, it is not because I see in it a panacea," he wrote. "My personal ideals go far beyond that. But whether we like it or not, it is coming. The colossal blunders of the ministries, and their increasingly frequent assumption of the right, under the shelter of the Emperor's signature, of modifying by mere decrees the fundamental laws of the Empire, render it unavoidable."[96]

On Sunday, April 21, Kropotkin addressed his biggest meeting in Chicago, sponsored by the local anarchist groups. Paying twenty-five cents a ticket, more than three thousand people packed the Central Music Hall to hear him hold forth on "Anarchism: Its Philosophy and Ideal." All the anarchists were there—Havel, the Isaaks, and their comrades—as well as society people, attracted by the prospect of seeing an authentic prince. On every seat there was a copy of *Free Society*, put there by the Isaaks' daughter Mary and her friend Sonia Edelstadt, a niece of the Jewish anarchist poet, David Edelstadt. The chairman was Clarence Darrow, the celebrated lawyer, who was then a Tolstoyan like Jane Addams. He introduced Kropotkin with the remark, "In Russia they exile their prophets. In this country we hang them." This reference to the Haymarket affair caused a stir in the assembly.[97]

On April 22 Kropotkin took the train to Urbana to speak at the University of Illinois on "The Modern Development of Socialism." His address was warmly received, the student newspaper finding it "of especial value in clearing up the haze of erroneous impressions which surrounds the subject of anarchists and anarchism." The next day he traveled to the University of Wisconsin at Madison and spoke on "Turgenev and Tolstoy," the lecture being reported "a success from every point of view."[98] On April 24 he was back in Chicago to attend a farewell reception arranged by the Industrial Art League. Declaring that his visit to America would remain one of the most pleasant recollections of his life, he expressed the hope that the land of Emerson, Thoreau, and Whitman would take a leading part in the socialist and anarchist movement. After his departure, the *Chicago Chronicle*, one of the leading dailies in the city, held a symposium on the effect of his visit. Only one contributor (Lucy Parsons) was an anarchist, yet nearly all agreed that Kropotkin's influence had been constructive and for the good.[99]

Kropotkin returned to the East through Indiana and Ohio, collecting data on American farming, as he had done while crossing Canada in 1897. He stopped for two days in Buffalo, where his friend Mavor had come down from Toronto to meet him.[100] Then he proceeded to New York City, sailing back to England in early May.

By all indications, Kropotkin's second American tour had been as successful as the first. According to Jane Addams, he had been "heard throughout the country with great interest and respect." As Abe Isaak, Jr., put it, he had given anarchist propaganda "a lively impetus," while gaining for himself "the honor and esteem of all intelligent people, and the love and friendship of all comrades." Writing in a similar vein, Harry Kelly called Kropotkin's visit a "triumphal procession," with "one continuous ovation from the day he landed till the day he sailed." He had traveled as far west as Chicago and Madison, addressing half a dozen universities as well as numerous educational and cultural groups. "Add to all this propaganda the countless number of people Kropotkin met and discussed with privately," noted Kelly, "the articles written and interviews granted to newspapermen, and it will convey a fair idea of the work this one man did in the two months of his stay in America."[101]

But the journey had taken its toll. In contrast to his first visit, Kropotkin's health had been adversely affected. In New York, as we have seen, he had contracted influenza, and he returned to England in a weakened condition. In November 1901 he suffered a severe heart attack, from which, he told the Swiss anarchist James Guillaume, he "nearly died." He placed much of the blame on "my trip to America," with its crowded and exhausting schedule of appearances.[102]

Health reasons alone would probably have deterred any repetition of the journey had something else not occurred to rule out future visits. In September 1901, four months after Kropotkin's departure, President McKinley was assassinated by a self-proclaimed anarchist named Leon Czolgosz. Rumors were soon afloat of an anarchist plot hatched by Kropotkin and Goldman, with Czolgosz as their instrument. Hull House was alleged to have been the scene of their "secret, murderous meetings" during Kropotkin's visit. The story was pure fabrication, yet Kropotkin was greatly disturbed, not least because of the repressions suffered by his Chicago comrades, including Havel and the Isaaks, who were thrown in jail and denied counsel until Jane Addams intervened in their behalf, an action that cost Hull House the backing of Mrs. Palmer.[103]

Kropotkin could never again visit the United States, for in 1903 a law was passed by Congress forbidding anarchists to enter the country. Once again, wrote Kropotkin to Goldman, bourgeois society "throws its hypocritical liberties over-board, tears them to pieces—as soon as people use those liberties for fighting that cursed society."[104] Yet the

anti-anarchist law, for all his bitter feeling against it, did not destroy
Kropotkin's affection for the United States. "Here is my opinion," he
wrote Max Nettlau in 1902. "From among a hundred men taken at
random in Europe, you will not find as many enthusiasts, ready to set
forth on untraveled paths, as in America. The dollar is nowhere given
so little importance: it is won or it is lost. In England, one values and
worships the pound, but definitely not in America. That is America.
*Any village in Oregon is better than the smallest hamlet in Ger-
many.*"[105]

Although Kropotkin never returned to the New World, his influence
continued to make itself felt. One by one, his books were published in
American editions, and his articles appeared and reappeared in the anarchist press, making him the most widely read anarchist writer in
America. His portrait was hung in anarchist clubs and schools, and a
number of anarchist groups and organizations adopted his name.
There was a Kropotkin Library at the Stelton colony in New Jersey, a
Kropotkin Group in New York composed of Russian immigrant workers, and a Kropotkin Branch of the Workmen's Circle in Los Angeles,
to cite only three examples.

In December 1912 a Seventieth Birthday Celebration was held in
Kropotkin's honor at Carnegie Hall. Sponsored by *Mother Earth* in
cooperation with the *Fraye Arbeter Shtime*, it featured musical events
and dramatic readings, in addition to speeches in English, French,
Spanish, Czech, and Yiddish. Similar meetings were held in Boston,
Chicago, and Toronto, all of which Kropotkin had visited during his
tours of North America. For the same occasion such anarchist journals
as *Mother Earth*, *Cronaca Sovversiva*, and *Golos Truda* devoted special issues to Kropotkin's life and ideas, with tributes by his principal
associates, and a Kropotkin Literary Society was organized by Jewish
anarchists to publish anarchist and socialist classics, some by Kropotkin himself. Moved by these fraternal gestures, Kropotkin sent the following letter to *Mother Earth*: "I need not tell you, nor could I word
it on paper, how deeply I was touched by all these expressions of sympathy, and how I felt that 'something brotherly' which keeps us, Anarchists, united by a feeling far deeper than the mere sense of solidarity
in a party; and I am sure that the feeling of brotherhood will have some
day its effect, when history will call upon us to show what we are
worth, and how far we can act in harmony for the reconstruction of
Society upon a new basis of equality and freedom."[106]

Until his death in Russia in 1921, Kropotkin regarded his American
comrades with profound affection. When Emma Goldman paid him a
visit in 1920, he asked to be remembered to his friends in the States,

sending "special love" to Harry Kelly.[107] When Kropotkin died, memorial meetings were held in cities from New York to Los Angeles. In 1923 a gifted anarchist printer in New Jersey, Joseph Ishill, put together a beautiful volume in his memory, with contributions by Goldman, Berkman, Voltairine de Cleyre, Rudolf Rocker, Saul Yanovsky, and other anarchist writers.[108] At the same time, anarchists in America, headed by Kelly, raised funds to support the Kropotkin Museum, established in Moscow to house his papers and memorabilia. In 1931, the tenth anniversary of Kropotkin's death, a memorial volume, edited by Gregory Maximoff, was published in Chicago, and the Detroit *Probuzhdenie* put out a special issue with a selection of Kropotkin letters edited by Max Nettlau. For the same occasion, the Free Society Group of Chicago organized a mass meeting to honor Kropotkin's memory, with Yanovsky and Clarence Darrow among the speakers.[109] Furthermore, on the centennial of Kropotkin's birth in 1942, a celebration took place in Los Angeles under the auspices of the Kropotkin Branch of the Workmen's Circle and the Rocker Publications Committee, which issued a brochure of tributes and recollections by Kropotkin's surviving colleagues.[110]

By his writings and personal example, Kropotkin influenced a whole range of well-known figures in American life, anarchist and nonanarchist alike. Berkman called him "my teacher and inspiration," while the civil libertarian Roger Baldwin, who edited a collection of Kropotkin's essays, wrote that Kropotkin's social philosophy "made an enduring mark on my thinking."[111] From his prison cell Bartolomeo Vanzetti invoked Kropotkin's concept of mutual aid as the basis of the future libertarian society.[112] In a similar vein, scholars and writers like Lewis Mumford, Will Durant, Ashley Montagu, and Paul Goodman expressed their indebtedness to Kropotkin's teachings, as did the muckraking journalist I. F. Stone, for whom "his vision of a voluntary society without police or oppression" has remained the "noblest human ideal."[113]

The social ferment of the 1960s saw a revival of interest in Kropotkin and his doctrines. His major works were republished and new biographies and anthologies of his writing appeared in print. In 1967 a group of New Left anarchists established a Kropotkin House in Duluth, Minnesota. An anarchist group formed in 1974 by students in London, Ontario, dubbed itself the Friends of Kropotkin. In 1975 a Kropotkin Society was started in Evansville, Indiana, with a journal entitled *Equality*. As of this writing, interest in Kropotkin and his work shows little sign of abating. His moral stature and vision of a free society continue to appeal to those, especially students, repelled by an increasingly conformist world. Kropotkin's emphasis on the natural and spontaneous, his criticism of arid ideological dogmas, his distrust of bureaucracy and standardization, his faith in voluntary cooperation and mutual aid, are leaving their mark on a new generation of idealists.

CHAPTER SIX

Stormy Petrel: Anatoli Zhelezniakov

"THE GUARD IS TIRED." With these words, uttered on the night of January 5, 1918, a young anarchist sailor named Anatoli Grigorievich Zhelezniakov dispersed the Constituent Assembly and carved a niche for himself in the history of the Russian Revolution.

When the tsarist regime collapsed in February 1917, Zhelezniakov, a disciple of Kropotkin and Bakunin, had been serving on a minelayer based in Kronstadt, the headquarters of the Baltic Fleet near the capital city of Petrograd. After the February Revolution, anarchists and other militants occupied the villa of P. P. Durnovo, the governor of Moscow during the Revolution of 1905, and converted it into a revolutionary commune and "house of rest," with rooms for reading and discussion and a garden used as a playground for their children. To hostile minds, however, the Durnovo villa had become a foul den of iniquity, "a sort of Brocken, where the powers of evil assembled, witches' Sabbaths were held, and there were orgies, plots, dark and sinister, and doubt-less bloody doings," as N. N. Sukhanov wrote in his notes on the Russian Revolution.[1] Yet the villa was left undisturbed until June 5, 1917, when a number of its anarchist occupants tried to seize the printing plant of a middle-class newspaper. The First Congress of Soviets, then in session in the capital, denounced the raiders as "criminals who call themselves anarchists,"[2] and on June 7, P. N. Pereverzev, the minister of justice in the Provisional Government, ordered the anarchists to evacuate the house immediately.

The next day fifty sailors, Zhelezniakov among them, rushed from Kronstadt to defend their fellow revolutionaries, who had meanwhile barricaded themselves in the villa against a government attack. For the next two weeks the anarchists remained entrenched in the villa, in defiance of both the Provisional Government and the Petrograd Soviet. But after some of them broke into a nearby jail and liberated the inmates, Minister Pereverzev ordered a raid on the house, during which an anarchist workman was killed and Zhelezniakov was taken captive, relieved of four bombs, and locked up in the barracks of the Preobrazhensky Regiment.

After a summary trial, the government sentenced him to fourteen years at hard labor and ignored all petitions from the Baltic sailors for his release. During the July Days demonstrations in the capital, a group of sailors came to the Tauride Palace to see Pereverzev in person. Finding him absent, they seized the minister of agriculture, Victor Chernov, the Socialist Revolutionary leader and future chairman of the Constituent Assembly, to whom Zhelezniakov, six months later, would address his order to disperse; and it was only an impromptu speech by Trotsky, who (in a phrase that was to become famous) praised the Kronstadt sailors as "the pride and glory of the Revolution," that saved Chernov from being lynched.[3]

A few weeks later, Zhelezniakov escaped from his "republican prison," as one anarchist journal called it,[4] and resumed his revolutionary activities. In a dramatic episode, he organized a mass demonstration of Kronstadt sailors at the American embassy to protest against the death sentence imposed on Tom Mooney in San Francisco, as well as the threatened extradition to California of Alexander Berkman, whom the authorities sought to implicate, with the same perjured evidence used against Mooney, in the Preparedness Parade bombing of July 22, 1916.[5]

In October 1917 Zhelezniakov cooperated wholeheartedly with the Bolsheviks in the overthrow of the Provisional Government. Although the crew of his minelayer elected him as their delegate to the Second Congress of Soviets, which met on October 25, 1917, he was busy that night leading a contingent of sailors in the storming of the Winter Palace that marked the demise of the Provisional Government.[6] After the October Revolution, Zhelezniakov was named as commander of the detachment guarding the Tauride Palace—"bandoleers of cartridges draped coquettishly across their shoulders and grenades hanging obtrusively from their belts," in the description of an eyewitness;[7] and it was in this capacity that he carried out (on Bolshevik orders) his historic mission of suppressing the Constituent Assembly, ending its life of a single day.

It seems fitting that an anarchist should have played this role. For the anarchists, as opponents of all government, rejected representative democracy almost as vehemently as they rejected the tsarist and proletarian dictatorships. Universal suffrage was counterrevolution, as Proudhon had said, and parliament a nest of fraud and compromise, an instrument of the upper and middle classes to dominate the workers and peasants. With few exceptions (Kropotkin among them) the anarchists scorned what they called the "parliamentary fetishism" of the other revolutionary groups and openly denounced the Constituent Assembly from the first.

During the Civil War that followed, Zhelezniakov fought in the Red Army as commander of a flotilla and later of an armored train. He took part in crucial campaigns against the Don Cossacks led by Ataman Kaledin and against generals Krasnov and Denikin. When Trotsky reorganized the Red Army, putting tsarist officers in positions of high authority and abolishing the system of self-government among the rank and file, Zhelezniakov protested vigorously, as did many other revolutionaries who opposed any return to old military methods. For this the Bolsheviks outlawed him, as they outlawed the anarchist Black Guards in Moscow and Nestor Makhno in the Ukraine.

Zhelezniakov, however, returned to Moscow illegally and discussed the matter with Sverdlov, chairman of the Soviet Executive Committee, who assured him that there had been a misunderstanding and offered him a high military position. Zhelezniakov declined and left for Odessa, where he resumed his activities against the Whites. But he was too effective a warrior to be let go so easily, and the following year, 1919, the Bolsheviks repeated their overtures. This time Zhelezniakov accepted, and he was appointed as commander of the armored train campaign against Denikin, who placed a reward of 400,000 rubles on his head.[8] Zhelezniakov fought bravely without injury until July 26, 1919, when he was killed near Ekaterinoslav by a shell of Denikin's artillery. He was twenty-four years old.

The Soviet government, though it had outlawed Zhelezniakov and declared him a traitor, now embraced him as one of its heroes. His body was brought to Moscow and buried with speeches and pomp. A statue of Zhelezniakov stands today in the city of Kronstadt—erected by the Bolsheviks in tribute to his role in the October Revolution and the Civil War. Poems and songs have been composed in his honor by Soviet writers and are recited and sung to this day ("Beneath the earth, overgrown with weeds, lies the sailor Zhelezniak, partisan"),[9] but without any hint that Zhelezniakov was an anarchist. On the contrary, the Communists claim him as one of their own and avoid mentioning his anarchist affiliations, calling him only a "revolutionary," a "hero," and a "martyr for the people." Soviet sources, in fact, say that he joined the Bolshevik party, but this is untrue. Though he participated in the October Revolution and fought in the Red Army, Zhelezniakov remained an anarchist to the last. As he told his comrade Volin: "Whatever may happen to me, and whatever they may say of me, know well that I am an anarchist, that I fight as one, and that *whatever my fate, I will die an anarchist.*"[10]

For all his revolutionary zealotry, Zhelezniakov had a gentler side. Hot-headed, militant, impulsive, he was also literate, idealistic, even aesthetic. During the summer of 1917, while imprisoned by the Provisional Government after the Durnovo villa affair, he wrote a remarkable poem, the only one of his that survives. First published in 1923 in the journal *Krasnyi Flot* (Red Fleet), it was reprinted in the 1970 edition of the annual Soviet literary anthology, *Den' poezii* (Poetry Day).[11] It is a moving poem, the quality of which my unrhymed literal translation can barely approximate:

> Falcon, falcon,
> Do not laugh at me now,
> That I should find my destiny in jail.
> I was higher than you in the heavens, above the earth,
> I was higher than you and the eagle.
>
> I saw many celestial bodies unknown to you,
> I learned many great secrets;
> I often spoke with the stars,
> I flew as high as the bright sun.
>
> But the day quickly passed and the next one came,
> And I burned with a rebellious flame.
> I was pursued by the enemies of freedom,
> My brothers were the wind and thunder.
>
> But once in the dark night of the steppe
> During a fatal storm I became weak
> And since then here I sit like a thief in his chains,
> Like an unfaithful and captured slave.
>
> Falcon, falcon, when you chance to fly
> Into the limitless and mountainous space—
> Don't forget to give the clouds my greetings,
> Tell all that I shall break my chains,
> That my life in jail is only a twilight nap,
> Only a spectral daydream.

CHAPTER SEVEN

Nestor Makhno: The Man and the Myth

NESTOR IVANOVICH MAKHNO, the anarchist partisan leader, was among the most colorful and heroic figures of the Russian Revolution and Civil War. His movement in the Ukraine represents one of the few occasions in history when anarchists controlled a large territory for an extended period of time. For more than a year he was a greater power on the steppe than either Trotsky or Denikin. A born military leader, he fought simultaneously on several fronts, opposing Reds as well as Whites, Austrian invaders and Ukrainian nationalists, not to speak of the countless bands of irregulars who crossed and recrossed the steppe in search of plunder and booty. According to Victor Serge, he was a "strategist of unsurpassed ability," whose peasant army possessed a "truly epic capacity for organization and battle." Emma Goldman called him "the most picturesque and vital figure brought to the fore by the Revolution in the South."[1]

Makhno was born on October 27, 1889, of a poor peasant family in the Ukrainian settlement of Gulyai-Polye, situated in Ekaterinoslav province between the Dnieper River and the Sea of Azov. He was barely a year old when his father died, leaving five small boys to the care of their mother. As a child of seven, Makhno was put to work tending cows and sheep for the local peasantry; he later found employment as a farm laborer and as a worker in a foundry. In 1906, at the age of seventeen, Makhno joined an anarchist group in Gulyai-Polye. Two years later he was brought to trial for participating in a terrorist attack that claimed the life of a district police officer. The court sentenced him to be hanged, but because of Makhno's youth this was commuted to an indefinite period in the Butyrki prison in Moscow.

Makhno proved a refractory inmate, unable to accept the discipline of prison life, and during the nine years of his detention he was often placed in irons or in solitary confinement. For a time, however, he shared a cell with an older, more experienced anarchist named Peter Arshinov, who taught him the elements of libertarian doctrine and confirmed him in the faith of Bakunin and Kropotkin.

Released from prison after the February Revolution of 1917, Makhno returned to his native village and assumed a leading role in community affairs. He helped organize a union of farm laborers and served as its chairman. Before long, he was elected chairman of the local union of carpenters and metalworkers and also of the Gulyai-Polye Soviet of Workers' and Peasants' Deputies. In August 1917, as head of the soviet, Makhno recruited a band of armed peasants and set about expropriating the estates of the neighboring gentry and distributing the land to the peasants. From that time, the villagers began to regard him as a new Stenka Razin or Emelian Pugachev, sent to realize their ancient dream of land and liberty.

Makhno's activities, however, came to a halt the following spring, when the Soviet government signed the Treaty of Brest-Litovsk and a large force of German and Austrian troops marched into the Ukraine. Makhno shared the indignation of his fellow anarchists at this compromise with German "imperialism," but his band of partisans was too weak to offer effective resistance. Forced into hiding, he made his way to the Volga River, then proceeded north to Moscow, where he arrived in June 1918.

During his short visit to the capital, Makhno had an inspiring audience with his idol, Peter Kropotkin, an encounter movingly described in Makhno's memoirs. He was also received in the Kremlin by Lenin, who sounded him out on the attitude of the Ukrainian peasantry towards the Bolsheviks, the military situation in the south, and the differences between the Bolshevik and anarchist conceptions of the revolution. "The majority of anarchists think and write about the future," Lenin declared, "without understanding the present. That is what divides us Communists from them." Though the anarchists were "selfless" men, Lenin went on, their "empty fanaticism" blurred their vision of present and future alike. "But I think that you, comrade," he said to Makhno, "have a realistic attitude towards the burning evils of the time. If only one-third of the anarchist-communists were like you, we Communists would be ready, under certain well-known conditions, to join with them in working towards a free organization of producers." Makhno retorted that the anarchists were not utopian dreamers but realistic men of action. After all, he reminded Lenin, it was the anarchists and Socialist Revolutionaries, rather than the Bolsheviks, who were beating back the nationalists and privileged classes in the Ukraine, "Perhaps I am mistaken," answered Lenin, who then offered to help Makhno return to the south.[2]

When Makhno returned to Gulyai-Polye in July 1918, the area was occupied by Austrian troops and by the militia of their Ukrainian puppet, Hetman Skoropadsky. Organizing a band of partisans under the anarchist banner, Makhno launched a series of raids against the Austrians and Hetmanites and against the manors of the nobility. Extraordinary mobility and a bag of clever tricks constituted Makhno's chief tactical devices. Traveling on horseback and in light peasant carts (*tachanki*) on which machine guns were mounted, his men moved swiftly across the steppe between the Dnieper and the Sea of Azov, swelling into a small army as they went and inspiring terror in their adversaries.

Previously independent guerrilla bands accepted Makhno's command and rallied behind his black banner. Villagers provided food and fresh horses, enabling the Makhnovists to travel forty or fifty miles a day with little difficulty. Turning up quite suddenly where least expected, they would attack the gentry and military garrisons, then vanish as quickly as they had come. In captured uniforms they infiltrated the enemy's ranks to learn their plans or to open fire at point-blank range. On one occasion, Makhno and his retinue, masquerading as Hetmanite guardsmen, gained entry to a landowner's ball and fell upon the guests in the midst of their festivities. When cornered, the Makhnovists would bury their weapons, make their way singly back to their villages, and take up work in the fields, awaiting a signal to unearth a new cache of arms and spring up again in an unexpected quarter. For Isaac Babel, in *Red Cavalry Tales*, Makhno was "as protean as nature herself. Haycarts deployed in battle array take towns, a wedding procession approaching the headquarters of a district executive committee suddenly opens a concentrated fire, a little priest, waving above him the black flag of anarchy, orders the authorities to serve up the bourgeoisie, the proletariat, wine and music. An army of tachankas possesses undreamed-of possibilities of maneuver."[3]

Small, agile, well-knit, Makhno was a resourceful leader who combined an iron will with a sense of humor, winning the unswerving devotion of his followers. In September 1918, after defeating a superior force of Austrians at the village of Dibrivki, his men gave him the affectionate title of *bat'ko*, their "little father." Two months later, the end of the First World War led to the withdrawal of Austrian and German troops from Russian territory. Makhno managed to seize some of their arms and equipment. He next turned his wrath upon the followers of the Ukrainian nationalist leader Petliura. At the end of December, he succeeded in dislodging the Petliurist garrison from Ekaterinoslav. His troops, with their weapons concealed inside their clothing, rode into the central railway station on an ordinary passenger train, took the nationalists by surprise, and drove them from the city. The next day, however, the enemy reappeared with reinforcements, and Makhno was compelled to flee across the Dnieper and return to his base in Gulyai-Polye. The Petliurists, in turn, were evicted by the Red Army shortly afterwards.

During the first five months of 1919, the Gulyai-Polye region was virtually free of political authority. The Austrians, Hetmanites, and Petliurists had all been driven away, and neither the Reds nor the Whites were strong enough to fill the void. Makhno took advantage of this lull to attempt to reconstruct society on libertarian lines. In January, February, and April, the Makhnovists held a series of Regional Congresses of Peasants, Workers, and Insurgents to discuss economic and military matters and to supervise the task of reconstruction.

The question which dominated the Regional Congresses was that of defending the area from those who might seek to establish their control over it. The Second Congress, meeting on February 12, 1919, voted in favor of "voluntary mobilization," which in reality meant outright conscription, as all able-bodied men were required to serve when called up. The delegates also elected a Regional Military Revolutionary Council of Peasants, Workers, and Insurgents to carry out the decisions of the periodic congresses. The new council encouraged the election of "free" soviets in the towns and villages—that is, soviets from which members of political parties were excluded. Although Makhno's aim in setting up these bodies was to do away with political authority, the Military Revolutionary Council, acting in conjunction with the Regional Congresses and the local soviets, in effect formed a loose-knit government in the territory surrounding Gulyai-Polye.

Like the Military Revolutionary Council, the Insurgent Army of the Ukraine, as the Makhnovist forces were called, was in theory subject to the supervision of the Regional Congresses. In practice, however, the reins of authority rested with Makhno and his staff. Despite his efforts to avoid anything that smacked of regimentation, Makhno appointed his key officers (the rest were elected by the men themselves) and subjected his troops to the stern military discipline traditional among the Cossack legions of the nearby Zaporozhian region. Yet the Insurgent Army never lost its plebeian character. All its officers were peasants or, in a few cases, factory or shop workers. One looks in vain for a commander who sprang from the upper or middle classes, or even from the radical intelligentsia.

For a time, Makhno's dealings with the Bolsheviks remained friendly, and the Soviet press extolled him as a "courageous partisan" and revolutionary leader. Relations were at their best in March 1919, when Makhno and the Communists concluded a pact for joint military action against the Volunteer Army of General Denikin. According to the agreement, the Insurgent Army of the Ukraine became a division of the Red Army, subject to the orders of the Bolshevik supreme command but retaining its own officers and internal structure, as well as its name and black banner.

Such gestures, however, could not conceal the underlying hostility between the two groups. The Communists had little taste for the autonomous status of the Insurgent Army or for the powerful attraction it exerted on their own peasant recruits. The Makhnovists, on their side, feared that sooner or later the Red Army would attempt to bring their movement to heel. As friction increased, the Soviet newspapers abandoned their eulogies of the Makhnovists and began to attack them as "bandits." In April 1919 the Third Regional Congress of Peasants, Workers, and Insurgents met in defiance of a ban placed on it by the Soviet authorities. In May two Cheka agents sent to assassinate Makhno were caught and executed. The final breach occurred when the Makhnovists called a Fourth Regional Congress for June 15 and invited the soldiers of the Red Army to send representatives. Trotsky, commander in chief of the Bolshevik forces, was furious. On June 4 he banned the congress and outlawed Makhno. Communist troops carried out a lightning raid on Gulyai-Polye and dissolved the agricultural communes set up by the Makhnovists. A few days later. Denikin's forces arrived and completed the job, liquidating the local soviets as well.

The shaky alliance was hastily resumed that summer, when Denikin's drive towards Moscow sent both the Communists and the Makhnovists reeling. During August and September Makhno's guerrillas were pushed back towards the western borders of the Ukraine. On September 26, however, Makhno launched a successful counterattack at the village of Peregonovka, near Uman, cutting the White general's supply lines and creating panic and disorder in his rear. This was Denikin's first serious reverse in his advance into the Russian heartland and an important factor in halting his drive towards the Bolshevik capital. By the end of the year, a counteroffensive by the Red Army had forced Denikin to beat a retreat to the shores of the Black Sea.

At the end of 1919, Makhno received instructions from the Red command to transfer his troops to the Polish front. The order was plainly designed to draw the Insurgent Army away from its home territory, leaving it open to the establishment of Bolshevik rule. Makhno refused to budge. Trotsky, he said, wanted to replace Denikin's forces with the Red Army and the dispossessed landlords with political commissars. Having vowed to cleanse Russia of anarchism "with an iron broom,"[4] Trotsky replied by again outlawing the Makhnovists. There ensued eight months of bitter struggle, with losses heavy on both sides. A severe typhus epidemic augmented the toll of victims. Badly outnumbered, Makhno's partisans avoided pitched battles and relied on the guerrilla tactics they had perfected in more than two years of civil war.

Hostilities were broken off in October 1920, when Baron Wrangel, Denikin's successor in the south, launched a major offensive, striking northwards from the Crimea. Once more the Red Army enlisted Makhno's aid, in return for which the Communists agreed to an amnesty for all anarchists in Russian prisons and guaranteed the anarchists freedom of propaganda on condition that they refrain from calling for the overthrow of the Soviet government.

Barely a month later, however, the Red Army had made sufficient gains to ensure victory in the Civil War, and the Soviet leaders tore up their agreement with Makhno. Not only had the Makhnovists outlived their usefulness as a military partner, but as long as the bat'ko was at large the spirit of anarchism and the danger of a peasant rising would remain to haunt the Bolshevik regime. On November 25, 1920, Makhno's commanders in the Crimea, fresh from their victory over Wrangel, were seized by the Red Army and shot. The next day, Trotsky ordered an attack on Makhno's headquarters in Gulyai-Polye, during which Makhno's staff were captured and imprisoned or shot on the spot. The bat'ko himself, however, together with a remnant of an army that had once numbered in the tens of thousands, managed to elude his pursuers. After wandering over the Ukraine for the better part of a year, the guerrilla leader, exhausted and suffering from unhealed wounds, crossed the Dniester River into Rumania and eventually found his way to Paris.

GIVEN his colorful personality and the rich drama of his career, it is small wonder that Makhno should be the subject of a growing literature. Until recently, however, accounts of his movement, with few exceptions, consisted of mixtures of fact and fiction, of hostile, sometimes vicious polemics, of sensationalist journalism or uncritical, romanticized portraits verging on hagiography. Perhaps it is inevitable that a glamorous and controversial figure of Makhno's stamp should lend himself to such treatment. To a degree, the problem stems from incomplete source material. The journals and manifestoes of the Makhno movement are hard to come by, having been in great part lost or destroyed in the turmoil of the Civil War. What is more, the relevant documents in Soviet archives remain inaccessible to Western specialists. Nor, to my knowledge, have the archives of Makhno's associate Volin (held by his sons in Paris) been made available to the scholar, though they are bound to include important material. Yet, for all these limitations, the sources are considerable and remain to be exhaustively tapped.

What do these sources include? To begin with, we have Makhno's personal memoirs through December 1918, published in a three-volume edition between 1929 and 1937, the last two volumes edited with prefaces and notes by Volin.[5] In addition, eleven Makhnovist proclamations were preserved by Ugo Fedeli, an Italian anarchist who obtained them in the 1920s during visits to Moscow, Berlin, and Paris, where he became personally acquainted with Makhno. These proclamations have been published in the original Russian and are also included in the English edition of Peter Arshinov's history of the Makhnovist movement.[6] Further archival materials, to be mentioned again later, are to be found in the Tcherikower Collection of the YIVO Institute for Jewish Research in New York. Moreover, Soviet histories and documentary collections, though invariably hostile and of limited worth, contain useful information, as do articles on Makhno in Soviet academic journals. Beyond this, additional documents and photographs remain in the hands of Makhno's surviving comrades in France and other countries. There are also the scattered files of Makhnovist newspapers in Western libraries, interviews with participants in the Insurgent Army and with people who knew Makhno in exile, the eyewitness histories of Arshinov and Volin, and the secondary accounts by David Footman, Michael Palij, and others.

To date, however, there has been no comprehensive study of Makhno based on the full range of available sources. As a result, a number of questions persist. Was Makhno a military dictator, as his detractors maintain? A bandit and counterrevolutionary, as Soviet writers describe him? A "primitive rebel," in Eric Hobsbawm's phrase?[7] Was he an incurable drunkard? An anti-intellectual? An anti-Semite? A pogromist? How critical were his military efforts in saving the Revolution from the Whites? Did his unsophisticated equipment and tactics doom him to defeat before a centralized professional army? How successful were his attempts to establish local self-management in the villages and towns of the Ukraine? What do we really know about him? How much is myth and fantasy, how much incontrovertible fact?

To answer these questions, one must come to grips with the underlying question of Makhno's anarchism. According to Emma Goldman, Makhno's object was to establish a libertarian society in the south that would serve as a model for the whole of Russia. Interestingly, Trotsky once noted that he and Lenin had toyed with the idea of allotting a piece of territory to Makhno for this purpose,[8] but the project foundered when fighting broke out between the anarchist guerrillas and the Bolshevik forces in the Ukraine.

But was Makhno in fact an anarchist, or merely another "primitive" rebel from the southern frontier, harking back to Razin and Pugachev with their vision of Cossack federalism and rough-and-ready democracy? The answer is that he was both. Nor is there any contradiction, for the Cossack-peasant rebellions of the seventeenth and eighteenth centuries possessed a strong egalitarian and antistatist character, their participants mounting an all-out attack upon the nobility and bureaucracy and detesting the state as an evil tyranny which trampled on popular freedoms. Makhno's anarchism was compatible with these sentiments and with peasant aspirations in general. The peasants wanted the land, and then to be left alone by gentry, officials, tax collectors, recruiting sergeants, and all external agents of authority. These were to be replaced by a society of "free toilers" who, as Makhno expressed it, would "set to work to the tune of free and joyous songs which reflected the spirit of the revolution."[9]

In this sense, Makhno was the very incarnation of peasant anarchism, the partisan leader in closest touch with the most cherished hopes and feelings of the village. He was, in George Woodcock's description, "an anarchist Robin Hood,"[10] a familiar figure in other peasant and artisan societies, notably in Spain and in Italy, where anarchism struck deep and lasting roots. (In Mexico, too, he had his counterparts in Emiliano Zapata and Ricardo Flores Magón.) To his supporters he was a modern Razin or Pugachev, come to rescue the poor from their oppressors and to grant them land and liberty. As in the past, his movement arose in the southern borderlands and was directed against the wealthy and powerful. Makhno, wrote Alexander Berkman, became "the avenging angel of the lowly, and presently he was looked upon as the great liberator, whose coming had been prophesied by Pugachev in his dying moments."[11]

Following the example of his predecessors, Makhno expropriated the landlords, removed the officials, inaugurated a Cossack-style "republic" on the steppe, and was revered by his followers as their good father. He called on the peasants to rise against the "golden epaulettes" of Wrangel and Denikin and to fight for free soviets and communes. At the same time he opposed the "Communists and commissars," just as Razin and Pugachev had opposed the "boyars and officials." The Bolsheviks, for their part, denounced him as a brigand, the epithet with which Moscow had maligned its guerrilla opponents since the seventeenth century. Furthermore, the same legends arose about Makhno as about Razin and Pugachev. As his wife told Emma Goldman, "there grew up among the country folk the belief that Makhno was invincible because he had never been wounded during all the years of warfare in spite of his practice of always personally leading every charge."[12]

There was, however, an important difference. Unlike Razin and Pugachev, and unlike his contemporary "atamans" in the Ukraine, Makhno was motivated by a specific anarchist ideology. Throughout his life he proudly wore the anarchist label as a mark of his opposition to authority. As early as 1906, it has been noted, he joined an anarchist group in Gulyai-Polye. His understanding of anarchism matured during his years in prison, under the tutelage of Arshinov, and was deepened by his contact with Volin, Aaron Baron, and other anarchist intellectuals who joined his movement during the Civil War. Of the older theorists, his main source of inspiration was Kropotkin, to whom he made a pilgrimage in 1918, as mentioned above, but he also strongly admired Bakunin, calling him a "great" and "tireless" rebel, and the stream of leaflets that issued from his camp often bore a Bakuninist flavor.

Makhno's anarchism, however, was not confined to verbal propaganda, important though this was to win new adherents. On the contrary, Makhno was a man of action who, even while occupied with military campaigns, sought to put his anarchist theories into practice. His first act on entering a town—after throwing open the prisons— was to dispel any impression that he had come to introduce a new form of political rule. Announcements were posted informing the inhabitants that they were now free to organize their lives as they saw fit, that his Insurgent Army would not "dictate to them or order them to do anything." Free speech, press, and assembly were proclaimed, although Makhno would not countenance organizations that sought to impose political authority, and he accordingly dissolved the Bolshevik revolutionary committees, instructing their members to "take up some honest trade."[13]

Makhno's aim was to throw off domination of every type and to encourage economic and social self-determination. "It is up to the workers and peasants," said one of his proclamations in 1919, "to organize themselves and reach mutual understanding in all areas of their lives and in whatever manner they think right." With his active support, anarchistic communes were organized in Ekaterinoslav province, each with about a dozen households totaling one hundred to three hundred members. There were four such communes in the immediate vicinity of Gulyai-Polye, Makhno's base of operations, and a number of others were formed in the surrounding districts. (Makhno himself, when time permitted, labored in one of the Gulyai-Polye communes.)

Each commune was provided with as much land as its members were able to cultivate without hiring additional labor. The land, as well as the tools and livestock, was allotted by decision of the Regional Congresses of Peasants, Workers, and Insurgents, and the management of the commune was conducted by a general meeting of its members. The land was held in common, and kitchen and dining rooms were also communal, though members who wished to cook separately or to take food from the kitchen and eat it in their own quarters were allowed to do so. Though only a few members actually considered themselves anarchists, the peasants operated the communes on the basis of full equality ("from each according to his ability, to each according to his need") and accepted Kropotkin's principle of mutual aid as their fundamental tenet. It is interesting to note that the first such commune, near the village of Pokrovskoye, was named in honor of Rosa Luxemburg, not an anarchist but a Marxist and recent martyr in the German revolution, a reflection of Makhno's undoctrinaire approach to revolutionary theory and practice.

In his efforts to reconstruct society along libertarian lines, Makhno also encouraged experiments in workers' self-management whenever the occasion offered. For example, when the railway workers of Aleksandrovsk complained that they had not been paid for many weeks, he advised them to take control of the railroad and charge the users what seemed a fair price for their services. Such projects, though they call for a closer examination by historians, were of limited success. They failed to win over more than a minority of workers, for, unlike the farmers and artisans of the village, who were independent producers accustomed to managing their own affairs, factory hands and miners operated as interdependent parts of a complicated industrial machine and floundered without the guidance of technical specialists. Furthermore, the peasants and artisans could barter the products of their labor, whereas the workers depended on wages for their survival. Makhno, moreover, compounded the confusion when he recognized all paper money issued by his predecessors—Ukrainian nationalists, Whites, and Bolsheviks alike. He never understood the complexities of an urban economy, nor did he care to understand them. In any event, he found little time to implement his economic programs. He was forever on the move. His army was a "republic on *tachanki*," as Volin described it, and "the instability of the situation prevented positive work."[14]

In the Ukraine in 1918-1920, as in Spain in 1936-1939, the libertarian experiment was conducted amid conditions of civil strife, economic dislocation, and political and military repression. It was therefore unable to endure. But not for want of trying, nor from any lack of devotion to anarchism. Through all Makhno's campaigns a large black flag, the classic symbol of anarchy, floated at the head of his army, embroidered with the slogans "Liberty or Death" and "The Land to the Peasants, the Factories to the Workers." The Cultural-Educational Commission, including Volin, Arshinov, and Baron, edited anarchist journals, issued anarchist leaflets, and delivered lectures on anarchism to the troops. Beyond this, the commission founded an anarchist theater and planned to open anarchist schools modeled on Francisco Ferrer's Escuela Moderna in Spain.

In one area, however, Makhno made a significant compromise with his libertarian principles. As a military leader, it has been noted, he was compelled to inaugurate a form of conscription in order to replenish his forces; and he is known on occasion to have imposed strict measures of military discipline, including summary executions. His violent tendencies, some maintain, were accentuated by bouts with alcohol. Volin underscores Makhno's drinking and carousing nature, and Victor Serge describes him as "boozing, swashbuckling, disorderly and idealistic."[15] Hostile observers have compared him to a Chinese warlord, insisting that his army was libertarian only in name. This, however, is not a true picture. Although military considerations inevitably clashed with Makhno's anarchistic doctrines, his army was more popular both in organization and social composition than any other fighting force of his day.

By all accounts, Makhno was a military leader of outstanding ability and courage. His achievement in organizing an army and conducting an effective and prolonged campaign is, apart from some of the successes of the Spanish anarchists in the 1930s, unique in the history of anarchism. He inherited a good deal of the Cossack tradition of independent military communities in the south and of their resentment of government encroachments. His guerrilla tactics of ambush and surprise were both a throwback to the Russian rebels of the past and an anticipation of the methods of combat later employed in China, Cuba, and Vietnam. But how critical were his efforts in saving the Revolution from the Whites? Volin flatly asserts that "the honor of having anni-hilated the Denikinist counter-revolution in the autumn of 1919 be-longs entirely to the Makhnovist Insurgent Army." David Footman writes more modestly that "there is some justification for the claim that Peregonovka was one of the decisive battles of the Civil War in the south."[16] In any case, the importance of the battle is beyond dis-pute.

Makhno, in short, was a thoroughgoing anarchist, who practiced what he preached insofar as conditions permitted. A down-to-earth peasant, he was not a man of words, not a phrasemaker or orator, but a lover of action who rejected metaphysical systems and abstract social theorizing. When he came to Moscow in 1918, he was disturbed by the atmosphere of "paper revolution" among the anarchists as well as the Bolsheviks.[17] Anarchist intellectuals struck him, in the main, as men of books rather than deeds, mesmerized by their own words and lacking the will to fight for their ideals. Nevertheless, he respected them for their learning and idealism and later sought their assistance in teaching his peasant followers the fundamentals of anarchist doc-trine.

Makhno's anti-intellectual streak was shared by his mentor Arshi-nov, a self-educated workman from the Ukraine like his pupil. Arshi-nov, however, went further. In his *History of the Makhnovist Move-ment* he not only criticizes the Bolsheviks as a new ruling class of intellectuals, a theory first put forward by Bakunin (speaking of Marx and his associates), developed by Machajski, and restated during the Revolution by Maximoff and other anarchist writers; he expresses contempt for anarchist intellectuals as well, calling them mere theorists who seldom acted but who "slept through" events of unparalleled his-torical significance and abandoned the field to the authoritarians.[18] This goes far to explain his *Organizational Platform* of 1926, endorsed by Makhno, which castigates do-nothing intellectuals and calls for ef-fective organization and action.[19]

This brings us to the vexed question of Makhno's alleged anti-Sem-itism, which future biographers must subject to careful scrutiny. Charges of Jew-baiting and of anti-Jewish pogroms have come from every quarter, left, right, and center. Without exception, however, they are based on hearsay, rumor, or intentional slander, and remain un-documented and unproved.[20] The Soviet propaganda machine was at particular pains to malign Makhno as a bandit and pogromist. But after meticulous research, Elias Tcherikower, an eminent Jewish his-torian and authority on anti-Semitism in the Ukraine, concluded that the number of anti-Jewish acts committed by the Makhnovists was "negligible" in comparison with those committed by other combatants in the Civil War, the Red Army not excepted.[21]

To verify this, I have examined several hundred photographs in the Tcherikower Collection, housed in the YIVO Library in New York and depicting anti-Jewish atrocities in the Ukraine during the Civil War. A great many of these photographs document acts perpetrated by the adherents of Denikin, Petliura, Grigoriev, and other self-styled "atamans," but only one is labeled as being the work of the Makhnovists, though even here neither Makhno himself nor any of his recognizable subordinates are to be seen, nor is there any indication that Makhno had authorized the raid or, indeed, that the band involved was in fact affiliated with his Insurgent Army.

On the other hand, there is evidence that Makhno did all in his power to counteract anti-Semitic tendencies among his followers. Moreover, a considerable number of Jews took part in the Makhnovist movement. Some, like Volin and Baron, were intellectuals who served on the Cultural-Educational Commission, wrote his manifestoes, and edited his journals, but the great majority fought in the ranks of the Insurgent Army, either in special detachments of Jewish artillery and infantry or else within the regular partisan units, alongside peasants and workers of Ukrainian, Russian, and other ethnic origin.

Makhno personally condemned discrimination of any sort, and punishments for anti-Semitic acts were swift and severe: one troop commander was summarily shot after raiding a Jewish town, and a soldier met the same fate merely for displaying a poster with the stock anti-Semitic formula, "Beat the Jews, Save Russia!" Makhno denounced Ataman Grigoriev for his pogroms and had him shot. Had Makhno been guilty of the accusations against him, surely the Jewish anarchists in his camp would have broken with his movement and raised their voices in protest. The same is true of Alexander Berkman, Emma Goldman, and others who were in Russia at the time, and of Sholem Schwartzbard, Volin, Senya Fleshin, and Mollie Steimer in Paris during the 1920s. Far from criticizing Makhno as an anti-Semite, they defended him against the campaign of slander that persisted from all sides.

Finally, the last years of Makhno's life deserve fuller treatment than they have received from historians. Of all the writers to date, Malcolm Menzies and Alexandre Skirda have provided the most satisfactory accounts of this period.[22] Yet even they have not told the full and dramatic story of Makhno's escape across the Dniester, his internment in Rumania, his escape to Poland, his arrest, trial, and acquittal, his flight to Danzig, renewed imprisonment and final escape (aided by Berkman and other comrades in Europe),[23] and his ultimate sanctuary in Paris, where he lived his remaining years in obscurity, poverty, and disease, an Antaeus cut off from the soil that might have replenished his strength. According to Berkman, Makhno in Paris dreamed of returning to his native land and "taking up again the struggle for liberty and social justice."[24] He had always hated the "poison" of big cities, cherishing the natural environment in which he was born. How ironic that he should have ended his days in a great foreign capital, working in an automobile factory, a restless consumptive for whom drink provided meager relief.

Yet he never lost his passion for anarchism, never abandoned the movement to which he had dedicated his life. He attended anarchist meetings (frequenting, among others, the Jewish Autodidact Club), defended the *Organizational Platform* of his old comrade Arshinov, and mingled with anarchists from all over the world, including a group of Chinese students and also Durruti and Ascaso from Spain, whom he regaled with his adventures in the Ukraine and offered his help when the moment for their own struggle should arrive. Though death intervened to prevent this, it is of interest that a number of veterans of his Insurgent Army did in fact go to fight in the Durruti column in 1936.[25] How fitting, then, that the Spanish comrades should have provided financial assistance when Makhno lay mortally ill with tuberculosis.

Makhno's final moments have been movingly conjured by Malcolm Menzies.[26] In July 1934, Makhno, forty-four years old, is lying at death's door in a Paris hospital. Overcome by fever, he lapses into semiconsciousness and dreams his last dream, a dream of his beloved countryside, of the open steppe covered with snow, a bright sun in an azure sky, and Nestor Ivanovich seated on his horse, moving in slow motion towards a cluster of mounted comrades waiting in the distance, who touch their caps in greeting at his approach. Time passes, the seasons change, spring arrives—Germinal!—the rebirth of hope, a landscape of green, the smell of fresh earth, a murmuring stream, and a fleeting, all too fleeting, glimpse of freedom. And then eternal silence. Makhno's body was cremated and the ashes interred in the Père-Lachaise Cemetery, not far from the mass grave of Paris Communards who were massacred there in 1871.

CHAPTER EIGHT

V. M. Eikhenbaum (Volin): The Man and His Book

VOLIN, LIKE his comrade Makhno, was one of the most celebrated figures in the Russian anarchist movement. He played an active part in both the 1905 and the 1917 revolutions, as well as in the revolutionary movement in exile. In 1905, as a Socialist Revolutionary, he was one of the founders of the St. Petersburg Soviet, and in 1917 he edited *Golos Truda* (The Voice of Labor), the principal anarcho-syndicalist journal of the revolutionary period. During the Civil War he helped found the Nabat (Alarm) Confederation in the Ukraine, edited its newspaper of the same name, and played an important role in the partisan movement led by Makhno.

Unlike Makhno, however, Volin was primarily an intellectual, a propagandist of the word rather than the deed. A prolific writer and lecturer, he was the theorist of "united anarchism" and the author of the most impressive anarchist-inspired history of the Russian Revolution, which has been translated into many languages. Speaker and editor, historian and journalist, educator and poet, Volin was a versatile man. His life, laden with hardship, was punctuated by arrests, escapes, and a number of brushes with death. One of the most effective critics of the Bolshevik dictatorship, he was twice imprisoned by the Soviet secret police and, Trotsky having ordered his execution, only narrowly escaped with his life. In prison and exile, in propaganda and action, he remained a devoted revolutionary, possessed of both moral and physical courage. He was, in Victor Serge's description, "completely honest, rigorous in his thinking, full of talent, of eternal youth and joy in struggle."[1] His *nom de guerre*, formed from the Russian word *volia*, meaning "freedom," fittingly evokes the ideal to which he dedicated his life.

Volin, the pseudonym of Vsevolod Mikhailovich Eikhenbaum, was born on August 11, 1882, into an educated family of assimilated Russian-Jewish intellectuals, who lived near the city of Voronezh in the black-earth region of south-central Russia. His paternal grandfather, Yakov Eikhenbaum, was a mathematician and poet;[2] his parents were both doctors. Living in comfortable circumstances, they employed Western tutors for the education of their two sons. Accordingly, Volin and his younger brother were brought up with a knowledge of French and German, which they could speak and write almost as fluently as their native Russian. The brother, Boris Eikhenbaum (1886-1959), was to become one of Russia's most distinguished literary critics, a founder of the Formalist school and an authority on Tolstoy and other writers.

Volin himself might have followed a similar path. He attended the gymnasium at Voronezh and enrolled in the law school of St. Petersburg University. There, however, he became immersed in revolutionary ideas; and in 1904, to his parents' distress, he abandoned his studies to join the Socialist Revolutionary party and engage in full-time agitation among the workers of the capital, with whom he had established tentative contact three years before, when he was nineteen.

Volin poured the whole strength of his idealistic nature into his new cause. He organized workers' study groups, started a library, and drew up a reading program, while giving private lessons to earn a living.[3] On January 9, 1905, he took part in the great protest march on the Winter Palace that was fired on by tsarist troops, leaving hundreds of victims in the snow. This was the famous "Bloody Sunday" which marked the beginning of the 1905 Revolution. He also took part (while still a Socialist Revolutionary) in the formation of the first St. Petersburg Soviet and in the Kronstadt rising of October 25, 1905, for which he spent a short term in the Peter-Paul fortress. Soon after his release, he became the object of a manhunt in the reaction which followed the revolution. Captured by the Okhrana in 1907, he was thrown into prison and ordered deported to Siberia, but succeeded in escaping to France.[4]

Volin's flight to the West opened a new phase in his political and intellectual development. In Paris he became acquainted with both French and Russian anarchists, including Sébastien Faure (with whom he was later to collaborate on the four-volume *Encyclopédie Anarchiste*) and Apollon Karelin, who presided over a small libertarian circle called the Brotherhood of Free Communists (Bratstvo Vol'nykh Obshchinnikov). In 1911 Volin joined Karelin's group, quitting the Socialist Revolutionary party for anarchism, to which he remained unswervingly devoted for the rest of his life.

A staunch antimilitarist, Volin in 1913 became an active member of the Committee for International Action Against War. After the outbreak of the First World War in August 1914, he stepped up his antimilitarist agitation, to the intense displeasure of the French authorities, who in 1915 decided to intern him for the duration of hostilities. Warned by friends, however, Volin fled to the port city of Bordeaux and shipped out as quartermaster aboard a freighter bound for the United States, leaving behind his wife and children.

Arriving in New York in early 1916, Volin joined the Union of Russian Workers of the United States and Canada, an anarcho-syndicalist organization with nearly ten thousand adherents. A capable writer and speaker, he joined the staff of its weekly newspaper, *Golos Truda*, and debated and lectured at many of its clubs and meeting halls, both in Canada and the United States. In December 1916, for example, he embarked on a tour of Detroit, Pittsburgh, Cleveland, and Chicago, speaking on such subjects as syndicalism, the general strike, the world war, and the labor movement in France.[5] With the outbreak of the February Revolution, however, Volin resolved to return to Russia at the first opportunity. In May 1917, assisted by the Anarchist Red Cross, the staff of *Golos Truda*, Volin among them, packed up their equipment and sailed home by the Pacific route, arriving in Petrograd in July. The following month they resumed publication of *Golos Truda* as the weekly organ of the Union of Anarcho-Syndicalist Propaganda, which spread the gospel of revolutionary syndicalism among the workers of the capital.

Volin now emerged as one of the leading anarchist intellectuals of the revolutionary period. At rallies and in factories and clubhouses he was a popular speaker, calling for workers' control of production in place of both capitalism and reformist trade unionism. Though he was of medium height and frail physique, his handsome, intelligent face with its prematurely greying beard and piercing dark eyes made him an impressive-looking figure; and with his cogent argumentation and emphatic gestures and witty, at times shattering, repartée—he reminded Victor Serge of the Old French rebel Blanqui—he held his listeners spellbound. Beginning with the second issue, he also assumed the editorship of *Golos Truda* (the first number was edited by Maksim Raevsky, who, for reasons still unexplained, suddenly dropped out of the movement). Under Volin's able direction, *Golos Truda* became the most influential anarcho-syndicalist journal of the Russian Revolution, with an estimated readership of twenty-five thousand. A selection of his own articles—which appeared in nearly every issue—was published in book form in 1919 under the title *Revolution and Anarchism*.[6]

Volin, meanwhile, had come into conflict with the fledgling Bolshevik administration. "Once their power has been consolidated and legalized," he wrote in *Golos Truda* at the end of 1917, "the Bolsheviks as state socialists, that is as men who believe in centralized and authoritarian leadership, will start running the life of the country and of the people from the top." The soviets, he went on to predict, would become mere "tools of the central government," and Russia would see the emergence of "an authoritarian political and state apparatus that will crush all opposition with an iron fist. 'All power to the soviets' will become 'all power to the leaders of the party.' "[7]

In March 1918 Volin was sharply critical of the Treaty of Brest-Litovsk, by which Russia ceded to Germany more than a quarter of its population and arable land and three-quarters of its iron and steel industry. Lenin insisted that the agreement, severe as it was, provided a desperately needed breathing spell in which to consolidate Bolshevik power. For the anarchists, however, the treaty was a humiliating capitulation to the forces of reaction, a betrayal of the worldwide revolution. Volin denounced it as a "shameful" act and called for "relentless partisan warfare" against the Germans.[8] Soon after this, he relinquished the editorship of *Golos Truda* and left for the Ukraine, stopping in his native district to visit his relatives, whom he had not seen in more than a decade.

Spending the summer of 1918 in the town of Bobrov, Volin worked in the educational section of the local soviet, helping to organize a program of adult education, including a library and a people's theater. In the fall he moved to Kharkov, where he became the guiding spirit of the Nabat Confederation and the editor of its principal journal. He also played a key role in its first general conference, held at Kursk in November 1918, which sought to draft a declaration of principles that would be acceptable to all schools of anarchist thought, individualist as well as communist and syndicalist.[9]

Ever since leaving *Golos Truda*, Volin had been evolving from anarcho-syndicalism towards a more ecumenical position that he called "united anarchism" (*edinyi anarkhizm*), a theory that would encourage all factions of the movement to work together in a spirit of mutual respect and cooperation within the framework of a single, unified, but flexible organization—a sort of model for the future libertarian society itself. Many of his former comrades, notably Gregory Maximoff and Mark Mratchny, found "united anarchism" a vague and ineffectual formula to which they were unable to subscribe. Mratchny, while he thought Volin "a fluent speaker and very knowledgeable," perceived "a certain shallowness in him. He spoke and wrote easily, but always on the surface and without real substance."[10]

Volin pressed forward with his idea. He saw the embodiment of united anarchism in the Nabat Confederation, with its center in Kharkov and branches in Kiev, Odessa, and other large southern cities, a single organization embracing all varieties of anarchism while guaranteeing autonomy to each individual and group. Apart from publishing *Nabat*, the confederation issued several regional papers, as well as brochures and proclamations, and had a flourishing youth organization in addition to a Union of Atheists. It presented an alternative social model to both the Bolsheviks and the Whites, who, needless to say, endeavored to suppress it.[11]

In the summer of 1919, as the Bolsheviks intensified their persecution of the anarchists and began to close their newspapers and meeting places, Volin went to Gulyai-Polye and joined the insurrectionary army of Makhno, for which the Nabat Confederation supplied ideological guidance. Volin, along with Peter Arshinov and Aaron Baron, served in the Cultural-Educational Commission, editing the movement's newspapers, drafting its proclamations and manifestoes, and organizing its meetings and conferences. Volin headed the educational section (as he had done in the Bobrov Soviet) during the summer and fall, besides serving for six months on the Military Revolutionary Council. The following year the Bolsheviks offered him the post of commissar of education for the Ukraine, which he abruptly refused, just as his mentor Kropotkin had refused Kerensky's offer to become minister of education in the Provisional Government of 1917.[12]

In December 1919 the Military Revolutionary Council sent Volin to Krivoi Rog to counter Ukrainian nationalist propaganda disseminated in the area by Petliura. On the way, however, he was stricken with typhus and forced to stop at a peasant village, whose inhabitants labored to revive his health. On January 14, 1920, while still bedridden, he was arrested by the Fourteenth Red Army and handed over to the Cheka. Trotsky, whom he had repeatedly criticized in *Nabat*, issued orders for his execution. But anarchists in Moscow, among them Alexander Berkman, recently arrived from the United States, circulated an appeal for his transfer to Moscow and presented it to Nicholas Krestinsky, secretary of the Communist party. Krestinsky, though he had known Volin as a fellow student at St. Petersburg University, rejected the appeal, insisting that Volin was a counterrevolutionary. But, under pressure from the anarchists and their sympathizers (Victor Serge among them), he finally yielded and ordered Volin transferred to Moscow's Butyrki prison.[13]

This occurred in March of 1920. Seven months later, as part of an accord between the Red Army and Makhno's Insurgent Army of the Ukraine, Volin was released. Having recovered from his bout with typhus, he went to the town of Dmitrov, north of Moscow, to pay his respects to Kropotkin, before returning to Kharkov to resume the publication of *Nabat*. Once back in the Ukraine, he began preparations for an All-Russian Congress of Anarchists to meet at the end of the year. In late November, however, Trotsky discarded his agreement with Makhno and ordered an attack on Gulyai-Polye, while the Cheka rounded up members of the Nabat Confederation assembled in Kharkov for the congress. Volin, with Baron and others, was carried off to Moscow and locked up again in Butyrki, from which he was transferred in turn to Lefortovo and Taganka, names that figure in Solzhenitsyn's writings on Soviet prisons.

Volin remained behind bars for more than a year. In July 1921, when the Red International of Trade Unions (the Profintern) was created in Moscow, a number of foreign delegates, disturbed by the persecution of the anarchists and the suppression of the Kronstadt rebellion, were persuaded by Emma Goldman, Alexander Berkman, and Alexander Schapiro to protest to Lenin and to Dzerzhinsky, the head of the Cheka. The French anarchist Gaston Leval, then a young delegate to the Profintern Congress, was permitted to visit Volin in prison, and Volin, speaking in flawless French, regaled him for over an hour with the story of his odyssey in the Ukraine.[14] Soon afterwards, Volin, Maximoff, and other anarchists staged an eleven-day hunger strike to dramatize their incarceration. Lenin finally agreed to release them, on condition of their perpetual banishment from Russia, and in January 1922 they left for Berlin.

Volin never returned to his native country. In Berlin, Rudolf Rocker and other prominent German anarchists helped him and his family get settled. Though only forty, Volin, with his receding hair and grizzled beard, looked much older, but his animated gestures and rapid movements quickly dispelled this impression. Rocker, who had to closet himself in his private study when he wanted to write, envied Volin's facility for concentration; he could go on with his writing, Rocker recalled, in the same small attic where he and his wife and five children had to eat and sleep and carry on their daily lives.[15]

Volin stayed in Berlin for about two years. There he published seven issues of *Anarkhicheskii Vestnik* (The Anarchist Herald), an organ of "united anarchism" in contrast to Maximoff's specifically anarcho-syndicalist journal *Rabochii Put'* (The Workers' Road), which appeared at the same time. Together with Berkman, he engaged in relief work to aid his imprisoned and exiled comrades. In 1922 he edited a slim but important volume, *Goneniia na anarkhizm v Sovetskoi Rossii* (The Repressions of the Anarchists in Soviet Russia), published in French and German as well as Russian, which provided the first documented information to the outside world of Bolshevik persecution of the anarchists. He also wrote a valuable preface to Arshinov's history of the Makhnovist movement and helped translate the book into German.[16]

In 1924 Volin was invited by Sébastien Faure to come to Paris and collaborate on the anarchist encyclopedia he was preparing.[17] Faure could make good use of a man with Volin's erudition, command of languages, and familiarity with anarchist history and theory. Volin accepted, moved to Paris, and wrote a number of major articles for the encyclopedia, some of which were published as separate pamphlets in several languages. Over the next dozen years, moreover, he contributed to a range of anarchist periodicals, including *Le Libertaire* and *La Revue Anarchiste* in Paris, *Die Internationale* in Berlin, and *Man!*, *Delo Truda*, and the *Fraye Arbeter Shtime* in the United States. He also published a volume of poetry,[18] dedicated to the memory of Kropotkin, who had died in 1921, and began to work on his monumental history of the Russian Revolution.[19]

Volin, however, was not immune from the factional quarrels that plagued the Russian anarchists in exile. In 1926 he broke with his old comrades Arshinov and Makhno over their controversial *Organizational Platform*, which called for a General Union of Anarchists with a central executive committee to coordinate policy and action.[20] In the dispute, Volin ranged himself with Alexander Berkman, Emma Goldman, Sébastien Faure, Errico Malatesta, Rudolf Rocker, and other notable anarchists from different countries. With a group of associates, he issued a scathing reply to Arshinov the following year, arguing that the *Organizational Platform*, with its appeal for a central committee, clashed with the basic anarchist principle of local initiative and was a reflection of its author's "party spirit" (Arshinov had been a Bolshevik before joining the anarchists in 1906).[21]

Volin felt vindicated in 1930 when Arshinov returned to the Soviet Union and rejoined the party—only to be purged by Stalin a few years later. With Arshinov gone, Galina Makhno urged Volin to visit her ailing husband, fatally stricken with tuberculosis. In 1934, on the eve of Makhno's death, the old friends were briefly reconciled, and Volin saw to the posthumous publication of the second and third volumes of Makhno's memoirs, to which he contributed prefaces and notes.[22]

During the late 1920s and 1930s, Volin continued to denounce the Soviet dictatorship, labeling Bolshevism "red fascism" and likening Stalin to Mussolini and Hitler.[23] In his small Parisian apartment he conducted an informal class on anarchism which drew young comrades of several nationalities, Marie Louise Berneri among them. To support his family, meanwhile, he tried his hand at a variety of jobs, working, among other things, as an agent for a newspaper clipping service and collaborating with Alexander Berkman on a Russian translation of Eugene O'Neill's *Lazarus Laughed*, commissioned by the Moscow Art Theater.[24]

After the outbreak of the Spanish Civil War in 1936, Volin accepted an invitation from the Confederación Nacional del Trabajo (CNT) to edit its Paris-based French periodical, *L'Espagne Anti-Fasciste*. He soon quit, however, when the CNT endorsed the popular front and supported the loyalist government. At this point, his life never easy, always on the edge of poverty,[25] Volin suffered a series of misfortunes, of which the death of his wife, following a nervous collapse, was the worst. Shortly afterwards, in 1938, he left Paris for Nîmes, to which his friend André Prudhommeaux, a well-known libertarian writer and the manager of a printing cooperative, had beckoned him. Volin took a seat on the editorial board of Prudhommeaux's weekly paper, *Terre Libre*, while continuing his study of the Russian Revolution, which he completed in Marseilles in 1940, after the outbreak of the Second World War.

VOLIN'S BOOK, *The Unknown Revolution*, is the most important anarchist history of the Russian Revolution in any language. It was written, as we have seen, by an eyewitness who himself played an active part in the events that he describes. Like Kropotkin's history of the French Revolution, it explores what Volin calls the "unknown revolution," that is, the social revolution of the people as distinguished from the seizure of political power by the Bolsheviks. Before the appearance of Volin's book, this theme had been little discussed. The Russian Revolution, as Volin saw it, was much more than the story of Kerensky and Lenin, of Social Democrats, Socialist Revolutionaries, or even anarchists. It was an explosion of mass discontent and of mass creativity, elemental, unpremeditated, and unpolitical, a true social revolution such as Bakunin had foreseen half a century before.

As a great popular movement, a "revolt of the masses," the Russian Revolution needed a Volin to write its history "from below," as Kropotkin and Jean Jaurès had done for France. "It is the whole immense multitude of men who are finally entering the limelight," Jaurès had remarked of 1789.[26] Such was also the case in Russia between 1917 and 1921, when the country underwent a vast upheaval encompassing every area of life and in which ordinary men and women played an essential part. A similar phenomenon occurred in Spain between 1936 and 1939. Russia and Spain, indeed, experienced the greatest libertarian revolutions of the twentieth century, decentralist, spontaneous, egalitarian, led by no single party or group but largely the work of the people themselves.

The most striking feature of this "unknown revolution," in Volin's interpretation, was the decentralization and dispersal of authority, the spontaneous formation of autonomous communes and councils, and the emergence of workers' self-management in town and country. Indeed, all modern revolutions have seen the organization of local committees—factory committees, housing committees, educational and cultural committees, soldiers' and sailors' committees, peasant committees—in an efflorescence of direct action on the spot. In Russia the soviets, too, were popular organs of direct democracy until reduced by the Bolsheviks to instruments of centralized authority, rubber stamps of a new bureaucratic state.

Such is Volin's central thesis. In rich detail he documents the efforts of workers, peasants, and intellectuals to inaugurate a free society based on local initiative and autonomy. Libertarian opposition to the new Soviet dictatorship, above all in Kronstadt and the Ukraine, receives extensive treatment. Volin presents a deeply sympathetic account of the Makhno movement, yet without glossing over its negative aspects, such as Makhno's heavy drinking and the formation of what some regard as a military camarilla around Makhno's leadership. (Volin, it has been noted, broke with Makhno over the *Organizational Platform*, and the resulting antagonism never completely abated.)

The book, however, is not without its shortcomings. In discussing the historical antecedents of the Russian revolutionary movement, Volin mentions the great peasant and Cossack rebellions of the seventeenth and eighteenth centuries only in passing, without taking account of their strongly antistatist character. For all their "primitive" qualities, the risings of Razin and Pugachev were anti-authoritarian movements for a decentralized and egalitarian society. Oddly enough, moreover, Volin omits the anarchists from his chapter on the 1905 Revolution, although it was in 1905 that the Russian anarchists played their first important role and emerged as a force to be reckoned with. (Volin, it is worth recalling, was a Socialist Revolutionary at the time, not converting to anarchism until 1911.)

Furthermore, Volin's discussion of the social revolution in 1917 needs amplification. Little is said of the worker and peasant movements outside Kronstadt and the Ukraine. The book also neglects the individualist anarchists, a fascinating if relatively small group, as well as the role of women in the anarchist and revolutionary movements. Surely the activities of women—on the bread lines and picket lines, in strikes and demonstrations, on the barricades and in guerrilla units, in winning over the soldiers and their male and female workmates, in creating free schools and day-care centers, in their overall drive for dignity and equality—form a major part of the "unknown revolution" with which Volin was so deeply concerned.

The book, it must be added, suffers from deficiencies of style. Volin, as George Woodcock has noted, was "not an elegant writer in the literary sense." He tended, rather, towards prolixity, and his history would have benefited from condensation.[27] Yet, for all these blemishes, *The Unknown Revolution* is an impressive work. It is a pioneering history of a neglected aspect of the Russian Revolution. With the partial exception of Arshinov's history of the Makhno movement and Maximoff's history of the Bolshevik repressions, there is no other book like it.[28]

Volin, as noted earlier, completed *The Unknown Revolution* in 1940 while living in Marseilles. When Victor Serge met him there that year, he was working in the office of a small movie house and living on practically nothing. After the Nazi invasion and the formation of the Vichy government, his position became increasingly precarious. He went from hiding place to hiding place, living in extreme poverty and in constant fear of arrest. Yet he refused to seek refuge across the Atlantic. He hoped to take part in the coming events in Europe, about which, noted Serge, he cherished a "romantic optimism."[29] Two of Volin's comrades, Mollie Steimer and Senya Fleshin, met him in Marseilles in 1941. They begged him to come away with them to Mexico, but to no avail. He was needed in France, Volin insisted, to meet with the youth and "prepare for the revolution when the war is over."[30]

Pursued by the authorities both as an anarchist and as a Jew, Volin somehow managed to evade their clutches. When the war finally ended he returned to Paris, but only to enter a hospital. For he had contracted tuberculosis and his days were numbered. He died on September 18, 1945. His body was cremated and the ashes buried in the Père-Lachaise Cemetery, close to the grave of Nestor Makhno, who had succumbed to the same disease eleven years before. The old comrades were thus reunited in death, their remains resting by those of the martyrs of the Paris Commune.

Part II : America

CHAPTER NINE

Proudhon and America

THE INFLUENCE of Pierre-Joseph Proudhon, the great French anarchist and social thinker, is a subject about which little has been written. His ideas on money and credit, on labor and capital, on individual sovereignty and voluntary cooperation, which he evolved in an uninterrupted flow of books and articles spanning the 1840s and 1850s, reached far beyond the borders of his native country, leaving an imprint on Russian populism, Spanish federalism, and disparate social movements around the globe.

In the United States, where his impact was greater than has been commonly supposed, Proudhon's views were given wide publicity. During the years preceding the Civil War, they were circulated by French and German exiles from the Revolution of 1848, most notably Claude Pelletier, Frédéric Tufferd, Joseph Déjacque, and Wilhelm Weitling; and with equal enthusiasm they were promoted by a circle of American-born Fourierists, mostly of New England origin, including Charles A. Dana, Parke Godwin, and Albert Brisbane. Brisbane actually visited Proudhon in a Parisian prison in 1848 and talked with him "by the hour" about his theories. "Proudhon and I," he later wrote, "agreed perfectly as to principles which in our opinion could be applied practically in various ways even in the present state of society."[1]

But it was Dana, a scion of the celebrated New England family, who claims priority in bringing Proudhon's ideas before the American public. Dana, a native of New Hampshire, was born in 1819. In 1842, after attending Harvard College, he joined Brook Farm, the famous transcendentalist and Fourierist community, where, associating with such luminaries as George Ripley, Theodore Parker, and Margaret Fuller, he lectured on diverse subjects, sang in the choir, and wrote for *The Dial* and *The Harbinger*.

In 1847 Dana left Brook Farm and joined the staff of Horace Greeley's New York *Tribune*. The next year, he embarked on an extended tour of Europe, then in the throes of revolution. In Paris he heard Proudhon speak in the National Assembly and became acquainted with his views at first hand. Proudhon, he found, was far from being "an atheist and a madman, a Communist burning to plunder the wealthy, the living incarnation of immorality, disorder, and folly," as newspapers on both sides of the Atlantic depicted him. On the contrary, though "always bold and often irreverent," he was a man devoted to the cause of justice, notable for his "love of freedom and hatred of hypocrisy," and possessed of "a remarkable degree of originality and vigor of mind as well as of honesty and moral courage."[2]

Deeply impressed, Dana published, on his return to New York in 1849, a series of articles on Proudhon for the *Tribune*, centering on his scheme for a mutual bank—a People's Bank, Proudhon called it—in which credit would be provided at cost, thereby stimulating production, eliminating poverty and unemployment, and achieving social and economic justice for all. Later the same year, Dana revised the articles for publication in *The Spirit of the Age*, a New York weekly edited by William Henry Channing, a former associate at Brook Farm. Nearly half of a century later, they were reprinted in pamphlet form by Benjamin Tucker as *Proudhon and His "Bank of the People."*

Dana, after 1849, did not pursue his interest in Proudhon. Appointed managing editor of the *Tribune*, a post which he held until 1862, he immersed himself in a wide range of social and political matters, the abolition of slavery being the most conspicuous. In 1863, at the height of the Civil War, he was appointed assistant secretary of war by Abraham Lincoln, a position in which he remained until the surrender of Lee at Appomattox. Returning to New York, Dana helped establish the daily *Sun*, of which he soon became the general editor. With his crisp style, broad erudition, and political contacts, he emerged, over the next generation, as a powerful force in American journalism. He died in 1897 at the age of seventy-eight.

IN THE MEANTIME, another group of American writers, anarchists rather than Fourierists, had been actively spreading the Proudhonian gospel. As early as 1849, the year in which Dana published his articles on Proudhon, William B. Greene of Massachusetts penned a similar series which, the following year, appeared in pamphlet form as *Mutual*

Banking. Greene, then thirty years old (the same age as Dana), was one of the most colorful American reformers of the period. A man of striking physical appearance and natural dignity, he had been born in the town of Haverhill in 1819, the son of Nathaniel Greene, postmaster of Boston and founder of the Boston *Statesman*, the leading Democratic paper in Massachusetts. More than six feet tall, slender and erect, Greene attended West Point, took part in the Florida war against the Seminoles, and then abruptly left the service to study at Harvard Divinity School. Thomas Wentworth Higginson, who encountered Greene around this time, thought him the "handsomest and most distinguished looking person I had ever met," with his military, "almost defiantly self-assertive" bearing, jet-black hair, and "eyes that transfix you with their blackness and penetration."[3]

Concluding his studies in 1845, Greene served as pastor of the Unitarian church in West Brookfield, Massachusetts. Increasingly, however, his interests shifted to social and economic issues; and in 1850, under the influence of Proudhon, he brought out his pamphlet on mutual banking, "the most important work on finance," wrote Benjamin Tucker, "ever published in this country."[4]

With the appearance of *Mutual Banking*, Greene succeeded Dana as Proudhon's leading American disciple. Not only was he active in disseminating Proudhon's ideas, but in 1850 and 1851 he petitioned the Massachusetts legislature—without result—for a mutual banking law on Proudhonian lines. Greene, however, differed from Proudhon in one important respect. Unlike his mentor, he championed the cause of women's rights, speaking out on the subject before the Massachusetts Constitutional Convention in 1853.[5] Later that year, he left for Paris and became personally acquainted with Proudhon, who confirmed him in the mutualist faith.[6]

Greene remained in France until 1861, when the outbreak of the Civil War drew him back to the United States. Offering his services to Governor Andrew (on whom Bakunin called during his sojourn in Boston), he was made colonel of the Fourteenth Massachusetts Infantry, which, stationed near Washington, became the First Massachusetts Artillery, entrusted with defending the capital against a threatened Confederate attack. By now Greene's hair and beard were grizzled, but he still had, a subordinate recalled, "the keenest black eyes ever put in mortal's head." Rapid of speech and action, scorning slow or clumsy movement in others, he was nevertheless "kind, patient, forgiving, and fatherly to his enlisted men."[7]

Greene served as a Union officer for little more than a year. He resigned his commission in October 1862, after a quarrel with Governor

Andrew, and thenceforth devoted his energies to economic and social reform. Returning to Boston, he emerged, together with Josiah Warren, Ezra Heywood, Lysander Spooner, and Stephen Pearl Andrews, in the forefront of the individualist anarchist movement in America, championing the cause of free speech, free credit, women's equality, and the amelioration of the condition of labor. In 1869 he became president of the Massachusetts Labor Union and was cofounder, with Ezra Heywood, of the New England Labor Reform League, an organization, thanks to Greene's efforts, permeated with Proudhonian ideas and dedicated, in the words of its charter, drafted by Heywood and Greene, to "the abolition of class laws and false customs, whereby legitimate enterprise is defrauded by speculative monopoly, and the reconstruction of government on the basis of justice and reciprocity."[8]

By 1873 Greene was serving as vice-president of the league—whose members included Warren, Andrews, and Benjamin Tucker—and was active at the same time in the French-speaking section of the International Working Men's Association in Boston. An imposing figure, he was the center of attention in any group in which he took part, often accompanied by his wife, Anna, from the prominent Shaw family of Boston, a woman as fair as he was dark, nearly as tall as he and quite as distinguished in appearance.[9] Still devoted to Proudhon, who had died in 1865, Greene translated several of his writings, including an essay on "The State" and an extract from *What Is Property?* in which Proudhon proclaimed himself an anarchist and condemned unearned property as "theft." Both translations appeared in Heywood's magazine *The Word* during the early 1870s.[10] In 1873, moreover, Greene, together with Heywood and Tucker, again petitioned the Massachusetts legislature for a mutual banking law. This duplication of his efforts of the 1850s met with the same lack of success. For the duration of his life, financial and labor reform remained Greene's overriding interests. He died, in England, in 1878, his last years clouded by the death of his daughter, Bessie, who was lost in a shipwreck.

BY THE TIME of his death, Greene had been replaced by Benjamin Tucker as the leading American apostle of Proudhon's doctrines. The son of a New Bedford whaling merchant, Tucker, as was noted in Chapter 2, was a student at MIT when, in 1872, he attended a convention of the New England Labor Reform League in Boston. It was his first encounter with the anarchists. Greene, serving as chairman and "strikingly handsome" in his black velvet coat, Tucker later recalled, made "an admirable presiding officer." At a table in the hall, where literature was displayed, Tucker bought Greene's *Mutual Banking* and

Warren's *True Civilization*, along with several pamphlets by Heywood and copies of *The Word*. Heywood, after the opening session, approached the young man and introduced him to Greene and Warren. Tucker was profoundly impressed. He afterwards looked back on that meeting as the "pivotal point" of his career. It was, noted Tucker's companion, Pearl Johnson, "one of the finest days of his life."[11]

It was through Greene, as Tucker acknowledged, that he first learned the theories of Proudhon, "though I was always a Proudhonian without knowing it." "I am indebted to Col. Greene's *Mutual Banking*," he said, "more than to any other single publication for such knowledge as I have of the principles of finance—the most compact, satisfactory, keen and clear treatise upon money extant." The better he came to know Greene, the more Tucker enjoyed his company. Before long, his admiration for his mentor was "unbounded." It was worthwhile, he thought, to go anywhere "if Col. Greene and his wife were going to be present, if for nothing more than to see them enter the room! Dignity and poise, gracious manners, kindliness, and all so well balanced in two stately and fine specimens of the human race."[12]

Inspired by Greene's example, Tucker went abroad in 1874, plunged into Proudhon's works, and returned to America a convert. At Greene's suggestion, in 1876 he translated *What Is Property?* in its entirety, a volume of more than four hundred pages. In 1877 and 1878 he followed this with part one of *The System of Economical Contradictions*, serialized in his own journal, the *Radical Review*, and with Proudhon's essay on "The Malthusians," which appeared in the Boston *Index*. In 1879, moreover, he translated Proudhon's debate on interest with the French economist Bastiat, which was published in the *Irish World* of New York.

When Tucker, in 1881, launched his remarkable journal *Liberty*, he continued his Proudhonian mission. Indeed *Liberty*, as Tucker himself noted, was "brought into existence almost as a direct consequence of the teachings of Proudhon" and "lives principally to emphasize and spread them."[13] Not only did a quotation from Proudhon—"Liberty, Not the Daughter but the Mother of Order"—adorn the paper's masthead, but its columns were stocked with articles about him and with further translations of his writings (including a previously unpublished play entitled *Galileo*), together with advertisements for his portrait that proclaimed him "the profoundest political philosopher and economist that has ever lived." Encouraged by *Liberty*, it might be added, a Proudhon discussion club was founded in Boston towards the end of 1887, with both anarchists and nonanarchists among the participants.[14]

Tucker's greatest ambition was to publish the complete works of Proudhon in English translation. This proved beyond his capacities. But additional works by the master were translated by Tucker's associates. The most notable of these was *The General Idea of the Revolution in the Nineteenth Century*, published by John Beverley Robinson of St. Louis in 1923. Tucker considered this Proudhon's greatest work, savoring in particular its passionate indictment of the state: "To be governed is to be kept in sight, inspected, spied upon, directed, law-driven, numbered, enrolled, indoctrinated, preached at, controlled, estimated, valued, censured, commanded, by creatures who have neither the right, nor the wisdom, nor the virtue to do so. To be governed is to be, at every operation, every transaction, noted, registered, enrolled, taxed, stamped, measured, numbered, assessed, licensed, authorized, admonished, forbidden, reformed, corrected, punished. It is, under pretext of public utility, and in the name of the general interest, to be placed under contribution, trained, ransacked, exploited, monopolized, extorted, squeezed, mystified, robbed; then, at the slightest resistance, the first word of complaint, to be repressed, fined, despised, harassed, tracked, abused, clubbed, disarmed, choked, imprisoned, judged, condemned, shot, deported, sacrificed, sold, betrayed; and, to crown all, mocked, ridiculed, outraged, dishonored. That is government; that is its justice; that is its morality."[15]

Robinson, an architect by profession and the author of a pamphlet based on Proudhon's economic ideas,[16] also translated an essay by Proudhon on "The Bank of the People," which appeared in 1927 in *Proudhon's Solution of the Social Problem*, an anthology edited by Henry Cohen, a Tuckerite from Denver, Colorado. Cohen's collection, in addition, contained reprints of Greene's *Mutual Banking* and Dana's *Proudhon and His "Bank of the People,"* along with other valuable material, including previously untranslated passages from *The System of Economical Contradictions*, rendered into English by Clarence Lee Swartz, yet another of Tucker's disciples. Swartz's own book, *What is Mutualism?*, acknowledges its debt to both Proudhon and Greene.[17] It might also be mentioned that Proudhon's *War and Peace* (whose title Tolstoy, an admirer of the French anarchist, borrowed for his famous novel) was translated in prison by Bartolomeo Vanzetti while awaiting execution.[18]

One final point must be noted. We have seen that it was Tucker, in 1896, who first issued Dana's *Proudhon and His "Bank of the People"* in pamphlet form, adding a preface, explanatory notes, and a descriptive subtitle ("Being a Defence of the Great French Anarchist, Showing the Evils of Specie Currency, and That Interest on Capital Can and

Ought to be Abolished by a System of Free and Mutual Banking"). In making the pamphlet available, Tucker's purpose was twofold. First, he considered the work "a really intelligent, forceful, and sympathetic exposition of mutual banking," to quote his own description, and therefore worthy of republication. His second object, however, was to unmask Dana as a "diabolical hypocrite."[19] For Dana, his radical past long since forgotten, had become a staunch defender of conservative interests, his latest target being William Jennings Bryan, the free-silver candidate for president in the 1896 national elections. Tucker, according to Henry Cohen, sent copies of Dana's pamphlet to newspaper editors in every city, and Dana, says Cohen, became the laughing stock of the country.[20]

But Tucker's star was also on the wane. Since the 1870s, he had translated Proudhon's writings, circulated his ideas, and preserved his memory, as Cohen put it, with "an ability and a devotion that have no parallel in any American reform movement."[21] For a generation, moreover, he had defended the cause of freedom against collectivist and statist encroachments. By the turn of the century, however, the heyday of individualist anarchism had passed; and in 1908, his storehouse of books and papers destroyed in a fire, Tucker departed for Europe, never to return.

From that moment, Tucker abandoned his role as a purveyor of mutualist ideas. Although he retained the anarchist label, he had come to believe that free banking, even if inaugurated, was no longer adequate to break the monopoly of capitalism or weaken the authority of the state. With the passage of time, Tucker grew increasingly pessimistic. The "monster, Mechanism," he wrote in 1930, "is devouring mankind."[22] By then he had outlived his reputation as a social thinker. His retirement, in Monaco, was virtually complete. Few people knew him or were acquainted with his work, and his death in 1939 passed almost unnoticed. He had lived to be eighty-five, and the global war that he had feared and predicted was looming on the horizon.

CHAPTER TEN

Benjamin Tucker and His Daughter

THE NAME OF Benjamin Tucker has already figured prominently in these pages. America's chief exponent of individualist anarchism, he was instrumental in bringing the ideas of Proudhon, Bakunin, Stirner, and other anarchists and near-anarchists before an inquisitive readership. His principal achievement was the publication of his journal *Liberty*, the best anarchist periodical in the English language, as Joseph Ishill rightly judged it.[1] Unlike Alexander Berkman, whose *Prison Memoirs of an Anarchist* has become a classic, Tucker had no great book smoldering inside him. Nor, in contrast to Emma Goldman or Johann Most, did he acquire a reputation as a speaker. (He held forth, on the contrary, only when the occasion demanded it, being "never as ill at ease," he confessed, as when standing on his feet before an audience.)[2]

But Tucker was an accomplished translator, whose renderings of Proudhon and Bakunin (to say nothing of Victor Hugo, Chernyshevsky, and Tolstoy) alone have earned him a place in the anarchist pantheon. More than that, he was a first-rate editor and writer, one of the finest journalists American radicalism has produced. Of *Liberty* he had particular cause to be proud. It was meticulously designed and edited, with a brilliant galaxy of contributors, not least among them Tucker himself. Its debut in 1881 was a milestone in the history of the anarchist movement, and it won an audience wherever English was read. As a publisher, moreover, Tucker issued a steady stream of books and pamphlets on anarchism and related subjects over a period of nearly thirty years. In doing so, noted an admirer, he accomplished "more practical work for the advancement of liberty than any other man, living or dead, with the possible exception of Proudhon."[3]

These words (by Laurance Labadie) were written in 1935. By then Tucker was practically forgotten, a man, said H. L. Mencken, who deserved "a great deal more fame than he has got."[4] And today, to the extent that he is remembered at all, it is not for any sensational deed, comparable to Berkman's assault on Henry Clay Frick, but rather for what he wrote and published, nearly all of it in his magazine *Liberty*. His life, admirable though it was, lacked dramatic quality. For excitement, color, or suspense, it cannot compare with that of Bakunin, Kropotkin, or Malatesta, still less of Durruti, Vanzetti, or Makhno. Events there were, to be sure: Tucker's early conversion to anarchism, his seduction by Victoria Woodhull, his controversy with Johann Most, to mention just a few. Yet these were merely ripples in an otherwise unbroken current. Tucker was a man of intellect rather than of action. His months and years were taken up mostly with the working out of his ideas and with the publication of his books and journals, *Liberty* above all else. This being so, historians have dwelled on Tucker's role as a publicist, to the neglect of his personal life. Little has been told about Tucker the man.

By examining the available sources, however, we can learn a great deal about the human side of Tucker, much of it of considerable interest. In physical appearance, he was a handsome man, 5′9″ tall and weighing about 165 pounds, with piercing dark eyes, dark brown hair, and a neatly trimmed beard and mustache. (He shed his beard in later years, but kept his mustache until the end.) Always impeccably dressed, he was seldom to be seen in his shirtsleeves or otherwise informally attired.

To match his well-groomed appearance, Tucker exhibited a meticulousness of mind and manner throughout his long life. There was in him to the end something aloof and shut in. He was without snobbery or racial and class bias, but he showed always the aristocratic stance of a member of the New England gentry. Though he had a large circle of acquaintances, he did not make friends easily, and few came to know him on intimate terms. George Schumm, William Bailie, and other close associates on *Liberty* always addressed him as "Mr. Tucker" in their letters.

These qualities were amply reflected in Tucker's writing. He possessed the virtues of discipline, stability, and high standards. He worked with great concentration, thoroughness, and attention to detail. His keenness of intellect, lucidity of style, and adherence to principle were proverbial. Not only did he have a sharp analytical mind and a true gift of literary craftsmanship, but he was in deadly earnest about what he thought and how he expressed it. And he was consistent to a fault. (Tucker's great weakness, a colleague observed, was his "fear of being inconsistent.")[5]

It is remarkable how little Tucker's ideas and prose changed over the course of his life, which stretched from antebellum Massachusetts to the Riviera on the eve of the Second World War. What he had to say he said straight out and confidently and well. But his candor was seldom tempered by tact. He was a bristlingly aggressive polemicist, sensitive to criticism and sure of his own high worth. Sure, also, of the rightness of his views, he seldom yielded an inch to his opponents. In his writing, said J. William Lloyd, a sometime contributor to *Liberty*, Tucker was "dogmatic to the extreme, arrogantly positive, browbeating and dominating, true to his 'plumb-line' no matter who was slain, and brooked no difference, contradiction or denial. Biting sarcasm, caustic contempt, invective that was sometimes almost actual insult, were poured out on any who dared criticize or oppose."[6]

For Tucker, as his companion Pearl Johnson said of him, was "first, last, and always a controversialist, and therein lay his strength."[7] He was forever correcting his adversaries, straightening them out, pointing out errors in their logic. With trembling fingers, friend and enemy alike must have opened each fresh issue of *Liberty*, fearing that "keen, clear-cut style," as C. L. Swartz described it, "that was the delight of his adherents and the despair of his opponents."[8] Not even his closest collaborators escaped his assaults ("How you do jump on a fellow!" J. B. Robinson protested).[9] Stephen Pearl Andrews, forty-two years his senior, Tucker took sharply to task for distorting the views of Proudhon. Andrews's reply was a model of conciliation: "You speak of my misrepresenting Proudhon. You will do me the justice to believe that if I have done so in any particular, it is because I have misapprehended him. That is entirely possible, as my examination was of course hurried. But you do not tell me upon what point, or points. If you choose to do so, and if I then see with you, I am entirely willing and desirous even to modify, in accordance with the truth. What we both want is the truth."[10]

For conciliation, however, Tucker had little regard. A "glittering icicle of logic," as a friend characterized him,[11] he delighted in argumentation, consuming inordinate energy in hairsplitting and sterile debate. He sent his "fine hard shafts among foes and friends with an icy impartiality," Voltairine de Cleyre remarked, "hitting swift and cutting keen—and ever ready to nail a traitor." Lizzie M. Holmes complained of the spirit of "intolerance, severity, and invective" with which Tucker's pronouncements were imbued. Why, she asked, should a lover of liberty show such a pugnacious disposition?[12] Tucker, as W. C. Owen put it, was one of those "cold enthusiasts" who keep their goal steadily in view, march directly towards it, and care nothing for popular applause or pecuniary gain. Tucker could not disagree. "This is the first time that I have been called a 'cold enthusiast,' " he wrote to Owen, "but I recognize that the expression hits the mark. To tell the truth, I am a little bit proud of my frigidity."[13]

That a coldness, not to say shallowness, of spirit pervaded much of Tucker's written work is hard to deny. Although he wielded a "forceful pen," as Emma Goldman noted, his was far from being a "large nature," and his attitude towards the communist anarchists, among whom she mingled, was "charged with insulting rancor." "No, I never see Tucker," she wrote in 1930, when they both resided on the Riviera. "I would not go around the corner to meet him. He was an old fogey before he grew old and is small in his attitude to other social schools."[14] The antipathy, it should be noted, was mutual. There was "never much love lost between us," Tucker remarked of Goldman, "although some of her qualities are excellent, and I am sorry that she has been treated so badly. I heard the other day, indirectly, that she intends to look me up on her return to the Riviera!! (Where to *hide*? that is the question. 'O for a lodge in some vast wilderness!')"[15]

To those who knew Tucker only through his writing, then, he might seem arrogant, vindictive, and cruel. One could not read an issue of *Liberty*, said J. William Lloyd, without getting the impression that he was "a fire-eater, most of the time angry." Yet nothing could be further from the truth. For all his acidity in print, Tucker was invariably cordial in private company. This surprised readers of *Liberty* when they met him for the first time. "Face to face," said Lloyd, "this tiger was a dove." Albert Chavannes found him "the mildest mannered pirate that ever cut a throat or sank a ship"; to C. L. Swartz he was "the most affable and polished gentleman and the warmest friend."[16]

What then accounts for the impression of coldness or aloofness that he left with so many others? According to his sister-in-law, Dr. Bertha F. Johnson, this was due merely to shyness on Tucker's part.[17] And shyness, too, may help to explain Tucker's inadequacy as a public speaker, as well as his frequent, "slightly nervous" laugh.[18] Tucker himself, in a letter to Jo Labadie, admitted that "I am as shy in getting acquainted with children as with grown people, which is equivalent to saying that I am very shy indeed."[19] Along with his shyness, moreover, went a lack of physical courage that dated from his early childhood. "Probably I do not need to remind you of the baby that I was in our boyhood days," he wrote to a cousin towards the end of his life, "averse to doing stunts, timid to the extreme in all muscular sports, and boo-hooing on the slightest provocation. I am the same coward still, and am ashamed of it now as I was ashamed of it then."[20]

Reserved as he was, however, there was a lighter side to Tucker's personality. He was far from being an ascetic, as Victor S. Yarros describes him.[21] He enjoyed plays and concerts. He knew and loved good food. "I was always an epicure," he wrote in 1936, "and even a gourmand, to the extent that I could afford, and sometimes to an extent that I could not afford."[22] For all his timidity, moreover, Tucker had several love affairs—with Victoria Woodhull and Sarah E. Holmes, for example—before he found the beautiful young woman with a "classic face" who became his much adored companion.[23]

It was his old associate George Schumm who recommended Pearl Johnson for work at Tucker's Unique Book Shop in New York City during the last two years of its existence (1906 to 1908). She was twenty-five years Tucker's junior, and he had known her mother's family during his boyhood in Massachusetts. Two years before his death, Tucker thanked Schumm for bringing them together. "That was without doubt the greatest stroke of luck that I have ever had in my life," Tucker wrote. "I realize it more and more as time goes on. How little we know of the future, and the surprises! A word drops, and a child is born. With all my heart I thank you!"[24]

The child was Oriole Tucker, who arrived in November 1908, ten months after the fire that wiped out her father's warehouse and ended his publishing venture of thirty years. Tucker was fifty-four years old, and his career as a publicist was over. Six weeks after Oriole's birth, the family sailed for Europe. Tucker never returned to the United States. Oriole was raised in France and in Monaco, where she lived until her father's death in 1939. She was Tucker's only child, and he was deeply devoted to her.[25] Bright and pretty, she spoke flawless French and English and became an accomplished pianist. Until the age of fifteen, she did not attend school. Her mother instructed her at home with textbooks furnished by the Calvert School in Baltimore. When she finally entered school, she made an outstanding record. At home, she was brought up in accordance with her parents' libertarian principles. She had a room of her own, said Tucker, "which is almost her castle, and which her father rarely enters, except under stress of necessity. There are four lines of Emerson which I am fond of quoting: 'When the Church is social worth, / When the State-house is the hearth, / Then the perfect state has come,— / The republican at home.' It has been my endeavor in my later years to realize *The Anarchist at home*, and it seems to me that my effort in this line has not been entirely in vain."[26]

On January 21, 1973, I visited Oriole Tucker at her home in Ossining, New York, with the object of interviewing her about her father, and especially about the personal side of his life. Married to Jean Riché, a French chef, she taught French at the Dobbs Ferry Middle School a few miles away. Her house stood on the site of the former Stillwater colony, a short-lived School of Living community founded by Ralph Borsodi in 1939. Across the road lived Beatrice Schumm Fetz, the daughter of Tucker's longtime associates George and Emma Schumm, while at the bottom of the hill stood the house of Margaret Noyes Goldsmith, a granddaughter of John Humphrey Noyes, the celebrated founder of the Oneida community.

Oriole was a fine-looking woman with remarkable eyes, a youthful appearance, and a vivid memory, particularly where her parents were concerned. I looked forward to coming back at a more advanced stage of my research, in order to talk to her again about her father. But she died suddenly in June 1974, at the age of sixty-five. Thus our conversation was never completed. What she told me during our meeting, however, is of great interest. Her words were as follows.

Oriole Tucker

I was born in New York City on November 9, 1908, delivered by Dr. E. B. Foote, Father's friend and fellow libertarian. I was named after J. William Lloyd's daughter, Oriole Lloyd. My parents had been hoping I would arrive on November 11, the anniversary of the Haymarket executions. After the disastrous fire in January 1908, Father had decided to move to France. He didn't want to start all over again. Besides, he loved France and always said he wanted to die in France. He and Mother went to Paris in the summer of 1908 and rented a house in the suburb of Le Vésinet, near Saint-Germain. They came back to the U.S. to have me born here (Mother was expecting a difficult birth and wanted the family on hand). But by Christmas I was in France, aged six weeks old. And there I stayed. When I was three and a half, Mother and I did come to the States for a few months to see her family. After the war, though, we never came back as a family. In 1936, I came by myself for three months. America had been as far away to me as the moon. It was a fairyland to me: Mother kept talking about it, tried to keep it alive, but to me all the names I heard seemed like people stepping out of mythology.

Mother—Pearl Johnson—was the daughter of a New England couple, Horace Johnson and Florence Hull, one of four daughters of

Moses Hull, a minister of advanced views who became a well-known spiritualist. Pearl went to the Sunrise Club in New York, and knew Bea Schumm. It was George Schumm who suggested her to Father to work in his bookshop a few years before I was born. One of Mother's sisters was Dr. Bertha Johnson. Fred Schulder, who worked as a salesman for *Liberty*, was Aunty Bertha's boyfriend. His son with Adeline Champney, Horace Champney, was the Quaker who sailed a boat to Vietnam a few years ago to protest against the war.

When Father's mother died, she left him a nice sum of money. He put it in an annuity and had a comfortable income thereafter of $1,650 a year. In New York he lived pleasantly, though not lavishly, in a two-room hotel suite. Another reason he decided to go to France was that he and the family could live rather well there on his income. My parents, incidentally, were never legally married. Yet they were the most monogamistic couple I ever saw, absolutely devoted to each other until the end. Oddly enough, they believed in having separate rooms and, if one had the means, even separate houses, coming together when you wanted to. They couldn't afford that though! I always liked the idea of my husband coming home at night and not having to plan and make a date to see him!

We lived in Le Vésinet the first six years, traveling a good deal. The winter following the outbreak of the war we stayed with Henry Bool in England,[27] and when we returned to France we moved to an apartment in Nice. We stayed there eleven years. But taxes were rising sharply in France, so we moved to Monaco, where we rented a nice house for thirteen years, and where Father died in 1939.

During the war, Father was anti-German from the start. The German government, German militarism, German regimentation—he hated them with a passion. And he loved France. France was the only thing that counted—French food, French wine, French newspapers and books. He wanted to be buried there. He never came back to the United States, and never wished to. He didn't speak French very well, but he read it easily. He had a great admiration for Clemenceau, to whom he bore a close physical resemblance.

After the war, Father was afraid of trouble. He was afraid, as a foreigner, of being disturbed. He wanted to be left alone. There was no contact with Emma Goldman or Alexander Berkman, who were living in southern France. Father disliked both of them. Mother had been friends with Emma Goldman in New York, and once she saw them on the street in Nice but decided not to approach them. John Henry Mackay[28] used to come down, and George Bernard Shaw came once for afternoon tea. When I was eighteen I gave French lessons to Henry

Cohen's sister. Pryns Hopkins,[29] who was living in Nice, came over to visit, and some nephew of Tolstoy's, but otherwise not many of Father's old friends.

In France the whole family lived an anarchistic life. When I asked a question—like how in the world would we get along without police—Father would say look it up on page so and so of *Instead of a Book*.[30] Mother, by contrast, would explain carefully. She was a born teacher and psychologist. But Father was a born nonteacher. He couldn't speak to a young person. Mother always gave me sensible answers. He had it all worked out—it was very discouraging to talk with him—he always had irrefutable arguments, he always seemed right. And that turned me off. He made no allowance for human feelings and frailties. Just hew to the line and let the chips fall where they may. Mother, too, said he had no psychological understanding of people. He had great affection and respect for me, but we couldn't discuss anything.[31]

Father, incidentally, believed in contracts. We had written contractual arrangements around the house. When I was eighteen, he wrote a whole contract about my paying a share of what I made from giving piano lessons. That might seem cold and calculating, yet it made everything clear and simple. He never would have entered my room without knocking, even when I was a little girl. He was old-fashioned in many ways. He rode in a car two or three times in Paris. But he was scared stiff of them. He thought they were dangerous. As a result, I disliked them too and didn't go in them for a long time.

Sometime during the 1920s Victor Yarros wrote an article on anarchism, virtually repudiating his whole connection with it, his whole past. This made Father furious. He wrote to him, and there was a bitter controversy. Around that same time, the Sacco-Vanzetti affair took place. That was the first blow to my good feeling about America. Father wrote a letter to an American paper blasting the travesty of justice that had taken place. The Spanish Civil War came during the last years of his life. He was certainly against Franco, but he didn't seem to get excited about it. He worried a great deal about the approaching world war, though. He thought we should escape to Denmark, where it was safe! We were scared stiff by Munich. Things got worse and worse. We didn't know what to do—to uproot him and come to America and go to live at Aunty Bertha's? It was really a blessing that he died when he did, you know. The very next day we packed up his books and papers. We came to New York on October 5, 1939. Mother went to Aunty Bertha's farm, and I stayed with George Macdonald,[32] a miserable isolationist to the nth degree! In 1940 we took an apartment on Amsterdam Avenue. Mother died there in 1948. I had married meanwhile.

Mother died when my first daughter was six or eight months old. We came up here in 1948. My older daughter Marianne has a brain like her grandfather, yet with such sympathy and understanding for everyone. Now she is twenty-five and getting an M.A. in social work in Baltimore. Her sister, twenty-three, is studying dance in Toronto.

Father's attitude towards communism never changed one whit, nor about religion. He was very consistent all his life. In his last months he called in the French housekeeper. "I want her," he said, "to be witness that on my death bed I'm not recanting. I do *not* believe in God!" I was interested, even sympathetic, in his ideas. But I was never really an anarchist. I don't think it would ever work. Neither did Father at the end. He was very pessimistic about the world and in his political outlook. But he was always optimistic about himself, always cheerful, happy; he never sat and brooded, but was content to look out at the view and at his books. He sang hymns from Sunday School—the *Rock of Ages* and that sort of thing—and couldn't keep a tune. He had a reputation as a cold person. But how he loved Mother! And he cried easily at anything noble.

CHAPTER ELEVEN

C. W. Mowbray: A British Anarchist in America

IT HAS ALREADY been noted that immigrants and visitors played a key role in shaping American anarchism. Among the Russians, as we have seen, Bakunin escaped to the United States in 1861, Kropotkin came to lecture in 1897 and 1901, and Emma Goldman and Alexander Berkman, arriving in the 1880s, remained until their deportation in 1919. The names of émigrés from other countries are hardly less familiar. From Germany came Johann Most and Rudolf Rocker, Otto Rinke and Josef Peukert, Robert Reitzel and Max Baginski, to say nothing of the Haymarket martyrs, Louis Lingg, August Spies, George Engel, and Adolph Fischer. From Italy came Luigi Galleani and Errico Malatesta, Pietro Gori and Saverio Merlino, Carlo Tresca and Armando Borghi, Nicola Sacco and Bartolomeo Vanzetti. From France came Joseph Déjacque and Anselme Bellegarrigue, Elisée and Elie Reclus, Clément Duval and Jules Scarceriaux. From Japan came Denjiro Kotoku, from India Har Dayal and M.P.T. Acharya, from Austria Rudolph Grossmann ("Pierre Ramus"), from Spain Pedro Esteve, from Mexico Ricardo and Enrique Flores Magón, from Rumania Joseph Ishill and Marcus Graham.

What then of Great Britain? The numbers here too are impressive. They include revolutionaries and pacifists, communists and syndicalists, individualists and mutualists, and some who moved from one school to another. But because their names are not so well known, little has been said of them as a group. Unlike other immigrants, moreover, they faced no language barrier and, mingling easily with native American anarchists, were less conspicuous as a national category. It is only when we enumerate them that their importance becomes apparent. Among the Chicago anarchists of the 1880s we find not only Samuel Fielden, son of a Chartist and formerly a Methodist preacher in Lancashire, but also William Holmes, secretary of the American Group, whose companion Lizzie M. Holmes was assistant editor of *The Alarm* under Albert Parsons, and Dr. James D. Taylor, who practiced medicine in the United States for half a century ("Chronic Disease and Its Cure by the Vacuum Method," ran his advertisement in *The Alarm*). In addition, General Matthew M. Trumbull, the Chicago attorney who defended the Haymarket anarchists in two widely distributed pamphlets, had been a Chartist before emigrating to America.

More than a few of the British expatriates had served their radical apprenticeship in William Morris's Socialist League. For example, Thomas H. Bell of Los Angeles had been a member of the Edinburgh branch, and William Bailie, a Belfast-born associate of Benjamin Tucker and biographer of Josiah Warren, had been active in the Manchester branch, arranging lectures by Morris and Kropotkin and other celebrated speakers. The German anarchist Max Metzkow, who figured (with Alexander Berkman) in the Homestead strike of 1892, had been a member of the London branch; and William Holmes contributed a "Chicago Letter" to the league's weekly organ, *The Commonweal*. During the early 1890s, it might be added, John C. Kenworthy (afterwards a prominent English Tolstoyan) started a Socialist League in New York with his compatriot William C. Owen and with the American architect John H. Edelmann, editor of *Solidarity*, with whom Kropotkin stayed during his 1897 visit. (After Edelmann's premature death in 1900, his companion, Rachelle Krimont, went to England to live at the Whiteway colony where she raised their two children.)

British-born anarchists were conspicuous among the contributors to Benjamin Tucker's *Liberty*. Apart from William Bailie, there were James L. Walker, the foremost Stirnerite in the United States (born in Manchester in 1845); Henry Bool, the Ithaca, New York, furniture dealer who helped finance Tucker's publishing ventures; the feminist poets Miriam Daniell and Helena Born, who had been socialists in Bristol before emigrating to America; the poet William A. Whittick; William Hanson, a Yorkshire-born watchmaker in Philadelphia; Alfred B. Westrup, a leading monetary reformer; and Archibald H. Simpson, a member of Tucker's circle in Boston after serving his anarchist apprenticeship in Chicago. (Simpson, Westrup, and Bool, and also W. C. Owen, eventually returned to England, where they spent their declining years.)

Britons were equally numerous among the social revolutionaries who followed Most, Bakunin, and Kropotkin. Suffice it to mention the Yorkshire shoemaker George Brown, a comrade of Voltairine de Cleyre's in Philadelphia; William MacQueen, an agitator in the Paterson strike of 1902, who had published *The Free Commune* in Manchester and Leeds at the end of the 1890s; the Dublin-born physician John Creaghe, who worked with W. C. Owen in the Flores Magón movement in California; and C. W. Mowbray, whose career will be traced in this chapter.

Though they settled mostly in the northeastern states, British-born anarchists were scattered across the country, living in Los Angeles and Chicago as well as in New York, Philadelphia, and Boston. They came from Ulster and Wales, Scotland and Yorkshire, Liverpool and London, to say nothing of the Continental exiles (Russians, Jews, Germans, Italians, Spaniards) for whom Britain was a way station to America. In addition to Dr. Creaghe, moreover, there were scores of Irish among them, such as Con Lynch and T. P. Quinn, Dr. Gertrude B. Kelly and her brother John F. Kelly (who broke with Tucker's *Liberty* and wrote for *The Alarm*), Eugene O'Neill's friend Terry Carlin, the militant socialist Patrick Quinlan, and the militant syndicalists Jay Fox, William Z. Foster (the future Communist leader), and Joseph O'Carroll, not to mention David Sullivan of the New York Ferrer Center, who proved to be a double agent.[1]

During the twentieth century a number of Britons took part in the anarchist schools and colonies at Stelton, New Jersey, and Lake Mohegan, New York: James and Nellie Dick, Fred Dunn (editor of *The Voice of Labour* in London during the First World War), Harry Clements (whose companion, Sonia, was the daughter of John and Rachelle Edelmann), William Stevens, Watkin Bannister, and William Bridge (grandfather of Joan Baez, the singer and social activist, whose mother and aunt attended the Stelton school). It might be noted that Harry Kelly, a founder of both the Stelton and Mohegan colonies, had a Cornish father (not Irish, as his name might suggest); and Leonard Abbott, another key figure in the Modern School movement, though of American parentage, was born and raised in England (he attended the Uppingham school) and nourished himself on Kropotkin, William Morris, and Edward Carpenter.

Some additional names may be mentioned to round out the picture. Charlotte Wilson, a founder of the London *Freedom* in 1886, spent her last years in the United States, although aloof from the anarchist movement.[2] John Turner of the Freedom Group made two extended lecture tours of the States, in 1896 and in 1903-1904, when he became the first person to be deported under the anti-anarchist law enacted after the assassination of President McKinley. The father of C. L. James, a prolific anarchist writer in Wisconsin, was the well-known English novelist and historian G.P.R. James. A. C. Cuddon, Josiah Warren's earliest British disciple, visited the Modern Times colony on Long Island in 1858 (whose members included the British-born Positivist Henry Edger). To these must be added Lizzie Turner Bell and Jessie Bell Westwater (wife and sister of Thomas H. Bell), Alfred Kinghorn-Jones of San Francisco and C. B. Cooper of Los Angeles, Archie Turner and Thomas Wright of the Road to Freedom Group in New York, and E. F. Mylius, deported from Britain on the eve of the First World War, who edited *The Social War* with Hippolyte Havel.

Before the turn of the century, passage to America was cheap and restrictions were minimal, so that more than a few British anarchists were able to visit the States for brief periods, among them Sam Mainwaring, Tom Cantwell, and Alfred Marsh, in addition to those already mentioned. Travel across the ocean was of course a two-way affair, and many American anarchists journeyed to Britain during this period. Lucy Parsons went in 1888, Emma Goldman in 1895 and 1899, Harry Kelly in 1895 and 1898 (working in the *Freedom* office until 1904), Voltairine de Cleyre in 1897 and 1903, Lillian Harman in 1898 (to assume the presidency of the Legitimation League), and Benjamin Tucker in 1889, when he visited William Morris at Hammersmith, dining with Belfort Bax, George Bernard Shaw, May Morris, and her husband H. H. Sparling, secretary of the Socialist League. The result was an interchange of personalities and a cross-fertilization of ideas that gave the anarchist movement a rich transatlantic dimension.

CHARLES WILFRED MOWBRAY arrived in the United States in the summer of 1894. A self-educated tailor from the London slums who had served in the army as a youth, Mowbray was a big, athletic-looking man in his late thirties, with black hair, blazing eyes, and a tempestuous eloquence that had stirred many an audience in Britain, where he had been a friend of William Morris and an active member of the Socialist League since its formation a decade before. On September 20, 1885, he had been roughed up and arrested for "obstructing a public thoroughfare" at Dod Street and Burdett Road, Limehouse, a site long used for open-air meetings until the London police began to interfere. In court the next morning Mowbray, "who had really done the most," as Morris confided to his wife, was set free, though a disturbance broke out in which Morris himself was nearly ordered detained by the presiding magistrate.[3]

This incident marked the beginning of a long free-speech fight, involving unemployment demonstrations and Haymarket protests among other issues. Mowbray, a militant agitator of the Johann Most stamp, was a central figure. On June 14, 1886, he was again arrested at a free-speech rally in Trafalgar Square and fined twenty shillings and costs. Undaunted, he organized a series of well-attended unemployment meetings at Norwich, where he had become secretary of the local Socialist League branch. "Socialism is going like wildfire," he reported to Morris in October 1886.[4]

On January 14, 1887, however, Mowbray and a young associate named Frederick Henderson were arrested following a meeting in the Norwich marketplace where, the authorities alleged, a bank and several shops were damaged by the crowd. Convicted of inciting to riot and "disturbing the public peace," Mowbray was sentenced to nine months and Henderson to four months in prison. But their efforts had not been for nothing. Morris, who followed the trial closely, noted in his diary that "there is a good deal of stir amongst the labourers about there; the place is wretchedly poor." The Socialist League organized a mass meeting in the Norwich marketplace to protest against the sentences, and a committee was appointed "to see after Mowbray's wife and children while he is in."[5]

When Mowbray came out, he resumed his agitation for the Socialist League, taking part in annual Paris Commune and Haymarket commemorations, side by side with Kropotkin, Malatesta, Louise Michel, and Saul Yanovsky, who had come to London from New York to edit *Der Arbeter Fraynd*, the Yiddish anarchist paper in Whitechapel. In November 1888 Mowbray returned to Norwich to chair a Haymarket meeting at which Lucy Parsons, on a lecture tour of the British Isles, spoke on "The Labor Movements in America," followed by the singing of her husband's favorite song, "Annie Laurie," and of William Morris's "No Master."[6]

An irrepressible firebrand, Mowbray had emerged from prison "more extreme than ever." He was convinced of the need to use dynamite and propaganda by the deed to destroy the capitalist system. Following the London dock strike of 1889, he declared that the city's slums should be set ablaze and their inhabitants settled in West End mansions. "I feel confident that a few determined men—and when I say determined, I mean men who are prepared to do or die in the attempt—could paralyse the forces of our masters, providing that they were acquainted with the power which nineteenth-century civilisation has placed within our reach," he wrote in November 1890. The following year, before a Haymarket gathering in London, he declared:

"We have heard much of the doctrine of brotherhood and love tonight, but the doctrine of hate and vengeance is just as necessary and right."[7]

The extremism of Mowbray's pronouncements led some to conclude—without evidence—that he was an *agent provocateur*, or at least a dupe of the police. Five months later, in April 1892, he again got into trouble during the so-called Walsall Affair, in which a group of anarchists were charged with a dynamite conspiracy directed against the tsar of Russia. When *The Commonweal*, the organ of the Socialist League and a paper with which Mowbray had been associated, published an article entitled "Are These Men Fit to Live?"[8]—referring to the Home Secretary and police officials who had conducted the investigation and the judge who had sentenced the four defendants to ten years in prison even though the instigator of the plot had been a police spy—Mowbray was arrested and charged with inciting to murder. On April 19, while Mowbray was in custody, his wife, the daughter of a French Communard, died of consumption at the age of thirty-five. Morris put up £500 bail so that Mowbray could attend the funeral, which served as the occasion for an anarchist demonstration in which Louise Michel and Malatesta took part. Soon afterwards, Mowbray was tried and acquitted, though David J. Nicoll, an associate on *The Commonweal*, received an eighteen-month term of penal servitude.

On November 11, 1892, Mowbray was again addressing a Haymarket anniversary meeting in London with Kropotkin, Malatesta, Yanovsky, and Louise Michel. The following summer he was excluded from the Zurich Congress of the Second International, along with Gustav Landauer and other anarchist delegates, who proceeded to hold a "counter-congress" of their own.[9] A year later, the Socialist League having disbanded and *The Commonweal* having ceased publication, Mowbray landed in America on a speaking tour.

During the summer and fall of 1894, Mowbray lectured in New York, Paterson, and other eastern cities with large immigrant and working-class populations. In the spirit of Bakunin and Most, he called for revolutionary action by all the disinherited elements of society, dismissing trade unionism of the "old sick benefit sort" as a failure. "We must denounce the brutal indifference of the employed to the sufferings of the unemployed—the criminals, the tramps, the casual laborers, the victims, in short, of the brutal system of class monopoly we are all suffering under," he declared. In Paterson, according to a French-language anarchist paper, Mowbray's audience was held in thrall for an hour and a half by "the charm of his passionate and sincere voice, piling argument upon argument." Mowbray, said an English associate, was "one of the greatest working-class orators who ever spoke in public."[10]

On November 11, 1894, the seventh anniversary of the Haymarket executions, Mowbray addressed memorial meetings at the Thalia Theatre and Clarendon Hall in New York, followed by similar meetings in Hoboken, Paterson, and Newark. He then spoke in Pittsburgh and Baltimore, before coming to Philadelphia in late December to address the Freiheit and Freie Wacht groups and the Ladies' Liberal League. So far, his tour had been "successful beyond my wildest hopes," he wrote. But on December 28 he received a setback. For when "the jolly comrade with the great head and greater heart," as Voltairine de Cleyre describes him, finished his lecture to the Ladies' Liberal League and was taking down names of persons who wished to form an anarchist group, he was arrested by detectives and charged with inciting to riot and sedition against the Commonwealth of Pennsylvania.[11]

De Cleyre, who had welcomed Mowbray on behalf of the Ladies' Liberal League, immediately organized a defense committee. Thanks to her efforts, Mowbray was quickly released and was able to proceed to Boston, where, in early 1895, he settled down to practice his trade. Though an admirer of Johann Most, Mowbray was also on friendly terms with Most's arch-rival in the German anarchist movement, Josef Peukert, whom he had met at Peukert's Autonomie Club in London. Peukert was now living in Chicago, and with his help Mowbray brought his family over from England in April 1895.[12]

It was not long before Mowbray resumed his agitational work, addressing German, Bohemian, and American groups throughout the Northeast. In the summer of 1895 he embarked on a speaking tour that took him as far west as St. Louis and Chicago. The Chicago police, however, with memories of Haymarket still fresh, decided there would be no "anarchy nonsense" preached in their city. Accordingly, they interrupted a speech in which Mowbray favored "battling on Bunker Hill under the red flag, not the Stars and Stripes, but the glorious red flag of triumph." A riot nearly occurred, and only the bandmaster prevented disaster by striking up the "Marseillaise," which was "taken up by every man on the grounds until there was one great chorus."[13]

Mowbray, thereafter, concentrated his propaganda on the East Coast, and primarily in Boston. Among his ablest converts there was a twenty-four-year-old printer from Missouri named Harry Kelly, who, with Joseph Cohen and Leonard Abbott, was to become a key figure in the Modern School movement and a founder of the Stelton and Mohegan colonies, which flourished in New Jersey and New York between the world wars. Kelly found Mowbray "a magnetic speaker" who was performing an "invaluable service" as an interpreter of anarchist theory to the working classes. To Emma Goldman, by contrast, Mowbray's lectures, for all their fiery rhetoric, were devoid of intellectual substance.[14]

Be that as it may, Kelly was presently the secretary of an anarchist-communist group in Boston, created largely through Mowbray's efforts. Kelly and Mowbray, in addition, served as secretaries of the Union Cooperative Society of Printers and the Union Cooperative Society of Journeymen Tailors, both of which became affiliated with the Central Labor Union of Boston and imbued it with an anarchist flavor. In the spring of 1895, at Mowbray's urging, Kelly traveled to London with a letter of introduction to John Turner, an active member of the Freedom Group and general secretary of the Shop Assistants' Union, which he had organized a few years earlier. Kelly remained in England more than three months, meeting Kropotkin, Malatesta, and other well-known figures and becoming the chief link between the anarchist-communist movements in Britain and the United States.

When Kelly returned to Boston, he was eager to start a journal to advance the ideas of the anarchist-communist school, a kind of American version of the London *Freedom*, founded in 1886 by Kropotkin, Charlotte Wilson, and their associates. For this purpose, seventy dollars was raised by holding a raffle in which the prize was a tailor-made suit. Kelly and Mowbray peddled the tickets among the Boston unions, in which they were now familiar figures, and bought material for the suit out of the funds collected. James Robb, another anarchist tailor, contributed the skills of his craft by sewing the prize suit.

Out of these efforts came *The Rebel* ("A Monthly Journal Devoted to the Exposition of Anarchist Communism"), launched on September 20, 1895. Edited and printed by Mowbray, Kelly, and Robb, together with Henry A. Koch, a Boston hatter, and N. H. Berman, a Russian-Jewish printer, it featured articles by Kropotkin and Louise Michel as well as by American anarchists who adhered to their economic theories. Voltairine de Cleyre, though not an advocate of communal property, became a major contributor, with essays on the Chicago martyrs, the Ladies' Liberal League, and a streetcar strike in Philadelphia.

Mowbray, at the same time, continued his lectures in Boston and other eastern cities. In 1896 he and Most were listed as speakers at a twenty-fifth anniversary celebration of the Paris Commune, and with Kelly he published a journal called *The Match*, which "sputtered for two numbers and went out."[15] A few years later, however, he moved to New York, and from there to Hoboken, where he opened a saloon and himself became a heavy drinker. Like John Turner, he was deported after the shooting of President McKinley. Back in London, he joined the Industrial Union of Direct Actionists, a federation of anarchist groups, and was again addressing meetings alongside Malatesta and Kropotkin, as he had done so often in the past. But before long he abandoned anarchism to become a tariff reform lecturer. He died of heart failure in December 1910 at Bridlington, Yorkshire, in a hotel where he was staying.[16]

CHAPTER TWELVE

Sacco and Vanzetti: The Italian Anarchist Background

NEARLY SEVENTY YEARS have passed since the arrest of Nicola Sacco and Bartolomeo Vanzetti, which sparked one of the most controversial episodes in American history. On April 15, 1920, a paymaster and his guard were shot to death during the robbery of a shoe factory in South Braintree, Massachusetts. Three weeks later, Sacco, a shoe worker, and Vanzetti, a fish peddler, both Italian immigrants and anarchists, were charged with participating in the crime. The following year they were brought to trial.

The trial, occurring in the wake of the Red Scare, took place in an atmosphere of intense hostility towards the defendants. The district attorney, Frederick G. Katzmann, conducted a highly unscrupulous prosecution, coaching and badgering witnesses, withholding exculpatory evidence from the defense, and perhaps even tampering with physical evidence. A skillful and ruthless cross-examiner, he played on the emotions of the jurors, arousing their deepest prejudices against the accused. Sacco and Vanzetti were armed; they were foreigners, atheists, anarchists. This overclouded all judgment. The judge in the case, Webster Thayer, likewise revealed his bias. Outside the courtroom, during the trial and the appeals that followed, he made remarks that bristled with animosity towards the defendants ("Did you see what I did with those anarchistic bastards the other day? I guess that will hold them for a while.")[1] When a verdict of guilty was returned, many believed that the men had been convicted because of their foreign birth and radical beliefs, not on solid evidence of criminal guilt.

In the aftermath of the trial, as legal appeals delayed sentencing, a mounting body of evidence indicated that the wrong men had been apprehended. Key prosecution testimony was retracted and new evidence was produced that was favorable to the defendants. Herbert Ehrmann, a junior defense attorney, built a strong case against the Morelli gang of Providence, which specialized in stealing shipments from shoe manufacturers.[2]

But the attitude of the authorities had become so rigidly set against the defendants that they turned a deaf ear to contrary views. Because of this, a growing number of observers, most of whom abhorred anarchism and had no sympathy with radical propaganda of any kind, concluded that the accused had not received a fair trial. The judge's bias against the defendants, their conviction on inconclusive evidence, their dignified behavior while their lives hung in the balance—all this attracted supporters, who labored to secure a new trial. At the eleventh hour, Governor Alvan T. Fuller conducted a review of the case, appointing an advisory committee, headed by President A. Lawrence Lowell of Harvard, to assist him. The Lowell Committee, as it became known, though finding Judge Thayer guilty of a "grave breach of official decorum" in his derogatory references to the defendants,[3] nevertheless concluded that justice had been done.

As events moved towards a climax, the case assumed international proportions, engaging the passions of men and women around the globe. Anatole France, in one of his last public utterances, pleaded with America to save Sacco and Vanzetti: "Save them for your honor, for the honor of your children and for the generations yet unborn."[4] In vain. On August 23, 1927, the men were electrocuted, in defiance of worldwide protests and appeals. By then, millions were convinced of their innocence, and millions more were convinced that, guilty or innocent, they had not received impartial justice.

With the passage of sixty years, one might have thought that everything that was likely to be known about the Sacco-Vanzetti affair had already been disclosed, every speculation laid to rest, every clue pursued to its inevitable dead end. Yet such a belief would be unwarranted. For, in spite of the unceasing flow of books about the case, it remains, as A. William Salomone has noted, a "great dark forest," large areas still unknown and unexplored.[5] A deeper knowledge of the anarchist dimension, for example, of the social, political, and intellectual world in which the defendants lived and acted, would go far to explain their behavior on the night of their arrest, as well as the determination of the authorities to convict them.

Anarchism, indeed, was Sacco and Vanzetti's strongest passion, the guiding beacon of their lives, the focus of their daily interests and activities. To ignore it, as many writers have done, is to forfeit any apprehension of their motives and aspirations, so crucial to understanding the case. "Both Nick and I are anarchists," Vanzetti declared, "the radical of the radical—the black cats, the terrors of many, of all the bigots, exploitaters [sic], charlatans, fakers and oppressors." "I am," he asserted, "and will be until the last instant (unless I should discover that I am in error) an anarchist-communist, because I believe that communism is the most humane form of social contract, because I know that only with liberty can man rise, become noble, and complete."[6]

Further statements of this kind, by Sacco as well as by Vanzetti, could be cited. What was the nature of the movement to which these men were so unswervingly devoted? Who were the Italian anarchists? Where did they come from? What did they want, and what did they achieve?

The first Italian anarchist groups in the United States sprang up during the 1880s, rooted in the large-scale immigration of the period. Most of the immigrants were of peasant and artisan stock, the anarchists not excepted. Their initial group, formed in 1885 in New York City, which became an active center of Italian anarchism in America, was called the Gruppo Anarchico Rivoluzionario Carlo Cafiero, Cafiero being one of the most famous anarchists in Italy during the late nineteenth century, an "idealist of the highest and purest type," in Kropotkin's description.[7] Another group of the same name was founded two years later in Chicago, the focus of Italian anarchism in the Midwest. The first newspaper published by the Italian anarchists in the United States appeared in 1888. Entitled *L'Anarchico* (The Anarchist), it was issued by the Cafiero group in New York.

From New York the movement spread rapidly as the immigrants increased in number. At first, it was concentrated in the large port cities on the eastern seaboard, where the newcomers tended to settle. By the early 1890s, accordingly, we find Italian anarchist groups in such places as Boston and Philadelphia in addition to New York. From the east, the movement gradually filtered westward, with circles appearing in Pittsburgh, Cleveland, and Detroit, as well as in Chicago. Finally by the mid-1890s, groups were established on the Pacific Coast, the first, in San Francisco, being founded in 1894.

Among the factors that spurred the formation of these groups was the Haymarket affair of 1886-1887. It is often said that the explosion in Chicago, which caused the death and injury of several policemen and led to the hanging of four anarchists and the suicide of a fifth in his cell, precipitated the downfall of the anarchist movement in the

United States. Yet precisely the opposite was the case. The Haymarket executions stimulated the growth of anarchism, among both immigrants and native-born Americans, and there was a swift rise in the number of Italian anarchist groups after 1887.

Another important stimulus was the arrival from Italy of a series of distinguished anarchist writers and speakers. Beginning in the 1890s, virtually every famous Italian anarchist visited the New World. Some stayed only three or four weeks, some several years, and a few, like Luigi Galleani and Carlo Tresca, remained for longer periods. The first major figure to arrive was Francesco Saverio Merlino, perhaps the most scholarly of the Italian anarchists, who landed in New York in 1892 at an early phase of the movement. Having lived in London for several years, Merlino, unlike other Italian anarchist leaders and many of the rank and file, was fluent in English. As a result, he was able to found not only one of the earliest Italian anarchist journals in this country, *Il Grido degli Oppressi*, but also the English-language *Solidarity*, directed towards native Americans as well as Italians who had acquired the language of their adopted land. Apart from launching these papers, Merlino conducted a speaking tour through the United States, remaining for some months in Chicago. His propaganda, both written and oral, gave anarchism a strong impetus, and it was unfortunate for the movement that he returned to Europe in 1893.[8]

But Merlino was only the first of a series of eloquent spokesmen. The second, Pietro Gori, who arrived in New York in 1895, had an even greater impact on the movement. Gori spent a year in the United States. Like Merlino, he was trained in the law, as Galleani was also. (The rank and file, as has been noted, were virtually all working people.) These leaders, coming from middle-class and upper-middle-class families, were akin to the Russian populists, those conscience-stricken noblemen, Bakunin and Kropotkin among them, who acknowledged a debt to the people and taught them the gospel of revolt. Gori, like them, came from a prosperous household; a university graduate, a lawyer by profession, he too cast his lot with the poor. A magnetic speaker, he was also a playwright and poet, whose works were read and performed at radical gatherings in America and Europe.

During his stay in the United States, Gori held between two hundred and four hundred meetings—estimates vary—in the space of a single year.[9] Accompanying himself on the guitar, he would begin to sing and thereby attract a crowd, who would stay to hear him lecture on anarchism. In this way he won many converts and started a number of anarchist groups. Gori resembled a Christian evangelist, wandering from town to town between Boston and San Francisco, preaching the gospel of anarchism, which for some fulfilled the needs of a religion. Tragically for the movement, he fell ill after his return to Europe and died in 1911, at the age of forty-five, depriving anarchism of one of its most beloved apostles.

After Merlino and Gori came Giuseppe Ciancabilla, one of the most articulate, if least well known, of the Italian anarchist visitors. Ciancabilla, who had been born in Rome (Gori hailed from Messina, Merlino from Naples, Galleani from the Piedmont, Tresca from the Abruzzi), arrived in America in 1898 and settled in Paterson, New Jersey, a major stronghold of Italian anarchism in the East. He soon became the editor of *La Questione Sociale*, a paper which Gori had helped to establish in 1895 and which was already the leading organ of Italian anarchism in the United States. Ciancabilla eventually drifted west, settling among the miners of Spring Valley, Illinois. After the assassination of President McKinley in 1901, when anarchist groups became the targets of police repression, Ciancabilla was expelled from Spring Valley, and then from Chicago. Driven from pillar to post, arrested, manhandled, evicted, he ended up in San Francisco, where Gori had lectured in 1895. He was editing a journal there called *La Protesta Umana* when he suddenly took ill and died in 1904, at the early age of thirty-two, one of the most capable of the Italian anarchists in America.[10]

We come now to Errico Malatesta, who, although the most celebrated of all the Italian anarchist leaders—the word "leaders" must be placed in quotes, as the anarchists at most recognized only mentors or guides—may be dealt with briefly, since his stay in America lasted only a few months. Disembarking in 1899, he took up the editorship of *La Questione Sociale*. He also addressed numerous meetings, in Spanish as well as in Italian, throughout the East. During one of his lectures, in West Hoboken, New Jersey, the representative of a rival faction, or an individual with some private grudge—the motives of this man, Domenico Pazzaglia, remain unclear—drew a pistol and fired at Malatesta, wounding him in the leg. Malatesta, though seriously injured, refused to press charges against his assailant. (Interestingly, the man who subdued Pazzaglia was none other than Gaetano Bresci, the anarchist from Paterson who went to Italy in 1900 and assassinated King Umberto at Monza.) On leaving America, Malatesta stopped briefly in Cuba before proceeding to London. A few years later he returned to his native country where, until the advent of Mussolini, he carried on his anarchist activities. He died, while under house arrest in Rome, in 1932.[11]

WE MUST LINGER somewhat longer over Luigi Galleani, who, during the first two decades of the twentieth century, was the leading Italian anarchist in America. One of the greatest radical orators of his time, Galleani inspired a far-flung movement that included Sacco and Vanzetti among its adherents. He also edited the foremost Italian-American periodical, *Cronaca Sovversiva*, which ran for fifteen years before its suppression by the American government.

Yet Galleani has fallen into oblivion. Today he is virtually unknown in the United States outside a small circle of scholars and a number of personal associates and disciples, whose ranks are rapidly dwindling. No biography in English has been devoted to him, nor is he so much as mentioned in most general histories of anarchism or in the comprehensive survey of American anarchism by William Reichert.[12] His writings, moreover, remained untranslated until the appearance in 1982 of *The End of Anarchism?*, which, distilling the essence of his faith, fills a conspicuous gap in the literature of anarchism available to English readers and restores a major figure in the movement to his proper historical place.[13]

Galleani was born on August 12, 1861, in the Piedmont town of Vercelli, not far from the city of Turin. The son of middle-class parents, he was drawn to anarchism in his late teens and, while studying law at the University of Turin, became an outspoken militant whose hatred of capitalism and government would burn with undiminished intensity for the rest of his life. Galleani refused to practice law, which he had come to regard with contempt, transferring his talents and energies to radical propaganda. Under threat of prosecution, he took refuge in France, but was soon expelled for taking part in a May Day demonstration. Moving to Switzerland, he visited the exiled French anarchist Elisée Reclus, whom he assisted in the preparation of his *Nouvelle géographie universelle*, by compiling statistics on Central America. He also assisted students at the University of Geneva in arranging a celebration in honor of the Haymarket martyrs, for which he was expelled as a dangerous agitator. He returned to Italy and continued his agitation, which got him into trouble with the police. Arrested on charges of conspiracy, he spent more than five years in prison and exile before escaping from the island of Pantelleria, off the coast of Sicily, in 1900.[14]

Galleani, now in his fortieth year, began an odyssey that landed him in North America. Aided by Reclus and other comrades, he first made his way to Egypt, where he lived for the better part of a year among a colony of Italian expatriates. Threatened with extradition, he moved to London, from which he soon embarked for the United States, arriv-

ing in October 1901, barely a month after the assassination of Mc-
Kinley. Settling in Paterson, Galleani assumed the editorship of *La
Questione Sociale*, then the leading Italian anarchist periodical in
America. Scarcely had he installed himself in this position when, in
June 1902, a strike erupted among the Paterson silk workers. Galleani,
braving the antiradical hysteria which followed the shooting of Mc-
Kinley, threw all his energies into their cause. In eloquent and fiery
speeches he called on the workers to launch a general strike and free
themselves from capitalist oppression. Paul Ghio, a visitor from
France, was present at one such oration. "I have never heard an orator
more powerful than Luigi Galleani," he afterwards wrote. "He has a
marvelous facility with words, accompanied by the faculty—rare
among popular tribunes—of precision and clarity of ideas. His voice is
full of warmth, his glance alive and penetrating, his gestures of excep-
tional vigor and flawless distinction."[15]

In the midst of the strike, during a clash between the workers and
the police, shots were fired and Galleani was wounded in the face. Indicted for inciting to riot, he managed to escape to Canada. A short
time after, having recovered from his wounds, he secretly recrossed the
border and took refuge in Barre, Vermont, living under an assumed
name among his anarchist comrades, who regarded him with intense
devotion.

The Barre anarchist group, one of the earliest in New England, had
been established in 1894. Its members were stone and marble cutters
from Carrara, who had virtually transplanted their way of life to the
United States, following the same occupations, customs, and beliefs as
in the old country. It was among these dedicated rebels that Galleani,
on June 6, 1903, launched *Cronaca Sovversiva*, the mouthpiece for his
incendiary doctrines and one of the most important and ably edited periodicals in the history of the anarchist movement. Its influence, reaching far beyond the confines of the United States, could be felt wherever
Italian radicals congregated, from Europe and North Africa to South
America and Australia. In 1906, however, during a polemical exchange with G. M. Seratti, the socialist editor of *Il Proletario* in New
York, the latter revealed Galleani's whereabouts (a charge also leveled
at the English writer H. G. Wells),[16] and Galleani was taken into custody. Extradited to New Jersey, he was tried in Paterson in April 1907
for his role in the 1902 strike. The trial, however, ended in a hung jury
(seven for conviction, five for acquittal), and Galleani was set free.

Galleani returned to Barre and resumed his propaganda activities.
Now in his late forties, he had reached the summit of his intellectual
powers. Over the next few years his fiery oratory and brilliant pen car-

ried him to a position of undisputed leadership within the Italian-American anarchist movement. Galleani had a resonant, lilting voice with a tremolo that captivated his audience. He spoke easily, powerfully, spontaneously, and his bearing was of a kind that made his followers, Sacco and Vanzetti among them, revere him as a kind of patriarch of the movement, to which he won more converts than any other single individual. Galleani was also a prolific writer, pouring forth hundreds of articles, essays, and pamphlets that reached tens, perhaps hundreds, of thousands of readers on several continents. Yet he never produced a full-length book: the volumes appearing over his signature, such as *Faccia a faccia col nemico*, *Aneliti e singulti*, and *Figure e figuri*, are collections of pieces previously published in *Cronaca Sovversiva*. In this respect he resembles Most, Malatesta, and Tucker (author of *Instead of a Book: By a Man Too Busy to Write One*), rather than Godwin, Proudhon, or Kropotkin.

The End of Anarchism?, Galleani's most fully realized work, itself began as a series of articles. In June 1907, shortly after Galleani's acquittal at Paterson, the Turin daily *La Stampa* published an interview with Saverio Merlino, who had meanwhile recanted his anarchism and joined the socialist movement. Merlino, whose interview was titled "The End of Anarchism," pronounced anarchism an obsolete doctrine, torn by internal disputes, bereft of first-rate theorists, and doomed to early extinction. Galleani was incensed. "The end of anarchism?" he asked in *Cronaca Sovversiva*, adding a question mark to the title of Merlino's interview. Just the opposite was true. In an age of growing political and economic centralization, anarchism was more relevant than ever. Far from being moribund, "it lives, it develops, it goes forward"[17]

Such was Galleani's reply to Merlino, elaborated in a series of articles in *Cronaca Sovversiva* between August 1907 and January 1908. Combining the spirit of Stirnerite insurgency with Kropotkin's principle of mutual aid, Galleani put forward a vigorous defense of communist anarchism against socialism and reform, extolling the virtues of spontaneity and variety, of autonomy and independence, of self-determination and direct action, in a world of increasing standardization and uniformity. A revolutionary zealot, he preached a militant form of anarchism that advocated the overthrow of capitalism and government by violent means, dynamite and assassination not excluded. He would brook no compromise with the elimination of economic and political oppression. Nothing less than a clean sweep of the bourgeois order would satisfy his thirst for the millennium.

Galleani produced ten articles in response to Merlino. He intended to write still more, but day-to-day work for the movement—editing *Cronaca Sovversiva*, organizing meetings, issuing pamphlets, embarking on coast-to-coast lecture tours—prevented him from doing so. In 1912 he moved *Cronaca Sovversiva* from Barre to Lynn, Massachusetts, where he had won a devoted following. When the First World War broke out in 1914, he opposed it, in contrast to Kropotkin, with all the strength and eloquence at his command, denouncing it in *Cronaca Sovversiva* with an oft-repeated slogan, "Contro la guerra, contro la pace, per la rivoluzione sociale!" (Against the war, against the peace, for the social revolution!) With America's entry into the conflict in April 1917, Galleani became the object of persecution. His paper was shut down and he himself was arrested on charges of obstructing the war effort. On June 24, 1919, he was deported to his native Italy, leaving behind his wife and five children.

Back in Turin, Galleani resumed publication of *Cronaca Sovversiva*. As in America, however, it was suppressed by the authorities. On Mussolini's accession to power in 1922, Galleani was arrested, tried, and convicted on charges of sedition, and sentenced to fourteen months in prison. Upon his release, he returned to his old polemic against Merlino, completing it in a series of articles in *L'Adunata dei Refrattari*, the journal of his disciples in America, who issued the entire work, old articles and new, as a booklet in 1925. Malatesta, whose conception of anarchism diverged sharply from that of Galleani, hailed it as a "clear, serene, eloquent" recital of the communist-anarchist creed.[18] But its publication did not endear Galleani to the Mussolini government. Arrested again in November 1926, Galleani was locked up in the same cell in which he had spent three months in 1892 and found it "as dirty and ugly" as before.[19] Soon afterwards, he was banished to the island of Lipari, off the Sicilian coast, from which he was later removed to Messina, and condemned to serve six months in prison, for the crime of insulting Mussolini.

In February 1930, Galleani, in failing health, was allowed to return to the mainland. Retiring to the mountain village of Caprigliola, he remained under the surveillance of the police, who seldom left his door and followed him even on his solitary walks in the surrounding countryside. Returning from his daily walk on November 4, 1931, Galleani collapsed and died. His anarchism, to the end, had burned with an unquenchable flame. Ever hopeful for the future, despite a life of bitter experience, he had remained faithful to the ideal that had inspired him for half a century.

SUCH WAS the figure who, more than any other, breathed life into the Italian anarchist movement in America. His disciples, nearly all of them manual laborers, numbered in the thousands. In New York they included garment and construction workers, in Paterson, workers in the great silk factories. We find them among the quarry workers of Barre, the shoe workers of Lynn, the construction workers of Boston, the cigar workers of Philadelphia and Tampa. They were numerous among the miners of Pennsylvania and Illinois; and in Chicago and Detroit, in San Francisco and Los Angeles, they were represented in a variety of trades, from barber and tailor to bricklayer and machinist.

But by no means all the Italian anarchists were disciples of Galleani. Ideologically, they fell into four categories: anarchist-communist, anarcho-syndicalist, anarchist-individualist, and just plain anarchist, without the hyphen. These categories overlapped; there were no hard-and-fast divisions between them. As followers of Galleani, Sacco and Vanzetti considered themselves anarchist-communists, rejecting not only the state but also the private ownership of property. The anarcho-syndicalists, among whom Carlo Tresca was a powerful influence, placed their faith in the trade-union movement, which was generally shunned by the anarchist-communists, who feared the emergence of a boss, a *padrone*, endowed with special privileges and authority. The third group, the individualist anarchists, were suspicious of both the communal arrangements of the anarchist-communists and the labor organizations of the anarcho-syndicalists, relying instead on the actions of autonomous individuals. Some of the more interesting, not to say exotic, Italian anarchist periodicals were published by individualists, such as *Nihil* and *Cogito, Ergo Sum* ("I think, therefore I am," with emphasis always on the "I"), both appearing in San Francisco early in the century, and *Eresia* in New York some twenty years later. Their chief prophet was the nineteenth-century German philosopher Max Stirner, whose book *The Ego and His Own* served as their testament. The fourth group, which deserves mention if only because it is so often neglected, consisted of anarchists who refused to attach any prefix or suffix to their label, calling themselves "anarchists without adjectives," not communist anarchists or syndicalist anarchists or individualist anarchists; and the figure whom they most admired was Malatesta, who preached an undogmatic brand of anarchism that encompassed a range of elements.

It has been noted that many of the Italian anarchists, and especially those of the Galleani school, tended to shun the trade unions. Because of this, the Italian anarchists did not play a conspicuous role in the organized American labor movement, differing in this respect from their Russian and especially their Jewish counterparts, who (as will be seen in the following chapter) were prominent in the textile unions, above all the International Ladies' Garment Workers' Union and the Amalgamated Clothing Workers of America. Not that the Italian anarchists were entirely absent from these unions, but their role was not a major one because of their suspicion of formal organizations that might harden into hierarchical and authoritarian shape, with their own bureaucrats, bosses, and officials. The Russian anarchists, by contrast, organized a Union of Russian Workers in the United States and Canada which boasted nearly ten thousand members. Avoiding this type of activity, the Italians contented themselves with participation in strikes and demonstrations. I have mentioned the Paterson strike of 1902, to which might be added the Lawrence strike of 1912 and another strike in Paterson in 1913. Sacco and Vanzetti both took part in strikes, Sacco at Hopedale in 1913, Vanzetti at Plymouth in 1916.

In forming groups, publishing newspapers, and agitating for better working conditions, the Italian anarchists were creating a kind of alternative society that differed sharply from the capitalist and statist society that they deplored. They had their own circles, their own beliefs, their own culture; they were building their own world in the midst of a system that they opposed and detested. Rather than await the millennium, they tried to live the anarchist life on a day-to-day basis within the interstices of American capitalism. They formed, in effect, tiny enclaves, little nuclei of freedom, as they saw it, which they hoped would spread and multiply, engulfing the entire country and the world. After ten or twelve hours in the factory or mine, they would come home, eat supper, then go to their anarchist club and begin to churn out their pamphlets and journals on makeshift presses. Aldino Felicani, treasurer of the Sacco-Vanzetti Defense Committee, is an example of such an anarchist; and the literature which he accumulated, extensive as it was, constituted a mere fragment of the output of these self-educated workers, a token of their idealism and dedication. Approximately five hundred anarchist newspapers were published in the United States between 1870 and 1940, in a dozen or more different languages. Of these the number of Italian papers—including the *numeri unici* issued on special occasions—approached a hundred, an astonishing figure considering that they were produced by ordinary workers in their spare time, mainly on Sunday and in the evening. And in addition to the newspapers and journals, of which more were issued by the Italians than by any other immigrant group, a flood of books and pamphlets rolled off the presses, comprising an immense alternative literature, the literature of anarchism.

Beyond their publishing ventures, the Italian anarchists engaged in a variety of social activities. Life was hard for these working-class immigrants, but there were many moments of happiness and laughter. They had their orchestras and theater groups, their picnics and outings, their lectures and concerts. Hardly a week went by that there was not some traditional social activity, but with a radical twist. Leafing through the old newspapers, one encounters a picnic at the restaurant of Mrs. Bresci, widow of the assassin of King Umberto, in Cliffside Park, New Jersey. (The police afterwards drove her out of town, and aided by her husband's former comrades, she eventually moved to California with her two daughters.) Picnics were important occasions, not merely to eat and drink and dance, but also to collect money for the movement. New York and New Jersey anarchists made excursions up the Hudson in rented steamboats, and when they reached Bear Mountain, or some other rural setting, out came the bread and wine, the accordions and mandolins, followed invariably by the collection.

Attending lectures was another popular activity among the Italian anarchists, and especially the lectures of Galleani, whom they prized above all other speakers. The lectures were held in rented halls and in anarchist clubhouses—that of the Gruppo Autonomo of East Boston, for example, or of the Gruppo Diritto all'Esistenza of Paterson, or of the Gruppo Gaetano Bresci of East Harlem, or perhaps of a Circolo di Studi Sociali, dozens of which flourished throughout the country. Open any anarchist newspaper and you will see them listed, with the weekly or monthly contributions of their members, usually only twenty-five or fifty cents. And yet it was these contributions that kept the Sacco-Vanzetti Defense Committee in operation through seven years of struggle in behalf of the accused men.

The Italian anarchists also had their dramatic societies, a particularly interesting aspect of the radical counterculture. Amateur theater groups in small towns and large cities put on hundreds of plays, some of them by Pietro Gori, such as *The First of May*. Another play that was frequently performed was called *The Martyrs of Chicago* and dealt with the Haymarket tragedy. There was a Pietro Gori theatrical society in New York which endured until the 1960s, dissolved only by the death and old age of its members.

Anarchist schools—often named after the Spanish educator Francisco Ferrer, executed in Barcelona in 1909—formed another part of this alternative culture. There were Italian and non-Italian Ferrer Schools in the United States, also called Modern Schools, a name that suggests what they were striving for—an education to suit the modern, scientific age, in contrast to that of the parochial schools, drenched in the spirit of religious dogma and superstition, or of the public schools, in which generals and presidents, conquest and war, were glorified and exalted. The Modern Schools were schools in which the children, educated in an atmosphere of freedom and spontaneity, would learn about working-class movements and revolutions, as well as how to think and live according to their own lights and in harmony with their neighbors. By the time of the First World War, at least two such schools conducted in Italian had been founded, in Paterson and in Philadelphia. Both were Sunday and evening schools, attended by adults and children alike.

And the anarchists also substituted their own commemorative dates and rituals for traditional religious and national holidays. Thus, instead of Christmas or Easter or Thanksgiving, the principal holidays for the anarchists were the anniversary of the Paris Commune on March 18, the day of working-class solidarity on May 1, and the anniversary of the Haymarket executions on November 11. Every year, in every part of the country, hundreds of meetings were held to commemorate these occasions. In a similar vein, one reads of Emma Goldman, on a nationwide speaking tour in 1899, stopping in Spring Valley, Illinois, among the Italian and French miners, who brought her their babies to be baptized—with the names not of religious saints but of rebels and popular heroes—and then remained to hear her speak on the emancipation of women and the "necessity of the unhampered development of the child."[20]

Such, then, was the character of the movement to which Sacco and Vanzetti adhered. They subscribed to its newspapers (their dues are recorded in the columns of *Cronaca Sovversiva*); they attended—religiously, one might almost say—the lectures of Galleani; they distributed the announcements of these lectures and circulated the literature of their movement; they frequented the concerts and picnics and acted in anarchist plays; they took part in demonstrations (Sacco, when arrested, had in his pocket the notice of a protest meeting at which Vanzetti was scheduled to speak) and agitated during strikes. Vanzetti, from his cell at Charlestown, wrote articles for the anarchist press, some of them appearing in *L'Adunata dei Refrattari*, a successor to *Cronaca Sovversiva* that ceased publication in 1971, after fifty years of existence.

Both men, it must also be noted, were social militants who advocated relentless warfare against government and capital. Far from being the innocent dreamers so often depicted by their supporters, they belonged to a branch of the movement that preached insurrectionary violence and armed retaliation, including the use of dynamite and assassination. Such activities, they believed, were replies to the monstrous violence of the state. The greatest bombthrowers and murderers were not the isolated rebels driven to desperation but the military resources of every government—the army, militia, police, firing squad, hangman. Such was the position of Sacco and Vanzetti, as well as of Galleani, who showered praises on every rebellious deed and glorified the perpetrators as heroes and martyrs, sacrificing their lives for the oppressed.

Sacco and Vanzetti, gentle in their daily lives, lofty in their ideals, may themselves have been involved in such activities,[21] though no reliable evidence has yet been offered to confirm this. Their explanations for being armed at the time of their arrest—Sacco worked as a night watchman in his factory, Vanzetti carried money when selling fish— are unconvincing; more likely, they carried guns because they were militants who believed in retaliatory action and who rejected docile submission to the state. At any rate, the image of "a good shoemaker and a poor fish peddler," which came to define the character of the two men, calls for revision.[22]

To the very end, Sacco and Vanzetti remained dedicated anarchists, continuing their work even in prison. Through their articles and letters, through their speeches in court, they were propagating the ideas of their creed. In doing so, they were at one with Malatesta, for whom the conquest of liberty demanded an unrelenting struggle. What mattered, Malatesta had written, was "not whether we accomplish anarchism today, tomorrow, or within ten centuries, but that we walk towards anarchism today, tomorrow, and always."[23]

CHAPTER THIRTEEN

Jewish Anarchism in the United States

WE TURN NOW to one of the largest and most active of the national elements which made up the anarchist movement in the United States. Anarchism, for all its international pretensions, for all its faith in the unity of mankind, has always been divided into national groups. There have been French anarchists and Spanish anarchists, Russian anarchists and Polish anarchists, Japanese anarchists and Chinese anarchists, Brazilian anarchists and Cuban anarchists. By the same token, there have also been Jewish anarchists, united by language and tradition in addition to their political beliefs. Nor should this be surprising. For anarchists, cherishing diversity against standardization and conformity, have always prized the differences among peoples—cultural, linguistic, historical—quite as much as their common bonds.[1]

It was not until the 1880s, following the first wave of mass immigration from tsarist Russia, that Jews began to play a significant role in the American anarchist movement. Before that time, Jewish anarchists were few in numbers and did not constitute a recognizable group. Isidore Stein, for one, was active in the German wing of the movement, becoming secretary of the New Haven Group of the International Working People's Association, founded in 1883. In later years other Jews made their mark in the English-speaking segment of the movement. Of these, Emma Goldman and Alexander Berkman were the most conspicuous, although Victor Yarros and Henry Cohen, both associated with Benjamin Tucker's journal *Liberty*, deserve mention, as do Herman Eich, the "ragpicker poet" of Portland, Oregon, and Sigismund Danielewicz, editor of *The Beacon* in San Diego and San Francisco.

This chapter, however, will confine itself to the Yiddish-speaking branch of the movement, which came into being as a direct consequence of the Haymarket affair of 1886-1887. The trial of the Chicago anarchists, prominently reported in the American press, kindled widespread interest in anarchist personalities and ideas. The unfairness of the proceedings, the savagery of the sentences (seven condemned to death and one to fifteen years in prison), the character and bearing of the defendants fired the imagination of young idealists, Jewish and non-Jewish alike, and won numerous converts to the cause.

The Haymarket trial precipitated the formation of the first Jewish anarchist group in the United States, the Pioneers of Liberty (Pionire der Frayhayt). This took place in New York on October 9, 1886, the day that sentence was pronounced on Albert Parsons, August Spies, and their associates. The founders, no more than a dozen in all, were rank-and-file workers whose names (Faltzblatt, Bernstein, Strashunsky, Yudelevich) remain obscure even to the specialist in Jewish radical history. They were soon joined, however, by a brilliant constellation of writers and speakers—Saul Yanovsky, Roman Lewis, Hillel Solotaroff, Moshe Katz, J. A. Maryson, David Edelstadt—who made the group one of the most remarkable in the history of the anarchist movement. All in their early or middle twenties—Yanovsky and Katz were born in 1864, Solotaroff and Lewis in 1865, Edelstadt and Maryson in 1866—they displayed, apart from unusual literary and oratorical skills, a vigor and dynamic energy that made a powerful impression on the immigrants of the Lower East Side, the predominantly Jewish quarter of New York in which the Pioneers of Liberty were located.[2]

The initial task of the Pioneers of Liberty, who affiliated themselves with the International Working People's Association, of which the Haymarket anarchists were also members, was to join the campaign to save their Chicago comrades from the gallows. To this end, they held meetings, sponsored rallies, and gathered funds for judicial appeals. In addition, they arranged a ball on the Lower East Side at which one hundred dollars was raised and sent to the families of the defendants.[3] At the same time, they began to spread anarchist propaganda among the Jewish immigrants, who were arriving in rapidly growing numbers. At their club on Orchard Street, in the heart of the Lower East Side, the Pioneers held weekly lectures and discussions that attracted an enthusiastic crowd. They also published literature in the Yiddish language, including a pamphlet on the Haymarket case, which culminated (on November 11, 1887) in the hanging of four of the defendants.[4]

Through their oral and written propaganda, the Pioneers of Liberty soon made themselves felt in other eastern cities with large Yiddish-speaking populations. Under the aegis of the Pioneers, workers' educational clubs sprang up in Baltimore, Boston, and Providence, among other places, while additional groups, mostly of mixed anarchist and socialist composition, began to take shape. Of these the most important was the Knights of Liberty (Riter der Frayhayt) of Philadelphia, founded in 1889 by anarchist workmen who, having lived in London before coming to the United States, adopted the name of the Jewish group in Whitechapel. The Knights, following the example of the Pioneers, launched a series of anarchist forums, held on Sunday afternoons, which were attended by hundreds of workers. Well-known anarchists from New York—Solotaroff and Lewis, Edelstadt and Katz—were invited to deliver lectures, while the Knights boasted oratorical talent of their own in the persons of Max Staller, Chaim Weinberg, and Isidore Prenner, who made "powerful, fiery speeches."[5]

The names "Pionire der Frayhayt" and "Riter der Frayhayt" not only underscored the dedication of the anarchists to freedom as the highest principle of their creed, but also reflected the influence of Johann Most and his newspaper *Freiheit* on the fledgling Jewish movement. Most, though himself a gentile, was the leading apostle of anarchism to the Jewish immigrants in America, holding a place comparable to that of Rudolf Rocker among the Jews of London's East End. Most's flaming oratory and acidic pen, his fervent advocacy of revolution and of propaganda by the deed, won him a large and devoted following among the Jewish militants, who came to regard him, in the words of Morris Hillquit, as their "high priest."[6]

In Most the Jewish anarchists found a formidable propagandist and agitator. He could enthrall with his revolutionary passion even those Jews—the vast majority—with only a shaky grasp of the German in which he spoke. His sharp phrases, noted Israel Kopeloff, a member of the Pioneers of Liberty in New York, had "the impact of the bombs and dynamite" of which he so often spoke; and he had only to give the word, so it seemed, and "the audience would rush to build barricades and begin the revolution." "It is an understatement," recalled Chaim Weinberg of Philadelphia, "to say that Most had the ability to inspire an audience. He electrified, all but bewitched, every listener, opponent as well as friend."[7]

Owing to Most's influence, the Jewish anarchists developed close ties with the German branch of the movement. Emma Goldman, under Most's tutelage, delivered her first anarchist speeches in German, and Alexander Berkman, a member of the Pioneers of Liberty from 1888, worked as a compositor on the *Freiheit*, which served as a clearing-house for anarchist readers of German. Inspired, at the same time, by

Russian populism, many of the Jewish anarchists, Goldman and Berkman among them, pored over Russian revolutionary literature and attended Russian radical gatherings, including those of the Russian Progressive Union in New York, of which Yanovsky and Kopeloff were active members.[8]

As has been noted, more than a few Jewish anarchists in the United States had served their radical apprenticeship in London, a stoppingplace for immigrants to the New World.[9] Over the years, ties between London and New York remained strong, and the Jewish anarchists in America continued to read and support the *Arbeter Fraynd* (Workers' Friend), published in the Whitechapel ghetto. They also read Benjamin Tucker's *Liberty*, published in Boston, and Dyer Lum's *The Alarm*, published in New York, if their English was up to it. What they lacked, however, was a journal of their own—printed in their own language and serving their own needs. To fill this gap, the Pioneers of Liberty announced, in January 1889, that they would presently start a weekly paper in New York, to be called the *Varhayt* (Truth).[10]

To edit the *Varhayt*, the Pioneers invited Joseph Jaffa of Whitechapel, a regular contributor to the *Arbeter Fraynd*. A former rabbinical student in Russia, Jaffa had lived in Paris before coming to London in 1886 and had a good command of French as well as English, from which he made translations into Yiddish. He had served as secretary of the International Working Men's Educational Club (the so-called Berner Street Club) and was a highly regarded figure in the movement, admired for his erudition and linguistic talent.[11] Jaffa, who accepted the invitation, proved himself a worthy choice. Aided by Isidore Rudashevsky as manager and by an editorial board composed of Katz, Solotaroff, Maryson and Lewis, all men of intellect and ability, he launched a publication of which the Pioneers of Liberty could be proud.

The *Varhayt*, which saw the light on February 15, 1889, was the first Yiddish anarchist periodical in the United States. Strictly speaking, in fact, it was the first in the entire world, as the *Arbeter Fraynd*, while founded in 1885, retained a mixed identity, part anarchist, part socialist, before adopting an unequivocally anarchist stand in 1892. The appearance of the *Varhayt* was therefore a major landmark in the history of the Jewish movement, both in America and abroad. In content, moreover, it maintained a remarkably high level for a neophyte paper, featuring articles by Johann Most and Peter Kropotkin, poems by David Edelstadt and Morris Rosenfeld, a digest of Marxian economics, as well as a serialization of Zola's novel *Germinal*, a favorite of anarchists and socialists of the period. An entire number (March 15,

1889) was devoted to the Paris Commune, commemorating its eighteenth anniversary. Letters to the editor, political and labor news, and essays by Yanovsky, Lewis, Solotaroff, and Katz, the leading lights of the Pioneers of Liberty, rounded out a readable journal.[12] It is surprising, therefore, that the *Varhayt* should have lasted only five months, twenty issues appearing in all. A shortage of funds appears to have been the cause of its demise. But it was succeeded, as will be seen in a moment, by the *Fraye Arbeter Shtime* (Free Voice of Labor), one of the longest-lived anarchist journals in history, enduring more than eighty-seven years.

During this initial period from 1886 to 1890, anarchism emerged as probably the largest and certainly the most dynamic movement among Jewish radicals in the United States. The Jewish anarchists, predominantly workers, took part in the first strikes against sweatshop labor and helped organize some of the first Jewish trade unions, such as those of the New York cloakmakers and kneepants workers. At the same time, they played an important role in the social and cultural life of the Lower East Side and of ghettos in other cities, organizing clubs, cooperatives, and mutual-aid societies, sponsoring lectures, picnics, and concerts, and commemorating the inauguration of the Paris Commune (March 18), the First of May, and the execution of the Haymarket martyrs (November 11). In so doing, they imparted a new revolutionary content to traditional popular activities, creating a kind of alternative society, or counterculture, which resembled that of their Italian comrades.

A conspicuous feature of this counterculture was militant atheism and antireligious propaganda. For the Jewish anarchists, attacks on religion were inseparable from attacks on government and capital. Just as every state, they insisted, was an instrument by which a privileged few wielded power over the immense majority, so every church was an ally of the state in the subjugation of humankind, spiritually as well as politically and economically. While retaining a devotion to the secular aspects of Yiddish culture, along with an intense consciousness of being Jewish, the anarchists were aggressive in their rejection of traditional Judaism. They upheld reason and science against ignorance and superstition, which to them lay at the root of every religion. Johann Most's *The God Pestilence*, translated into Yiddish in 1888, played a key role in this antireligious propaganda. Moreover, each year, beginning in 1889, the Pioneers of Liberty published a four-page antireligious journal on Yom Kippur, the most sacred of Jewish holidays, and printed antireligious tracts based on a parody of Jewish liturgy and ritual.[13] Additional literature of this type, such as Benjamin Feigenbaum's *Passover Hagadah According to a New Version*, was imported from London and distributed in large quantities.

The most dramatic antireligious weapon, however, during this early stage of the movement, was the Yom Kippur ball. Featuring dancing, merrymaking, and atheistic harangues, it openly travestied the Jewish Day of Atonement, thereby arousing the fury of the orthodox community, for whom nothing could be a more direct attack upon their faith. On the occasion of New York's first Yom Kippur ball, held in 1889, the owner of Clarendon Hall on East Thirteenth Street, under pressure from conservative Jewry, broke his contract with the anarchists and denied them entry. The festivities were transferred to the Fourth Street Labor Lyceum, where Johann Most, Saul Yanovsky, and Roman Lewis were the principal speakers, followed by singing, dancing, and recitations in Russian, German, and Yiddish.[14]

Thereafter Yom Kippur balls took place every year, in New York and in other cities. Tickets to the 1890 ball in Brooklyn bore the following text: "Grand Yom Kippur Ball. With theatre. Arranged with the consent of all new rabbis of liberty. Kol Nidre Night and Day. In the year 6651 [a misprint for 5651], after the invention of the Jewish idols, and 1890, after the birth of the false Messiah, the Brooklyn Labor Lyceum, 61-67 Myrtle Street, Brooklyn. The Kol Nidre will be offered by John Most. Music, dancing, buffet, 'Marseillaise,' and other hymns against Satan."[15] In Baltimore, the same year, a debate was scheduled between anarchist and orthodox speakers on the question, "Are religion and socialism compatible?" An audience of 1,000 gathered to hear the proceedings. The orthodox speaker went first, presenting his case without incident, but when the anarchist, Dr. Michael Cohn, rose to speak, the audience grew agitated, someone shouted "Fire!" and the meeting broke up amid confusion.[16]

The anarchists, however, were undeterred. In 1891, Yom Kippur balls were held in Baltimore, New York, Philadelphia, Providence, Boston, Chicago, and St. Louis. In New York, Solotaroff and Lewis were the main speakers, with the usual music, entertainment, and buffet. In Providence and Boston, Moshe Katz delivered a lecture—billed as a "Kol Nidre Sermon"—on the evolution of religion, apparently without disturbance. In Philadelphia, however, the police raided the premises and arrested two participants, Isidore Prenner and I. Appel, who were jailed for inciting to riot.[17]

The Yom Kippur balls, in the end, proved counterproductive, alienating not only the more pious Jews, whose religious sensibilities were outraged, but also their less observant brethren, for whom the impious festivities of the anarchists were a senseless mockery of hallowed traditions. Nevertheless, the influence of the anarchists continued to grow. To many among the radical youth of the ghetto, the socialists and other moderates seemed tame and colorless beside these apostles of wholesale revolution, who put forward the exciting idea of complete emancipation as an immediate possibility. As the anarchists saw it, no meaningful improvement could be obtained within the framework of the capitalist system, and the workers would remain oppressed if they did not defend their interests by direct action, including violence if necessary. Over and over they underscored the futility of the ballot and the need for armed insurrection to overthrow the established order. To rely on gradual reform—on reformist "gibberish" (*knakeray*), as they put it[18]—was tantamount to capitulation. They were impatient for the millennium, for the "new deliverance from Egypt," as Most termed it,[19] which they expected at any moment. Any policy, any action that tended to delay its arrival gave succor to the enemy and prolonged the enslavement of the poor.

Small wonder that such a philosophy should have captured the imagination of Jewish militants. In the totality of its rejection of existing conditions, in the fervor with which it assaulted conventional values, religious as well as social and economic, it spoke directly to the desire of young idealists for a world of freedom and justice constructed on new foundations. Besides, as Morris Hillquit noted, anarchism was a "romantic movement, filled with thrilling conspiracies and acts of heroism and self-sacrifice."[20] As such, it attracted a growing number of youthful rebels, disdainful of gradualist methods.

Before 1890, anarchists and socialists dealt with each other on more or less amicable terms. Although they competed for the allegiance of Jewish workers, the lines between them were not yet sharply drawn. Many belonged to the same organizations (for example, the United Hebrew Trades), and it was still possible for them to seek common ground for discussion. In November 1888, anarchists and socialists sponsored a joint meeting to memorialize the Chicago martyrs on the first anniversary of their hanging. After this, however, the gap between them steadily widened. In 1889 and 1890, public debates took place between their leading spokesmen—Saul Yanovsky vs. Louis Miller, Hillel Solotaroff vs. Michael Zametkin, Roman Lewis vs. Abraham Cahan—on fundamental questions of tactics and organization.[21]

In spite of growing divisions, however, anarchists and socialists endeavored to work together, hoping to avoid a split in the ranks of Jewish labor. In a conciliatory spirit, the anarchists proposed the establishment of a bipartisan weekly newspaper, on the lines of the London *Arbeter Fraynd*, with an editor from each faction in charge. On the initiative of the Pioneers of Liberty and the Knights of Liberty, a convention was summoned to discuss the matter. The socialists, despite misgivings, accepted the call, and on December 25, 1889, the meeting opened in the hall of the Essex Street Market, decorated for the occasion with red flags, portraits of the Haymarket martyrs, and a banner inscribed "Neither God Nor Master!"[22] It was the first conference of Jewish radicals in America, the forty-seven delegates representing thirty-one organizations—groups, trade unions, educational clubs—in Baltimore, Philadelphia, Boston, Chicago, and other cities, in addition to New York itself. Both sides had mobilized their forces, and the delegates, evenly divided between the two camps, included such figures as Lewis, Solotaroff, and Katz for the anarchists, Hillquit, Zametkin, and Miller for the socialists.[23]

From the outset it was evident that no agreement would be forthcoming. The anarchists, favoring a joint newspaper, argued that the workers should acquaint themselves with all streams of radical thought, if only to choose intelligently among them. The socialists, however, branded a nonparty paper as *"pareveh lokshn"* (neutral noodles, i.e., neither dairy nor meat), a term imported from London, where it had been used to deride the *Arbeter Fraynd*. An effective journal, they maintained, must have a consistent point of view, with a clear stand on basic social, political, and economic issues. Would it make sense, they asked, to reject violence and uphold the ballot in one article while condoning terrorism and decrying elections in another? Such a publication, far from uniting the workers, would leave them in hopeless confusion.

After six days of bitter debate, the issue was put to a vote. The anarchists were narrowly defeated, by a margin of twenty-one to twenty. Then the gathering, recalled Abraham Cahan, broke up amid "a wild scene of mutual recriminations."[24] The breach between anarchism and socialism had become irreparable. Thereafter, all attempts at cooperation were abandoned as useless, and there was nothing left but war between the two camps.

The socialists, after leaving the hall, immediately opened discussions on launching their own paper; two months later, the *Arbeter-Tsaytung*, a weekly, began to appear. Not to be outdone, the anarchists made plans for a publication of their own. On January 17, 1890, the Pioneers of Liberty called a meeting, attended by representatives of the Knights of Liberty and other groups, to consider the matter, agreeing, among other things, on a name for the new journal: *Fraye Arbeter Shtime*. On behalf of the Pioneers of Liberty, Moshe Katz and H. Mindlin wrote to Morris Winchevsky in London, inviting him to serve as editor. Winchevsky, as much a socialist as an anarchist, quickly declined, and the post went to Roman Lewis.

To raise funds to launch the paper, some of the best anarchist speakers—Lewis and Katz of New York, Prenner and Weinberg of Philadelphia—set out on tours of the East and Middle West. In the meantime, an interim paper, *Der Morgenshtern* (The Morning Star), began to appear on a weekly basis. Running from January 17 to June 20, 1890, it was edited by Dr. Abba Breslavsky, a young physician who hovered between anarchism and socialism. The publisher, an anarchist, was Ephraim London (father of the future socialist congressman Meyer London), who operated a small printing shop on the Lower East Side. *Der Morgenshtern*, though it boasted a rich fare of articles and poems as well as a serialization of Chernyshevsky's *What Is to Be Done?*, was only a stopgap enterprise. Barely two weeks after it ceased publication, the *Fraye Arbeter Shtime* made its debut.

The founding of the *Fraye Arbeter Shtime* was a milestone in the history of the movement. Appearing on Independence Day, July 4, 1890, it was destined to survive, with a few interruptions, for nearly nine decades. When it ceased publication, in December 1977, it was the oldest Yiddish newspaper in the world, antedating Cahan's *Daily Forward* by seven years. The *Fraye Arbeter Shtime* played a vital role in the Jewish labor movement in America; and throughout its long life it maintained a high literary standard, featuring some of the finest writers and poets in the history of Yiddish radical journalism.[25]

Claiming to represent thirty-two Jewish workers' associations, the *Fraye Arbeter Shtime*, published weekly at 184 East Broadway, combined the functions of a labor paper, a journal of radical opinion, a literary magazine, and a people's university. It contained articles by Most and Kropotkin, translations from Turgenev's *On the Eve*, popularizations of material from the natural and social sciences (including Marx's *Capital*), and poems by Edelstadt, Rosenfeld, and Joseph Bovshover, bemoaning the wretchedness of the sweatshops and painting alluring images of a classless and stateless millennium in which hunger and poverty, exploitation and oppression, would cease to exist. Edelstadt, moreover, produced a series of poetic tributes to the Haymarket anarchists, whose martyrdom remained a powerful inspiration. Parsons's last words on the gallows—"Let the Voice of the People Be Heard!"—adorned the paper's masthead.

Roman Lewis, the first editor, was himself a regular contributor, his articles covering a wide range of subjects. An energetic young man, as fluent in Russian as in Yiddish, he was an effective fund-raiser for the paper and a popular speaker at radical gatherings. Nevertheless, for reasons that remain obscure, his tenure lasted only six months. Resigning at the end of 1890, he took a post with the cloakmakers' union and later went over to the socialists. Still later, he turned to politics and was elected an assistant district attorney in Chicago on the Democratic ticket.[26]

Replacing Lewis was Dr. J. A. Maryson, a prolific essayist and translator, one of the few members of the Pioneers of Liberty—Alexander Berkman was another—who gained sufficient mastery of English to carry on propaganda in that language. Maryson's successor, after a brief interval, was the poet David Edelstadt, summoned from Cincinnati to fill the post.[27] One of the first of the Yiddish "labor poets," Edelstadt had made his debut in the *Varhayt* and contributed to *Der Morgenshtern*, becoming the bard of the Jewish working class. Emma Goldman thought him "a great poet and one of the *finest* types of Anarchists that ever lived."[28] A buttonhole maker by trade, "a child of poverty, a dreamer of struggle," as he describes himself in one of his verses, he experienced at first hand the miseries of sweatshop life that he so hauntingly evokes in his poems. These poems—"In Kamf," "Vakht Oyf," "Natur un Mensh" are among the most famous—won immediate popularity among the Yiddish-speaking workers. Set to music, they were sung at picnics and rallies and wherever Jewish laborers gathered.

Edelstadt, with his "fine idealistic nature,"[29] set a distinctive stamp on the *Fraye Arbeter Shtime* during this initial phase of its existence. But his career was abruptly cut short. Stricken with tuberculosis, then endemic among toilers in the sweatshops, he was compelled, in October 1891, to quit his post and move to Denver in search of a cure. The disease, however, had progressed too far and though he continued to send poems to the paper for several months, his strength in the end gave out. He died in October 1892 at the age of twenty-six.[30] During the next few years, Edelstadt groups sprang up in Chicago, Boston, and other cities; an Edelstadt Singing Society was formed in New York; and over Edelstadt's grave in Denver a headstone was erected, placed there, in the words of his niece, by "the working people who loved him and whom he had tried to defend and enlighten."[31]

Edelstadt's passing was a blow to the Jewish movement. The *Fraye Arbeter Shtime*, however, carried on under Solotaroff and Moshe Katz, a capable young man of twenty-seven, soon to acquire a reputation as a translator of anarchist classics, including Kropotkin's *Conquest of Bread*, Jean Grave's *Moribund Society and Anarchy*, and Alexander Berkman's *Prison Memoirs of an Anarchist*.[32] Each December, moreover, following a tradition begun in 1889 when anarchists and socialists met to debate the establishment of a joint newspaper, the *Fraye Arbeter Shtime* held a conference on the Lower East Side to discuss the major questions facing the movement, such as the efficacy of Yom Kippur balls and the attitude of anarchists towards organized labor.[33] In 1891, it might be added, the editors received a visit from Elisée Reclus, the celebrated French anarchist and geographer, who urged them to organize schools for children to be conducted on libertarian lines.[34]

Another key event of the period was the attempt by a Pioneers of Liberty member, Alexander Berkman, on the life of Henry Clay Frick, manager of the Carnegie steel works near Pittsburgh. Berkman's act, which occurred during the Homestead strike of 1892, drew a mixed reaction from his comrades. To some, according to Joseph Cohen, a future editor of the *Fraye Arbeter Shtime*, Berkman's name became "a kind of talisman, a source of inspiration and encouragement."[35] Others, however, were more critical; and a few severed ties with the movement and repudiated terrorism wherever it might occur, but especially in democratic America.

At the time of Berkman's act, the *Fraye Arbeter Shtime* was already in serious trouble. Dependent on the support of indigent workers, it had faced financial problems from the start. A wage dispute with its typesetters compounded the paper's difficulties, and in May 1892 it suspended publication for ten months. No sooner did it revive, in March 1893, than the country was hit by a depression. The paper held on until April 1894, when it was forced again to halt publication.[36]

With the suspension of the *Fraye Arbeter Shtime* in 1894, the first phase of the history of Jewish anarchism in America came to an end. It was followed by a period of marking time that lasted until 1899, when the revival of the paper stirred new life into the movement. During this interval, Jewish anarchism remained in the doldrums. The Pioneers of Liberty, the Knights of Liberty, and other groups faded away, along with the International Working People's Association, which maintained a shadowy existence until its final disappearance before the First World War. Yet activity did not cease altogether. Lectures and meetings continued, if not on the scale of the past. Each year, moreover, the Jewish anarchists of northeastern cities sent delegates to New York to gather and hold discussions.[37] But most important was the appearance, beginning in 1895, of *Di Fraye Gezelshaft* (The Free Society), a thirty-two-page monthly cultural and literary journal, with offices at 202 East Broadway. Its editor, M. Leontieff (the pseudonym of Lev Solomon Moiseev), though only twenty-three years old, was well versed in European literature and had contributed to the *Fraye*

Arbeter Shtime in the months preceding its suspension. A construction engineer by profession, he was to acquire a worldwide reputation in his field, supervising the erection of the Manhattan and Williamsburg bridges in New York. Assisted by Maryson, Katz, and Solotaroff, Leontieff made *Di Fraye Gezelshaft* a first-rate publication, with articles by the leading Yiddish anarchist writers, along with translations from such prominent European anarchists as Kropotkin, Grave, Reclus, and Sébastien Faure.[38]

Aside from *Di Fraye Gezelshaft*, visitors from abroad imparted life to the flagging movement. This was especially true of Peter Kropotkin, who came for the first time in 1897 and lectured in New York and other cities. He also attended private gatherings arranged by his comrades, including one at the home of Solotaroff, where the Dreyfus case and other issues of the day were discussed. Of all the major theorists of anarchism, none, not even Most, exerted a more powerful influence on the Jewish adherents than Kropotkin, whose visit provided a badly needed lift. Yet it was not until the resurrection of the *Fraye Arbeter Shtime*, after a five-year hiatus, that the movement recovered its former health. This took place in October 1899, with Saul Yanovsky at the helm. Yanovsky's tenure lasted till 1919, spanning the first two decades of the new century. This period, as we shall see, marked the heyday not only of the *Fraye Arbeter Shtime* but of the Jewish anarchist movement as a whole.

YANOVSKY had been born in the Russian town of Pinsk in 1864. Although the son of a rabbi, he rejected religion at an early age—"all hokum," he contemptuously called it.[39] Emigrating to America in 1885, he worked at various jobs in the clothing industry (shirtmaker, cloakmaker, capmaker) until he was fired for demanding better conditions. Stirred by the fate of the Haymarket martyrs, he joined the Pioneers of Liberty, wrote for the *Varhayt*, and became, in his own description, an "outspoken anarchist," a proponent of terrorism and insurrection.[40]

Yanovsky's pen attracted attention, and in 1889 he was invited to London to edit the *Arbeter Fraynd*. His arrival, according to Rudolf Rocker, "opened a new epoch in the Jewish labor movement" of that city.[41] An eloquent speaker, he often shared the platform with Kropotkin, Errico Malatesta, and Louise Michel, appearing at Haymarket, May First, and Paris Commune memorials. His pamphlet *Vos viln di anarkhistn?*, published by the *Arbeter Fraynd* press in 1890, was among the first expositions of anarchism in Yiddish and expressly designed for a working-class audience. "His language was natural and alive," observed Rocker, "and he made his readers think." Yanovsky, in Rocker's opinion, was "the ablest propagandist in speech and print" among the Whitechapel Jews at that time.[42]

After five years in England, Yanovsky returned to the United States, settling as before in New York. Small, dark, intense, with a mustache and imperial beard, he once again became a familiar figure in Jewish anarchist circles, lecturing to eager audiences throughout the Northeast. Yet there was a negative side to Yanovsky's character that impaired his effectiveness within the movement. Narrow, sarcastic, intolerant, he was tactless in his dealings with others, unsparing in his criticisms of friend and foe alike. "Why are you wasting paper?" he asked a young poet who had shown him samples of his work. After a piano concert, he asked the soloist why he did not play the violin. "I don't know the violin," said the pianist. "And the piano you know?" retorted Yanovsky.[43] Such barbs, remarked Joseph Cohen, won Yanovsky more than a few enemies, even within his own movement.[44] Goldman criticized his "despotic methods"; Berkman thought him rigid and "dictatorial." "He was a clever fellow," recalled another comrade, "but very sharp in his manner. He could give you such a dig that you could see stars!"[45]

And yet, whatever his personal shortcomings, Yanovsky was a highly capable editor and administrator. On this even his enemies agreed. Invited to revive the *Fraye Arbeter Shtime* after its insecure beginnings, he put the paper on a solid footing, lending it a stability it had previously lacked. Endowed with an eye for literary talent, he opened its columns to a host of gifted writers and to fresh views on many subjects. To the roster of anarchist contributors, which included Kropotkin, Solotaroff, and Most, he added such names as Rudolf Rocker, Max Nettlau, Abraham Frumkin, Emma Goldman, and Voltairine de Cleyre, an American of gentile origins who had learned Yiddish in the Philadelphia ghetto.[46] For Jewish workers hungry for culture, he published translations of August Strindberg and Henrik Ibsen, Bernard Shaw and Oscar Wilde, Leonid Andreev and Olive Schreiner, Octave Mirbeau and Bernard-Lazare. In addition, he published such notable Yiddish writers as Avrom Reisen and H. Leivick, whose contributions made the *Fraye Arbeter Shtime* one of the most readable papers of the day. Yanovsky's own column, "Oyf der Vakh" (On Watch), became a particular favorite, celebrated for its trenchant wit.[47] Under Yanovsky, according to one authority, the *Fraye Arbeter Shtime* came to occupy "an enviable position in Yiddish letters."[48] Its circulation mounted steadily, exceeding twenty thousand on the eve of the First World War.[49]

Yanovsky, it must be added, gave the *Fraye Arbeter Shtime* a new direction. Before its suspension in 1894, the paper, imbued with millenarian expectations, had scorned piecemeal reform in favor of wholesale revolution and the total destruction of the existing system. Yanovsky himself, like the majority of his Jewish comrades, had been an ardent disciple of Johann Most and a defender of propaganda by the deed.[50] By now, however, the apocalyptic fervor of the 1880s and 1890s, the belief that the social revolution was imminent and physical force unavoidable, had begun to fade. For the solution of social problems, Yanovsky concluded, anarchism needed a more constructive approach. Terrorism he had come to oppose with every fiber of his being. For him, a friend recalled, anarchism was "a philosophy of human dignity and cooperation, of love and brotherhood, not bombs."[51] "Direct action," as the *Fraye Arbeter Shtime* put it, no longer meant violence or subversion, but rather the founding of libertarian schools, the fostering of workers' unions, the establishment of cooperative organizations of every type.[52] Outraged by the assassination of President McKinley in 1901, Yanovsky insisted that anarchism, above everything else, called for harmony and "peace among men." Despite this, the offices of the *Fraye Arbeter Shtime*, now at 185 Henry Street, were invaded and wrecked by an angry mob and Yanovsky himself was cornered and beaten.[53]

Another sign of the shift to a more pragmatic, less quixotic, position was the softening of antireligious agitation, so conspicuous a feature of the movement in its formative period. For those, as one announcement put it, who would "rather dance and be merry than fast and atone for their past sins," Yom Kippur balls continued to take place.[54] But they were far from being as numerous as before the turn of the century, nor, one suspects, indulged in with comparable zeal. The pogroms in Kishinev and other Russian cities between 1903 and 1906 had a sobering effect, turning more than a few Jewish anarchists back to their roots. After Kishinev, remarked Israel Kopeloff, "my previous cosmopolitanism, internationalism, and similar views vanished at one blow, like the contents of a barrel with the bottom knocked out."[55] Hillel Solotaroff, one of the most dedicated figures in the movement, experienced a reawakening of the national feeling that had led him, as a youth in Russia, to join the Am Olam (Eternal People) colonization society, under whose auspices he had emigrated to America. Together with Kopeloff and Moshe Katz, fellow veterans of the Pioneers of Liberty era, he veered towards Zionism as the answer to Jewish survival.[56]

Yet another area in which a more pragmatic approach was manifested was the labor movement. The anarchists, during the Yanovsky period, took part in the organization of unions in all trades in which Jewish workers were employed, from bookbinding and cigarmaking to tailoring and housepainting. They were especially active in the International Ladies' Garment Workers' Union and in the Amalgamated Clothing Workers of America, participating in strikes, rooting out corruption, and fighting against bureaucracy and indifference. For all their militancy, they no longer disdained partial economic gains, as many had done in the past. As Rocker noted, "the old slogan, 'The worse the better,' was based on an erroneous assumption. Like that other slogan, 'All or nothing,' which made many radicals oppose any improvement in the lot of the workers, even when the workers demanded it, on the ground that it would distract the mind of the Proletarist, and turn it away from the road which leads to social emancipation. It is contrary to all the experience of history and psychology; people who are not prepared to fight for the betterment of their living conditions are not likely to fight for social emancipation. Slogans of this kind are like a cancer in the revolutionary movement."[57]

Given this new attitude, it is not surprising that the anarchists should have taken an active part in the Workmen's Circle, the socialist-oriented Jewish fraternal order in the United States and Canada, with its emphasis on life insurance, sickness and accident benefits, burial plots, and educational and cultural programs.[58] By the 1920s, some two dozen anarchist branches had been established, including the Naye Gezelshaft Branch of New York, the Radical Library Branch of Philadelphia, the Frayhayt Branch of Baltimore, and the Kropotkin Branch of Los Angeles.

The Jewish anarchists, moreover, engaged in a whole range of cooperative ventures, most notably the housing cooperatives of the International Ladies' Garment Workers' Union near New York's Pennsylvania Station and of the Amalgamated Clothing Workers on the Lower East Side and in the Bronx. In Philadelphia, by the same token, Chaim Weinberg, a member of the now defunct Knights of Liberty, organized a Jewish Workers' Cooperative Association, which sponsored lectures, distributed literature, opened a cooperative shoe store and bakery, and succeeded in attracting nearly nine hundred members.[59] Similarly, the Stelton colony in New Jersey, itself largely founded by Jewish anarchists, boasted a cooperative food store, garment factory, and jitney service, in addition to a children's school on the model of Francisco Ferrer's Escuela Moderna in Barcelona.[60]

The Yanovsky era saw the rapid expansion of Jewish anarchism throughout America. After the revival of the *Fraye Arbeter Shtime*, new groups sprang up, new periodicals appeared, and the movement attained its fullest flowering. In New York alone at least ten Jewish groups came into being between 1900 and 1918,[61] with a total of some five hundred members. Spurred by a wave of immigration from Russia following the Revolution of 1905, similar growth took place in other cities; and in December 1910 a Jewish anarchist federation, the Federirte Anarkhistishe Grupen in Amerike (Federated Anarchist Groups in America), was formed at a convention in Philadelphia, arranged by the Radical Library, which had replaced the Knights of Liberty as the leading Jewish group of that city.[62]

The proliferation of Jewish groups was accompanied by an increase in the number of anarchist publications in the Yiddish language. As the following list indicates, twelve of the twenty Yiddish anarchist periodicals in the United States were started during the first two decades of the twentieth century:

YIDDISH ANARCHIST PERIODICALS IN THE UNITED STATES

Di Abend Tsaytung. New York, 1906. Daily. Published by the *Fraye Arbeter Shtime*. Edited by Saul Yanovsky.

Der Anarkhist. Philadelphia, 1908. Monthly. Published by the Group of Anarchist Communists.

Behind the Bars. New York, 1924. Published by the Anarchist Red Cross Society. In English and Yiddish. Only one number appeared (January 1924).

Broyt un Frayhayt. Philadelphia, 1906. Weekly. Edited by Joseph J. Cohen.

Fraye Arbeter Shtime. New York, 1890-1977. Weekly, then fortnightly and monthly. Edited by David Edelstadt, Saul Yanovsky, et al.

Di Fraye Gezelshaft. New York, 1895-1900. Monthly. Edited by M. Leontieff.

Di Fraye Gezelshaft. New York, 1910-1911. Monthly. Edited by Saul Yanovsky.

Di Fraye Tsukunft. New York, 1915-1916. Irregular. Published by the Anarchist Federation of America.

Dos Fraye Vort. New York, 1911. Monthly. Published by the Federated Anarchist Groups in America, Edited by J. A. Maryson.

Di Frayhayt. New York, 1913-1914. Monthly. Published by the Federated Anarchist Groups in America. Edited by L. Barone.

Frayhayt. New York, 1918. Monthly. Edited by Jacob Abrams et al.

*Lebn un Kamf. New York, 1906. Edited by Julius Edelsohn.

Der Morgenshtern. New York, 1890. Weekly. Edited by Abba Braslavsky.

*Di Shtime fun di Rusishe Gefangene. New York, 1913-1916? Monthly. Published by the Anarchist Red Cross. Edited by Alexander Zager.

*Der Shturm. New York, 1917-1918. Fortnightly? Edited by Jacob Abrams et al.

Di Sonrayz Shtime. Alicia, Michigan, 1934. Published at the Sunrise Co-operative Farm Community. Only one issue appeared (May 19, 1934).

Tfileh Zakeh. New York, 1889-1893. Issued annually (on Yom Kippur) by
the Pioneers of Liberty Group.
Varhayt. New York, 1889. Weekly. Published by the Pioneers of Liberty
Group. Edited by Joseph Jaffa.
Der Yunyon Arbeter. New York, 1925-1927. Weekly. Published by the Anar-
chist Group, I.L.G.W.U. Edited by Simon Farber.
*Zherminal. Brooklyn, N.Y., 1913-1916? Monthly. Published by the Ger-
minal Group. Edited by Zalman Deanin.

*I have been unable to locate copies of these journals.

Yanovsky himself edited two of the new papers, in addition to the
Fraye Arbeter Shtime. The first, *Di Abend Tsaytung*, was apparently
designed to compete with Abraham Cahan's successful *Jewish Daily
Forward*; but, lacking sparkle and substance, it failed after two
months. The second, *Di Fraye Gezelshaft*, a literary monthly on the
pattern of its namesake of the 1890s, proved more durable, surviving
a year and a half. Of all the Yiddish journals, however, only the *Fraye
Arbeter Shtime* was able to maintain a prolonged existence.

Nevertheless, a passion to educate and uplift drove the anarchist
presses at a furious pace. Beyond the newspapers and journals, a flood
of books and pamphlets saw their way into print. The Fraye Arbeter
Ferlag of Newark, New Jersey, for example, published Yiddish translations of Kropotkin, Malatesta, and other leading anarchist writers;
the Germinal Publishing Association of Brooklyn brought out a new
Yiddish translation of Kropotkin's *Appeal to the Young*; the Fraye Gezelshaft Group of Winnipeg issued a Yiddish version of Kropotkin's
Place of Anarchism in Socialistic Evolution; and the Broyt un Frayhayt
Bibliotek of New York published translations of Voltairine de Cleyre's
Direct Action, Maria Goldsmith's *Anarchism and Revolutionary Syndicalism*, and the courtroom speech of Matryona Prisiazhniuk, a Russian anarchist who, condemned to death in 1909, committed suicide
in her cell.[63] Children as well as adults devoured Darwin, Spencer, and
other famous scientists and writers. "Think of it!" exclaimed the police
commissioner of New York. "Herbert Spencer preferred to a fairy
story for boys and girls."[64] To satisfy their hunger for learning, Jewish
anarchists in a number of cities organized libraries, reading rooms, and
literary clubs, while on the Lower East Side the bookstore of Max Maisel, a devoted anarchist and bibliophile, became a hub of intellectual
activity, with a huge stock of radical works in Yiddish, some of them—
by Kropotkin, Thoreau, and Oscar Wilde—published by Maisel himself.[65]

Kropotkin remained by far the most popular anarchist writer, idolized by his Jewish disciples. On his second visit to the United States, in

1901, he lectured before overflow audiences in several cities—though, as noted in Chapter 5, when the *Fraye Arbeter Shtime* planned a supplement with a group of his photographs he put a stop to it, refusing, he told Yanovsky, to be made into "an icon."[66] After Kropotkin returned to England, the Jewish anarchists sent money to assist his activities in behalf of the blossoming anarchist movement in Russia. When revolution erupted in 1905, they redoubled their efforts, supporting the Russian anarchist press and welcoming a series of Russian revolutionaries—Nicholas Chaikovsky, Maxim Gorky, Gregory Gershuni, Catherine Breshkovskaya, Chaim Zhitlovsky—who came to America on fund-raising tours.[67] In 1907, after the revolution was suppressed, an Anarchist Red Cross was organized to send aid to political prisoners. Headquartered in New York, with branches in Philadelphia, Baltimore, Chicago, and Detroit, it issued appeals, circulated petitions, and organized banquets ("peasant balls" and "prisoner balls") to collect money and clothing for Russian revolutionaries in jail and exile.[68]

While continuing to follow events in Russia with passionate interest, the Jewish anarchists threw themselves into other causes. In 1911 they protested against the execution of Denjiro Kotoku and his anarchist associates in Tokyo. In 1912 they supported the textile strikers in Lawrence, Massachusetts, and in 1913, in Paterson, New Jersey. They raised funds for the Mexican Revolution, and especially for the movement led by Ricardo and Enrique Flores Magón in southern California. And, as before, they organized picnics and excursions, concerts and theatrical performances, for the benefit of their newspapers and journals.

Throughout these years, March 18, May 1, and November 11 remained red-letter days on the anarchist calendar. And on December 7, 1912, as noted earlier, a Seventieth Birthday Celebration was held in Kropotkin's honor in Carnegie Hall, arranged by the *Fraye Arbeter Shtime* together with Emma Goldman's *Mother Earth*. For the occasion, the *Fraye Arbeter Shtime* devoted a special issue to Kropotkin's life and ideas, and a Kropotkin Literary Society (Kropotkin Literatur-Gezelshaft) was established to publish anarchist and socialist classics in Yiddish translation, including works by Kropotkin himself. With J. A. Maryson as secretary-treasurer and Max Maisel among its participants, it attracted members from Jewish groups all over the country and, in the first decade of its existence, brought out seven volumes of Kropotkin, a one-volume collection of Bakunin, and a three-volume edition of Marx's *Capital*, as well as Proudhon's *What Is Property?*, Stirner's *The Ego and His Own*, and other works.[69]

With the outbreak of the First World War, the anarchist movement entered a critical period. When Kropotkin declared his support for the Entente, fearing that German militarism might prove fatal to social progress in Europe, his position was vigorously debated in the *Fraye Arbeter Shtime*, leaving scars that never completely healed. Yanovsky at first opposed the fighting and signed an International Manifesto on the War, together with Joseph Cohen, Alexander Berkman, Emma Goldman, and other prominent anarchists on both sides of the Atlantic, declaring that the responsibility for all wars rested "solely in the existence of the State."[70] Yanovsky, however, opened his paper to differing opinions on the question and himself, influenced by Kropotkin, shifted his stand in favor of an Allied victory.[71]

The Bolshevik Revolution was another source of bitter contention. All anarchists, of course, welcomed the overthrow of the tsar with jubilation, some hoping that the United States would undergo a similar social and political upheaval.[72] But the seizure of power by the Bolsheviks, in November 1917, evoked a mixed response. While Goldman sang the praises of Lenin and Trotsky ("who hold the world in awe by their personality, their prophetic vision, and their intense revolutionary spirit"), Yanovsky criticized Lenin as a "Mephistopheles" and foresaw the creation of a new dictatorship that boded ill for the future of Russia.[73]

In the midst of this controversy, Yanovsky resigned as editor of the *Fraye Arbeter Shtime*. By then—the year was 1919—anarchism had fallen on hard times. Repressions and deportations during and immediately following the war deprived the movement of some of its most dedicated activists, Goldman and Berkman among them. The pull of Communism also took its toll. Many saw the Russian Revolution as the coming of the workers' millennium and flocked to their homeland—only to disappear in the prisons and execution chambers of the secret police. Declining immigration and restrictions on eastern Europeans reduced potential Yiddish-speaking recruits to a trickle. In the meantime, the older generation of anarchists was beginning to fade, while their children, born and bred in the United States, were becoming assimilated and entering the mainstream of American life. The movement was plunged into a period of stagnation from which it never recovered.

YANOVSKY, after quitting the *Fraye Arbeter Shtime*, assumed the editorship of *Gerekhtikayt* (Justice), the weekly Yiddish organ of the International Ladies' Garment Workers' Union, a post that he held until 1926. Under his direction, it became one of the "liveliest and best edited labor papers in America," in the opinion of a leading authority.[74]

The *Fraye Arbeter Shtime*, in his absence, went through a difficult period, with an editorial committee in charge. Readership fell off and old financial troubles returned. To take matters in hand, a new Jewish anarchist federation, the Yidishe Anarkhistishe Federatsie fun Amerike und Kenede, was formed in 1921, which issued appeals and organized picnics and banquets. Contributions came in from all parts of North America. By the mid-1920s the paper was again on a secure footing.

To succeed Yanovsky, the federation's choice fell upon Joseph Cohen, a strong and able individual, who took up his duties in 1923. Cohen was a cigarmaker from Philadelphia, where, converted to anarchism by Voltairine de Cleyre, he had emerged as a leading figure in the Jewish movement. He was not only the driving force of the Radical Library Group and of the Philadelphia Modern School, but a founder of the Stelton colony in New Jersey and afterwards of the Sunrise colony in Michigan. He was also the author of four books (including a history of Jewish anarchism in America)[75] and countless articles that chronicle these ventures in which he played so central a part.

Cohen's personality, however, had a sharp edge. Like Yanovsky, he possessed a streak of intolerance and even arrogance that earned him the reproach of not a few of his comrades. Alexander Berkman accused him—as Berkman had accused Yanovsky—of dictatorial behavior. "He will stop at nothing," wrote Berkman to Michael Cohn, "in order to make his job safe, not for democracy but autocracy." To Berkman, moreover, Cohen lacked a clear point of view: "He now writes as an Anarchist, again as a parliamentarian, and then again one does not know what he stands for. I think under his editorship the F.A.S. lacks a real and definite face. And that is bad for a paper."[76]

Berkman's appraisal was unfair. During Cohen's tenure, the *Fraye Arbeter Shtime* maintained a high journalistic level, if not as high as under Yanovsky. It carried essays and articles by prominent writers—Berkman himself and Goldman, Nettlau and Rocker, Maximoff and Volin—and remained a treasure-house of information on the anarchist movement, both in America and abroad. In addition, it published valuable jubilee issues and special supplements,[77] as well as a short-lived English page, designed for younger readers unfamiliar with Yiddish,[78] and a number of books and pamphlets in English, such as Nettlau's *Errico Malatesta* (1924) and Berkman's *Now and After: The ABC of Communist Anarchism* (1929).[79]

Beyond all this, the Jewish anarchists sent money to the Kropotkin Museum in Moscow, established after their mentor's death in 1921,[80] contributed to a fund for aging anarchists in Europe, among them Nettlau, Malatesta, and Volin,[81] and took part in rallies and protests in behalf of Sacco and Vanzetti, another Haymarket affair in its impact on the anarchist movement. Between 1923 and 1927, moreover, they joined forces with their erstwhile socialist rivals to prevent a Communist takeover in the clothing unions. Towards this end, the Anarchist Group of the International Ladies' Garment Workers' Union launched a weekly paper, *Der Yunyon Arbeter* (The Union Worker), which demanded that the union remain free of party control and denounced the "arrogance" (*khutspah*) of Communist officials and their fraudulent election practices, including hooliganism and "gangster" methods.[82]

With the aid of their socialist allies, the anarchists succeeded in blocking the Communist effort to capture the garment unions. In the process, however, they became enmeshed in the union hierarchy. Some, indeed, rose to high office, Morris Sigman becoming president of the ILGWU, Rose Pesotta and Anna Sosnovsky vice-presidents. Yanovsky, as we have seen, edited the union paper *Gerekhtikayt*, and was succeeded by another anarchist, Simon Farber, formerly editor of *Der Yunyon Arbeter*. These developments were part of the evolution of Jewish anarchism, since the beginning of the century, towards a more pragmatic, less militant position. Anarchists who had previously condemned reformism adopted a conciliatory attitude. Some, indeed, questioned the efficacy of revolution in the light of events in Soviet Russia.[83]

This process accelerated during the New Deal of the 1930s, when more than a few Jewish anarchists voted (for Roosevelt) for the first time. Jewish anarchism, as a result, lost its identity as a revolutionary, anti-establishment movement. After defeating the Communists, anarchists and socialists remained on friendly terms. The *Fraye Arbeter Shtime*, while it continued to pay tribute to Haymarket and the Paris Commune, refrained from criticizing the ILGWU or the Amalgamated Clothing Workers union, which supported the paper with subscriptions and with advertisements on May Day, Labor Day, and other special occasions, including the annual fund-raising banquet.

The concerns of the Jewish anarchists during the 1920s and 1930s were not very different from those of the socialists and liberals. They covered the whole range of problems that confronted the world between the two wars: the growth of the Bolshevik dictatorship, the rise of Mussolini and Hitler, the plight of political exiles in Europe, the martyrdom of Sacco and Vanzetti, and the overriding questions of violence, revolution, and war. For a brief moment the anarchists could exult in the Spanish Revolution and hope that their cause had gained a new lease on life. But the victory of Franco in 1939 came as a devastating blow. Hope turned to bitter disappointment. The coming of the Second World War and the massacre of the Jews in Europe seemed to many the ultimate madness. Rocker, who had immigrated to America in 1933, a refugee from Nazi Germany, came to believe that Hitler had to be defeated by force of arms if freedom was to survive. So far as German militarism and regimentation were concerned, Rocker admitted, Kropotkin had, a quarter century before, "judged things better than I and others did."[84]

Meanwhile, the editorship of the *Fraye Arbeter Shtime* had been changing hands. Joseph Cohen left in 1932 to found the Sunrise colony in Michigan[85] and was replaced by an editorial committee that included Yanovsky, Michael Cohn, and Abraham Frumkin. In 1934 a new editor, Mark Mratchny, was appointed, who served until 1940. A veteran of the Russian Revolution, a friend of Berkman and Goldman, Mratchny was intelligent and well educated, trained in psychoanalysis, the master of several languages, and highly qualified for the position. He was deeply interested in developments in Spain, which received broad coverage in the paper. The defeat of Spain, he later recalled, was "a crushing disappointment to me." Afterwards anarchism seemed a hollow shell. "I felt like a rabbi in an empty synagogue. So I resigned from the *Fraye Arbeter Shtime* and from the movement."[86]

The end of the 1930s also saw the passing of Saul Yanovsky. One of the last survivors of the Pioneers of Liberty, he had been an anarchist since the 1880s and his tenure as editor of the *Fraye Arbeter Shtime* had marked the high point of the Jewish movement. During the 1920s and 1930s he remained an active figure, lecturing from coast to coast to raise money for the paper. Though his strength had begun to wane, his tongue was as sharp as ever. "Yanovsky is getting old and more cynical," wrote Michael Cohn to Berkman in 1930. "He curses and cusses privately and openly everything and everybody."[87]

In 1938 Yanovsky made his last extended lecture tour, traveling as far as California. Thomas H. Bell, who had encountered him in London half a century before and thought him "the most wonderful young man I had ever met in my life," was present when Yanovsky spoke in Los Angeles. What Bell now beheld was "a shrunken old man, crotchety often and very bitter-tongued sometimes. But I took him in my arms and hugged him close and kissed his shrunken old cheeks with the very warmest feelings." Bell then remarks: "We become in our old age crabby, blind, deaf, lame or asthmatic. And our movement is now completely overwhelmed in a gigantic world-wide wave of reaction. But, ah, when I look back to the glorious days and the glorious comrades of our young movement, I am stirred to the depths by affection and pride.[88] Yanovsky, an incessant smoker, died of lung cancer the following year.

But the *Fraye Arbeter Shtime* carried on under a succession of new editors. After Mratchny came Dr. Herman Frank, a devotee of Gustav Landauer, followed in turn by Solo Linder, formerly active in the London movement, then by Isidore Wisotsky, an oldtime Wobbly and anarcho-syndicalist in the days of the First World War. As the years passed and readership declined, the paper showed increasing signs of age, changing from a weekly to a fortnightly, then from a fortnightly to a monthly. Gone were the ghettos and sweatshops in which the Jewish immigrants had lived and toiled. Gone, too, lamented Wisotsky, were "the dreamer, the revolutionist, the Socialist, the Anarchist, the I.W.W., the Idealist, the agitator, the free thinker, and the Missionary of yesterday."[89]

By the 1970s circulation of the *Fraye Arbeter Shtime* had fallen to less than two thousand. Then, after languishing for several years, the paper took on a new vitality when Ahrne Thorne, converted to anarchism during the Sacco-Vanzetti agitation, assumed the editorship in March 1975. A printer by trade and a journalist by avocation, Thorne had a craftsman's eye for handsome typography and a practiced ear for good writing. During his tenure, the journal regained its former place in the Yiddish intellectual and cultural world, savored for the quality of its articles and the range of its subjects, from literature and economics to labor and world affairs.

But time was taking its inexorable toll. Readers of Yiddish were dying out. Aging Jewish anarchists retired to Florida and California. The Jewish Anarchist Federation dissolved in 1966, and anarchist branches of the Workmen's Circle disbanded or merged with nonanarchist branches. The Kropotkin Branch of Los Angeles was the last to go, closing its doors in 1975 after more than fifty years of activity. The *Fraye Arbeter Shtime*, too, was on its last legs. In May 1977 it held its last annual banquet, an event recorded in the *New York Times*.[90] In December of that year it ceased publication, the victim of mounting costs and declining circulation. At the time of its demise, after eighty-seven years, it was the world's oldest Yiddish publication and, apart from the London *Freedom*, founded in 1886, the oldest anarchist journal in existence. It was also the last of the foreign-language anarchist papers in the United States, *L'Adunata dei Refrattari*, its Italian counterpart, having folded in 1971.[91]

The closing of the *Fraye Arbeter Shtime* marked the end of the Jewish anarchist movement in America. The Jewish anarchists, during nearly a hundred years of activity, had compiled an impressive record.

Not only did they have the courage to reject accepted standards and to suffer hardship for the sake of principles they believed to be right, but within their circles and groups, their newspapers and forums, they found a rich social and cultural life, a spirit of warmth, of camaraderie, of high-minded devotion to a common cause. Moreover, by defying the conventions of the prevailing social and political system, they obtained a glimpse of that freer world towards which they had so ardently aspired.

CHAPTER FOURTEEN

Alexander Berkman: A Sketch

MORE THAN a century after his birth and a half-century after his death, Alexander Berkman is beginning to receive the recognition he deserves. His name, until recently, had been little known outside anarchist circles. He is seldom mentioned in histories of the United States, and then only in connection with the Homestead steel strike of 1892, when he tried to assassinate Henry Clay Frick. But the revival of interest in anarchism during the past decades has begun to acquaint a broader public with Berkman's life and ideas; and with the reprinting of his prison memoirs and of his primer of communist anarchism, it remains only to reissue his Russian diary to complete his trilogy of major writings.[1]

For Berkman was much more than "the man who shot Frick." Between his release from prison in 1906 and his deportation to Russia in 1919, he was, with Emma Goldman, the leading figure in the American anarchist movement, the editor of its foremost periodical, a gifted writer and speaker, and the martyr of prolonged imprisonment for a cause that he cherished as "the very finest thing that humanity has ever thought of."[2] A man of uncompromising integrity, he showed none of the duplicity or thirst for power with which so many revolutionists have been tainted. To Victor Serge he was the lone survivor of a generation of idealists that had passed into history.[3] Exiled from America, exiled from Soviet Russia, he spent his last years in southern France, clinging to his faith in the ultimate triumph of his ideal. Berkman was a "transparently honest man," wrote H. L. Mencken, yet "we hunt him as if he were a mad dog—and finally kick him out of the country.

And with him goes a shrewder head and a braver spirit than has been seen in public among us since the Civil War."[4]

Berkman, the youngest of four children, was born of well-to-do Jewish parents in Vilna, Russia, on November 21, 1870. His father, a wholesaler in the shoe industry, was prosperous enough to be allowed to move to St. Petersburg, a privilege restricted to the upper echelons of Jewish merchants and professionals. Sasha (the Russian diminutive of Alexander) grew up in comfortable surroundings—complete with servants and a summer house near the capital—and attended a classical gymnasium reserved for the privileged elements of society. Yet at a very early age he was astir with dreams of revolt. The decade of the 1870s, particularly in St. Petersburg, saw the growth of Russian populism, which culminated in 1881 with the assassination of the tsar. Sasha's geography lesson was interrupted by the exploding bombs, which shattered the windows of his classroom. At home that evening his parents spoke in hushed tones, but his older brother, who sympathized with the revolutionists, came to his bedside and thrilled him with "mysterious, awe-inspiring words: Will of the People—tyrant removed—Free Russia."[5]

Young as he was, Sasha was deeply moved by the martyrdom of the populists, five of whom were hanged for their part in the assassination. He was inspired by their idealism and courage, and from that time forward their example lingered in his thoughts, remaining fresh a decade later when he resolved to assassinate Frick. A special source of inspiration was his mother's youngest brother, the "Uncle Maxim" of his prison memoirs, who was banished to Siberia when Sasha was entering gymnasium. Documents in Berkman's archives reveal that "Uncle Maxim" was none other than Mark Natanson, one of the most famous of the revolutionary leaders, whose populism was strongly tinged with anarchist sympathies and who was admired by his comrades for his organizing abilities, clear-headedness, and self-sacrifice, traits that his nephew exhibited in abundant measure. A founder of the Chaikovsky circle (of which Peter Kropotkin was a member) and of the Land and Freedom society, the largest populist organization of the 1870s, Natanson afterwards became a key figure in the Socialist Revolutionary party, a staunch antimilitarist during the First World War, a leader of the Left Socialist Revolutionaries during the Russian Revolution, and a severe critic of the Bolshevik dictatorship, which drove him into exile in Switzerland, where he died in 1919.

Such was "Uncle Maxim," whom Berkman later called "my ideal of a noble and great man."[6] And Berkman's own career was to follow a similar path. At school he was considered one of the ablest students, though "too rebellious." At the age of twelve he wrote an essay denying the existence of God. At fifteen, already reading revolutionary literature, he was demoted for "precocious godlessness, dangerous tendencies, and insubordination."[7] By then he was living in Kovno, a town in the Jewish Pale of Settlement, where the family had moved after his father's untimely death deprived them of the right to live in the capital. The following year his mother died also, leaving Sasha an orphan. Six months later, in February 1888, he left for America to begin a new life.

ON NOVEMBER 11, 1887, just three months before his departure, the Haymarket anarchists had died on the gallows, and when Berkman arrived in New York the case was still being passionately discussed. Berkman, for whom the memory of the martyred Russian populists remained unfaded, was deeply affected by the hangings. He immediately flung himself into anarchist agitation, first in the principal Jewish group, the Pioneers of Liberty, then in the German *Freiheit* group led by Johann Most, the dominant figure in the immigrant wing of the movement.

The next few years, during which Berkman and Emma Goldman began their lifelong friendship, passed in relative quiet. But in 1892, after Sasha, Emma, and a young anarchist painter[8] had opened a lunchroom in Worcester, Massachusetts, the news broke of the shooting of workers at the Carnegie steel mills in Homestead, Pennsylvania, near Pittsburgh. Berkman, emulating his populist heroes, acquired a pistol and set out for Homestead to kill Frick, Carnegie's autocratic manager, whose elegant mansion with its remarkable collection of paintings still graces Fifth Avenue in New York. It was Frick who, by importing a private army of Pinkertons to break the strike, had precipitated the bloodshed. To Berkman, moreover, Frick was a symbol of capitalist oppression, whose removal, he thought, would rouse the people against the injustice of the existing order. Berkman's attempt, that is to say, was an act of propaganda by the deed, a solitary American *attentat* at a time when a rash of political assassinations had broken out all over Europe.

But it failed to awaken the people, just as it failed to eliminate Frick, who, though wounded by pistol and dagger, made a quick recovery. Berkman, however, paid dearly. For fourteen years (he went in at twenty-one and came out at thirty-five) he was immured in the Western Penitentiary of Pennsylvania, in Allegheny City, an experience hauntingly described in his *Prison Memoirs of an Anarchist*, published six years after his release. Yet prison, for all its stifling brutality, saw Berkman's character grow and mature. He was able to read Pushkin, Go-

gol, Turgenev, Hugo, and Zola, history and poetry, philosophy and religion—and by so doing, to develop his feeling for language and his latent ability to write. Prison, moreover, served to strengthen his anarchist convictions. "My youthful ideal of a free humanity in the vague future," he wrote to Emma Goldman after nearly ten years behind bars, "has become clarified and crystallized into the living truth of Anarchy, as the sustaining elemental force of my every-day existence."[9]

Berkman's survival of prison, with its long stretches of solitary confinement, bears witness to his indomitable spirit. Yet he emerged on the edge of collapse. Tormented by nightmares of the past, assailed by doubts for the future, he struggled to readjust to life. After a period of deep inner turmoil when at times he considered suicide, his spirits at last began to revive. By writing his prison memoirs he helped rid himself of the phantoms of Allegheny City, and before long he could again devote his energies to the cause of social justice. "I feel," he remarked, "like one recovering from a long illness: very weak, but with a touch of joy in life."[10]

With the death of Johann Most in 1906 (shortly before Berkman's release from prison), Berkman, together with Emma Goldman, became the leading figure in the American anarchist movement. Addressing meetings, organizing demonstrations, editing periodicals, and agitating among the workers and unemployed, he did more than any of his associates, apart from Goldman herself, to futher the libertarian cause. Under his editorship, Goldman's *Mother Earth* became the foremost anarchist journal in the United States and one of the best produced anywhere in the world. In view of his crushing imprisonment, Emma later recalled, he "surprised everybody by the vigour of his style and the clarity of his thoughts."[11] In addition to his chores on her journal, he edited and corrected the proofs of Goldman's *Anarchism and Other Essays* (published by the Mother Earth press in 1910), as he was to do with all her future books, including her memorable autobiography, *Living My Life*.

Berkman, at the same time, was active in other areas of work. In 1910 and 1911 he helped organize the Ferrer School in New York, which encouraged a libertarian spirit among its students, and he served as one of its first teachers. During the next few years, moreover, he presided over demonstrations for the unemployed and agitated for such causes as the Lawrence textile strike of 1912 and the Ludlow massacre of 1914. With the outbreak of the First World War, he organized antimilitarist rallies in New York and made extended lecture tours through the country, trying to arouse public opinion against the growing war hysteria. Towards the end of 1915 he went to California to campaign for the release of David Caplan and Matthew Schmidt, who had been jailed for their complicity with the McNamara brothers in bombing the Los Angeles Times Building five years before. And in January 1916 he launched in San Francisco his own revolutionary paper, *The Blast*, which, during its eighteen-month existence, became second only to *Mother Earth* as the most influential anarchist journal in America.

The Blast, however, proved an unfortunate title. On July 22, 1916, a bomb exploded during the San Francisco Preparedness Parade, killing ten and injuring forty, and the police tried to implicate Berkman, who was innocent of any connection with the affair. Their efforts, however, were unsuccessful, and the blame was pinned on two labor militants, Thomas Mooney and Warren Billings (neither of whom was an anarchist), who, as Richard Frost shows in his exhaustive study of the case, were convicted on the basis of perjured testimony and fabricated evidence.[12]

As in the Haymarket tragedy, it was never discovered who actually threw the bomb, yet Billings was sentenced to life imprisonment and Mooney to death by hanging. Berkman, as Frost also shows, was one of the first to come to their aid, raising funds, securing attorneys, and setting in motion a nationwide campaign in their defense. At Berkman's instigation, anarchists (among them Anatoli Zhelezniakov) even demonstrated outside the American embassy in Petrograd in the midst of the Russian Revolution, causing President Wilson to intervene in the case and secure a commutation of Mooney's sentence.[13] Without Berkman's assistance, Mooney and Billings might have suffered the fate of Parsons and Spies, of Sacco and Vanzetti. As it was, they were not released until 1939, having spent more than two decades in prison for a crime they did not commit.

In 1917, on America's entry into the war, Berkman returned to New York to agitate against conscription. He was soon arrested, tried, and sentenced to two years in Atlanta Federal Prison, seven months of which he spent in solitary confinement for protesting against the beating of his fellow inmates. He emerged, said Goldman, who herself was jailed for denouncing the draft law, "with the horrors of his experience burned into his soul" and nearer to collapse, both physically and morally, than he had been after fourteen years in Western Penitentiary.[14]

But the government, swept by a wave of anti-revolutionary hysteria, was not content until he was driven out of the country. And in December 1919 he and Goldman were deported to Russia. At a farewell dinner in Chicago on the eve of their departure, they were told the news of the death of Frick, whom Berkman had tried to kill more than a quarter century before. "Deported by God," was Berkman's comment. Frick, added Emma, was but a man "of the passing hour. Neither in life nor in death would he have been remembered long. It was Alexander Berkman who made him known, and Frick will live only in connexion with Berkman's name. His entire fortune could not pay for such glory."[15]

IN JANUARY 1920 Berkman, now nearly fifty, returned to the land he had left in his youth a generation before. Having lost none of his passion for freedom and justice, he plunged with renewed energy into revolutionary activity, cooperating with the Bolsheviks in cultural if not political endeavors. For several months he and Goldman traveled through the country, from Archangel to Odessa, collecting material for the Museum of the Revolution in Petrograd. It was not long, however, before the methods of the Soviet government dampened his enthusiasm. He was stunned by the wholesale arrests of Russian anarchists, the dispersal of Makhno's guerrilla army, and the conversion of the local soviets into tools of the state apparatus. The Bolsheviks, he complained, while ruling in the name of the workers, were in fact destroying the popular initiative and self-reliance on which the success of the revolution depended.[16]

The final blow came with the suppression of the Kronstadt rising in March 1921. This, to Berkman, "symbolized the beginning of a new tyranny."[17] At the end of the year, his illusions shattered, Berkman decided to emigrate. "Grey are the passing days," he recorded in his diary. "One by one the embers of hope have died out. Terror and despotism have crushed the life born in October. The slogans of the Revolution are forsworn, its ideals stifled in the blood of the people. The breath of yesterday is dooming millions to death; the shadow of today hangs like a black pall over the country. Dictatorship is trampling the masses under foot. The Revolution is dead; its spirit cries in the wilderness. . . . I have decided to leave Russia."[18]

Once more in exile, a man without home or country, Berkman continued to work for the movement to which he had dedicated his life. After a brief stay in Stockholm, he went to Berlin, where he mingled in anarchist circles and published several pamphlets on Bolshevik Russia and the Kronstadt rebellion. In 1925 he moved to France, where he was to live out the rest of his life. To an old friend in Chicago he complained of "the inner struggles, the feeling of lonesomeness of soul and the mental travail of these days of disillusionment and reaction."[19] But he refused to despair. He threw himself into relief work in behalf of his comrades, organizing a fund for aging European anarchists (such as

Errico Malatesta, Sébastien Faure, and Max Nettlau) and becoming secretary and treasurer of a committee to aid anarchist prisoners in Russia, as well as the editor of its bulletin. In addition, he helped gather material on political persecution under the Bolshevik regime (*Letters from Russian Prisons*, published in 1925) and the same year brought out his own Russian diary, *The Bolshevik Myth*, one of the earliest and most penetrating accounts of emerging Soviet totalitarianism.

In 1926, Berkman, then living near Paris, was invited by the Jewish Anarchist Federation of New York to write a primer of anarchism. He consented, as Goldman explained,[20] for two reasons. First, to correct the distortions of anarchism in the mind of the average citizen, to whom it was synonymous with terrorism and chaos. To dispel this misconception, wrote Berkman to Nettlau, the foremost historian of anarchism, would require "a book that *any* person can read and understand. An ABC of Anarchism." In the second place, Berkman felt, it was necessary to reexamine the anarchist position in the light of the Russian Revolution, the chief lesson of which, he wrote, was that authoritarian methods "cannot lead to liberty, that methods and aims are in essence and effects identical."[21]

Such were the goals of *Now and After*, whose subtitle, *The ABC of Communist Anarchism*, gives a clearer idea of its contents. Berkman was not an original theorist. His ideas were drawn largely from Kropotkin and other founding fathers of the movement. But he was a lucid and gifted writer with a firm and fluent command of his subject. H. L. Mencken, himself no mediocre stylist, praised Berkman's ability to write "simple, glowing and excellent English."[22] The result was a classic, ranking with Kropotkin's *Conquest of Bread* as the clearest exposition of communist anarchism in English or any other language. Above all, for Berkman, "the idea was the thing."[23] To prepare men and women for a freer life, he believed, it was necessary to eliminate their authoritarian prejudices and nourish a new idea, a spirit of cooperation and mutual aid, that would enable them to live in harmony and peace. Towards that end his own small book, indeed his whole libertarian career, was an important contribution.

When *Now and After* was published in 1929, Berkman had only seven years to live. Under constant threat of expulsion by the French government, he earned a precarious living from translating, editing, and occasional ghostwriting for American and European publishers, an income that had to be supplemented by gifts from his comrades and friends. By the early 1930s his health began to fail and his letters complained of depression and fatigue. In early 1936 he underwent two operations for a prostate condition, which left him in chronic pain.

Finally, on June 28, 1936, suffering from his illness and unwilling to exist through the generosity of others, he shot himself to death in his Nice apartment. He died just three weeks before the outbreak of the Spanish Civil War, which, as Emma Goldman suggests, might have revived his spirits and given him a new lease on life.[24]

"To be a *man*," said Berkman, "a complete MAN," was the highest aim of life.[25] And he himself provided an outstanding example. "A rare person has left us," wrote his comrade Rudolf Rocker, "a great and noble character, and a real man. We bow quietly before his grave and swear to work for the ideal which he served faithfully for so many years."[26]

CHAPTER FIFTEEN

Ricardo Flores Magón in Prison

THE CAREER of Ricardo Flores Magón, the foremost Mexican anarchist of the twentieth century, involves a paradox. On the one hand, he must be counted among the martyrs of the Mexican Revolution. His movement, embodied in the Partido Liberal Mexicano, set in motion the forces that, in May 1911, drove Porfirio Díaz into exile. And his journal, *Regeneración*, which in the early stages of the Revolution reached a circulation of nearly thirty thousand, played an important part in rousing the Mexican laborers, rural as well as urban, against the Díaz dictatorship and in pushing the Revolution in a more egalitarian direction than it might otherwise have taken. Under the banner of "Land and Liberty," the Magonista revolt of 1911 in Baja California established short-lived revolutionary communes at Mexicali and Tijuana, having for their theoretical basis Kropotkin's *Conquest of Bread*, a work which Flores Magón regarded as a kind of anarchist bible and which his followers distributed in thousands of copies. Today the memory of Flores Magón is honored throughout Mexico. His remains rest in the Rotunda of Illustrious Men in Mexico City. In all parts of the country streets and squares bear his name, and Mexicans pay him homage as a great "precursor" of their Revolution,[1] one of the major social upheavals of the century.

And yet, the greater part of Flores Magón's adult life was spent not in Mexico but in the United States. When released from the Belén Prison in Mexico City towards the end of 1903, Flores Magón, threatened with further persecution, decided to leave the country and continue his agitation from across the border. On January 4, 1904, at the age of thirty, he crossed the Rio Grande at Laredo, Texas, never to see his homeland again. He spent the next nineteen years in the United States, more than half of them in prison. He was jailed in Missouri, in California, in Arizona, in Washington, and in Kansas, where he died at Leavenworth Penitentiary in 1922. His odyssey, as a friend remarked, had led "directly to the Cross."[2]

What began for Flores Magón as a struggle against Díaz thus became a simultaneous struggle against American political repression. Hounded by the police, by private detectives, by postal and immigration officials, he was driven from city to city, a prey to periodic arrests and under constant threat of deportation. Between 1904 and 1907 he lived in El Paso, San Antonio, St. Louis, Toronto, Montreal, and Los Angeles. In San Antonio an attempt was made on his life; in Los Angeles he was beaten by the police; in St. Louis and El Paso the offices of his newspaper were raided and its files and equipment confiscated. From 1907 to 1910 he found himself behind bars in Los Angeles and in Arizona.

It was during these years in the United States that Flores Magón's libertarian philosophy achieved its fullest flowering. By the same token, his movement fired the imagination of American anarchists and the Industrial Workers of the World. Both Emma Goldman and Alexander Berkman spoke and wrote in his behalf, raising funds for *Regeneración* and for lawyers and bail when Flores Magón and his associates were arrested. Additional money came from the Anarchist Red Cross in New York, thanks in part to the efforts of Lucy Parsons, the widow of the Haymarket martyr Albert R. Parsons. Voltairine de Cleyre, another prominent American anarchist, also collected funds for her Mexican comrades, to whom she dedicated her last poem, "Written-in-Red," published in *Regeneración* six months before her death.[3] Furthermore, two California anarchists, the German-born Alfred G. Sanftleben and the English-born William C. Owen, edited the English page of *Regeneración*, while the ranks of the Liberal army in Baja California included hundreds of American anarchists and Wobblies, among them Frank Little and Joe Hill, the most celebrated martyrs to the IWW cause.

On August 3, 1910, Ricardo Flores Magón was released from prison after three years of confinement for violating American neutrality laws. Six months later, his followers launched their revolt in Baja California, stirring high hopes among his American friends. Emma Goldman, in Los Angeles, spoke in support of his cause, cheered by a jubilant crowd who broke into radical songs. Jack London, after the capture of Mexicali, sent Flores Magón a message of encouragement: "We socialists, anarchists, hoboes, chicken-thieves, outlaws and undesirable citizens

of the United States are with you heart and soul in your effort to overthrow slavery and autocracy in Mexico."⁴ By the end of May, however, the rising had petered out; and on June 22, 1911, Flores Magón
was again convicted of infringing neutrality regulations. He was sentenced to one year and eleven months in the federal penitentiary on
McNeil Island, Washington, where the gloom of prison life was relieved by visitors from nearby Home colony, the leading anarchist
community on the West Coast. In January 1914, having completed his
sentence, Flores Magón went to work on a cooperative farm near Los
Angeles, resuming publication of *Regeneración* on a hand press with a
barn for an office. In February 1916, however, he was again arrested
and condemned to one year on McNeil Island, although execution of
the sentence was postponed. "Our crime?" he wrote to *The Blast*,
Berkman's paper in San Francisco. "Our refusal to accept the authority
of any Gods in heaven or on earth. 'Neither God nor Master!' is our
motto."⁵

Flores Magón's final arrest came on March 21, 1918, when he and
his colleague Librado Rivera fell victim to the antiradical hysteria that
swept the United States during the First World War. The occasion was
the publication, over their signatures, of a manifesto urging the anarchists and workers of the world to prepare for the coming social revolution. "Activity, activity, and more activity is what we must have at
this moment," the manifesto declared. "Let each man and each woman
that loves the anarchist ideal spread it with tenacity, without thinking
of danger or taking notice of ridicule or considering the consequences.
To work, comrades, and the future will be our ideal."⁶ Convicted under the Espionage Act of obstructing the war effort, Flores Magón received an appalling twenty-year sentence (Rivera was given fifteen
years) plus the one-year term that had been deferred in 1916. "A sentence of twenty-one years," he wrote to a friend at Home colony, "is a
sentence of life for a man as old and worn out as I am."⁷

On November 3, 1919, because of his declining health, Flores Magón was transferred from McNeil Island to the larger federal prison
and drier climate at Leavenworth, where Rivera soon followed him.
Ralph Chaplin, the Wobbly poet, who occupied an adjoining cell,
found Flores Magón "gentler, and fiercer, by nature than any man I
had ever met," although his face and manner were "those of a saint
rather than a soldier." Serving as prison librarian, he impressed "all of
us as the highest type of revolutionary idealist," and "though he was
broken in health by many years of imprisonment, his zeal for human
betterment was still unabated."⁸

While imprisoned at Leavenworth, Flores Magón began a long correspondence with "Ellen White," the pseudonym of Lilly Sarnoff, a young New York anarchist and member of the defense committee working for his release. Sarnoff, born in Russia in 1899, came to the United States in 1905 with fresh memories of the anti-Jewish pogroms she had witnessed. Joining the anarchist movement as a young girl, she was active in behalf of political prisoners and wrote poems and sketches for a number of American anarchist periodicals, including *The Road to Freedom* and *Man!* After Flores Magón's death, she threw herself into the campaign to save Sacco and Vanzetti, corresponding with them and visiting them in prison, as she had done with Flores Magón. For many years she was a member of the Ferrer colony at Stelton, New Jersey, where she continued to reside, with her companion Louis G. Raymond, until her death in 1981. In 1971 she published a booklet of poems, the first of which tells of Flores Magón and his calvary in America, where "rebels are not wanted," but "only those of small minds, crafty men, and ignorant."9

Over a two-year period from October 6, 1920, to November 12, 1922 (only nine days before his death), Ricardo Flores Magón wrote more than forty letters to Sarnoff (all have been preserved and all but one are on deposit in the International Institute of Social History in Amsterdam). All of the letters, together with others to Harry Weinberger, Flores Magón's indefatigable attorney, and to such friends as Nicolás T. Bernal, Gus Teltsch, and Rose Bernstein, were published in a Spanish translation in 1925 by the Grupo Cultural "Ricardo Flores Magón" of Mexico City.10 In 1976 the Tierra y Libertad Group of Mexico City issued a new Spanish translation of the letters to Sarnoff, followed by facsimile copies of the originals.11

The letters to Sarnoff are of considerable interest. For, apart from revealing the horrors of prison life during the Palmer era, they discuss at some length the major issues—the attitude towards the Bolshevik Revolution and the prospects of a libertarian alternative—which preoccupied the entire anarchist movement in the aftermath of the war. Like most anarchists, including Goldman and Berkman, Flores Magón had at first hailed Lenin and Trotsky as heralds of a new dawn of liberty and justice. By 1920, however, he was denouncing them for "killing" the revolution and imposing a new dictatorship upon the people. Tyranny, he declared, cannot but lead to tyranny, and "I am against despotism whether exercised by the workers or the bourgeoisie." But he never lost his faith that a genuine revolution was in the offing. "History," he asserted, "is already writing the last lines of the period which had its cradle in the ruins of the Bastille, and is about to open a new period, whose first chapter will be known by generations to come as the gropings of the human race upon the road to freedom."[12]

Flores Magón's letters, moreover, possess genuine literary merit, being written in a glowing if excessively florid style reflecting an age of romantic revolutionism that has since passed into history. W. C. Owen is justified in calling Flores Magón "one of the most powerful writers the revolutionary movement has produced."[13] For his literary talent, combined with his idealism and moral fervor, made *Regeneración* one of the outstanding anarchist journals of the period, winning him a devoted following both in Mexico and the United States. And his letters to Sarnoff and other comrades, distinguished by the same poetic eloquence and burning idealism as his writings in Spanish, reveal a remarkable command of the English language. In some respects, including the use of archaic or nonexistent words ("intermeddle," "candorous," "emphemerous"), they resemble the prison letters of Vanzetti, published in 1928.[14]

In spite of his transfer to Leavenworth, Flores Magón's health continued to deteriorate. Yet Weinberger, for all his strenuous efforts, was unable to secure his release. (Rejecting Weinberger's appeal, Attorney General H. M. Daugherty wrote of Flores Magón that he was "a dangerous man because of the seditious and revolutionary doctrines which he asserts and practices, and his determination not to abide by the laws of this country.")[15] Nor would Flores Magón recant his anarchist beliefs or make a personal appeal for pardon, preferring death to the ignominy of begging for mercy from the state. "When I die," he wrote in December 1920, "my friends will perhaps inscribe on my tomb, 'Here lies a dreamer,' and my enemies, 'Here lies a madman.' But no one will be able to stamp the inscription, 'Here lies a coward and a traitor to his ideals.' "[16]

In the early hours of November 21, 1922, Ralph Chaplin was awakened by the night orderly and informed that Flores Magón had died of heart failure in his cell. He was forty-nine years old and in the fifth year of his sentence. Some, including Librado Rivera, were convinced that he had been murdered, but Chaplin believed that a sudden physical collapse had indeed ended his life.[17] At any rate, it was the prison that had killed him. The authorities, by ignoring Weinberger's petitions for clemency and by failing to provide Flores Magón with adequate medical attention, had in effect condemned him to death. On hearing the news, Berkman, who himself had spent sixteen years in American prisons, wrote: "Ricardo was a splendid man and most devoted comrade. Those prison doctors—I know them—they'd swear you are well when you are breathing your last."[18] With the death of Flores Magón, the Red Scare had claimed another victim.

Thus it was only as a corpse that Ricardo Flores Magón, after two decades in exile, could return to his native country. When his body was brought back to Mexico, throngs of workers and peasants, with red and black flags, lined the railroad tracks as the special train with his flower-enshrouded coffin went from town to town on its way to the capital. To W. C. Owen, it was the courage and integrity of Flores Magón that inspired such devotion among his compatriots. "The man was so obviously sincere," wrote Owen, "so set in his conviction that, whoever else might be tamed into silence, he must speak; so intense in his determination to play out his part in the great struggle for the overthrow of human slavery, which he individually, at any cost, must fight out to the bitter end."[19]

In January 1923 Flores Magón was given a public funeral, one of the largest ever held in Mexico City. Like the funeral of Kropotkin in Moscow two years before, it became a political demonstration, with banners bearing the legend, "He Died for Anarchy." On May 1, 1945, the day of international working-class solidarity, his remains were interred in the national pantheon. "The Mexican state gave its blessing to the man who had cursed the existence of the State," an American historian has remarked. "It was a generous but ironic compliment."[20]

CHAPTER SIXTEEN

Mollie Steimer: An Anarchist Life

ON JULY 23, 1980, Mollie Steimer died of heart failure in the Mexican town of Cuernavaca, ending a life of uninterrupted activity in behalf of the anarchist cause. At the time of her death, Steimer was one of the last of the prominent figures closely associated with Emma Goldman and Alexander Berkman. She was also one of the last of the oldtime anarchists with an international reputation, the survivor of a remarkable company of Russian political exiles in Mexico that included such diverse figures as Jacob Abrams, Victor Serge, and Leon Trotsky.

When her heart gave out, Steimer was eighty-two years old. Born on November 21, 1897, in the village of Dunaevtsy in southwestern Russia, she had emigrated to the United States in 1913 with her parents and five brothers and sisters. Only fifteen when she arrived in the New York ghetto, she immediately went to work in a garment factory to help support her family. She also began to read radical literature, starting with Bebel's *Women and Socialism* and Stepniak's *Underground Russia* before discovering the works of Bakunin, Kropotkin, and Goldman. By 1917 Mollie had become an anarchist. With the outbreak of the Russian Revolution, she plunged into agitational activity, joining a group of young anarchists gathered around a clandestine Yiddish journal called *Der Shturm* (The Storm). Plagued by internal dissension, the Shturm group reorganized itself towards the end of the year, adopting the name of Frayhayt (Freedom) and launching a new journal under that title, of which five numbers appeared between January and May of 1918, with cartoons by Robert Minor and articles by Maria Goldsmith and Georg Brandes, among others. For its motto the editors chose Henry David Thoreau's celebrated dictum, "That government is best which governs not at all" (in Yiddish: "Yene regirung iz di beste, velkhe regirt in gantsn nit"), an extension of Jefferson's "That government is best which governs least."

The Frayhayt group consisted of a dozen or so young men and women, workers of east European Jewish origin, who met regularly at 5 East 104th Street in Harlem, where several of them, including Steimer, shared a six-room apartment. The most active figure in the group, apart from Mollie herself, was Jacob Abrams, thirty-two years old, who had immigrated from Russia in 1906.[1] In 1917, as secretary of the Bookbinder's Union, Abrams had labored to prevent the extradition of Alexander Berkman to San Francisco, where the authorities were seeking to implicate him in the famous Mooney-Billings dynamiting affair. Another member of the group was Abrams's wife Mary, a survivor of the tragic Triangle Shirtwaist fire in 1911, from which she managed to escape with minor injuries by jumping out of a window. The rest included Hyman Lachowsky, a printer, Samuel Lipman, twenty-one years old and more a Marxist than an anarchist, Lipman's girlfriend Ethel Bernstein, her sister Rose Bernstein, Jacob Schwartz, Sam Hartman, Bernard Sernaker (whose daughters, Germinal and Harmony, attended the Ferrer School at Stelton), Clara Larsen, Sam and Hilda Adel (uncle and aunt of the writer Leon Edel), and Zalman and Sonya Deanin.

The group, as a collective, edited and distributed their newspaper in secret. This was necessary because it had been outlawed by the federal government for its opposition to the American war effort, not to speak of its anticapitalist, prorevolutionary, and pro-Soviet orientation ("The only just war is the social revolution," proclaimed its masthead). Printing the paper on a hand press, the group folded it tightly and stuffed it at night into mailboxes around the city. Federal and local officials soon became aware of their activities but were unable to track the group down, until an incident occurred that catapulted Abrams, Steimer, and their comrades into the headlines—and also landed them in jail.

What provoked the incident was the landing of American troops in Soviet Russia during the spring and summer of 1918. Viewing the intervention as a counterrevolutionary maneuver, the members of the Frayhayt group resolved to stop it. With this object, they drafted two leaflets, one in English and one in Yiddish, appealing to the American workers to launch a general strike. "Will you allow the Russian Revolution to be crushed?" the English leaflet asked. "YOU; yes, we mean YOU, the people of America! THE RUSSIAN REVOLUTION CALLS TO THE WORKERS OF THE WORLD FOR HELP. The Russian Revolution cries:

'Workers of the world! Awake! Rise! Put down your enemy and mine!' Yes, friends, there is only one enemy of the workers of the world and that is capitalism.'' The Yiddish leaflet bore a similar message: "Workers, our reply to the barbaric intervention has to be a general strike! An open challenge will let the government know that not only the Russian worker fights for freedom, but also here in America lives the spirit of revolution. Do not let the government scare you with their wild punishment in prisons, hanging and shooting. We must not and will not betray the splendid fighters of Russia. Workers, up to fight!"[2]

Both leaflets were printed in five thousand copies. Steimer distributed most of them at different places around the city. Then, on August 23, 1918, she took the remainder to the factory in lower Manhattan where she worked, distributed some by hand, and threw the rest out of a washroom window on an upper floor. Floating to the street below, they were picked up by a group of workmen, who immediately informed the police. The police in turn notified American military intelligence, which sent two army sergeants to the building. Going from floor to floor, they encountered a young worker named Hyman Rosansky, a recent recruit of the Frayhayt group, who had been helping with the distribution of the leaflets. Rosansky admitted his involvement, turned informer, and implicated the rest of his comrades.

Steimer was quickly taken into custody, along with Lachowsky and Lipman. The same day, police raided the headquarters of the group on East 104th Street, wrecking the apartment and arresting Jacob Abrams and Jacob Schwartz, who were beaten with fists and blackjacks on the way to the station house. When they arrived, further beatings were administered. Schwartz was spitting blood. Soon afterwards, Lachowsky was brought in bruised and bleeding, with tufts of hair torn from his head.[3] During the next few days, the rest of the group were rounded up and questioned. A few were released, but Abrams, Steimer, Lachowsky, Lipman, and Schwartz, along with a friend named Gabriel Prober, were indicted on charges of conspiracy to violate the Sedition Act, passed by Congress earlier that year. Rosansky, who had cooperated with the authorities, was granted a postponement of his hearing.

The Abrams case, as it came to be known, constitutes a landmark in the repression of civil liberties in the United States. The first important prosecution under the Sedition Act, it is cited in all standard histories of the subject as one of the most flagrant violations of constitutional rights during the Red Scare hysteria that followed the First World War.[4]

The trial, which lasted two weeks, opened on October 10, 1918, at the Federal Court House in New York. The defendants were Abrams,

Steimer, Schwartz, Lachowsky, Lipman, and Prober. Schwartz, however, never appeared in court. Severely beaten by the police, he was
removed to Bellevue Hospital, where he died on October 14, while the
trial was in progress. Official records attribute his death to Spanish
influenza, an epidemic of which was raging. According to his comrades, however, Schwartz had been brutally murdered. His funeral became a political demonstration; and on October 25 a memorial meeting, chaired by Alexander Berkman, was held in his honor at the
Parkview Palace. It was attended by twelve hundred mourners, who
heard speeches by John Reed, who had himself been arrested for condemning American intervention in Russia, and Harry Weinberger, the
defense attorney in the Abrams case, who had previously represented
Berkman and Goldman in their 1917 trial for opposing military conscription. He would shortly serve as counsel for Ricardo Flores Magón
in his bid to secure release from prison.

The Abrams case was tried before Judge Henry DeLamar Clayton,
who for eighteen years had represented Alabama in Congress. Clayton
proved to be another Gary or Thayer, the judges in the Haymarket and
Sacco-Vanzetti cases. He questioned the defendants about their "free
love" activity, and he mocked and humiliated them at every turn. "You
keep talking about producers," he said to Abrams. "Now may I ask
why you don't go out and do some producing? There is plenty of un-
tilled land needing attention in this country." When Abrams, at another point, called himself an anarchist and added that Christ was also
an anarchist, Clayton interrupted: "Our Lord is not on trial here. You
are." Abrams began to reply: "When our forefathers of the American
Revolution"—but that was as far as he got. Clayton: "Your what?"
Abrams: "My forefathers." Clayton: "Do you mean to refer to the
fathers of this nation as your forefathers? Well, I guess we can leave
that out, too, for Washington and the others are not on trial here."
Abrams explained that he had called them that because "I have respect
for them. We are a big human family, and I say 'our forefathers.' Those
that stand for the people, I call them fathers."[5]

Weinberger, the defense attorney, tried to show that the Sedition Act
was meant to penalize activities which hindered American conduct of
the war, and that since American intervention was not directed against
the Germans or their allies, then opposition to it by the defendants
could not be construed as interference with the war effort. This argument, however, was thrown out by Judge Clayton with the remark that
"the flowers that bloom in the spring, tra la, have nothing to do with
the case." The *New York Times*, praising the judge's "half-humorous
methods," declared that he deserved "the thanks of the city and of the

country for the way in which he conducted the trial." Upton Sinclair, by contrast, said that Clayton had been imported from Alabama to make Hester Street safe for democracy.[6]

Before the conclusion of the trial, Mollie Steimer delivered a powerful speech in which she explained her political beliefs. "By anarchism," she declared, "I understand a new social order, where no group of people shall be governed by another group of people. Individual freedom shall prevail in the full sense of the word. Private ownership shall be abolished. Every person shall have an equal opportunity to develop himself well, both mentally and physically. We shall not have to struggle for our daily existence as we do now. No one shall live on the product of others. Every person shall produce as much as he can, and enjoy as much as he needs—receive according to his need. Instead of striving to get money, we shall strive towards education, towards knowledge. While at present the people of the world are divided into various groups, calling themselves nations, while one nation defies another—in most cases considers the others as competitive—we, the workers of the world, shall stretch out our hands towards each other with brotherly love. To the fulfillment of this idea I shall devote all my energy, and, if necessary, render my life for it."[7]

With Clayton on the bench, the outcome of the trial was predictable. The jury found all but one of the defendants guilty (Prober was cleared on all counts). On the day of sentencing, October 25, Samuel Lipman stepped forward and began to address the court about democracy. "You don't know anything about democracy," interrupted Judge Clayton, "and the only thing you understand is the hellishness of anarchy."[8] Clayton sentenced the three men, Lipman, Lachowsky, and Abrams, to the maximum penalty of twenty years in prison and a $1,000 fine; Steimer received fifteen years and a $500 fine. (Rosansky, in a separate proceeding, got off with a three-year term.)

The barbarity of the sentences for the distribution of leaflets shocked liberals and radicals alike. A group of faculty members at the Harvard Law School, headed by Zechariah Chafee, protested that the defendants had been convicted solely for advocating nonintervention in the affairs of another nation, in short, for exercising the right of free speech. "After priding ourselves for over a century on being an asylum for the oppressed of all nations," declared Professor Chafee, "we ought not suddenly jump to the position that we are only an asylum for men who are no more radical than ourselves. Suppose monarchical England had taken such a position towards the republican Mazzini or the anarchist Kropotkin!"[9]

Joining Chafee in drafting a petition for amnesty was "the whole legal staff at Harvard," including such distinguished jurists as Roscoe Pound and Felix Frankfurter. Similar petitions were signed by Norman Thomas, Hutchins Hapgood, Neith Boyce, Leonard Abbott, Alice Stone Blackwell, Henry Wadsworth Longfellow Dana, and Bolton Hall. In Detroit, Agnes Inglis, the future curator of the Labadie Collection at the University of Michigan, worked in behalf of the defendants. An Italian anarchist of the same city wrote a play about the case and acted in it with his comrades.[10]

In addition, two organizations in New York came to the aid of the prisoners, who appealed their conviction to the U.S. Supreme Court. The first, the League for the Amnesty of Political Prisoners, chaired by Pryns Hopkins, with M. Eleanor Fitzgerald as secretary and Leonard Abbott, Roger Baldwin, Lucy Robins, Margaret Sanger, and Lincoln Steffens as members of the advisory board, issued a leaflet on the case, *Is Opinion a Crime?* The second group, the Political Prisoners Defense and Relief Committee, was organized by Sam and Hilda Adel, along with other former members of the Frayhayt group, supported by the *Fraye Arbeter Shtime*, the Workmen's Circle, and the Bookbinders' Union, of which Abrams had served as secretary. In 1919 it issued a thirty-two-page pamphlet entitled *Sentenced to Twenty Years Prison*, which constitutes a valuable source of information about the case. (A Russian translation was published by the Union of Russian Workers in the United States and Canada.)

Meanwhile, the four anarchists were released on bail to await the results of their appeal. Steimer immediately resumed her radical activities. Over the next eleven months she was arrested no fewer than eight times, kept in the station house for brief periods, released, then rearrested, sometimes without charges being preferred against her. On March 11, 1919, she was arrested at the Russian People's House on East 15th Street during a raid by federal and local police that netted 164 radicals, some of whom were later deported on the *Buford* with Goldman and Berkman. Charged with inciting to riot, Steimer was held for eight days in the notorious Tombs prison before being released on $1,000 bail, only to be arrested again and taken to Ellis Island for deportation. Locked up for twenty-four hours a day, denied exercise and fresh air and the right to mingle with other political prisoners, she went on a hunger strike until the authorities eased the conditions of her confinement. "The entire machinery of the United States government was being employed to crush this slip of a girl weighing less than eighty pounds," Emma Goldman complained.[11]

The government, however, was not yet ready to deport the twenty-one-year-old prisoner, whose case remained before the courts. Released from Ellis Island, Mollie was kept under constant surveillance. In the fall of 1919, when Goldman returned to New York after completing a two-year sentence in the federal penitentiary at Jefferson City, Missouri, Mollie took the opportunity to call on her. It was the beginning of a lasting friendship. Mollie reminded Emma of the Russian women revolutionaries under the tsar, earnest, ascetic, and idealistic, who "sacrificed their lives before they had scarcely begun to live." In Emma's description, Mollie was "diminutive and quaint-looking, altogether Japanese in features and stature." She was a wonderful girl, Emma added, "with an iron will and a tender heart," but "fearfully set in her ideas." "A sort of Alexander Berkman in skirts," she jested to her niece Stella Ballantine.[12]

Soon after her meeting with Goldman, Steimer was again arrested. She was imprisoned in the workhouse on Blackwell's Island, where she remained for six months, from October 30, 1919 to April 29, 1920. Locked up in a filthy cell, isolated once more from her fellow prisoners and barred from all contact with the outside world, she protested by singing "The Anarchist March" and other revolutionary songs at the top of her lungs and by staging another hunger strike.[13]

During this period, word came that the Supreme Court had upheld the conviction of Mollie and her comrades. Two justices, however, Louis Brandeis and Oliver Wendell Holmes, issued a strong dissenting opinion, agreeing with the defendants that their aim had been to help Russia and not to impede the war effort. "In this case," wrote Holmes, "sentences of twenty years' imprisonment have been imposed for the publishing of two leaflets that I believe the defendants have had as much right to publish as the Government has to publish the Constitution of the United States, now vainly invoked by them."[14]

When the Supreme Court announced its decision, Abrams, Lipman, and Lachowsky jumped bail and tried to escape to Mexico from New Orleans. Spotted by federal agents, their boat was stopped at sea, the men were removed and were taken to the federal prison in Atlanta, from which Berkman had just been released, pending his deportation to Russia. Like Berkman, Abrams and his comrades spent two years in Atlanta prison, from December 1919 to November 1921. Steimer, who had been informed of their escape plans, had refused to cooperate because it meant forfeiting $40,000 in bail contributed by ordinary workers. To deceive the men and women who had come to their aid, she felt, would be a dishonorable act. In April 1920 she was transferred from Blackwell's Island to Jefferson City, Missouri, where Goldman had been confined before her deportation with Berkman in December 1919.

Mollie remained in Jefferson City for eighteen months. Since the time of the trial, her life had been full of tragedy. Apart from her repeated incarcerations, one of her brothers had died from influenza and her father had died from the shock that followed her conviction. Yet she refused to despair. In a letter to Weinberger she quoted from a poem by Edmund V. Cooke:

> You cannot salt the eagle's tail,
> Nor limit thought's dominion;
> You cannot put ideas in jail,
> You can't deport opinion.

Weinberger, meanwhile, with the support of the Political Prisoners Defense and Relief Committee, had been trying to secure the release of his clients on condition of their deportation to Russia. Abrams and Lipman favored such an arrangement, but Lachowsky and Steimer were on principle opposed to deportation. Mollie was particularly adamant. "I believe," she told Weinberger, "that each person shall live where he or she chooses. No individual or group of individuals has the right to send me out of this, or *any* country!" She was concerned, moreover, for the other political prisoners in America who must remain behind bars. "They are my comrades, too, and I think it extremely selfish and contrary to my principles as an Anarchist-Communist to ask for my release and that of three other individuals at a time when thousands of other political prisoners are languishing in the United States jails."[15]

Abrams, exasperated by Steimer's stubborn adherence to principle, offered Weinberger a word of advice. "She must be approached like a good Christian," he wrote, "with a bible of Kropotkin or Bakunin. Otherwise you will not succeed."[16] In due course, an agreement was concluded, and Weinberger obtained the release of the four prisoners, with the stipulation that they must leave for Russia at their own expense and never return to the United States. The Political Prisoners Defense and Relief Committee took up a collection to pay for their transportation, and in November 1921 Steimer and the others arrived at Ellis Island to await deportation. They were not in the least upset about leaving America. On the contrary, they were eager to return to their homeland and to work for the revolution. As their comrade Marcus Graham wrote: "In Russia their activity is yet more needed. For there, a government rules masquerading under the name of the 'proletariat' and doing everything imaginable to enslave the proletariat."[17]

Although Mollie's friends and entire family were in the United States, her heart was light at the prospect of returning to Russia. "I shall advocate my ideal, Anarchist Communism, in whatever country I shall be," she told Harry Weinberger five days before her deportation. Two days later, on November 21, 1921, a farewell dinner was held at the Allaire Restaurant on East 17th Street in honor of the four young anarchists, with speeches by Weinberger, Leonard Abbott, Harry Kelly, Elizabeth Gurley Flynn, Norman Thomas, and others. From her cell on Ellis Island, Mollie sent an appeal to all "freedom-loving Americans" to join the social revolution.[18]

ON NOVEMBER 24, 1921, Mollie Steimer, Samuel Lipman, Hyman Lachowsky, and Jacob Abrams, accompanied by his wife, Mary, sailed for Soviet Russia on the SS *Estonia*. The *Fraye Arbeter Shtime* issued a warning. Despite their opposition to American intervention and their support of the Bolshevik regime, the paper predicted, they would not receive the welcome they expected, for Russia was no longer a haven for genuine revolutionaries but rather a land of authority and repression.[19] The prediction was soon to be borne out. Victims of the Red Scare in America, they became victims of the Red Terror in Russia. Arriving in Moscow on December 15, 1921, they found that Goldman and Berkman had already departed for the West, disillusioned by the turn the revolution had taken. (Steimer's disappointment in missing them, she wrote Weinberger, was "very deep.")[20] Kropotkin had died in February, and the Kronstadt rebellion had been suppressed in March. Makhno's insurgent army had been dispersed, hundreds of anarchists languished in prison, and the workers' and peasants' soviets had become instruments of party dictatorship, rubber stamps for a new bureaucracy.

Amid the gloom, however, there were some bright spots. Abrams organized the first steam laundry in Moscow, operating it in the basement of the Soviet foreign ministry. At the same time, he was able to work with his anarcho-syndicalist comrades at the Golos Truda publishing house, which had not yet been suppressed. Lipman was reunited with his sweetheart Ethel Bernstein, who had been deported with Berkman and Goldman on the *Buford*. Always closer to Marxism than to anarchism, he completed a course of study in agronomy and in 1927 joined the Communist party. Lachowsky, unhappy in Moscow, returned to his hometown of Minsk to find work as a printer. And Steimer met Senya Fleshin, who became her lifelong companion.

Three years older than Mollie, Senya had been born in Kiev on December 19, 1894, and had emigrated to the United States at the age of sixteen, working at the office of Goldman's *Mother Earth* until he returned to Russia in 1917 to take part in the revolution. He had been active in the Golos Truda group in Petrograd and afterwards in the Nabat Confederation in the Ukraine. Writing in the confederation's journal in March 1919, he chastised the Bolsheviks for erecting a "Chinese wall" between themselves and the people.[21] In November 1920, the confederation was broken up and Senya, along with Volin, Mark Mratchny, and Aaron and Fanny Baron, were arrested and transferred to a prison in Moscow. Released soon after, he returned to Petrograd to work at the Museum of the Revolution. It was here that he met Steimer shortly after her arrival from America, and the two fell immediately in love.

Deeply disturbed by the suppression of their movement, Senya and Mollie organized a Society to Help Anarchist Prisoners, traveling about the country to assist their incarcerated comrades. On November 1, 1922, they were themselves arrested on charges of aiding criminal elements in Russia and maintaining ties with anarchists abroad (they had been corresponding with Berkman and Goldman, then in Berlin). Sentenced to two years' exile in Siberia, they declared a hunger strike on November 17 in their Petrograd jail, and were released the next day. They were forbidden, however, to leave the city and were ordered to report to the authorities every forty-eight hours.

Before long, Senya and Mollie resumed their efforts in behalf of their imprisoned comrades. On July 9, 1923, their room was raided and they were again placed under arrest, charged with propagating anarchist ideas, in violation of Art. 60-63 of the Soviet Criminal Code. Sequestered from their fellow prisoners, they again declared a hunger strike. Protests to Trotsky by foreign anarcho-syndicalist delegates to a congress of the Red International of Trade Unions (Profintern) soon brought about their release. This time, however, they were notified of their impending expulsion from the country. From Moscow came Jack and Mary Abrams and Ethel Bernstein to bid them farewell. On September 27, 1923, they were placed aboard a ship bound for Germany.[22]

Upon landing, Senya and Mollie went straight to Berlin, where Alexander Berkman and Emma Goldman were awaiting them. They arrived half-starved and penniless and without a permanent passport. For the next twenty-five years they lived as "Nansen" citizens, anarchists without a country, until they acquired Mexican citizenship in 1948. From Berlin Mollie sent two articles to the London *Freedom*, "On Leaving Russia" (January 1924) and "The Communists as Jailers" (May 1924), in which she described her recent experience. When deported from America two years before, her "heart was light," she said, but she was "deeply grieved" to be deported from Russia, even though the "hypocrisy, intolerance, and treachery" of the Bolsheviks "aroused in me a feeling of indignation and revolt." In her homeland, she declared, a great popular revolution had been usurped by a ruthless political elite. "No, I am NOT happy to be out of Russia. I would rather be there helping the workers combat the tyrannical deeds of the hypocritical Communists."[23]

In Berlin, and afterwards in Paris, Senya and Mollie resumed the relief work that had led to their deportation. Together with Berkman, Goldman, Alexander Schapiro, Volin, and Mratchny, they served on the Joint Committee for the Defense of Revolutionaries Imprisoned in Russia (1923-1926) and the Relief Fund of the International Working Men's Association for Anarchists and Anarcho-Syndicalists Imprisoned in Russia (1926-1932), sparing no effort to maintain a steady flow of parcels and messages of encouragement to their imprisoned and exiled comrades. Their archives, housed at the International Institute of Social History in Amsterdam, bulge with letters from Siberia, the White Sea, and Central Asia, from such exotic-sounding places as Pinega, Minusinsk, Ust-Kulom, Narym, and Yeniseisk, which made up the Gulag Archipelago. Some of the letters were from anarchists they had known in America.

In Paris, to which Senya and Mollie moved in 1924, they lived in a room with Volin and his family, before moving in with yet another Russian anarchist fugitive, Jacques Doubinsky. In 1927 they joined Volin, Doubinsky, and Berkman in forming the Mutual Aid Group of Paris to assist fellow anarchist exiles, not only from Russia but also from Italy, Spain, Portugal, and Bulgaria, penniless, without legal documents, and in constant danger of deportation, which in some cases would have meant death.

At the same time, they joined Volin, Berkman, and others in denouncing the *Organizational Platform* drawn up by another Russian exile, Peter Arshinov, with the encouragement of Nestor Makhno. To Senya and Mollie, the *Organizational Platform*, with its call for a central executive committee, contained the seeds of authoritarianism and clashed with the basic anarchist principle of local autonomy. "Alas," wrote Mollie in November 1927, "the entire spirit of the 'platform' is penetrated with the idea that the masses MUST BE POLITICALLY LED during the revolution. There is where the evil starts, all the rest . . . is mainly based on this line. It stands for an Anarchist Communist Workers' Party, for an army . . . for a system of defense of the revolution which will inevitably lead to the creation of a spying system, investigators, prisons and judges, consequently a TCHEKA."[24]

In order to earn a living, Senya had meanwhile taken up the profession of photography, for which he exhibited a remarkable talent; he became the Nadar of the anarchist movement, with his portraits of Berkman, Volin, and many other comrades, both well known and obscure, as well as a widely reproduced collage of the international anarchist press. In 1929 Senya was invited to work in the studio of Sasha Stone in Berlin. There, assisted by Mollie, he remained until 1933, when Hitler's rise to power forced them to return to Paris, where they continued to live until the outbreak of the Second World War.

During these years of exile in the 1920s and 1930s, Senya and Mollie received a steady stream of visitors—Harry Kelly, Rose Pesotta, Rudolf and Milly Rocker, among others—some of whom recorded their impressions of their old friends. Kelly, for example, found Mollie "as childlike in appearance as ever, and as idealistic too." Goldman, however, thought her "narrow and fanatical," while Senya was always "ill and broken." Emma again compared Mollie to Berkman as a young militant and "a fanatic to the highest degree. Mollie is a repetition in skirts. She is terribly sectarian, set in her notions, and has an iron will. No ten horses could drag her from anything she is for or against. But with it all she is one of the most genuinely devoted souls living with the fire of our ideal."[25]

The most emotional reunion of these years came in 1926, when Jack and Mary Abrams arrived from Russia, disenchanted with the Soviet system. For several weeks the four old comrades shared Senya and Mollie's room in Volin's flat, talking over old times and wondering what the future held in store, until the Abramses went on to Mexico, where they lived out the remainder of their lives. As for the other defendants in the 1918 trial, Lachowsky had moved to his native Minsk and was never heard from again, while Lipman worked as an agronomist until Stalin's Great Purge, when he was arrested and shot. His wife Ethel was sent to a Siberian prison camp for ten years and now resides in Moscow, alone and impoverished. Their only child, a son, was killed at the front during the war against Hitler.[26]

The outbreak of the war in 1939 found Senya and Mollie in Paris. At first they were not molested, but before long their Jewish origins and anarchist convictions caught up with them. On May 18, 1940, Mollie was placed in an internment camp, while Senya, aided by French comrades, managed to escape to the unoccupied sector of the country. Somehow, Mollie secured her release, and the two were reunited in Marseilles, where they saw their old friend Volin for the last time in the autumn of 1941. Soon afterwards, they crossed the Atlantic and settled in Mexico City. "How my heart aches for our forsaken beloved ones," wrote Mollie to Rudolf and Milly Rocker in December

1942. "Who knows what will become of Volin, of all our Spanish friends, of our Jewish family! It *is* maddening!"[27]

For the next twenty years Senya operated his photographic studio in Mexico City under the name SEMO—for Senya and Mollie. During this time they formed a close relationship with their Spanish comrades of the Tierra y Libertad group, while remaining on affectionate terms with Jack and Mary Abrams, notwithstanding Jack's friendship with Trotsky, who had joined the colony of exiles in Mexico. Shortly before his death in 1953, Abrams was allowed to enter the United States to have an operation for throat cancer. "He was a dying man who could hardly move," their friend Clara Larsen recalled, "yet he was guarded by an FBI agent twenty-four hours a day!"[28]

Mollie, however, never returned to America. Friends and relatives had to cross the border and visit her in Mexico City or Cuernavaca, to which she and Senya retired in 1963. When deported from the United States, Mollie had vowed to "advocate my ideal, Anarchist Communism, in whatever country I shall be." In Russia, in Germany, in France, and now in Mexico, she remained faithful to her pledge. Fluent in Russian, Yiddish, English, German, French, and Spanish, she corresponded with comrades and kept up with the anarchist press around the world. She also received many visitors, including Rose Pesotta and Clara Larsen from New York.

In 1976 Mollie was filmed by a Dutch television crew working on a documentary about Emma Goldman, and in early 1980 she was filmed again by the Pacific Street Collective of New York, to whom she spoke of her beloved anarchism in glowing terms. In her last years, Mollie felt worn and tired. She was deeply saddened by the death of Mary Abrams in January 1978. Two years later, not long after her interview with Pacific Street films, she collapsed and died of heart failure in her Cuernavaca home. To the end, her revolutionary passion had burned with an undiminished flame. Senya, weak and ailing, was crushed by her sudden passing. Lingering on less than a year, he died in the Spanish Hospital in Mexico City on June 19, 1981.

Part III : Europe and the World

CHAPTER SEVENTEEN

The Paris Commune and Its Legacy

THE PARIS COMMUNE of 1871 was a pivotal event in modern history. The greatest urban insurrection of the nineteenth century, a shot heard around the world whose echoes have not died away, it made anarchists of Peter Kropotkin and Errico Malatesta and launched anarchist movements throughout the European continent. Although succeeded by an era of reaction and by the demise of the First International, it inspired eloquent and influential essays by Kropotkin and Bakunin, as well as one of Marx's best-known works, *The Civil War in France*, second only to the *Communist Manifesto* as his most powerful political tract.

At the time of its outbreak, friend and foe alike saw the Commune as an episode of the greatest importance, not only for France but for Europe as a whole. More than a century of historical perspective has reinforced this impression. The Commune, indeed, was an event of worldwide significance, whose impact was perhaps even greater abroad than within France itself, where it left scars that never completely healed. It showed how a war, especially a losing war, can trigger the outbreak of social rebellion, an example to be repeated in Russia, Spain, and China in the following century. For it was the defeat at Sedan, the conditions of the siege, and the humiliation of surrender that reawakened the revolutionary fervor of the workers, reviving the tradition of 1793 and 1848 and creating the climate for a popular revolutionary explosion. With its acts of heroism and self-sacrifice, with its pioneering measures of reform, the Commune became a source of inspiration for future generations. To this day the Mur des Fédérés in the Père-Lachaise Cemetery, where 147 Communards were massacred in the Bloody Week of May, remains a place of pilgrimage for social-ists, anarchists, and communists alike.

The defeat of the Commune, however, became an object lesson for those who sought to learn from its mistakes. It has been argued by anarchists as well as by Marxists that had the Communards seized the initiative and marched on Versailles, the outcome might have been dif-ferent. Although the majority held back for fear of provoking a civil war, some activists in the Commune (chiefly the Blanquists) urgently pleaded for such a course on the grounds, as Engels was to put it, that "the defensive is the death of every armed rising." Marx agreed. "If they are defeated," he wrote of the Communards in April 1871, "only their 'good nature' will be to blame."[1] But this is extremely doubtful. For though it is true that the failure of the Communards to take the offensive ensured their ultimate defeat, a march on Versailles had little chance of success, given the encirclement of Paris by Prussian troops. Bismarck would hardly have stood by and allowed a revolutionary movement to take possession of France.

Why then has this relatively brief episode—the Commune lasted only seventy-two days, from March 18 to May 28—been the object of such prolonged controversy? Was it the end of an old revolutionary tradition or the beginning of something new? This question is one of the many still in dispute. Yet the answer is plain: it had elements of both. With its tenacious parochialism, its proliferation of sections and clubs, its sans-culotte ideology, its Committee of Public Safety, its slo-gans of Liberty, Equality, Fraternity and of the Declaration of the Rights of Man, it was a throwback to the past. On the other hand, its rejection of centralized authority and its experiments in women's rights and workers' control pointed the way to the future. It was a bridge between the French and Russian revolutions, the echo of the first and the precursor of the second, the end of a dying epoch and the start of a new one that has yet to run its course.

What in fact happened in Paris in 1871? Was the Commune a work-ing-class government? A dictatorship of the proletariat? A negation of the state? Such were the respective descriptions of Marx, Engels, and Bakunin. Of the three famous revolutionaries, however, only Bakunin was a consistent supporter of the Commune. More than that, he took a personal part in its predecessors at Lyons and Marseilles in the fall of 1870. Marx, by contrast, remained strongly opposed to a revolt in Paris until its actual eruption. The establishment of a Commune, Marx believed, would be "desperate folly," and he warned the workers against any premature rising. Only after it was under way did he throw his support behind it, delivering an eloquent tribute that was at the same time an obituary: "Workingman's Paris with its Commune will forever be celebrated as the glorious harbinger of a new society. Its martyrs are enshrined in the great heart of the working class."

The principles of the Commune were eternal, said Marx. They could never be crushed, but would assert themselves again and again until the workers had been emancipated. Bakunin shared this view. Both men saw the Commune as the prototype of a new society. For Bakunin, however, it was not a proletarian dictatorship, nor any government at all, but rather the "bold and outspoken negation of the state," inaugurating "a new era of the final emancipation of the people and of their solidarity."[2] For James Guillaume, Bakunin's Swiss associate, the Commune constituted a "federalist revolution," paving the way for a "true state of anarchy, in the proper sense of the word." Kropotkin, in the same vein, hailed the Commune as the "precursor of a great social revolution . . . the starting point for future revolutions."[3]

YET NEITHER the anarchists nor the Marxists can claim the Commune as their exclusive property. Its program had no clear-cut identity to which any single label could apply. On the contrary, the Commune defies neat ideological or partisan classification. Reflecting a variety of interests and aspirations, it was all things to all men. Recent research has reemphasized its complexity. It exhibited both centralist and federalist, both authoritarian and libertarian, tendencies. It saw utopianism mixed with practical experimentation, patriotism combined with visions of universal brotherhood. In its social composition it was a mixture of workers and professionals, of tradesmen and artisans. Bakuninists and Marxists, Proudhonists and Blanquists, Republicans and Jacobins all played a part.

Its roots, however, were deeply embedded in local particularism; its thrust was overwhelmingly decentralist and libertarian; and its tactics were those of improvisation and direct action. For most laboring people, in France as elsewhere, the ideal society remained a direct democracy of councils, clubs, and communes, an anti-authoritarian commonwealth in which workers, artisans, and peasants might live in peace and contentment, with full economic and political liberty organized from below, a vision conjured by rebels and dissenters since the Middle Ages.

In keeping with this vision, the Commune established local control over economic, educational, and cultural as well as political and military affairs. It expropriated the clergy and converted the churches into social forums. It abolished the police and the army, assigning their duties to ordinary citizens—to "the people in arms"—with elected officers. It made public offices elective and limited their salaries to work-ers' wages. Given its brief existence and its overriding preoccupation with food and defense, its measures of reform were impressive. Rents were suspended and the payment of debts spread out. Free schools were opened and an artists' council established (Proudhon's friend Courbet was at its head). Essential public services—post, sewerage, gas, transportation—were kept running efficiently.

In the field of labor and industry the reforms were particularly re-markable. Fines were abolished in the factories. Night work was abol-ished in the bakeries. The ten-hour day was introduced in some shops. Above all, the Commune showed that ordinary workers were capable of running their own affairs. The stonecutters inaugurated a program of insurance. Unemployed women set up cooperative workshops. Trade unions and factory councils sprang up in every district. Factories abandoned by their owners were occupied and converted into workers' cooperatives, anticipating the experiments in workers' self-manage-ment of the Russian and Spanish revolutions. "We believe," pro-claimed a workers' club in December 1870, "that workers have the right today to take possession of the tools of production, just as in 1789 the peasants took possession of the land."4 Such declarations were repeated many times during the course of the Commune, for ex-ample by the Union of Women for the Defense of Paris: "We consider that the only way to reorganize labor so that the worker enjoys the product of his work is by forming free producers' cooperatives which would run the various industries and share the profits." This declara-tion called further for "the abolition of all competition between men and women workers, since their interests are absolutely identical and their solidarity is essential to the success of the final and universal strike of Labor against Capital."5

SUCH were the features of the Commune which made it an event of unparalleled significance for the development of European anarchism and socialism. Nor is it surprising that its participants included follow-ers of Proudhon (who himself had died in 1865), among them Cour-bet, Longuet, and Vermorel. The influence of Proudhon—unquestion-ably greater than that of Marx—was reflected in the title of "Federals" by which the Communards were known. As George Woodcock has observed, the Commune's proclamation of April 19, 1871, which de-manded "the absolute autonomy of the Commune extended to all the localities in France, assuring to each its integral rights and to every Frenchman the full exercise of his aptitudes, as a man, a citizen, and a laborer," might have been written by Proudhon himself.6

A number of Bakuninist anarchists also took part, such as the brothers Elisée and Elie Reclus, Elie becoming the director of the Bibliothèque Nationale. In addition, there were future anarchists like Louise Michel and near-anarchists and libertarian socialists like Benoît Malon, Gustave Lefrançais, Arthur Arnould, and Eugène Varlin. Varlin, who was captured by Versailles troops, tortured, mutilated, and shot, becoming one of the Commune's most famous martyrs, had written in 1870 that "the coming revolution must free the workers radically from all forms of capitalism or political exploitation and establish all social relationships on the basis of the principle of justice."[7] Other well-known activists included the Italian revolutionary Amilcare Cipriani and Emile Henry's father, Fortuné Henry, who were afterwards driven into exile.

The Commune gave a strong impetus to the anarchist movements in Italy, Spain, and Switzerland, as well as in France itself. Moreover, the doctrines of anarchist-communism and propaganda by the deed both grew directly out of the Commune and were evolved in the 1870s by Kropotkin, Malatesta, and Paul Brousse, all of whom became anarchists in the wake of the Commune. In its original sense, in fact, propaganda by the deed meant not individual acts of terror but the seizure of a town or locality as the base for a social revolution on the lines of the Commune of Paris. More than a few Communard militants fled across the borders into Spain, Switzerland, and Italy, where they stimulated local anarchist movements as well as the formation of an anti-authoritarian International.

More than anything else, the Commune was the inspiration of the emerging libertarian movement. For anarchists of all countries it was the spontaneous expression of federalist and antistatist ideals, a model of social revolution and of the coming libertarian order. "Society in the future," wrote Bakunin in *The Paris Commune and the Idea of the State*, "ought only to be organized from the bottom upwards, by the free association and federation of the workers, in associations first, then in communes, regions, nations, and finally in a great international and universal federation. It is only then that the true and vital order of liberty and general happiness will be realized."

The Commune, as we have seen, had a similar impact on Kropotkin's thinking, providing the model for the social revolution that he elaborated in *Words of a Rebel*, *The Conquest of Bread*, and *Fields, Factories and Workshops*. His own career as an anarchist coincided exactly with the fifty years between the Paris Commune of 1871 and the Kronstadt Commune of 1921. It was in 1871, following the suppression of the Commune of Paris, that he renounced his scientific pursuits and dedicated himself to the revolutionary cause. As a member of the Chaikovsky circle from 1872 to 1874, he lectured to workers and peasants on the lessons of the Commune; and after his imprisonment in St. Petersburg he tapped out a history of the Commune to the excited occupant of an adjoining cell. Kropotkin recognized the limitations of the Commune, which "could be nothing but a first attempt." He saw that it did not break completely with the state and that authoritarian revolutionary groups had tarnished its libertarian character. Nevertheless, he cherished it as the first heroic effort "to put an end to the ignoble bourgeois exploitation, to rid the people of the tutelage of the state, and to inaugurate in the evolution of the human race a new era of liberty, equality, and solidarity."[8]

THE BRIEF COURSE of the Commune saw innumerable acts of courage by anonymous as well as celebrated heroes: a worker sitting calmly in a newspaper kiosk outside Montparnasse Station, long after his comrades had evacuated, deliberately loading and firing at a detachment of Versailles troops, then walking slowly away after his ammunition had run out; Charles Delescluze, in his top hat and frock coat with red sash, mounting the barricades on the eve of defeat, his aging body forming a silhouette in the setting sun for the Versailles sharpshooters; Louise Michel running down a street on March 18, shouting "Treason!" and preventing the removal of the guns on the heights of Montmartre; Louise Michel and Elizabeth Dmitrieff, after all hope had vanished, carrying supplies, caring for the wounded, and taking up arms behind the barricades. Such acts made the Commune an inspiring if ultimately tragic affair, creating a legend both in France and abroad. "History," declared Marx, "has no comparable example of such greatness." "They were madmen," said the painter Renoir, "but they had in them that little flame that never dies."[9]

But the Commune had its darker side too, its moments of treachery and intolerance, however obscured by the subsequent reverence for its memory within revolutionary circles. It had its villains as well as its heroes, among whom anti-Semitism and anti-intellectualism reared their heads in anticipation of the Action Française and twentieth-century fascism. Despite their proclamation of equal incomes, the leaders of the Commune voted themselves a salary of fifteen francs a day, well above that of the average worker and on a par with that of factory foremen or senior officers of the National Guard. Over the opposition of such libertarians as Courbet, Malon, Lefrançais, and Arnould, a Committee of Public Safety was established and censorship of the press imposed, with twenty-seven papers of all political stripes suppressed.

Félix Pyat and especially Raoul Rigault marred the noble image of the Commune by arbitrary arrests and executions and by the taking of hostages, a tactic vigorously opposed by Lefrançais and Delescluze. More than four hundred persons were arrested during the first ten days of the Commune alone, and the Archbishop of Paris and a number of priests were taken out and shot.

Yet all this pales beside the atrocities of the national government. The repressions were led by General Gallifet, a brutal officer who boasted of having taken no prisoners in the Mexican War. Twice as many people were killed in Paris during one week as in the country at large throughout the whole French Revolution. More than 25,000 were butchered, 5,000 deported, 50,000 arrested, 14,000 imprisoned, and thousands more driven into exile. "I have just returned from Paris," wrote Adolphe Thiers to his foreign minister in Versailles, "where I have seen some terrible sights. Come, my friend, and share our satisfaction."[10]

The scale and savagery of the repressions were out of all proportion to the nature of the revolt itself, standing in sharp contrast to the jubilee atmosphere of the preceding weeks. For the Commune had been a collective holiday, an explosion of joyful high spirits, a "festival of the oppressed," as Lenin called it, marked by intense feelings of fraternity, solidarity, generosity, and hope. All this added to the tragedy and made the ending all the more unbearable. "The Communards," wrote Kropotkin, "were slashed, stabbed, shot, and disemboweled by the murderers of Versailles." Some 3,000 died in the forts and prisons; there were mass shootings in the Satory depot; at each captured barricade the defenders were massacred; 147 were shot at the Mur des Fédérés.

Hysteria and rumor caused the slaughter of additional innocents. Women carrying milk bottles were shot in the back as incendiaries (*pétroleuses*). "Did a hand appear at a shutter, the window was riddled with bullets," wrote Voltairine de Cleyre. "Did a cry of protest escape from any throat, the house was invaded, its inhabitants driven out, lined against the walls, and shot where they stood."[11] In the aftermath, the authorities received nearly 400,000 denunciations, mostly anonymous yet often acted upon. Louise Michel was deported to New Caledonia, where she was converted to anarchism. Elizabeth Dmitrieff, seriously wounded, escaped to Switzerland, then returned to her native Russia, married a political exile, and died an early death in Siberia. Meanwhile, the London *Times* protested against "the inhuman laws of revenge under which the Versailles troops have been shooting, bayonetting, ripping up prisoners, women and children during the last six days. So far as we can recollect there has been nothing like it in history."[12] And yet, Bakunin wrote, because the Commune was "massacred and drowned in blood by the executioners of monarchic and clerical reaction, it has become all the more lively and powerful in the imagination and heart of the European proletariat."

THE COMMUNE of Paris must not be seen as an isolated event. Rather, it was part of a larger movement, both in area and in time, extending through southwestern Europe during the early 1870s. In fact it had already become a movement within France itself before spreading beyond its borders. And it started not in Paris but in Lyons, the most revolutionary of the provincial cities, in September 1870, following the collapse of the Second Empire. News of the Lyons Commune touched off a chain reaction up and down the Rhone valley and through Provence. During the fall and winter, there were risings in Marseilles, Toulouse, Narbonne, Cette, Perpignan, Limoges, Saint-Etienne, Le Creusot, and other towns. The movement was sporadic and short-lived—in some places the Commune never really got off the ground—but it was of great significance nevertheless, especially in Lyons and Marseilles, where it flared up anew after the Paris Commune was established in the spring.[13]

In the South, however, Bakuninists played a more prominent role than in the capital. In Marseilles three of Bakunin's followers, Gaston Crémieux, Charles Alerini, and André Bastelica, were at the center of events; and in Lyons it was Bakunin himself and his associate Albert Richard who stood at the helm. After seizing the town hall with the help of General Cluseret, Bakunin's first act was to proclaim the abolition of the state. Wall posters to that effect were put up on September 25, 1870:

ARTICLE 1: The administrative and governmental machinery of the state, having become impotent, is abolished.

ARTICLE 2: All criminal and civil courts are hereby suspended and replaced by the People's justice.

ARTICLE 3: Payment of taxes and mortgages is suspended. Taxes are to be replaced by contributions that the federated communes will have collected by levies upon the wealthy classes, according to what is needed for the salvation of France.

ARTICLE 4: Since the state has been abolished, it can no longer intervene to secure the payment of private debts.

ARTICLE 5: All existing municipal administrative bodies are hereby abolished. They will be replaced in each commune by committees for the salvation of France. All governmental powers will be exercised by these committees under the direct supervision of the People.

ARTICLE 6: The committee in the principal town of each of the nation's departments will send two delegates to a revolutionary convention for the salvation of France.

ARTICLE 7: This convention will meet immediately at the town hall of Lyons, since it is the second city of France and best able to deal energetically with the country's defense. Since it will be supported by the People, this convention will save France.

TO ARMS!!![14]

From southern France the communalist movement crossed the frontiers into Italy and Spain, where its tremors had immediately been felt. In Italy it took the form of a rising in Bologna in 1874, in which Bakunin played his last active role, and had its final echo in the Benevento insurrection of 1877, led by Bakunin's young disciples, Malatesta, Cafiero, and Stepniak. In Spain the "cantonalist" movement of 1873-1874 was directly inspired by the events in France, especially in Lyons and Marseilles, from which a number of refugees (Alerini and Paul Brousse among them) fled across the Pyrenees and took part in the formation of communes as well as in the Barcelona general strike of July 1873.

More than this, however, Paris was part of a broader tradition of revolutionary communes in different parts of the world and spread out over two centuries: France in 1793, 1848, and 1871; Russia in 1905, 1917, and 1921; Italy in 1874, 1877, and 1920; Germany in 1918-1919; Spain in 1873-1874 and 1936-1939; Central and Eastern Europe after the Second World War—East Berlin and Poznan, Budapest and Prague. To these might be added the Paris upheaval of 1968, with its attack on centralized authority and appeals for workers' control, and the little-known Shanghai Commune of 1967, established "on the model of the Paris Commune of 1871," according to its student and worker participants.[15]

For all their diversity, these events possessed a number of common features. They occurred, for the most part, not in the advanced industrial countries (as Marx expected) but rather (as Bakunin foresaw) in relatively backward and peripheral areas with artisan and peasant economies and strong regionalist traditions. All were social revolutions, revolutions from below, decentralist, federalist, and libertarian, directed against authoritarian and oligarchical regimes. All saw a host of councils and committees spring spontaneously into life in the vacuum of fallen governments which, as Kropotkin wrote of 1871, "evap-

orated like a pond of stagnant water in a spring breeze." All were profoundly egalitarian, exhibiting the same festive atmosphere, the same
high spirits and exhilaration, the same generosity and heroism. All
were stamped out with savage brutality followed by periods of intense
reaction. Yet all created martyrs to inspire rebellions in the future.

IN RUSSIA, too, as in Italy and Spain, the Commune had an immediate
impact, above all on the young populists who "went to the people" in
1873 and 1874 to stir them to social rebellion. In the wake of the Commune, as we have seen, Kropotkin became a lifelong anarchist; and
Peter Lavrov, who played a personal role in the Commune, called it
"the first, though still pale, dawn of the proletarian republic."[16] During the Revolution of 1905, a group of anarchists, calling themselves
Communards, tried to convert the town of Bialystok into a "second
Paris Commune." By the same token, during the Revolution of 1917
anarchists in Moscow and Petrograd sought to transform the twin cap-
itals into egalitarian communes modeled on an idealized image of
1871. "Through a Social Revolution to the Anarchist Commune," was
the battle cry of the Petrograd Federation of Anarchists.[17]

Lenin, too, following Marx, regarded the Commune as the first
modern revolution, the first stage in a historical process of which the
Russian Revolution was the second. In April 1917 he carried *The Civil
War in France* with him to the Finland Station, and he incorporated the
communal program in his *April Theses* and *State and Revolution*.
When Lenin died his body was wrapped in a Communard flag; and
forty years later Soviet cosmonauts carried portraits of Marx and
Lenin and a ribbon from a Communard banner on their journey into
outer space. From the libertarian perspective, however, after the October Revolution the ideals of 1871 were betrayed, and the Commune
became the anarchists' answer to the Bolshevik dictatorship.

Kronstadt 1921 was the last episode in Russia of the communalist
tradition. There were differences, of course, between Kronstadt and
Paris. Kronstadt was a smaller affair, lasting two weeks rather than
two months and involving proportionately fewer casualties, Moreover,
the rebels were opposing a socialist (at least in name) regime. Yet the
similarities were so striking that anarchists in Petrograd called Kronstadt the "Second Paris Commune." There was the same libertarian
atmosphere, the same rejection of centralized power, the same spontaneous formation of councils and committees, the same appeal for
workers' control, the same acts of heroism, the same failure to take the
offensive, and the same bloody outcome. By a curious irony, even the
dates coincided: Paris rose on March 18,1871; Kronstadt fell on

March 18, 1921, fifty years later to the day. Alexander Berkman perceived the parallel: "The victors are celebrating the anniversary of the Commune in 1871. Trotsky and Zinoviev denounce Thiers and Gallifet for the slaughter of the Paris rebels."[18]

But the example of Paris survived. Communes sprang up in Barcelona in 1936, in Budapest in 1956, and in Prague in 1968—all of them crushed by the Marxists themselves, who thereby demonstrated their revolutionary bankruptcy. "Some defeats are really victories," said Karl Liebknecht on the eve of his murder in 1919, "while some victories are more shameful than any defeats."[19] A fitting epitaph for the communal risings from Paris to Prague. Their tradition, moreover, survives as an alternative to centralized government. So, at least, Kropotkin believed: "Breaking the chains of the state and overthrowing its idols, mankind will march towards a better future, no longer knowing either masters or slaves, keeping its veneration for the noble martyrs who paid with their blood and suffering for those first attempts at emancipation which have lighted our way in our march towards the conquest of freedom."

CHAPTER EIGHTEEN

Paul Brousse: The Possibilist Anarchist

AMONG THE MANY notable individuals attracted to anarchism by the Paris Commune was the French physician Paul Brousse. Though largely forgotten today, a century ago Brousse was one of the most active and esteemed figures in the international anarchist movement, playing a major role in the anti-authoritarian wing of the First International and in the French, Spanish, Swiss, and German anarchist movements during their formative years. Through his companion, Natalia Landsberg, the daughter of a tsarist police official who herself became an ardent anarchist, he was also in close touch with the Russian anarchist exiles in Switzerland during the 1870s. He spoke at Bakunin's funeral in 1876 and collaborated with Kropotkin in editing the Swiss anarchist journal *L'Avant-Garde* in 1877 and 1878. Along with Kropotkin, moreover, he took part in formulating two of the central anarchist doctrines of the late nineteenth century, communist anarchism and propaganda by the deed.

Brousse is interesting, too, because of the unusual direction which his political development followed. From an uncompromising anarchist militant in his early years, a proponent of insurrectionism and revolt, he evolved towards a moderate form of socialism known as "possibilism" and ended up, after the turn of the century, as president of the Paris Municipal Council and a member of the French Parliament. As an apostate from anarchism Brousse incurred the hostility of his libertarian comrades, while as a reformist and former anarchist he was anathema to the Marxists, who resented the support that he commanded within the Second International, of which he was a founding member.

Brousse was born to a comfortable middle-class family at Montpellier, in southern France, on January 23, 1844. His grandfather was a grain merchant and his father a physician who headed the chemistry department in the medical school of Montpellier University. Young Brousse himself enrolled in this school and worked as a hospital intern during a cholera epidemic in 1867, for which he was granted exemption from all university fees. Completing his studies, he began his medical practice and political career at the same time, contributing in 1870 to the radical paper *Les Droits de l'Homme*, edited by his future rival, Jules Guesde.

As has been noted, it was the Commune of Paris that made Brousse—like Kropotkin, Malatesta, and many others—an anarchist. A supporter of the communal movement and a member of the Montpellier section of the International Working Men's Association, which was outlawed after the crushing of the Commune, he was arrested in 1872 and sentenced to four months in prison. Escaping to Spain, which was beginning to feel the impact of the communal revolt across the border, he met two other exiles, Charles Alerini and Camille Camet, both devoted Bakuninists who had taken part in the inauguration of revolutionary communes in southern France. In April 1873 the three expatriates founded a French-language section of the International at Barcelona, and Brousse became editor of its journal, *La Solidarité Révolutionnaire*, which was smuggled into France where it helped keep the International alive.[1]

By this time, the communal movement had taken root in Spain, and on June 20, 1873, a group of Internationalists, Brousse among them, seized the town hall of Barcelona, determined, as Brousse later told Kropotkin, "to make the Revolution or die."[2] Their attempt, though quickly dispersed, was followed a month later by a general strike, which collapsed when the government began drafting workers into the army. The failure of the general strike, in which Brousse took an active part, had a profound effect on the young insurrectionist, and throughout the rest of his career he resolutely opposed it as a revolutionary weapon.

Following the removal from power in July 1873 of Francisco Pi y Margall, an exponent of Proudhon's federalist ideas, a military reaction set in, and Barcelona ceased to be a revolutionary sanctuary. Accordingly, Brousse made his way to Switzerland, together with Alerini, Camet, and García Viñas, a leader of the Barcelona section of the International. Brousse's flight marked the beginning of his six-year involvement in the Jura Federation and Anti-Authoritarian International, during which he emerged in the forefront of the European anarchist movement. Brousse was then thirty years old. Of medium height, with penetrating brown eyes, black beard, and flowing black hair, he made a strong impression on all who met him, including Kropotkin, who describes him in his *Memoirs of a Revolutionist* as a "young doctor, full of mental activity, uproarious, sharp, lively, ready to develop any idea with a geometrical logic to its utmost consequences, powerful in his criticisms of the state and state organization; finding enough time to edit two papers, in French and in German, to writes scores of voluminous letters, to be the soul of the workmen's evening party; constantly active in organizing men, with the subtle mind of a true 'southerner.' "[3]

Settling in Bern, Brousse immediately plunged himself into agitation and propaganda on behalf of the Jura Federation, the nucleus of the international anarchist movement. Among the most able of the French exiles in Switzerland, he was an uncompromising libertarian, opposed to universal suffrage, which he attacked, in the spirit of Proudhon, as "the brutality of mere numbers" and a device of privileged society to keep the workers in subjection. He was equally opposed to any central organization in the International, and it was for his unremitting criticisms of Marx and the General Council that he had been ousted from the Montpellier section in September 1872, the same month that Bakunin and Guillaume were expelled from the International at its congress in the Hague.

Soon after his arrival in Bern, Brousse organized a local French-language section of the Jura Federation, creating a stronghold of anarchist influence where none had existed before. At the same time, he sought to win the support of German-speaking workers in Switzerland, and at the 1874 congress of the Jura Federation at La Chaux-de-Fonds it was decided, largely on Brousse's insistence, that a German flysheet be printed to supplement the *Bulletin* of the Federation. In January 1875, again largely through Brousse's efforts, a small German study group was formed in Bern, which, in October of the same year, issued what was perhaps the first German anarchist program, calling for the overthrow of the state by means of a social revolution.[4] In March 1876, moreover, the group organized a public procession to commemorate the fifth anniversary of the Paris Commune. The procession, however, was broken up by a hostile crowd of burghers, enraged by the sight of the red flag, then the anarchist as well as the socialist symbol.

On July 15, 1876, began the appearance of *Die Arbeiter-Zeitung*, demanding the "complete, definitive, absolute emancipation of all workers."⁵ Financially supported by Natalia Landsberg, the paper was edited by Brousse with the cooperation of Kropotkin and three German exiles, Emil Werner, Otto Rinke, and August Reinsdorf, who were among the principal founders of the German anarchist movement. Brousse and Kropotkin wrote most of the articles in French, which Werner translated into German. In addition to being distributed in Switzerland, the paper was smuggled across the border and became the main vehicle of anarchist propaganda in Germany until it ceased publication the following year.

Meanwhile, on July 1, 1876, Bakunin had died in Bern. His funeral on July 3 became a political demonstration, with speeches by Brousse, Guillaume, Elisée Reclus, Adhémar Schwitzguébel, and Nicholas Zhukovsky. It was at this point that Brousse began to develop in earnest the theory of propaganda by the deed, which was to play a major role in the anarchist movement until the turn of the century. The term itself is usually attributed to Malatesta, who used it that year in a letter to Carlo Cafiero. But the idea, nurtured by the communalist insurrections in France and Spain, had already been expressed in Brousse's *Solidarité Révolutionnaire* during the summer of 1873. At that time Brousse envisioned the establishment of communes in cities throughout Europe, and the role of the commune as "the vehicle of the revolution" became central to his theory of anarchism.

Brousse's revolutionary extremism and emphasis on propaganda by the deed won him increasing support and made him a serious challenge to James Guillaume, the unofficial leader of the Jura Federation, with his more moderate proto-syndicalist position. Brousse was essentially a pragmatist, however, and propaganda by the deed did not mean individual assassinations, with which it became synonymous in succeeding decades, but rather local demonstrations, insurrections, and other forms of collective direct action, as exemplified by the Commune of 1871.

It was in this sense that the phrase was employed in Brousse's *Arbeiter-Zeitung* in 1876 and 1877; and in this form it was put into practice on March 18, 1877, in a second memorial procession in Bern on behalf of the Paris Commune. Kropotkin, Schwitzguébel, and George Plekhanov took part, in addition to Brousse himself, who composed a militant song, the *Red Flag*, for the occasion. (Plekhanov, the "father of Russian Marxism," was then a young Bakuninist, and the demonstration at the Kazan Cathedral in St. Petersburg in which he had been involved the previous December may be regarded as an early instance of propaganda by the deed in its original sense.) The Bern demonstration, which was followed by a visit to Bakunin's tomb, was dispersed by the police. A more dramatic example of propaganda by the deed occurred the following month with the Benevento rising in Italy, headed by Malatesta, Cafiero, and Stepniak, but this too was quickly suppressed.[6]

Apart from propaganda by the deed, Brousse was also one of the first exponents of communist anarchism, of which Kropotkin, though not its originator, became the leading theorist. As with propaganda by the deed, the first explicit mention of communist anarchism was made in 1876, by François Dumartheray, another prominent French exile in Switzerland, and was elaborated by Brousse in *Die Arbeiter-Zeitung*. It was formulated—again like propaganda by the deed—simultaneously and independently in Italy, and in October 1876 was incorporated into the official program of the Italian Federation. At the Verviers Congress of the Anti-Authoritarian International, both Brousse and Andrea Costa came out strongly in favor of communist anarchism, in contrast to the Spanish anarchists Viñas and Morago, who clung to Bakunin's collectivism, by which individuals are rewarded according to work rather than need. By that time, however, most Bakuninists outside of Spain were moving from collectivist to communist anarchism, and there is reason to believe that Bakunin himself, who died on the eve of its formulation, would have followed the same path.

By the middle of 1877 Brousse's attention was turning increasingly from Switzerland to France, from the Jura Federation and the international movement to the revival of anarchism in his native country. The Jura Federation was already in decline, the movement in Bern had collapsed, and the *Arbeiter-Zeitung* was shut down. That year, with Kropotkin's help, Brousse started the lively journal *L'Avant-Garde*, whose motto took the form of a poem:

> Lève-toi, peuple puissant!
> Ouvrier, prends la machine!
> Prends la terre, paysan!
>
> (Rise, people, in your might!
> Worker, take the machine!
> Take the land, peasant!)

Circulated clandestinely in France as well as distributed legally in Switzerland, *L'Avant-Garde* was uncompromising in its militancy, demanding the complete destruction of the state and its replacement by a society based on "the free formation of human groups around each need, each interest, and the free federation of these groups."[7]

In 1879 Brousse in turn assisted Kropotkin in launching *Le Révolté*, one of the most influential anarchist journals of the nineteenth century. In June of that year, however, Brousse was arrested and expelled from Switzerland. He traveled to Brussels, from which he was evicted after seven weeks, then lived in London for almost a year before returning to France and beginning a new phase of his radical career.

JUST AS Brousse's anarchism spanned the decade of the 1870s, his possibilism spanned the decade of the 1880s. Reexamining his anarchist beliefs, he abandoned propaganda by the deed and came to accept the usefulness of piecemeal reform, for which he had previously expressed contempt. When he returned to France in 1880, he had even abandoned his hostility to electoral action and no longer insisted on abstention from the vote. "The ideal," he wrote in 1883, "should be divided into several practical stages; our aims should, as it were, be *immediatised* so as to render them *possible*."[8] Brousse had become, in short, a leading advocate of reformist and municipal socialism. He founded the Possibilist party, the strongest socialist movement in France during the 1880s, and was instrumental in the formation of the Second International in 1889.

This development, however, was not as inconsistent as might appear. For Brousse, as his biographer David Stafford makes clear,[9] retained many of his earlier presuppositions. His transition from anarchism to possibilism was not a sudden conversion, not a sharp break with the past, but rather a continuation of his communalist program in a nonrevolutionary form. His early faith in local action, in the commune as the embryo of a libertarian society, survived in his new program of reform at the municipal level, a kind of "socialism in one city" that would eventually encompass the whole land. For the commune as the vehicle of working-class revolution he substituted the commune as the vehicle of working-class reform.

Brousse never returned to the anarchist movement. Like Costa and Guesde, like Plekhanov and Axelrod, he shed an early adherence to Bakuninism to become the founder of a socialist political movement. But his transition differed from theirs in an important respect: he did not forsake anarchism for Marxism. On the contrary, he remained as uncompromising in his anti-centralism, anti-authoritarianism, and anti-Marxism as he had been during his Bakuninist days in the First International; moreover, his aversion to elites of every kind and to abstract theoretical systems he retained as an integral component of his possibilist creed. Marx was "not infallible," Brousse insisted. "He is not a God." Brousse, reported Engels, was "the greatest muddlehead I have ever encountered, removing the anarchy from anarchism but retaining all other phrases and especially tactics."[10]

With the founding of the Second International, Brousse was at the peak of his influence. But the following year, 1890, the possibilist movement split apart when the followers of Jean Allemane, who advocated the general strike and opposed the admission of intellectuals and professionals into the party, broke away. In the remaining two decades of his life, Brousse became increasingly isolated, and his influence in the socialist movement waned. In July 1890, as vice-president of the Paris Municipal Council, he approved the organization of a reception in honor of two infantry battalions that had taken part in the suppression of the Commune of 1871; and in 1899 he approved the entry of Millerand into the French government—the first socialist to accept a ministry under the Third Republic—on the ground that "the safety of the Republic is the supreme law."[11]

By 1905 Brousse had become president of the Paris Municipal Council, and in this capacity was host to Alfonso XIII of Spain, which provoked the renewed enmity of his former anarchist comrades and led Guillaume to sever all relations with him. Afterwards Brousse fell into almost total obscurity. Losing his parliamentary seat in 1910, he was made director of a state mental hospital. He died, a forgotten figure, in 1912.

CHAPTER NINETEEN

The Martyrdom of Gustav Landauer

OVER THE LAST two decades, Gustav Landauer, the German anarchist and martyr, has had a remarkable revival. In 1969 the Austrian radio dedicated a program to him under the title of "Murder in Munich: The Life and Work of Gustav Landauer." In Tel Aviv an anarchist group was named in his honor (his influence on the Israeli communitarian movement has been considerable). And in April 1974 a well-attended session was devoted to his life and thought at an anarchist conference in New York.

At the same time, Landauer has inspired a spate of books and articles in several languages. To replace the older studies by Max Nettlau and Augustin Souchy, written in German but published in Spanish and Swedish and long out of print,[1] four full-length biographies have appeared,[2] and further studies of Landauer's life and ideas are in progress. As for Landauer's own writings, several anthologies were published in German in the 1960s and 1970s, with useful introductions and notes,[3] and a number of his longer works have been reprinted, including his essays on Shakespeare and his collection of letters from the French Revolution, reissued after forty years by the original publishers, Rütten and Loening.[4] Some of Landauer's most important writings were long ago translated into Spanish by Diego Abad de Santillán, who introduced him to a large audience in Spain and Latin America. In English, moreover, we have a translation of his *Aufruf zum Sozialismus* (1911) and excerpts from his essay *Die Revolution* (1908), in addition to his pamphlet *Social Democracy in Germany*, first published by Freedom Press of London in 1896,[5] although a proper collection of his principal essays and letters is long overdue.

Why the renewed interest in Landauer? What makes him an important figure (Rudolf Rocker called him a "spiritual giant")?[6] In the first place, his tragic and brutal death at the hands of the soldiers of emergent totalitarianism continues to arouse both indignation and compassion. He was the most famous anarchist martyr of the German revolution in the wake of the First World War. Endowed with remarkable gifts of character, intellect, and personal distinction, he was also the most influential German anarchist intellectual of the twentieth century, with the possible exception of Rocker himself. His work was praised by such eminent German writers as Ernst Toller, Hermann Hesse, and Arnold Zweig. He edited *Der Sozialist* (Berlin, 1891-1899, 1909-1915), one of the most impressive radical periodicals in modern German history. Although his novel *The Preacher of Death* (1893) is diffuse, meandering, and repetitious, he was a sensitive critic of drama and poetry, producing original essays on Shakespeare, Goethe, Hölderlin, Strindberg, and Walt Whitman. He also composed what the German writer Hans Blüher called the finest love letters of the twentieth century.[7] He was in close touch with writers of the German Expressionist movement, above all with Toller and Georg Kaiser, and he played an active part in the avant-garde German theater, being affiliated with the Neue Freie Volksbühne movement from 1892 until his death in 1919.

Beyond this, Landauer made his mark as a prolific translator of both anarchist and nonanarchist writers. He rendered into German portions of Proudhon's *War and Peace* and *General Idea of the Revolution in the Nineteenth Century*, as well as a number of Kropotkin's major works, including *Mutual Aid, Fields, Factories and Workshops*, and *The Great French Revolution*. He translated Etienne de la Boétie's *Discourse of Voluntary Servitude*, Oscar Wilde's *The Picture of Dorian Gray* and *The Soul of Man under Socialism*, the essays of George Bernard Shaw, and the poems of Whitman, of whom he was a devoted and lifelong enthusiast. (In *Leaves of Grass* he saw reflected his own mystical belief that man carries the world within himself, and as education minister in Bavaria in 1919 he proposed to introduce Whitman's poetry into the syllabus of every schoolchild.) Finally, he produced a modern rendition of the sermons and essays of Meister Eckhart, the German medieval mystic, whose philosophy Landauer greatly admired.

Landauer is well known, too, for his friendship with the Jewish mystical philosopher Martin Buber. Under Landauer's influence, Buber became a libertarian and a member of Landauer's Socialist Bund. It was Buber who first published *Die Revolution* and who painstakingly collected and edited Landauer's writings and correspondence after his death. Moreover, the chapter on Landauer in Buber's *Paths in Utopia* remains one of the few serious appraisals in English.[8]

Landauer, then, was an extremely versatile figure. Journalist and philosopher, novelist and critic—his range of interests was impressive. This perhaps accounts for the different perspectives from which his biographers have viewed him. For Ruth Hyman he was a "philosopher of utopia," for Charles Maurer a "mystical anarchist," for Eugene Lunn a "romantic socialist," for Wolf Kalz a "cultural socialist and anarchist." Landauer, however, used a different label, calling himself an "anarchist-socialist." "Anarchy," he wrote, "is the expression of the liberation of man from the idols of the state, the church, and capital; socialism is the expression of the true and genuine community among men, genuine because it grows out of the individual spirit."[9] Influenced by such diverse thinkers as Spinoza and Schopenhauer, Nietzsche and Ibsen, Proudhon and Bakunin, Kropotkin and Tolstoy, he was at once a socialist and an individualist, a romantic and a mystic, a militant and an advocate of passive resistance. He was also indebted to the Arts and Crafts movement of Ruskin and Morris, and to the Garden City movement of Geddes and Howard. Yet, for all these disparate elements, he was able to work out a coherent social philosophy and theory of revolution.

LANDAUER was born on April 7, 1870, of a middle-class Jewish family in Karlsruhe in southwestern Germany, a region with a long history of social dissent dating from the Middle Ages, and in which two other leading German anarchists, Johann Most and Rudolf Rocker, were born and raised. Eighteen-seventy saw the outbreak of the Franco-Prussian War, which marked the emergence of Germany as a centralized military power. Against this expanding Leviathan Landauer was to fight throughout his fifty-year life. At the same time, he also opposed the centralized and statist version of socialism embodied in the German Social Democratic party, with its hierarchical and authoritarian character. "What we fight," he asserted, "is State Socialism, levelling from above, bureaucracy; what we advocate is free association and union, the absence of authority, mind freed from all fetters, independence and well-being of all."[10]

In 1892, having studied at the universities of Heidelberg, Berlin, and Strassburg, Landauer joined a dissident Marxist group in Berlin known as "Die Jungen" (Rudolf Rocker was also a member), which had been expelled from the Social Democratic party the previous year.

Assuming the editorship of the group's weekly paper, *Der Sozialist,* he evolved a decentralist and anti-authoritarian critique of Marxism along the lines of Bakunin and Kropotkin, calling for the replacement of the state with a federation of autonomous communes organized from below.

Like Kropotkin and William Morris, Landauer admired the decentralized communal life of the Middle Ages, a "totality of independent units," he called it, a "society of societies."[11] Although he accepted the notion of class struggle, he was repelled by the dogmatic rigidity of Marxist theory, as well as by all centralized bureaucratic authority, economic as well as political. In 1893 he was one of the dissidents— Rosa Luxemburg was another—excluded from the Zurich Congress of the Second International, which caused the veteran Italian revolutionary Amilcare Cipriani to walk out, protesting, "I go with those you have banished, with the victims of your intolerance and brutality."[12] Landauer was again expelled—together with Errico Malatesta, Ferdinand Domela Nieuwenhuis, and other anarchist delegates—from the London Congress in 1896, the last time that the anarchists sought admission to the gatherings of the Socialist International. In his *Aufruf zum Sozialismus,* published in 1911, Landauer went so far as to call Marxism "the plague of our time and the curse of the socialist movement."[13]

In 1893, after the Zurich Congress, Landauer published his novel *The Preacher of Death,* but his literary activities were interrupted by a term in prison for disseminating "seditious materials" in *Der Sozialist,* the appearance of which was temporarily suspended. Though sent to jail a number of times—once for criticizing the Berlin chief of police— he continued to publish *Der Sozialist* until the end of the decade. Under Landauer it was a journal of high intellectual quality, if limited agitational value. For its increasing theoretical and philosophical orientation prevented it from winning a large working-class audience. Its appeal was more and more to intellectuals and professionals rather than to factory hands and farmers. This provoked dissension among the working-class members of its staff, who objected that the paper was losing its effectiveness as an instrument of anarchist propaganda. Though Landauer tried to alter his approach, he did not go far enough, and in 1899 dwindling readership forced *Der Sozialist* to cease publication.

By that time Landauer had come to abandon his frontal assaults upon capitalism and the state. Previously, his thinking had been dominated by the revolutionary anarchism of Bakunin and Kropotkin. Not that he lost interest in these figures. Of Bakunin he remarked, "I have loved and admired him from the first day I came across him," and in 1901 he wrote an afterword to a biographical sketch of the Russian anarchist by Max Nettlau.[14] During the next few years, moreover, he translated several of Kropotkin's most important books. Yet after the turn of the century he fell more and more under the influence of Tolstoy and especially of Proudhon, whom he called "the greatest of all the socialists."[15] He drew increasingly on Proudhon's mutualism in forming his own philosophy, adopting the notion of a People's Bank that would enable the small producer to obtain cheap credit as well as facilitating the fair exchange of his products. More and more his emphasis was on a peaceful social revolution and on the importance of libertarian education, especially as developed by Francisco Ferrer and his movement of Modern Schools. While he remained devoted to Kropotkin, it was less for the militant and revolutionary aspects of his thinking than for his ethical approach, his theory of mutual aid, and his stress on decentralized cooperative production.

Blending the federalist principles of Kropotkin and Proudhon, Landauer called for a society based on voluntary cooperation and mutual aid, "a society of equalitarian exchange based on regional communities, rural communities which combine agriculture and industry."[16] He spoke less and less of class struggle; and "direct action" now meant the creation of peaceful cooperatives combined with passive resistance to authority rather than armed rebellion or acts of propaganda by the deed. For Landauer, moreover, "general strike" came to mean not the cessation of work but the continuation of work for one's own benefit and under one's own self-management. Viewing the state as the negation of love and humanity, he called for its gradual replacement by voluntary communities. He appealed to the workers, peasants, and intellectuals alike to awaken from their stupor and opt out of the state system of coercion, exploitation, and injustice by forming their own rural and urban communes.

Socialism for Landauer was no longer the inauguration of something new all at once, not a sudden apocalyptic act, but the discovery and development of something already present and growing, something "always just beginning" and "always moving." His idea resembled the IWW slogan of "building the new society within the shell of the old." In his best-known writings, *Die Revolution* and *Aufruf zum Sozialismus*, he called on the people to create a free society "outside" and "alongside" the existing one; he urged them to "step outside capitalism" and "begin to be human beings"—to create what we would now call an alternative society in the form of libertarian enclaves within the established order that would serve as an inspiration and a model for others to follow. In other words, he conceived of revolution no longer as a violent mass upheaval but as the peaceful and gradual creation of a counterculture.

In formulating this conception, Landauer was strongly influenced by the sixteenth-century French writer de la Boétie and his criticism of the "voluntary servitude" of the masses.[17] La Boétie had said that the people should withdraw their support from authoritarian institutions and form their own libertarian ones; if no one will obey the tyrant his power will vanish. Dropping out of centralized, coercive, and bureaucratic society now became Landauer's principal message. His Socialist Bund, founded in 1908, was intended to be the beginning of such an alternative society, consisting of natural and voluntary bodies that the anarchists were to call "affinity groups" during the Spanish Civil War. At the same time, the Socialist Bund was to be a libertarian alternative to the authoritarian and hierarchical Social Democratic party. By 1911 it had twenty groups in Berlin, Zurich, and other German and Swiss cities, and even one in Paris.

But though Landauer had become a spokesman for voluntary co-operation and passive resistance, he never entirely repudiated mass revolution. He never rejected spontaneous popular insurrection; and though he opposed individual terrorism, he always retained a sympathy for the terrorists and understood the despair that drove them to act. First and foremost, however, he believed that there had to be a spiritual revolution within the individual. The social problem, he said, cannot be solved by violence or by the seizure of power. For the true social revolution is one of spiritual rejuvenation. What is needed, he wrote, is "a rebirth of the human spirit." A fundamental transformation of society can occur only when "we are seized by the spirit, not of revolution, but of regeneration." As he put it in his most famous and often-quoted passage, "the state is a condition, a certain relationship between human beings, a mode of human behavior; we destroy it by contracting other relationships, by behaving differently."[18]

DURING THE YEARS preceding the First World War, Landauer was a familiar figure within German artistic and intellectual circles. Tall, thin, and narrow-shouldered, with fine features and expressive eyes, he often wore a long cape and an old-fashioned hat. His full beard and long dark hair gave him the appearance of an Old Testament prophet. Thoughtful, intense, always searching for the truth, Landauer avoided all dogmas. "One felt when he spoke," wrote Rocker, "that every word came from his soul, bore the stamp of absolute integrity."[19] But he was a prophet without honor in his own country. He earned the undying hatred of many of his compatriots by his opposition to the war and his admission of German aggression. "War is an act of power, of murder, of robbery," he wrote as early as 1912 in anticipation of the American writer Randolph Bourne. "It is the sharpest and clearest expression of the state."[20] (Compare Bourne's famous dictum of 1918: "War is the health of the state.") At Christmas 1916 Landauer wrote a letter to Woodrow Wilson emphasizing the need not only for the conclusion of peace but also for a league of nations to control arms and ensure the protection of human rights throughout the world.

When revolution broke out in Bavaria on November 7, 1918, the first anniversary of the Bolshevik Revolution, Landauer was summoned to Munich by his friend Kurt Eisner, socialist president of the new Bavarian republic. Landauer, however, did not become a member of Eisner's cabinet, as is sometimes asserted. Rather, together with his comrades Erich Mühsam and Ernst Toller, he played a central role in a movement to organize councils of workers, farmers, soldiers, and sailors to launch the kind of federalist society that he had so long been advocating. He served with Mühsam in the Revolutionary Workers' Council and in the Central Workers' Council of Bavaria. He continued to favor a system of councils and cooperatives, based on autonomy and self-management, over either a parliamentary government or a proletarian dictatorship with state control of industry and agriculture.

Differing sharply with Mühsam on this point, Landauer had been critical of the revolutionary dictatorship created in Russia by Lenin, writing in 1918 that the Bolsheviks were "working for a military regime which will be much more horrible than anything the world has ever seen."[21] In place of the Marxist vision of state socialism and a dictatorship of the proletariat, Landauer continued to press for a decentralized society of free cooperatives and communities with local control and workers' self-management from below. Not that he expected the stateless millennium to be achieved overnight. "It does not occur to me to desire a finished result," he said. "I will always see something beyond the end. I am concerned with the process, and we are at last in the process."[22]

But his hopes, however limited, were disappointed. Following the assassination of Eisner (whose death came hard upon the murders of Rosa Luxemburg and Karl Liebknecht in Berlin), Landauer became minister of education in a new Council Republic proclaimed in Munich on April 7, 1919, his forty-ninth birthday. (One of his assistants was a young anarchist, Ret Marut, later to become a famous novelist as "B. Traven.")[23] This was a fitting post for a disciple of Ferrer, for a man who set so high a value on education to achieve the spiritual revolution of his dreams. But his tenure in office lasted only one week, collapsing when the Communists assumed power. Although he drew up a program of libertarian education for citizens of all ages, adults as well as children, it was never put into practice.

On May 1, 1919, the minister of defense in Berlin, Gustav Noske, sent Freikorps units to crush the Bavarian revolution. The following day Landauer was arrested. "Now is the time to bring forth a martyr of a different kind," he had written in 1911, "not a heroic but a quiet, unpretentious martyr, who will provide an example of the proper life."[24] Landauer himself now became such a martyr. In the prison courtyard an officer stepped up and struck him across the face, the signal for a savage massacre. Set upon by the troops, Landauer was beaten with truncheons and rifle butts, kicked, stomped, and trampled upon. "Kill me, then!" he exclaimed. "To think that you are human beings!"[25] At that he was shot to death. His body was stripped and thrown into a wash house. (Erich Mühsam was to suffer the same fate at the hands of the Nazis in 1934.)

Noske, a Social Democrat, congratulated the commander of the punitive force for the "discreet and wholly successful way in which you have conducted your operation in Munich." The soldier who shot Landauer was acquitted of all charges after claiming that he was merely "following orders." The officer who struck Landauer across the face was fined five hundred marks. Another officer was given five weeks in jail, not for murdering Landauer but for stealing his watch. The officer in charge was never brought to trial. A monument to Landauer, erected by the Anarcho-Syndicalist Union with contributions from the workers of Munich, was torn down by the Nazis after Hitler came to power. It has yet to be rebuilt.

CHAPTER TWENTY

Brazilian Anarchists

APART FROM Argentina, Brazil has produced the largest anarchist movement in Latin America. Its adherents were mostly immigrants, or children of immigrants, who came not only from Portugal, Spain, and Italy, but also from Germany, Austria, and other European countries between the 1880s and the First World War. During this period, more than a million immigrants entered Brazil from Italy alone, thousands of whom became anarchists or close sympathizers, so that anarchism outstripped socialism as the dominant radical ideology among prewar Brazilian workers and intellectuals. Until the 1920s most Brazilian trade unions were anarcho-syndicalist in orientation, and long afterwards they retained strong libertarian tendencies. Brazilian communism, moreover, sprang mainly from the anarchist movement, rather than from social democracy, giving the Brazilian Communist party a marked libertarian cast, particularly during its early years, which it lost only with the consolidation of Stalinism in the 1930s.

That Brazil, given its size and population, should have boasted a vigorous anarchist movement is perhaps not surprising. Nevertheless, one cannot but be impressed by its remarkable range and vitality and by the lofty idealism of its adherents. The origins of the movement can be traced to the 1870s and 1880s, when the doctrines of Proudhon and Bakunin inspired the formation of anarchist groups all over the world. Furthermore, the Haymarket executions of 1887 left a permanent mark on the Brazilian movement, which was shortly to have its own martyrs, the first being Polinice Mattei, stabbed to death in 1898 when he shouted "Viva l'anarchia!" at a political rally.[1]

In Brazil, as elsewhere, Haymarket was followed by the proliferation of anarchist groups and by the appearance of anarchist publications, in Italian as well as in Portuguese. Moreover, in 1890 Dr. Giovanni Rossi, an Italian agronomist and utopian visionary, founded the Cecilia colony in Paraná, one of the first anarchist communities in Latin America.[2] The next two decades saw an influx of European anarchist literature in several languages, not only by Proudhon, Bakunin, and Kropotkin, but also by Reclus, Malatesta, Jean Grave, and such lesser-known but influential writers as Saverio Merlino, Charles Malato, and Augustin Hamon.

As in Portugal and Spain, anarchism in Brazil often assumed an ascetic, quasi-religious form, marked by uncompromising dedication to principle, intense anticlericalism, vegetarianism, and renunciation of alcohol and tobacco. Apart from publishing their own journals, Brazilian anarchists served on the editorial staffs of labor, free-thought, and other radical periodicals that were launched around the turn of the century. They played a leading role in the formation of labor organizations, above all the Confederação Operária Brasileira (Brazilian Confederation of Labor), which, founded in 1906, attracted shoemakers, printers, masons, carpenters, fishermen, dockworkers, textile workers, and hotel and restaurant workers, as well as teachers, journalists, and poets. These self-educated workers, photographed at labor conferences in their high white collars, dark neckties, and frock coats, make an exotically attractive spectacle. Beyond their role in May Day rallies, strikes, and the movement for an eight-hour day, they organized antimilitarist demonstrations, libertarian schools, theatrical performances, musical concerts, and lectures on the sciences and arts.

Brazil, it is no exaggeration to say, produced some of the most colorful figures in the entire history of anarchism. Among them was Oreste Ristori, who was deported from Argentina after emigrating from Italy at the turn of the century. In an effort to escape, he jumped off the ship into a small boat, breaking both his legs. So great were his powers of persuasion that the doctor was converted to anarchism by the time he had finished treating him. Ristori went to Uruguay, and then to Brazil, where in São Paulo he founded the Italian-language weekly *La Battaglia*. In 1936, after his second expulsion from the country, he went to fight in Spain. With the victory of Franco and the suppression of the anarchists, Ristori returned to his native Italy and joined the antifascist resistance. After four years of fighting, he was captured and shot by the Germans in 1944.

Assisting Ristori on *La Battaglia* was Gigi Damiani, who had spent several terms in prison or under house arrest in Italy before he emigrated to Brazil in 1899. On his arrival he was again imprisoned for his anarchist beliefs. After his release, he learned the trade of painter and worked on stage sets for São Paulo theaters while assisting at *La Battaglia* and other anarchist papers. Not much of a talker, he was remembered by comrades for his "ironic smile."[3] Deported to Italy in 1919, he worked on the *Umanità Nova*, in close association with Malatesta.

Everardo Dias was two years old when brought to Brazil from Spain in 1887, the year of the Haymarket executions. Becoming an anarchist as a young man, he joined with Ristori and Benjamin Mota in the Association of Free Thought and edited its fortnightly journal, *O Livre Pensador* (Free Thought), which promoted the ideas of Darwin, Spencer, and Ferrer, and attacked the obscurantism and despotism of the Catholic church, as well as the "tyranny of tobacco" and of alcohol, "the most evil drink ever invented by man."[4]

Florentino de Carvalho, who also emigrated from Spain, got a job with the police but was converted to anarchism by Kropotkin's *Conquest of Bread*—a sort of anarchist bible in Spain and Latin America—which he had chanced upon in a São Paulo bookshop in 1902. Quitting the police, he worked as a stevedore and printer in the port city of Santos, where he became a labor organizer, hunted by his former colleagues. Yet he found the opportunity to read, write, and teach, and to speak at anarchist meetings, where his dark hair and blazing eyes reminded his comrades of Nietzsche.

Neno Vasco, who emigrated from Portugal in 1901 and joined a group of Italian anarchists in São Paulo, came from a wealthy family and earned a degree in law. Although he possessed none of Carvalho's oratorical gifts—he was too shy even to face an audience—his articles and plays and his journals *Aurora* (Dawn) and *A Terra Livre* (Free Earth) won him a reputation as the most cultivated anarchist in Brazil. A linguist and orthographer, he devised a modernized system of spelling from which many changes were later adopted by the Brazilian Academy of Letters.

Another gifted linguist was Paulo Berthelot—his passion was Esperanto—who came to Brazil from Paris in 1907. He soon left the coastal cities for the interior to learn from the Indian tribesmen about their stateless cooperative life, but he came down with fever and died in 1910. He was thirty years old.

Edgard Leuenroth, "a man of saintly character"[5] who became São Paulo's leading anarchist, was born in Brazil in 1881, the son of an immigrant pharmacist from Germany and a Brazilian mother. Leuenroth became a typographer, editor, librarian, and union organizer, and in 1905 joined Vasco and Manuel Moscoso in launching *A Terra*

Livre, one of the major anarchist journals in the country. In 1906, it is interesting to note, *A Terra Livre* ran a series of articles on the revolutionary struggles in Russia, appealing for financial assistance, which drew a letter of thanks from Peter Kropotkin.[6]

Apart from Leuenroth, two other native Brazilians merit attention: Fábio Luz, a well-known novelist trained in medicine, who held the post of school inspector in the Federal District and who preached the doctrines of anarchism throughout his life, and José Oiticica, poet, linguist, philosopher, the son of a senator in the northeastern state of Algosa. Oiticica, after being educated in medicine and law, founded a school in Rio before being appointed director of a municipal school in Laguna. He came to anarchism not so much by studying its classics as by evolving his own ideas about society and the state. Returning to Rio after two years in Laguna, he discovered to his amazement that the anarchists, whom he had previously regarded as mere bomb-throwers, had been advocating essentially the same ideas. Consequently he embraced their cause as his own, becoming one of its most energetic advocates. His libertarianism, however, was tainted with controversy. "I do not seek the democratization of aristocrats," he once remarked, "What I seek is the aristocratization of democrats. What I desire is to give them intelligence, culture, love of eternal beauty, of imperishable art." To those who found such statements condescending, even more disturbing was Oiticica's reference to Trotsky, Zinoviev, and Kamenev as the "three Jewish leaders" of the Bolshevik dictatorship.[7]

The response of the Brazilian anarchists to the Russian Revolution differed little from that of their comrades in other countries. At first, with few exceptions, they welcomed the Bolshevik insurrection with enthusiasm, hailing Lenin and Trotsky as colleagues who shared the ultimate anarchist vision of stateless communism. Through the influence of anarchism, they believed, Bolshevism had been transformed from an authoritarian philosophy into a libertarian one, and they condoned the "dictatorship of the proletariat" as a temporary expedient for combatting landlords, capitalists, and other counterrevolutionary elements that were seeking to regain power. In Rio and São Paulo between 1917 and 1919 anarchists mounted a series of strikes and demonstrations with the hope of achieving a general strike that, following the Bolshevik example, would overturn the capitalist system. They denounced the Allied intervention in Russia, sang the "Internationale," and marched through the streets (led by girls in red blouses) to celebrate the coming order. Anarchists in Rio de Janeiro, among them Oiticica, hatched an abortive conspiracy in November 1918 to seize key points around the city and overthrow the government, along the lines of the Bolshevik coup a year before.

By 1921, however, many had become disillusioned, for news had been reaching them of the suppression of their anarchist comrades, the crushing of the Kronstadt rebellion, and the growing bureaucratism and despotism of the Soviet government. On November 7, 1920, the third anniversary of the Bolshevik seizure of power, the anarchist journal *A Plebe* (The People) launched an all-out campaign against Bolshevism. Nevertheless, more than a few anarchists cast their lot with the fledgling Brazilian Communist party or became fellow travelers, counterparts of the "Soviet anarchists" in Russia.

Efforts at fomenting a revolution within Brazil had meanwhile been unsuccessful. Anarchists continued to be hounded and persecuted by the authorities. Charged with dynamite plots and conspiracies, they were arrested, held incommunicado, beaten, starved, tortured, shot, deported. Strikers were fired upon, blacklisted, and dismissed from their jobs. Journals were suppressed, presses smashed, meeting places and cultural centers closed down. Supporters of Bolshevism called on the workers to forsake the antipolitical and decentralist principles of anarchism for the more disciplined methods of Communism. The ensuing contest for mass support did much to disrupt the revolutionary movement and undermine the unity of Brazilian labor.

To make matters worse, the anarchists were divided from within. They quarreled not only about the nature of the Bolshevik dictatorship but also about the relationship between the anarchist movement and the industrial working class. Individualists castigated collectivists, anarchist-communists lashed out at anarcho-syndicalists. One anarchist-communist, echoing Bakunin on his Marxist antagonists, prophesied that if syndicalism should ultimately prevail, there would emerge a corps of "union functionaries who would dedicate all their energies to the constitution of a new state, and as a consequence promote a new economic inequality alongside its political inequality. In the place of the bourgeois class would stand the class of functionaries."[8]

Such disputes could not be resolved. From the 1920s on the influence of anarchism in Brazil dwindled, and what had once been a flourishing movement shrank to the proportions of a sect. But Leuenroth, Oiticica, and their associates refused to abandon the struggle. They took an active part in the movement to save Sacco and Vanzetti, and later fought in the streets against the Green Shirts and other fascist groups. In São Paulo and Rio de Janeiro small anarchist circles survived beyond the Second World War, remaining faithful to their ideal until the end. The last embers were crushed by the military dictatorship that came to power in 1964.

CHAPTER TWENTY-ONE

An Australian Anarchist: J. W. Fleming

THIS GALLERY of anarchist portraits concludes with a sketch of J. W. Fleming, "our most active comrade" in Australia, as Emma Goldman described him.[1] A man of strong character and militant temper, Fleming was a dedicated spirit of the kind without which no social movement can prosper. From his platform on the Yarra Bank, Melbourne's equivalent of Hyde Park, he held forth every Sunday in behalf of the workers and the unemployed. His courage and strength of will were proverbial. For nearly sixty years, despite harassment, persecution, and arrest, he carried on his self-appointed mission. Small wonder, then, that he should have been called the "most tenacious and enduring agitator" in the history of Australian anarchism.[2]

John William Fleming was born in Derby, England, in 1863 or 1864,[3] the son of an Irish father and an English mother, who died when he was five years old. His father, a worker, took part in a strike in Derby, and a grandfather, during the 1840s, agitated for the repeal of the Corn Laws. Chummy, as the boy was called, went to work at the age of ten in a Leicester boot factory, learning the trade that he would pursue for the rest of his life. In his teens, already a religious skeptic, he attended lectures by the leading freethinkers of the day—Charles Bradlaugh, George Jacob Holyoake, and Annie Besant—when they passed through the Midlands on their speaking tours.[4] He himself remained a lifelong secularist, raising his voice for anticlericalism and free thought long after anarchism had replaced atheism as his primary ideological commitment.

Beyond this, little is known of Fleming's formative years. When an uncle invited him to Australia, he decided to emigrate, arriving in Melbourne in 1884 and obtaining work as a bootmaker. He was twenty years old. Almost immediately, he was drawn to the secularist movement, which had attracted him as a youth in England. Nearly all anarchists were atheists or agnostics, and more than a few came to anarchism through the free-thought movement. Such was the case with Fleming. Not only did he join the Melbourne branch of the Australasian Secular Association, founded in 1882, but in October 1884 he attended the Second Australasian Free Thought Conference in Sydney.[5]

At the same time, Fleming threw himself into another cause—the movement for the unemployed—that was to occupy him throughout his career. In 1885, barely a year after his arrival, he took part in an unemployment demonstration in Melbourne, which ended with a march on the Treasury building, a banner demanding "Bread or Work" at the lead. Reaching its destination, the procession was attacked by the police, and Fleming and several others were arrested. Fleming, because of his youth, was discharged by the court with the advice to "stick to his last." At once, however, he set about collecting money to get his companions out of jail.[6]

Following this incident, the first of his numerous brushes with the law, Fleming left Melbourne for Ballarat, where he plied his bootmaker's trade, served as secretary of the local branch of the Australasian Secular Association, and took part in free-thought agitation. On one occasion he was stoned in Main Street along with a comrade named William Lee. By the time he returned to Melbourne, some six months later, two important events had taken place. The first was the formation of the Melbourne Anarchist Club, the first anarchist group in Australia. The club, established on May 1, 1886, was an offshoot of the Melbourne branch of the Australasian Secular Association, and Fleming joined it in September of that year.[7] The second event, on May 4, 1886, was the Haymarket explosion in Chicago, which, as we have seen, had a profound effect on the anarchist movement throughout the world. Fleming, after joining the Melbourne Anarchist Club, addressed a meeting to protest the conviction of the Chicago anarchists, and afterwards, with a group of fellow workers, sent a petition to President Cleveland against the impending executions. These efforts were unavailing, but for the rest of his days Fleming, recalling the "horrible murder of our comrades," cleaved to the ideal for which Parsons, Spies, Lingg, Engel, and Fischer went to the grave.[8]

Fleming continued to participate in the Melbourne Anarchist Club until July 1890, shortly before it disbanded owing to factional disputes. In addition, he was a founder of the Victoria bootmakers' union, campaigning for better working conditions for its members, who in 1890 chose him as their delegate to the Melbourne Trades Hall Council. The following year he was elected president of the union, as well as of the Fitzroy branch of the Progressive Political League, a forerunner of the Australian Labour Party.[9] He was also a founding member of the Australian Socialist League, a counterpart of William Morris's organization in England, and took part in the Knights of Labour, inspired by the American organization of the same name. In 1890, at a meeting of the Melbourne branch of the Knights, Fleming proposed the formation of a committee of labor and radical representatives to arrange a May First demonstration in Victoria; and it was he, two years later, who led the first May Day procession in Melbourne.[10]

Beyond all this, during these early years, Fleming found time for other activities. He took part in antisweating agitation, supported the formation of cooperatives, collected funds for the London dockworkers during their strike of 1889, campaigned for the Sunday opening of the Melbourne public library, spoke out for the village settlement movement, and agitated for free speech, free thought, militant unionism, and the single tax.

For his role in these activities Fleming suffered unremitting persecution. He was beaten by hired thugs, threatened with arrest, and occasionally locked up in jail. But he also commanded respect. His patent honesty and untiring efforts in behalf of the workers won him the friendship of Lord Hopetoun, the governor of Victoria, who sent Fleming gifts of money and champagne to be distributed among the unemployed. The friendship, it was said, extended to visits to Fleming's little house in Carlton, a suburb of Melbourne, which doubled as his bootmaker's establishment and where he lived a bachelor's life for half a century. (It was at this "dingy little shop of Mr. Fleming, who acts as the mouthpiece and guardian of the unemployed," reported a Melbourne newspaper, that the governor's largesse was handed out.)[11]

Fleming's gifts were those of an activist rather than of a theorist or writer. His contributions to the anarchist press, while spanning almost half a century, consisted entirely of letters to the editor, commenting on events of the day. Nevertheless, he possessed an ease with words that manifested itself not only in his correspondence, both public and private, but still more in his appearances at open-air gatherings and in lecture halls throughout Victoria. Indeed, Fleming's chief claim to distinction was as a radical speaker. On this all sources are agreed. No sooner had he arrived in Melbourne, in 1884, than he began to attend Sunday afternoon meetings on the North Wharf near Queen's Bridge, a popular outdoor forum; and before long he himself ventured onto the podium, speaking on a diversity of subjects ranging from atheism and unemployment to women's rights and the single tax. In June 1887 he addressed two thousand listeners on the question, "Should Men Starve to Celebrate the Queen's Jubilee?" In July his subject was "Reform or Revolution?" and the audience had grown to three thousand.[12]

Alarmed by the increasing crowds, the Melbourne Harbour Trust issued a summons against Fleming for trespassing on the wharf on Sunday, December 12, 1887. Discharged with a warning, he returned the following week. Under pressure from the authorities, however, he soon moved to a new speakers' corner located on the bank of the Yarra River, which flows through the city. There he erected a platform from which he would regularly hold forth on Sunday afternoons for sixty years. Plainly dressed in a worn felt hat, he spoke under a tall elm tree on a rostrum built of stone and earth raised about two feet off the ground. From the tree hung a bright red banner inscribed with the word "Anarchy" in bold letters. Sometimes a placard was also displayed, with the motto "No God, No Authority." A small table stood nearby, piled high with anarchist books. To signal that he was about to begin speaking, Fleming would ring a little bell and the crowd would gather about him. A small man with a thick mustache, regular features, sallow complexion, and "friendly-warm eyes," he seemed far from being a revolutionary firebrand, as he was commonly described in the press. Nor was he a great "screamer," one listener recalled, not a "shouter of words." On the contrary, he spoke in a "soft, gentle voice," in measured but impassioned tones, rising to anger only when dwelling on "the iniquity of parasite classes, autocrats, and humbug."[13]

Fleming's principal theme as a speaker, especially after the turn of the century, was the futility of parliamentary politics and of piecemeal reform. Having long since abandoned remedial measures, he pinned his hopes on direct action, including armed insurrection if necessary. He refused to compromise with the capitalist system, convinced that the salvation of the workers could be achieved only by destroying it root and branch. On this point he was emphatic. Political action, far from improving the lot of the workers, would divert them from the sole path to emancipation, the path of social revolution.

For the rapidly growing Labour Party Fleming had particular contempt. Its leaders, he declared, were feasting on the vitals of Australia, "the workers' paradise and mecca of that foolish fetish, the Labour Party Swindle." Melbourne itself was swarming with "degenerate cadgers. Self-respect is very rare. Since the advent of the labour politician, a generation of weaklings, inborn serfs, made between sleeping and waking, are trampling the liberties our fathers gave to us, liberties soaked with their red, warm blood, destroyed, put aside to appease political poltroons masquerading as labour champions."[14]

Fleming's intemperate language was bound to arouse animosity. Uncompromising and defiant, an irritant to conservatives and liberals alike, he was frequently heckled, interrupted, struck with fists, and pushed off the speaker's stand. In 1904, owing to his attacks on Labour officials ("fat old Carr," "senile old imbecile"),[15] he was expelled from the Melbourne Trades Hall Council, on which he had represented the bootmakers' union since 1890. Fleming attributed his expulsion to his anarchist beliefs, which no political party could stomach. "I am in the company of Tolstoy, Spencer, and the most advanced thinkers of the world," he asserted. "Workers will never get their rights while they look to Parliament. A general strike would be more effective than all the Parliaments in the world. ... We have been hanged in Chicago, electrocuted in New York, guillotined in Paris, and strangled in Italy, and I will go with my comrades. I am opposed to your Government and your authority. Down with them. Do your best. Long live Anarchy!"[16]

Fleming refused to desist. The Sunday following his expulsion, he addressed the largest audience he had ever had on the Yarra Bank, between eight and ten thousand people "listening to Anarchy."[17] Over the next decade he persisted in denouncing what he termed "the shysters in the political labour movement," the party bosses and officials who were selling the workers' birthright for a mess of pottage. In 1910 he excoriated the Labour premier of South Australia for ordering the police "to bludgeon the strikers at Adelaide." In 1911 he lashed out at the "fallacy of political action," insisting that genuine change could be secured only "through direct action followed by active revolt." In 1912, addressing a meeting of the unemployed in Richmond Town Hall, he called again for a strategy of direct action, urging his listeners to become "window smashers rather than endure hunger." And in 1913, citing the Mexican Revolution as a model, he proclaimed that "action alone would succeed and politics always fail. Down with politics! Down with Politicians!"[18]

Try as he might, however, Fleming was unable to turn the tide. Year after year, Labour continued to gain ground at the expense of the anarchists and other militants. That he faced an uphill struggle Fleming was fully aware, but he refused to allow himself to become discouraged. "There are only a few of us in Melbourne to keep Anarchy to the front," he admitted in 1904, "but we are sowing the seeds for the future harvest."[19]

Stubbornly, indefatigably, Fleming carried on his labors. Each year, flourishing his scarlet banner, he led the May Day procession through Melbourne, between ten and twenty thousand marchers with brass bands and decorated floats, ending up at the Yarra Bank where Fleming would address the crowd. The 1913 demonstration Fleming considered particularly successful, "as I was not mobbed nor interrupted" (in prior years he had been stoned and his flag "torn to pieces").[20] Each year, moreover, he took part in commemorations of the launching of the Paris Commune (March 18) and of the hanging of the Chicago martyrs (November 11). In 1910 the latter was held in the auditorium of the Trades Hall Council, from which Fleming had been expelled six years before. The Council, however, raised no objection, and the meeting was a "huge success," concluding with "three ringing cheers for our departed comrades, and for Anarchy and insurrection."[21]

To give the movement a further boost, Fleming, in 1908, invited Emma Goldman, one of anarchism's most talented speakers, to conduct an extended tour of Australia. A keen admirer of his American comrade, he had lauded her in his Yarra Bank speeches, corresponded with her for several years, and distributed her journal *Mother Earth* at his meetings since its inception in 1906. Excited at the prospect, Goldman began to raise money for the fare. With her lover Ben Reitman at her side, she remarked, the voyage would be "a joy and give me a much needed rest," remote from the attentions of the American authorities. Reitman, too, was "wild with the idea." He could talk of nothing else and was eager to start at once. In preparation for the visit, Goldman shipped 1,500 pounds of literature to Victoria, where there were "new friends to win, fresh minds and hearts to awaken." By April 1909 they were ready for the journey, their trunks packed, and a grand farewell party arranged. On the eve of their departure, however, Goldman was stripped of her American citizenship and had to cancel the trip lest she be forbidden to reenter the country. The tour was abandoned at great financial loss to *Mother Earth*, as well as to Fleming and his associates, who had completed all the necessary arrangements.[22]

Fleming and Goldman were never to meet, though he continued to sell *Mother Earth* at his meetings and corresponded with her until her death in 1940. He also sold other anarchist periodicals, including the London *Freedom* and *The Herald of Revolt*, published by Guy Aldred before the First World War. "You may be sure, dear comrade, I will do my best to push your paper," he wrote to Aldred in 1912, "but Australians don't read revolutionary literature. Tom Mann described them as mutton heads, which I think about correct." That year, said Fleming, every city in Australia was holding unemployment meetings, and yet there were no strikes. "The capitalist need only threaten, and obedience immediately comes forth. Conscription, the cherished weapon of the oppressors, is firmly rooted. Children fourteen years of age are imprisoned in a military fort over a hundred miles from Melbourne. That is what Labour government has brought Australia to. Oh, hell, can these human weeds become virile? I am shouting Anarchy."[23]

He was shouting in vain. With the outbreak of the First World War, Australia threw itself into the fray on the side of the British motherland. Fleming, like Goldman in America, clung to his antimilitarist principles. The war, as he saw it, was a capitalist struggle for power and profit, with the workers serving as cannon fodder, so that it was absurd to regard a victory for either side as preferable. Kropotkin's support of the Allies came to him as a shock. "I regret to think that after all these years, having accepted Kropotkin as teacher and guide, he should so disappoint us," wrote Fleming to Goldman in November 1914. "I feel oppressed."[24]

Fleming raised his voice in opposition—"The Rich Man's War and the Poor Man's Fight" was the title of one of his lectures in 1915. Summoned to court for utterances against the war, he was defended by a socialist lawyer, Marshall Lyle, and the charges were dismissed. Soon afterwards, however, he was fined for "discouraging recruiting" during a speech on the Yarra Bank. ("Why should you go and fight?" he was reported as saying. "Would you be any worse off if the Germans were in power than the rotters you have to put up with at present?") For the rest of the war Fleming kept up his antimilitarist crusade, suffering rough treatment from his opponents. He was taunted, stoned, knocked down, threatened with being thrown in the river, and on one occasion actually thrown in and pulled out by his socialist friend, Percy Laidler, who for years past had struggled at his side for the unemployed.[25]

When the war came to an end, Fleming was in his mid-fifties, the "last of the Mohicans" of Australian anarchism, as a British anarchist has called him.[26] Yet more than three decades of life still remained to him; and though the pace of his activity declined, he was never content to be idle. On the contrary, he continued to march every year on May First and to speak every Sunday from his Yarra Bank stand, where his red flag and little bell were familiar features. During the 1920s he spoke out in behalf of Sacco and Vanzetti, taking part in the worldwide campaign to prevent their execution. As the years passed, he harked back to his old free-thought message, his main target being the Catholic church, which, according to a regular listener, he "attacked virulently." On one such occasion a gang of youths from a neighboring Catholic parish rushed his platform and began to rough him up, but other speakers and listeners rallied to his aid and chased the marauders off. Fleming, shaken but unhurt, regained the podium and, in response to inquiries, said: "I'm all right. There appears to be only one casualty. I've lost my spectacles. They are probably in Mannix's museum by now." (Mannix was the Catholic Archbishop of Melbourne.)[27]

When the Great Depression struck, Fleming resumed his campaign for the unemployed. "Australia is down and out, with no sign of improvement," he wrote to Goldman in 1933. "The workers will submit to any injustice, compulsory arbitration is their only outlook. Voltaire once stated the world was full of fools, and he would leave the world as wicked and foolish as he found it." Voltaire, said Fleming, was right. Half a million men were out of work, and thirty thousand children were leaving school every year with no prospect of employment, all the result of "trusting the political prostitutes"of the Labour Party. Nor were the Communists any better: "The Communists go one further than the Labour men, endeavoring to get on the workers' backs. I sometimes think that life is a farce and all things show it. I used to believe it but now I know it." As for his fellow anarchists, their ranks were rapidly dwindling. Some had joined the Communists, others the Labour Party for political jobs. "Many of the old comrades are dead," wrote Fleming, "and I am the last of that proud race. The young today are duds, who have no wish to be free. Anarchism cries in the wilderness."[28]

Nor did matters improve as time elapsed; in some ways, indeed, they grew worse. Yet Fleming carried on as in the past. Week after week, year after year, he spoke out against government and religion. "I continue to keep the Anarchist flag flying," he declared. "I always say that I shall die an Anarchist and an Atheist, because that is based on reason and common sense." Nor did he have any regrets. On the contrary, he looked back with satisfaction on the life that he had led. "I have lived my life," he wrote to Goldman, echoing the title of her autobiography. "My small effort is not like yours, but it is an effort."[29]

With the outbreak of the Second World War, however, Fleming was overwhelmed with doubt. Would the "age of reason" never come? he asked. "Human nature does not change. The painful experience of the last wholesale butchery has been lost. Another flock of sheep are being prepared. Humans have lost their reason, and are tamely submitting to command, marching to death; man is a muff by nature, and has every appearance of remaining a muff. The dawning of Liberty, which was so promising when I was young, has departed. . . . The facts speak for themselves. The world is full of fools. My mark is to attack the hocus-pocus called God, and its comrade, authority. After all, authority comes from God. Anarchism exposes the swindle which the swarm of vermin fatten on. Plato wrote that the senate was corrupt; the politicians were bribed; the people were fools. The few thought, but the many never. I am seventy-six. My days are done. I have lived my life. I have kept the flag of anarchism flying. Long live Anarchy!"[30]

Fleming had lost his former optimism. There was no more talk of "sowing the seeds" of the workers' millennium. Rather, his mood was one of resignation, with little hope for the future. For another decade, however, he carried on his weekly forum, "grinding out old phrases and issuing futile challenges to the powers that be."[31] The last press report on his activity appeared in 1947, when Fleming was eighty-three: "Yes, 'Chummy' is still dishing it out from the same old rock platform, under the same old elm, under the same red banner, proclaiming Anarchy to the four winds. . . . Chummy, the last of the old time ranters, has stuck it out for over fifty years."[32]

Fleming died at his home in Carlton on January 25, 1950. His whole life had been devoted to the cause that he had espoused in his youth. In accordance with his wishes, his body was cremated. At the end of April, three months after his death, his friends suddenly recalled that Fleming had asked that his ashes be scattered on the Yarra Bank on May Day. They did not, however, have the ashes. "Does it matter what ashes they are?" asked Percy Laidler. A member of the butchers' union took the hint and, on May First, brought along a tin of ashes. At Yarra Bank Laidler got up and made a speech about Fleming, punctuating it by throwing handfuls of ashes, which blew in the Melbourne wind all over the crowd.[33] Thus did Chummy, heretic to the end, take part in his last May Day ceremony.

Notes

ONE : THE LEGACY OF BAKUNIN

1. E. Lampert, *Studies in Rebellion* (London, 1957), p. 118.
2. E. H. Carr, *Michael Bakunin* (New York, 1961), p. 196.
3. M. A. Bakunin, *Sobranie sochinenii i pisem, 1828-1876*, ed. Iu. M. Steklov, 4 vols. (Moscow, 1934-1936), IV, 154-55; *The "Confession" of Mikhail Bakunin*, tr. Robert C. Howes, with an introduction and notes by Lawrence D. Orton (Ithaca, 1977), p. 92.
4. Eugene Pyziur, *The Doctrine of Anarchism of Michael A. Bakunin* (Milwaukee, 1955), p.1.
5. Iu. M. Steklov, *Mikhail Aleksandrovich Bakunin*, 4 vols. (Moscow, 1926-1927), III, 112.
6. Carr, *Michael Bakunin*, p. 175.
7. M. A. Bakunin, *Oeuvres*, 6 vols. (Paris, 1895-1913), II, 399; Steklov, *Mikhail Aleksandrovich Bakunin*, I, 189.
8. Peter Kropotkin, *Memoirs of a Revolutionist* (Boston, 1899), p. 288.
9. Pyziur, *Doctrine of Anarchism*, p. 10.
10. *Dissent*, January-February 1968, pp. 41-44.
11. George Woodcock, *Anarchism* (Cleveland, 1962), p. 155.
12. Frantz Fanon, *The Wretched of the Earth* (New York, 1966), p. 88.
13. Herbert Marcuse, *One-Dimensional Man* (Boston, 1964), pp. 256-57.
14. Max Nomad, *Apostles of Revolution* (Boston, 1939), p. 127; Karl Marx, *L'Alliance de la démocratie socialiste et l'Association Internationale des Travailleurs* (London, 1873), p. 48.
15. M. A. Bakunin, *Gesammelte Werke*, 3 vols. (Berlin, 1921-1924), III, 120-21.
16. Régis Debray, *Revolution in the Revolution?* (New York, 1967), pp. 95-116.
17. Carr, *Michael Bakunin*, p. 181.
18. Ibid.
19. *Archives Bakounine*, vol. VI: *Michel Bakounine sur la guerre franco-allemande et la révolution sociale en France, 1870-1871*, ed. Arthur Lehning (Leiden, 1977), p. 45.

20. Paul Avrich, *The Russian Anarchists* (Princeton, 1967), p. 129.

21. Ibid.

22. Steklov, *Mikhail Aleksandrovich Bakunin*, I, 343-45; III, 118-27.

23. M. A. Bakunin, *Izbrannye sochineniia*, 5 vols. (Petrograd, 1919-1922), I, 237.

24. Bakunin, *Gesammelte Werke*, III, 35-38, 82.

25. The burden of authorship now seems to have been Nechaev's, though Bakunin may have had a hand in its composition or revision (see Chapter 3).

26. Eldridge Cleaver, *Soul on Ice* (New York, 1968), p. 12; George L. Jackson, *Blood in My Eye* (New York, 1972), p. 3.

27. Avrich, *The Russian Anarchists*, p. 200.

28. Ibid., p. 231.

29. Pyziur, *Doctrine of Anarchism*, p. 5.

30. Rudolf Rocker, *Anarcho-Syndicalism* (Indore, n.d.), p. 88.

31. Bakunin, *Oeuvres*, IV, 376.

32. Bakunin to Elisée Reclus, February 15, 1875, in James Guillaume, *L'Internationale: Documents et souvenirs (1864-1878)*, 4 vols. (Paris, 1905-1910), III, 284-85; K. J. Kenafick, *Michael Bakunin and Karl Marx* (Melbourne, 1948), p. 304.

33. G. P. Maximoff, ed., *The Political Philosophy of Bakunin* (New York, 1953), p. 48.

TWO : BAKUNIN AND THE UNITED STATES

1. *Kolokol* (London), November 22, 1861.

2. See E. H. Carr, "Bakunin's Escape from Siberia," *Slavonic Review* 15 (January 1937): 377-88; and *Libero International* (Kobe), no. 5 (September 1978). In Yokohama, by an odd coincidence, Bakunin ran into Wilhelm Heine, a fellow participant in the Dresden rising of 1849.

3. *San Francisco Evening Bulletin*, October 16, 1861; Alexander Herzen, *My Past and Thoughts*, tr. Constance Garnett, 6 vols. (London, 1924-1927), V, 137.

4. *Pis'ma M. A. Bakunina k A. I. Gertsenu i N. P. Ogarevu*, ed. M. P. Dragomanov (St. Petersburg, 1906), p. 191. [Hereafter cited as *Pis'ma*.]

5. Bakunin to Herzen and Ogarev, October 15, 1861, *Pis'ma*, p. 189. Carr gives both $250 and $300 as the sum borrowed from Rev. Koe: "Bakunin's Escape from Siberia," p. 383, and *Michael Bakunin* (New York, 1961), p. 247.

6. *Pis'ma*, p. 189.

7. Carr, *Michael Bakunin*, p. 252; Herzen, *My Past and Thoughts*, V, 131-32.

8. *Pis'ma*, pp. 189-90; Herzen, *My Past and Thoughts*, V, 131.

9. *Pis'ma*, pp. 191-92; Max Nettlau, *Michael Bakunin: Eine Biographie*, 3 vols. (London, 1896-1900), I, 138-40; V. Polonskii, *Mikhail Aleksandrovich Bakunin: Zhizn', deiatel'nost', myshlenie*, 2 vols. (Moscow, 1922-1925), II, 347-48.

10. *New York Times* and *New York Tribune*, November 16, 1861.

11. The passenger list of the *Champion*, as printed in the *New York Tribune* of November 16, 1861, gives his name as "M. Bakonnia."

12. See Bakunin to Solger, October 14, 1844, and Bakunin to Emma Herwegh, October 18, 1847, in Bakunin, *Sobranie sochinenii i pisem, 1828-1876*, ed. Iu. M. Steklov, 4 vols. (Moscow, 1934-1936), III, 236-38, 267-68.

13. Ibid., III, 467; *Dictionary of American Biography*, XVII, 393-94. See also A. E. Zucker, ed., *The Forty-Eighters: Political Refugees of the German Revolution*

of 1848 (New York, 1950), pp. 124, 343-44; and Carl Wittke, *Refugees of Revolution: The German Forty-Eighters in America* (Philadelphia, 1952), pp. 310-11.

14. When Bakunin visited Solger's New York home he wrote a note to Herzen and Ogarev, to which Solger and Kapp appended their greetings. See Bakunin to Herzen and Ogarev, December 3, 1861, *Pis'ma*, p. 193.

15. Zucker, *The Forty-Eighters*, pp. 307-308; Wittke, *Refugees of Revolution*, pp. 43, 62-63. See also Edith Lenel, *Friedrich Kapp* (Leipzig, 1935).

16. M. A. Bakunin, *Oeuvres*, 6 vols. (Paris, 1895-1913), I, 50. On Sumner see the fine two-volume biography by David H. Donald, *Charles Sumner and the Coming of the Civil War* and *Charles Sumner and the Rights of Man* (New York, 1960, 1970).

17. Boston, 1872-1877. On Wilson see Richard H. Abbott, *Cobbler in Congress: The Life of Henry Wilson, 1812-1875* (Lexington, Ky., 1972); and *Dictionary of American Biography*, xx, 322-25.

18. Jósef Hordyński, *History of the Late Polish Revolution, and the Events of the Campaign* (Boston, 1832); Martin P. Kennard, "Michel Bakounin," manuscript in Harvard Library, published by Oscar Handlin, "A Russian Anarchist Visits Boston," *New England Quarterly* 15 (March 1942): 104-109.

19. Kennard describes Solger as "a valued friend" who, like Bakunin, "had been compelled to flee, a political refugee from the absolutism of his fatherland" ("Michel Bakounin," p. 105).

20. Ibid., p. 107. By a remarkable coincidence, while Bakunin was visiting Kennard at his jewelry firm, they encountered the Austrian officer who had conducted him to prison in 1849, and who had now come to Boston to enter a Massachusetts unit of the Northern Army.

21. *Pis'ma*, p. 120.

22. Handlin, "A Russian Anarchist," p. 108.

23. Bakunin, *Oeuvres*, I, 172.

24. Ibid., I, 21-22; Handlin, "A Russian Anarchist," p. 107.

25. Bakunin, *Oeuvres*, I, 22.

26. *Pis'ma*, p. 190.

27. Van Wyck Brooks, *The Flowering of New England, 1815-1865*, rev. ed. (New York, 1937), p. 150.

28. Samuel Longfellow, ed., *Life of Henry Wadsworth Longfellow*, 3 vols. (Boston, 1886), II, 371.

29. Handlin, "A Russian Anarchist," p. 107. Contrast Carr, *Michael Bakunin*, p. 261: "Bakunin never acquired more than a smattering of spoken English."

30. Carr, *Michael Bakunin*, pp. 251-55; Handlin, "A Russian Anarchist," p. 105.

31. Handlin, "A Russian Anarchist," p. 106; Annie Longfellow Thorp, "A Little Person's Memories of Great People," Longfellow Papers, Craigie House, Cambridge, published by David Hecht, " 'Laughing Allegra' Meets an Ogre," *New England Quarterly* 19 (June 1946): 243-44.

32. *Pis'ma*, pp. 190-91.

33. Carr, *Michael Bakunin*, p. 247; Handlin, "A Russian Anarchist," p. 107.

34. Nettlau, *Michael Bakunin*, I, 138-40; *New York Times*, December 15, 1861; M. Bakunin, "Herzen," *Archives Bakounine*, ed. Arthur Lehning, v (Leiden, 1974), p. 23.

35. Bakunin to P. P. Lialin, February 27, 1862, in M. K. Lemke, *Ocherki osvoboditel'nogo dvizheniia "shestidesiatykh godov"* (St. Petersburg, 1908), pp. 133-35.

36. Bakunin, *Oeuvres*, IV, 289; Handlin, "A Russian Anarchist," p. 109.

37. Bakunin, *Oeuvres*, I, 12-13, 171. Emphasis in original. See also Hans Rogger, "Russia and the Civil War," in *Heard Round the World*, ed. Harold Hyman (New York, 1969), pp. 177-256.

38. Bakunin, *Oeuvres*, I, 174; IV, 448.

39. Quoted in Max M. Laserson, *The American Impact on Russia: Diplomatic and Ideological, 1789-1917* (New York, 1950), p. 171.

40. Handlin, "A Russian Anarchist," p. 108; Carr, *Michael Bakunin*, p. 491.

41. Bakunin, *Oeuvres*, I, 28-30. Emphasis in original. Bakunin's esteem for local self-government was influenced by, among others, Proudhon, de Tocqueville, and John Stuart Mill.

42. Ibid., I, 28-29. Emphasis in original. This, as David Hecht points out in *Russian Radicals Look to America, 1825-1894* (Cambridge, Mass., 1947), pp. 58-60, was written twenty-five years before Frederick Jackson Turner enunciated his famous "safety-valve" theory of American social stability.

43. Bakunin, *Sobranie sochinenii i pisem*, IV, 154-55; *The "Confession" of Mikhail Bakunin*, tr. Robert C. Howes, with an introduction and notes by Lawrence D. Orton (Ithaca, 1977), p. 92.

44. *Pis'ma*, p. 190.

45. Handlin, "A Russian Anarchist," p. 108.

46. Bakunin, *Oeuvres*, I, 29-30.

47. Ibid., I, 157-58.

48. Ibid., I, 171-74.

49. M. Bakunin, *God and the State* (New York, 1970), p. 32.

50. Bakunin, *Oeuvres*, I, 287-89; *Archives Bakounine*, vol. III: *Gosudarstvennost' i anarkhiia*, ed. Arthur Lehning (Leiden, 1967), 45. On another occasion, though praising educational advances in America and Switzerland, Bakunin nevertheless argued that "children of the bourgeoisie" enjoyed a higher education while those "of the people" received a "primary education only, and on rare occasions a bit of secondary education." *Oeuvres*, V, 324.

51. Bakunin to Reclus, February 15, 1875, in James Guillaume, *L'Internationale: Documents et souvenirs (1864-1878)*, 4 vols. (Paris, 1905-1910), III, 284-85.

52. Quoted by Charles Shively, introduction to S. P. Andrews, *The Science of Society* (Weston, Mass., 1970, reprint of the Benjamin Tucker edition of 1888), p. 21.

53. See, for example, M. Bakunin, "Gospel of Nihilism," *The Word*, April 1880.

54. Donald Drew Egbert and Stow Persons, eds., *Socialism and American Life*, 2 vols. (Princeton, 1952), I, 207.

55. *Liberty*, January 7 and 21, and March 18, 1882.

56. Tucker's involvement with Peter Kropotkin is detailed in Chapter 5.

57. Serialized in *Liberty*, May 17, 1884 ff., and issued in book form in 1886.

58. *Liberty*, June 7, 1890. Yarros also wrote essays for *Liberty* on Chernyshevsky and Herzen.

59. Ibid., November 26, 1881. Tucker's sources probably included J.W.A. von Eckardt, *Russia before and after the War*, tr. Edward Fairfax Taylor (London and Boston, 1880), with a 48-page chapter on Bakunin; and an article on Bakunin by E. de Laveleye in the *Revue des Deux Mondes* of the same year. In 1908, it might be added, Tucker published an American edition of Paul Eltzbacher's *Anarchism* (translated from the German by Tucker's associate Steven T. Byington), which contains a valuable chapter on Bakunin and his ideas.

60. *Liberty*, November 26, 1881.

61. Ibid., July 22, 1882. A leading authority on Tucker calls its publication "a landmark in anarchist propaganda." James J. Martin, *Men against the State: The Expositors of Individualist Anarchism in America, 1827-1908*, rev. ed. (Colorado Springs, 1970), p. 219. Another translation of *God and the State*, by Marie Le Compte, was serialized in the San Francisco *Truth* in 1883 and 1884, but Tucker's became the standard English version, reappearing in several editions, both in Britain and the United States, over the ensuing decades. In the United States it was reissued in 1896 by E. H. Fulton of Columbus Junction, Iowa, as Liberty Library No. 2; in 1900 by Abe Isaak (a Russian Mennonite turned anarchist) of San Francisco, as Free Society Library No. 4; and in 1916 (as amended by Max Nettlau) by Emma Goldman's Mother Earth Publishing Association, which incorrectly labeled it the "first American edition." Much to Tucker's consternation, the Liberty Library and Free Society editions failed to credit him with the translation, erroneously attributing it to Cafiero and Reclus, who had merely contributed the preface.

62. *Liberty*, September 18, 1886-June 18, 1887. Excerpts in Spanish appeared in the anarchist journal *El Despertar* (New York), June 1 and 15, 1892.

63. *The Alarm*, January 23, 1886.

64. *Freedom* (London), September-October 1900. In 1901, to mention another example, Abe Isaak's *Free Society* appealed for funds to decorate and maintain Bakunin's grave. *Free Society* (Chicago), August 4, 1901.

65. M. Bakunin, *Gott und der Staat* (Philadelphia, 1884), published by the Verlag der Gruppe II, I.A.A. [Internationale Arbeiter-Assoziation]; *Freiheit* (New York), May 2-June 13, 1891, then in pamphlet form as Internationale Bibliothek No. 17 (New York, 1892). Bakunin was often quoted by Most, the leading German anarchist in America, whose Pittsburgh Manifesto of October 1883 drew heavily on Bakuninist ideas.

66. *Dělnicke Listy* (New York), January 18, 1896 ff., reproduced in pamphlet form as *Bůh a stát* (New York, 1896); *Bog i gosudarstvo* (New York, 1918), published by the Union of Russian Workers of New York City; *Fraye Arbeter Shtime*, 1900-1901.

67. For example, *Freiheit*, March 16 and April 6, 1895, printed a German translation of three lectures delivered by Bakunin in May 1871 at Courtelary in the Swiss Jura, reissued as a pamphlet entitled *Drei Vorträge*. A Spanish translation appeared in *El Esclavo* of Tampa, Florida, in 1895, and a Czech translation in *Dělnicke Listy* in 1895 and also as a pamphlet, *Tři přednáški* (New York, 1895). Bakunin's essays and speeches also appeared in such journals as *Il Grido degli Oppressi* (New York, 1892-1894), *Germinal* (Paterson, N.J., 1899-1902), *Volné Listy* (New York, 1890-1917), *Di Fraye Tsukunft* (New York, 1915-1916), *Free Society* (San Francisco, Chicago, New York, 1897-1904), *Mother Earth* (New York, 1906-1917), and *Why?* (Tacoma, 1913-1914).

68. *Golos Truda* (New York, 1911-1917); *Khleb i Volia* (New York, 1919). See also *Rabochaia Mysl'* (New York), August 1916, which invoked Bakunin and Herzen's slogan "To the People!" According to one authority, the first Russian paper in the United States, *Svoboda*, was published in California during the 1870s by a follower of Bakunin. L. Lipotkin [Lazarev], "Russkoe anarkhicheskoe dvizhenie v Severnoi Amerike: Istoricheskii ocherk," manuscript, International Institute of Social History, Amsterdam, p. 111.

69. M. Bakunin, *Izbrannye sochineniia*, vol. 1 (New York, 1920), with an introduction by V. Cherkezov. See also *Tak govoril Bakunin* (Bridgeport, Conn., n.d.

[1919?]), first published in Paris in 1914 by the Bratstvo Vol'nykh Obshchinnikov. A Yiddish collection of Bakunin's writings, *Geklibene shriften*, was published in New York in 1919 by the Kropotkin Literary Society, with a biographical sketch by Rudolf Rocker.

70. Quoted in Rudolf Rocker, *Anarcho-Syndicalism* (Indore, n.d.), p. 88.

71. See Emily C. Brown, *Har Dayal: Hindu Revolutionary and Rationalist* (Tucson, 1975), pp. 116-17.

72. *Mother Earth*, May 1914; *The Modern School*, June 1, 1914. Havel produced a small pamphlet for the occasion, *Bakunin, May 30, 1814-July 1, 1876* (New York, 1914), published by the Centenary Commemoration Committee. For a similar celebration in Paris, see Paul Avrich, *The Russian Anarchists* (Princeton, 1967), p. 114 and illustration 7.

73. Vanzetti to Alice Stone Blackwell, September 15, 1925, *The Letters of Sacco and Vanzetti*, ed. Marion Denman Frankfurter and Gardner Jackson (New York, 1928), p. 169.

74. (Glencoe, Ill., 1953); (Milwaukee, 1955).

75. For example, Sam Dolgoff, ed., *Bakunin on Anarchy* (New York, 1972); Arthur Lehning, ed., *Michael Bakunin: Selected Writings* (New York, 1973); Michael Confino, ed., *Daughter of a Revolutionary: Natalie Herzen and the Bakunin/ Nechayev Circle* (La Salle, Ill., 1974); and Anthony Masters, *Bakunin: The Father of Anarchism* (New York, 1974). In 1961 E. H. Carr's *Michael Bakunin* was reissued by Vintage Books of New York, and in 1970 Bakunin's *God and the State* was reprinted—for the first time since the Mother Earth edition of 1916—by Dover Publications of New York. The first English translation of Bakunin's *Statehood and Anarchy* appeared in New York in 1976, and his *Confession* was published in an English translation by Cornell University Press in 1977. See Paul Avrich, "Bakunin and His Writings," *Canadian-American Slavic Studies* 10 (Winter 1976): 591-96.

76. *Freedom*, April 3, 1976.

THREE : BAKUNIN AND NECHAEV

1. I am indebted to the following works for this reappraisal of the Nechaev affair: *Archives Bakounine*, vol. IV: *Michel Bakounine et ses relations avec Sergej Nečaev, 1870-1872*, ed. Arthur Lehning (Leiden, 1971); Michael Confino, ed., *Daughter of a Revolutionary: Natalie Herzen and the Bakunin/Nechayev Circle* (La Salle, Ill., 1974); Confino, ed., *Violence dans la violence: Le débat Bakounine-Nečaev* (Paris, 1973); Stephen T. Cochrane, *The Collaboration of Nečaev, Ogarev and Bakunin in 1869: Nečaev's Early Years* (Giessen, 1977); Philip Pomper, *Sergei Nechaev* (New Brunswick, N.J., 1979). See also Aileen Kelly, *Mikhail Bakunin: A Study in the Psychology and Politics of Utopianism* (Oxford, 1982).

2. Confino, ed., *Violence dans la violence*, pp. 31-32.

3. Max Nomad, *Apostles of Revolution* (Boston, 1939), p. 216.

4. Filippo Michele Buonarroti, *Conspiration pour l'égalité dite de Babeuf* (Brussels, 1828).

5. Franco Venturi, *Roots of Revolution* (New York, 1960), p. 87. Among the Decembrists Nechaev singled out a certain Panov, who "alone, in entering the palace to slaughter the entire family of Tsar Nicholas with all of the household, possessed the genuine thought, feeling, and aspiration of the *muzhik*. Oh, if he had

only succeeded!" Quoted by Philip Pomper, "Nechaev and Tsaricide," *Russian Review* 33 (April 1974): 131.

6. Ibid., pp. 295-98.

7. Avrahm Yarmolinsky, *Road to Revolution* (New York, 1962), p. 136.

8. Venturi, *Roots of Revolution*, p. 337.

9. Ibid., p. 363. See also Deborah Hardy, *Petr Tkachev: The Critic as Jacobin* (Seattle, 1977), pp. 133-36.

10. Nomad, *Apostles of Revolution*, p. 222.

11. Confino, ed., *Daughter of a Revolutionary*, p. 20.

12. E. H. Carr, *Michael Bakunin* (New York, 1961), p. 393; Confino, ed., *Violence dans la violence*, p. 20.

13. Nicolas Walter, foreword to the Kropotkin Lighthouse Publications edition of the *Catechism* (London, 1971). See also Walter's "The Doomed Man: Sergei Nechayev (1847-1882)," *Freedom*, December 11, 1982. For a full English translation of the *Catechism* see Confino, *Daughter of a Revolutionary*, pp. 221-30.

14. Confino, ed., *Violence dans la violence*, p. 41.

15. Carr, *Michael Bakunin*, p. 393.

16. Bakunin to Ogarev, January 12, 1870, in Confino, *Daughter of a Revolutionary*, p. 151.

17. Confino, ed., *Violence dans la violence*, p. 53.

18. Bakunin to Alfred Talandier, July 24, 1870, in Confino, ed., *Daughter of a Revolutionary*, p. 307; Yarmolinsky, *Road to Revolution*, p. 163.

19. The letter in the original Russian with a French translation is in Lehning, ed., *Michael Bakounine et ses relations avec Sergej Nečaev*, pp. 103-34, 221-54. For a full English translation see Confino, ed., *Daughter of a Revolutionary*, pp. 238-80.

20. Arthur Lehning, *From Buonarroti to Bakunin* (Leiden, 1970), p. ix.

21. Carr, *Michael Bakunin*, p. 193; Bakunin, *Gesammelte Werke*, 3 vols. (Berlin, 1921-1924), III, 35-38, 82, 90-99; C. E. Black, ed., *Rewriting Russian History* (New York, 1962), p. 297.

22. K. J. Kenafick, *Michael Bakunin and Karl Marx* (Melbourne, 1948), pp. 132-33; Confino, ed., *Daughter of a Revolutionary*, pp. 323-24.

23. Venturi, *Roots of Revolution*, pp. 386-87; Yarmolinsky, *Road to Revolution*, p. 165.

24. Nomad, *Apostles of Revolution*, p. 251.

25. M. P. Sazhin, *Vospominaniia* (Moscow, 1925), p. 65.

26. Confino, ed., *Violence dans la violence*, p. 67.

27. E. H. Carr, *The Romantic Exiles* (London, 1933), p. 290; Albert Camus, *The Rebel* (New York, 1956), pp. 160-62.

28. Eldridge Cleaver, *Soul on Ice* (New York, 1968), p. 12. Cf. George L. Jackson, *Blood in My Eye* (New York, 1972), p. 3; and Huey Newton, interview in *Playboy*, May 1973, p. 90. Renato Curcio, a leader of the Red Brigades in Italy during the 1970s, likewise cited the *Catechism* with approval and modeled his revolutionary organization after that of Nechaev. See Curtis Pepper, "The Possessed," *New York Times Magazine*, February 18, 1979.

29. *New York Times*, February 23, 1974.

30. George Woodcock and Ivan Avakumović, *The Anarchist Prince* (London, 1950), p. 360; Peter Kropotkin, *Memoirs of a Revolutionist* (Boston, 1899), pp. 304-305.

31. H. E. Kaminski, *Bakounine: La vie d'un révolutionnaire* (Paris, 1938), p. 339.

FOUR : KROPOTKIN'S ETHICAL ANARCHISM

1. P. Kropotkin, "An Appeal to the Young," in *Kropotkin's Revolutionary Pamphlets*, ed. Roger N. Baldwin (New York: 1927), pp. 261, 279.

2. P. Kropotkin, *Memoirs of a Revolutionist* (Boston, 1899), p. 226.

3. Ibid., p. 240.

4. Errico Malatesta, in *Peter Kropotkin: The Rebel, Thinker, and Humanitarian*, ed. Joseph Ishill (Berkeley Heights, N.J., 1923), p. 39.

5. Kropotkin, *Memoirs of a Revolutionist*, pp. 216-17.

6. Ibid., p. 287.

7. P. Kropotkin, *Mutual Aid* (London, 1972), p. 18.

8. Ibid., p. 19.

9. Ibid., p. 31n.

10. T. H. Huxley, "The Struggle for Existence: A Programme," *The Nineteenth Century*, February 1888.

11. Kropotkin, *Mutual Aid*, p. 71.

12. Ibid., p. 30.

13. Ibid., p. 69. Cf. Kropotkin's *Modern Science and Anarchism* (New York, 1908), p. 44.

14. Kropotkin, *Mutual Aid*, p. 22.

15. P. Kropotkin, *Ethics: Origin and Development* (New York, 1924), p. 22.

16. Kropotkin, *Mutual Aid*, p. 245.

17. P. Kropotkin, *The Conquest of Bread* (London, 1972), p. 49.

18. Ibid., p. 46.

19. Ibid., p. 63.

20. Kropotkin, *Memoirs of a Revolutionist*, p. 119.

21. Kropotkin, *The Conquest of Bread*, p. 197.

22. Ibid., p. 139.

23. P. Kropotkin, *Fields, Factories and Workshops*, rev. ed. (London, 1913), p. 23; *The Conquest of Bread*, p. 164.

24. Kropotkin, *The Conquest of Bread*, p. 104.

25. Lewis Mumford, *The City in History* (London, 1966), p. 585.

26. Kropotkin, *The Conquest of Bread*, p. 53.

27. P. Kropotkin, "Anarchist Communism," in *Kropotkin's Revolutionary Pamphlets*, ed. Baldwin, p. 71.

28. Kropotkin, *The Conquest of Bread*, p. 172.

29. Ibid., pp. 124, 136.

30. Ibid., p. 140.

31. Kropotkin, *Fields, Factories and Workshops*, p. 383.

32. P. Kropotkin, *In Russian and French Prisons* (London, 1887); Baldwin, ed., *Kropotkin's Revolutionary Pamphlets*, pp. 219-35.

33. Kropotkin, *Memoirs of a Revolutionist*, p. 291.

34. Introduction to Baldwin, ed., *Kropotkin's Revolutionary Pamphlets*, p. 7.

35. Kropotkin, "The Spirit of Revolt," in ibid., pp. 40-41.

36. Fritz Fischer, *Germany's Aims in the First World War* (London, 1967).

37. P. Kropotkin, "A Letter on the Present War," *Freedom*, October 1914.

38. N. N. Sukhanov, the left Menshevik chronicler of 1917, in his *Notes on the Revolution* (in Russian).

39. Alexander Berkman, *The Bolshevik Myth (Diary 1920-1922)* (New York, 1925), p. 75; Paul Avrich, ed., *The Anarchists in the Russian Revolution* (Ithaca, 1973), pp. 147-48.

40. Aaron Baron, quoted in Victor Serge, *Memoirs of a Revolutionary, 1901-1941* (London, 1963), p. 124.

41. Georg Brandes, introduction to Kropotkin's *Memoirs of a Revolutionist*, p. xxxiii.

42. Kropotkin, *Ethics*, p. viii. According to the writer Ivan Bunin, Kropotkin had wasted his life "on revolutionary dreams of an anarchistic paradise," ending in "hunger and cold by the dim light of a smoky torch, in the midst of the long-awaited revolution, over a manuscript on human ethics!" Bunin, *Memories and Portraits* (Garden City, N.Y., 1951), pp. 199-201.

43. Mumford, *The City in History*, pp. 585-86.

44. Kropotkin, *The Conquest of Bread*, p. 111.

45. These words, though written by the Italian anarchist Carlo Cafiero, were approved and published by Kropotkin in his Geneva journal *Le Révolté* in December 1880.

46. See Olga Lang, *Pa Chin and His Writings* (Cambridge, Mass., 1967).

47. Kropotkin, *The Conquest of Bread*, p. 48.

48. Kropotkin, "Anarchist Morality," in *Kropotkin's Revolutionary Pamphlets*, ed. Baldwin, p. 113.

49. See James W. Cain, "Kropotkin House, Duluth," *Anarchy*, no. 84 (February 1968): 48-53.

50. Vernon Richards, ed., *Errico Malatesta: His Life and Ideas* (London, 1965), p. 261; Stepniak [S. M. Kravchinskii], *Underground Russia* (London, 1883), p. 89; Ishill, ed., *Peter Kropotkin*, pp. 12-17, 25.

51. Keir Hardie, quoted in Woodcock and Avakumović, *The Anarchist Prince*, p. 226.

52. P. Kropotkin, "Law and Authority," in *Kropotkin's Revolutionary Pamphlets*, ed. Baldwin, p. 205.

53. Quoted in Camillo Berneri, *Peter Kropotkin: His Federalist Ideas* (London, 1942), pp. 10-11.

54. J. S. Mill, *Principles of Political Economy* (London, 1923), pp. 210-11.

55. *Centennial Expressions on Peter Kropotkin, 1842-1942* (Los Angeles, 1942), p. 11.

56. Kropotkin, *The Conquest of Bread*, p. 49.

57. N. M. Pirumova, *Petr Alekseevich Kropotkin* (Moscow, 1972). For an appraisal of this work see Paul Avrich, "A New Soviet Biography of Kropotkin," *The Match!* (Tucson), January 1975.

FIVE : KROPOTKIN IN AMERICA

1. David Hecht, "Kropotkin and America," *Bulletin of the American Association of Teachers of Slavic and East European Languages* 10 (September 15, 1952): 5-7.

2. See P. Kropotkin, *The Great French Revolution, 1789-1793* (London, 1909), pp. 21-22, 141-42.

3. P. Kropotkin, *Russian Literature* (New York, 1905), pp. 4, 223-24.

4. P. Kropotkin, *Memoirs of a Revolutionist* (Boston, 1899), p. 440.

5. P. Kropotkin, *Mutual Aid* (London, 1972), pp. 25, 70, 89.

6. P. Kropotkin, *The Conquest of Bread* (London, 1972), p. 120; Kropotkin, *Fields, Factories and Workshops*, rev. ed. (London, 1913), pp. 62, 147-57.

7. P. Kropotkin, "Affaires d'Amérique," *Bulletin de la Fédération Jurassienne*, August 5, 1877. Cf. *Le Révolté*, December 23, 1882.

8. Harry Kelly, "Reminiscences and Reflections on Peter Kropotkin," *Centennial Expressions on Peter Kropotkin, 1842-1942* (Los Angeles, 1942), p. 27.

9. *The Commonweal*, October 22, 1887; *Freedom*, December 1898; Paul Avrich, *The Haymarket Tragedy* (Princeton, 1984), p. 436.

10. Quoted in James J. Martin, *Men against the State: The Expositors of Individualist Anarchism in America, 1827-1908*, rev. ed. (Colorado Springs, 1970), pp. 219-20; *Liberty*, October 29, 1881; June 10, 1882 ff.; February 17, 1883; March 6, 1886 ff.

11. Anna Strunsky Walling, "Three Contacts with Peter Kropotkin," *Mother Earth*, December 1912; Elizabeth Gurley Flynn, *The Rebel Girl: An Autobiography* (New York, 1973), p. 48. The first American translation, by Marie Le Compte, appeared in the San Francisco *Truth* from January 5 to 26, 1884. Afterwards there were numerous pamphlet editions in a variety of languages.

12. Emma Goldman, *Living My Life* (New York, 1931), p. 509.

13. I. Rudash, "Peter Kropotkin's Two Visits to America," *Man!*, March 1935.

14. See *Il Grido degli Oppressi*, June 14, 1893; *Solidarity*, July 29, 1893; *The Firebrand*, October 4, 1896. It was hoped in 1893 that Kropotkin might attend an International Anarchist Conference in Chicago, and there were erroneous reports the same year that he attended the unveiling of the Haymarket monument in Chicago's Waldheim Cemetery.

15. James Mavor, *An Economic History of Russia*, 2 vols. (London and Toronto, 1914).

16. James Mavor, *My Windows on the Street of the World*, 2 vols. (London and Toronto, 1923), I, 371; *Report of the Sixty-Seventh Meeting of the British Association for the Advancement of Science, Held at Toronto in August 1897* (London, 1898), pp. 648-49, 722-23.

17. P. Kropotkin, "Some of the Resources of Canada," *The Nineteenth Century*, March 1898, pp. 494-514. The diary is preserved among Kropotkin's papers in the Tsentral'nyi Gosudarstvennyi Arkhiv Oktiabr'skoi Revoliutsii, Moscow.

18. Kropotkin, *Memoirs of a Revolutionist*, p. 277.

19. Kropotkin to Geddes, November 27, 1897, Geddes Papers, National Library of Scotland, Edinburgh; George Woodcock and Ivan Avakumović, *The Anarchist Prince* (London, 1950), pp. 273-75. See also Kropotkin's Canadian diary, August 5, 1897, quoted in Natalia Pirumova, *Petr Alekseevich Kropotkin* (Moscow, 1972), p. 157. A Soviet edition of Kropotkin's memoirs contains a sketch he made of a Canadian landscape on September 5, 1897: *Zapiski revoliutsionera*, ed. V. A. Tvardovskaia (Moscow, 1966), p. 472.

20. Kropotkin, "Some of the Resources of Canada," pp. 494-96, 503-504.

21. George Woodcock and Ivan Avakumović, *The Doukhobors* (New York, 1968), pp. 130-32; Mavor, *My Windows*, II, 1.

22. Kropotkin, "Recent Science," *The Nineteenth Century*, November 1897, pp. 799-820; Kropotkin, "Some of the Resources of Canada," p. 514.

23. *When the Iron Is White* (Toronto, 1943), p. 5. I am grateful to Ahrne Thorne, the last editor of the *Fraye Arbeter Shtime*, for calling my attention to this anonymous pamphlet.

24. Kropotkin to Geddes, November 27, 1897; Kropotkin, "Some of the Resources of Canada," p. 495.

25. Kropotkin to Georg Brandes, June 28, 1898, *Correspondance de Georg Brandes*, ed. Paul Krüger, 2 vols. (Copenhagen, 1952-1956), II, 122; Kropotkin, "Some of the Resources of Canada," p. 494; Kropotkin, "On the Present Condition in Russia," *The Outlook*, January 8, 1898, p. 117.

26. A. Levin, "A derinerung vegn Pyotr Kropotkin," *Fraye Arbeter Shtime*, April 10, 1936; Johann Most, "Peter Krapotkin," *Freiheit*, October 30, 1897. Cf. Max Baginski, "John Most," *Mother Earth*, April 1906.

27. *New York Herald*, October 24, 1897.

28. Interview with Laurance Labadie, Suffern, N.Y., March 22, 1975; note entered by Jo Labadie on his copy of the San Francisco *Truth* of August 1884, which bears a portrait of Kropotkin.

29. Kropotkin, *Memoirs of a Revolutionist*, p. 490; Harry Kelly, "Roll Back the Years: Odyssey of a Libertarian," manuscript, Avrich Collection, Library of Congress, Chapter 8, p. 1.

30. Harry Kelly to Joseph J. Cohen, October 18, 1943, Cohen Papers, Bund Archives, New York; Kelly to John N. Beffel, July 7, 1948, Beffel Papers, Archives of Labor History and Urban Affairs, Wayne State University; *New York Herald*, October 24, 1897.

31. *New York Herald*, October 24, 1897.

32. Kelly, "Roll Back the Years," Chapter 8, pp. 1, 6; *New York Herald*, October 25, 1897.

33. *Liberty*, September 3, 1881; *New York Times*, October 25, 1897; *New York Herald*, October 25, 1897. See also *The World* (New York), October 25, 1897.

34. *New York Herald*, October 25, 1897; Stepniak [S. M. Kravchinskii], *Underground Russia* (London, 1883), p. 90.

35. Rudash, "Kropotkin's Two Visits"; Voltairine de Cleyre, "American Notes," *Freedom*, February 1898.

36. *Free Society*, December 17, 1897; *Freedom*, February 1898; Woodcock and Avakumović, *The Anarchist Prince*, p. 275.

37. P. Kropotkin, "La tuerie de Hazleton," *Les Temps Nouveaux*, October 9-15, 1897; Woodcock and Avakumović, *The Anarchist Prince*, p. 276. See also Kropotkin, "The Development of Trade-Unionism," *Freedom*, March 1898.

38. "Kropotkin in Boston," *Free Society*, November 14, 1897, quoted from the *Boston Herald*.

39. S.C.B., "Boston Letter," *Free Society*, December 12, 1897; Kropotkin to Geddes, November 27, 1897. Because of his crowded schedule, Kropotkin declined an invitation from his old friend William Bailie to speak before the Central Labor Union of Boston (Kropotkin to Bailie, November 5, 1897, Bailie Papers, Avrich Collection, Library of Congress). Bailie, a former member of the Manchester branch of the Socialist League, had emigrated to America in 1892 and joined the circle around Tucker's *Liberty*.

40. P. Kropotkin, *Kommunizm i anarkhiia* (St. Petersburg, 1906), p. 11; *Mutual Aid* (London, 1902).

41. Norton to S. G. Ward, November 28, 1897, *Letters of Charles Eliot Norton*, ed. Sara Norton and M. A. DeWolfe Howe, 2 vols. (Boston, 1913), II, 255.

42. Max Nettlau to Benjamin R. Tucker, March 22, 1937, Tucker Papers, New York Public Library.

43. Levin, "A derinerung vegn Pyotr Kropotkin." Apparently Kropotkin under-

stood Yiddish from his knowledge of German and his contacts with the Jewish anarchists of London.

44. S. Yanovsky, "Kropotkin as I Knew Him," in *Peter Kropotkin: The Rebel, Thinker, and Humanitarian*, ed. Joseph Ishill (Berkeley Heights, N.J., 1923), pp. 131-32.

45. *Sturmvogel* (New York), November 15, 1897; *New York Tribune*, November 20, 1897; Kropotkin to Geddes, November 27, 1897.

46. Rudash, "Kropotkin's Two Visits." This group, located in Geneva, issued pamphlets by Jean Grave, Elisée Reclus, Johann Most, and Kropotkin himself. See Paul Avrich, *The Russian Anarchists* (Princeton, 1967), p. 38.

47. Rudash, "Kropotkin's Two Visits."

48. Ibid; Woodcock and Avakumović, *The Anarchist Prince*, p. 276; *Centennial Expressions*, p. 27. See also *New York Times*, November 23, 1897.

49. *Freedom*, January 1898.

50. Kropotkin to Geddes, November 27, 1897.

51. *The World*, November 22, 1897.

52. Kropotkin to Geddes, November 27, 1897; John H. Edelmann, "Solidarity," *Solidarity*, July 15, 1898; Kelly to Beffel, July 7, 1948. *Solidarity*, however, was able to publish only eight additional numbers before running out of money again. Edelmann died two years later at the age of forty-eight.

53. Goldman, *Living My Life*, p. 252; *Freedom*, January 1898. Contrast Martin A. Miller, *Kropotkin* (Chicago, 1976), p. 171. According to Miller, who cites a letter from Kropotkin to Peter Lavrov, Kropotkin had a mixed reception in America and his lectures in New York and Boston were poorly attended. This, however, conflicts with other available evidence.

54. *Free Society*, January 16, 1898.

55. Goldman, *Living My Life*, p. 253. Yet when young Will Durant called on Kropotkin in 1912, he was scolded for "lecturing so much about sex." *Mother Earth*, October 1912.

56. Mavor, *My Windows*, II, 93; Roger N. Baldwin, "The Story of Kropotkin's Life," in *Kropotkin's Revolutionary Pamphlets*, ed. Roger Baldwin (New York, 1927), p. 25.

57. Robert Erskine Ely, "Prince Kropotkin," *Atlantic Monthly*, September 1898, pp. 338-446. At Kropotkin's suggestion, Page solicited articles on China from the anarchist geographer Elisée Reclus, which appeared in the same issue.

58. Kropotkin to Brandes, September 22, 1898, *Correspondance de Georg Brandes*, II, 132. "Around One's Life" (*Autour d'une vie*) became the title of the French edition, though Elisée Reclus suggested still another title, "Memoirs of an Anarchist." Reclus to Kropotkin, August 28, 1898, *Correspondance d'Elisée Reclus*, 3 vols. (Paris, 1911-1925), III, 213.

59. Mavor, *My Windows*, II, 93.

60. Kropotkin to Brandes, March 28, 1901, *Correspondance de Georg Brandes*, II, 171.

61. Quoted in Woodcock and Avakumović, *The Anarchist Prince*, p. 284; Harry Kelly, "American Notes," *Freedom*, July 1901.

62. Baldwin, ed., *Kropotkin's Revolutionary Pamphlets*, p. 26; Kropotkin, *Russian Literature*.

63. Leo Weiner, *Anthology of Russian Literature*, 2 vols. (New York and London, 1902); *Archibald Cary Coolidge: Life and Letters*, ed. H. J. Coolidge and

R. H. Lord (Boston and New York, 1932), p. 45: Kropotkin, *Russian Literature*, p. 39.

64. Baldwin, ed., *Kropotkin's Revolutionary Pamphlets*, p. 26.

65. "Comrade Kropotkin at Boston," *Free Society*, March 17, 1901; Harry Kelly, "Kropotkin in America," *Freedom*, March-April 1901, based on accounts in the *Boston Post* and *Boston Transcript*.

66. *Free Society*, March 17, 1901; *Freedom*, March-April 1901. For the printed text of Kropotkin's lecture, which differs in many details from the newspaper summaries, see Baldwin, ed., *Kropotkin's Revolutionary Pamphlets*, pp. 114-44.

67. *Boston Post*, quoted in *Freedom*, March-April 1901.

68. *Freedom*, July 1901.

69. Baldwin, ed., *Kropotkin's Revolutionary Pamphlets*, p. 26; *New York Times*, March 30, 1901.

70. Goldman, *Living My Life*, p. 287; Hippolyte Havel, "Emma Goldman," in Goldman, *Anarchism and Other Essays* (New York, 1910), pp. 29-30. Among those who assisted Emma Goldman was the Austrian anarchist Rudolf Grossmann, who later became known as "Pierre Ramus." Grossmann to Joseph Ishill, January 3, 1924, Ishill Papers, Harvard University.

71. Goldman, *Living My Life*, p. 361.

72. I. Ulman, "Kropotkin in New York," *Discontent*, April 24, 1901; *New York Times*, March 31, 1901.

73. *Freedom*, July 1901; Ulman, "Kropotkin in New York"; Alexis C. Ferm to Sasha Hourwich, May 23, 1951, Modern School Collection, Rutgers University.

74. George D. Herron, "Kropotkin as a Scientist," *Mother Earth*, December 1912: Ulman, "Kropotkin in New York."

75. Ulman, "Kropotkin in New York"; *New York Times*, April 1, 1901.

76. *Freedom*, July 1901.

77. Johann Most, "Eine Stunde mit Peter Kropotkin," *Freiheit*, April 13, 1901. See also Rudolf Rocker, *Johann Most; Das Leben eines Rebellen* (Berlin, 1924), pp. 396-99.

78. Baldwin, ed., *Kropotkin's Revolutionary Pamphlets*, pp. 26-27; Woodcock and Avakumović, *The Anarchist Prince*, p. 285. According to Kropotkin's daughter, it was her father who induced Booker T. Washington to write his memoirs. Interview with Alexandra Kropotkin, New York, March 10, 1965.

79. Goldman, *Living My Life*, p. 287.

80. S. Yanovsky, "Kropotkin kakim ia ego znal," in *P. A. Kropotkin i ego uchenie: Internatsional'nyi sbornik posviashchennyi desiatoi godovshchine smerti P. A. Kropotkina*, ed G. P. Maximoff (Chicago, 1931), p. 216.

81. "A 'Real Revolutionist,'" *Weekly People*, April 6, 1901.

82. Yanovsky, "Kropotkin kakim ia ego znal," p. 216. According to Woodcock and Avakumović, *The Anarchist Prince*, p. 278, the two men had actually met when Kropotkin wandered into De Leon's office while looking for Johann Most's *Freiheit*, and they had a pleasant and cordial conversation.

83. *Die Autonomie*, September 24, 1892. Cf. *Solidarity*, October 8, 1892.

84. Goldman, *Living My Life*, p. 169; Maximoff, ed., *P. A. Kropotkin i ego uchenie*, p. 226. For a different version see Baldwin, ed., *Kropotkin's Revolutionary Pamphlets*, pp. 25-26.

85. Alexander Berkman to Carl Nold, August 18, 1902, in Berkman, *Prison Memoirs of an Anarchist* (New York, 1912), p. 442. Cf. *Mother Earth Bulletin*, February 1918, where Emma Goldman refers to this incident.

86. Interview with Grace Umrath (a granddaughter of the Isaaks), New York, September 24, 1974; Abe Isaak, Jr., "Kropotkin in Chicago," *Free Society*, May 5, 1901.

87. Goldman, *Living My Life*, pp. 375-76; Jane Addams, *Twenty Years at Hull House* (New York, 1910), p. 402. As late as 1932, Edmund Wilson saw in the polygon room a portrait of Kropotkin among the "patron-saints and heroes of Hull House." Wilson, *The American Earthquake* (Garden City, N.Y., 1958), p. 449.

88. Alice Hamilton, *Exploring the Dangerous Trades* (Boston, 1943), p. 86. Dr. Hamilton was a leading authority on industrial poisons.

89. *Free Society*, May 5, 1901. Kropotkin remained a devotee of *Free Society* until it ceased publication in 1904, and kept in touch with Abe Isaak, whom he sent inscribed copies of his writings. He was especially impressed by C. L. James's "History of the French Revolution," serialized in *Free Society* in 1901 and published in book form the following year.

90. James W. Linn, *Jane Addams: A Biography* (New York, 1935), p. 197; Goldman, *Living My Life*, p. 361. Cf. Fernand Planche and Jean Delphy, *Kropotkine* (Paris, 1948), p. 108, where the incident is misdated as November 11, the anniversary of the Haymarket hangings.

91. Hippolyte Havel, "Kropotkin the Revolutionist," *Mother Earth*, December 1912.

92. Graham Taylor, *Pioneering on Social Frontiers* (Chicago, 1930), p. 317.

93. *Free Society*, May 5, 1901; P. Kropotkin, "Russia and the Student Riots," *The Outlook*, April 6, 1901, pp. 760-64; Kropotkin, "The Present Crisis in Russia," *North American Review*, May 1901, pp. 711-23.

94. Kropotkin, "The Present Crisis in Russia," pp. 717, 723.

95. Konstantin Pobedonostsev, "Russia and Popular Education," *North American Review*, September 1901, pp. 349-54.

96. Kropotkin, "Russian Schools and the Holy Synod," ibid., April 1902, pp. 518-27. See also James W. Hulse, *Revolutionists in London* (Oxford, 1970), pp. 169-70.

97. Sonia Edelstadt Keene to Paul Avrich, December 9, 1974, Avrich Collection, Library of Congress; Hutchins Hapgood, *The Spirit of the Ghetto* (New York, 1902), p. 149. See also *Lucifer*, April 27, 1901, and *Freiheit*, April 27, 1901.

98. Woodcock and Avakumović, *The Anarchist Prince*, pp. 286-87.

99. *Free Society*, May 5 and 19, 1901.

100. Mavor, *My Windows*, II, 93.

101. Addams, *Twenty Years at Hull House*, p. 402; *Free Society*, May 5, 1901; *Freedom*, July 1901.

102. Kropotkin to Guillaume, December 12, 1901, *Probuzhdenie*, February 1931.

103. Hamilton, *Exploring the Dangerous Trades*, p. 86; Linn, *Jane Addams*, p. 219.

104. Quoted in Richard Drinnon, *Rebel in Paradise* (Chicago, 1961), p. 94. Cf. Kropotkin to Goldman, December 16, 1903, Tamiment Library, New York University.

105. Derry Novak, ed., "Une lettre inédite de Pierre Kropotkine à Max Nettlau," *International Review of Social History* 9 (1964): 268-85; English translation in P. A. Kropotkin, *Selected Writings on Anarchism and Revolution*, ed. M. A. Miller (Cambridge, Mass., 1970), pp. 303-304. Emphasis in original.

106. *Mother Earth*, January 1913. See also Goldman, *Living My Life*, p. 510.

107. Emma Goldman to Stella Ballantine, November 4, 1920, Lillian D. Wald Papers, Columbia University.

108. Ishill, ed., *Peter Kropotkin*.

109. Maximoff, ed., *P. A. Kropotkin i ego uchenie; Probuzhdenie*, February 1931; *The Road to Freedom*, March 1931.

110. *Centennial Expressions.* Cf. the centennial issue of the *Fraye Arbeter Shtime*, published in December 1942.

111. Alexander Berkman, "Looking Backward and Forward," *Mother Earth*, December 1912; *Centennial Expressions*, p. 36.

112. *The Letters of Sacco and Vanzetti*, ed. Marion Denman Frankfurter and Gardner Jackson (New York, 1928), p. 108. Vanzetti (pp. 176, 275) also praised Kropotkin's history of the French Revolution and his *Encyclopaedia Britannica* article on anarchism.

113. *I. F. Stone's Bi-Weekly*, December 1971; interview with Harold Hayes, Channel 13, New York, February 3, 1975.

SIX : STORMY PETREL: ANATOLI ZHELEZNIAKOV

1. N. N. Sukhanov, *The Russian Revolution, 1917*, tr. and ed. Joel Carmichael (New York, 1955), p. 306.

2. *Izvestiia Petrogradskogo Soveta*, June 9, 1917.

3. Sukhanov, *The Russian Revolution*, p. 446.

4. *Golos Anarkhii* (Saratov), September 21, 1917.

5. *Bulletin of the Relief Fund of the International Working Men's Association for Anarchists and Anarcho-Syndicalists Imprisoned or Exiled in Russia* (edited by Alexander Berkman), March 1927.

6. I. E. Amurskii, *Matros Zhelezniakov* (Moscow, 1968), pp. 121-27; Norman Saul, *Sailors in Revolt: The Russian Baltic Fleet in 1917* (Lawrence, Kans., 1978), pp. 176, 188-89.

7. I. N. Steinberg, quoted in John Keep, *The Russian Revolution: A Study in Mass Mobility* (New York, 1976), p. 329.

8. *Goneniia na anarkhizm v Sovetskoi Rossii*, ed. Volin et al. (Berlin, 1922), p. 53.

9. "Lezhit pod kurganom, zarosshim bur'ianom, matros Zhelezniak, partizan" (Mikhail Golodnoi).

10. Volin, *The Unknown Revolution, 1917-1921*, rev. ed. (Detroit and Chicago, 1974), p. 238. Emphasis in original.

11. *Den' poezii* (Leningrad, 1970), pp. 30-31.

SEVEN : NESTOR MAKHNO: THE MAN AND THE MYTH

1. Victor Serge, *Memoirs of a Revolutionary, 1901-1941* (London, 1963), p. 121; Emma Goldman, *My Disillusionment in Russia* (London, 1925), p. 166.

2. N. Makhno, *Pod udarami kontr-revoliutsii (aprel'-iiun' 1918 g.)* (Paris, 1936), p. 93.

3. Isaac Babel, "Discourse on the Tachanka," *The Collected Stories* (Cleveland, 1960), pp. 83-86. I have altered the translation slightly.

4. P. A. Arshinov, *History of the Makhnovist Movement (1918-1921)* (Detroit and Chicago, 1974), p. 121; Volin: *The Unknown Revolution, 1917-1921* (Detroit and Chicago, 1974), pp. 307-308.

283

5. N. Makhno, *Russkaia revoliutsiia na Ukraine (ot marta 1917 g. po aprel' 1918 g.); Pod udarami kontr-revoliutsii (aprel'-iiun' 1918 g.); Ukrainskaia revoliutsiia (iiul'-dekabr' 1918 g.)*; reprinted in a one-volume edition in 1977. Volume 1 has been translated into French, German, Spanish, and Italian.

6. "Proclamations of the Machno Movement, 1920," *International Review of Social History*, 1968, part 2; Arshinov, *History of the Makhnovist Movement*, pp. 265-84. Fedeli was himself the author of a short but useful study of the Makhnovshchina: *Della insurrezione dei contadini in Ucraina alla rivolta di Cronstadt* (Milan, 1950).

7. Eric Hobsbawm, *Primitive Rebels* (New York, 1959), pp. 183-86.

8. L.Trotsky, *Stalinism and Bolshevism* (New York, 1937), pp. 22-23.

9. Paul Avrich, ed., *The Anarchists in the Russian Revolution* (Ithaca, 1973), p. 132.

10. George Woodcock, *Anarchism* (Cleveland, 1962), p. 419.

11. Alexander Berkman, *The Bolshevik Myth (Diary 1920-1922)* (New York, 1925), p. 191.

12. Goldman, *My Disillusionment in Russia*, pp. 148-49. As with Razin and Pugachev, songs about Makhno are still sung in the Soviet Union.

13. Volin, *The Unknown Revolution*, p. 631.

14. Ibid., p. 633.

15. Serge, *Memoirs of a Revolutionary*, p. 161.

16. Volin, *The Unknown Revolution*, p. 625; David Footman, *Civil War in Russia* (London, 1961), p. 276.

17. Makhno, *Pod udarami kontr-revoliutsii*, p. 93.

18. Arshinov, *History of the Makhnovist Movement*, p. 242.

19. *Organizatsionnaia platforma vseobshchego souiza anarkhistov* (Paris, 1926).

20. Makhno himself rejected such charges as "vicious rumors" spread by "political agents or charlatans." *The Road to Freedom*, November 1927. See also Alexander Berkman, "Some Bolshevik Lies about the Russian Anarchists," *Freedom*, April 1922.

21. Volin, *The Unknown Revolution*, pp. 698-700. See also *Man!*, September-October 1934.

22. Malcolm Menzies, *Makhno: Une épopée* (Paris, 1972), pp. 213-52; Alexandre Skirda, *Nestor Makhno: Le cosaque de l'anarchie* (Paris, 1982).

23. Alexander Berkman to Ben Capes, August 25, 1924, Berkman Archive, International Institute of Social History; Berkman to Minna Lowensohn, May 2, 1925, Lowensohn Papers, Avrich Collection, Library of Congress.

24. Quoted in Michael Palij, *The Anarchism of Nestor Makhno, 1918-1921* (Seattle, 1976), p. 243.

25. Abel Paz, *Durruti: Le peuple en armes* (Paris, 1972), pp. 117-20; L. Mercier Vega, *L'Increvable anarchisme* (Paris, 1970), p. 4.

26. Menzies, *Makhno*, pp. 251-52.

EIGHT : V. M. EIKHENBAUM (VOLIN): THE MAN AND HIS BOOK

1. Victor Serge, "In Memory: Boris [sic] Voline," *Politics*, February 1946.

2. In 1840, according to one authority, Yakov Eikhenbaum published an acclaimed Yiddish poem about a chess game. Harold Schefski, "Eikhenbaum, Boris

Mikhailovich," *The Modern Encyclopedia of Russian and Soviet Literature*, VI, 110.

3. M.S. [Mollie Steimer], "Life of a Russian Anarchist," *Freedom*, November 17, 1945. On Volin's life and career see also Mollie Steimer, "A Memorial Tribute to Vsevolod Eikhenbaum Voline," in *Fighters for Anarchism: Mollie Steimer and Senya Fleshin*, ed. Abe Bluestein (New York, 1983), pp. 70-79; G. P. Maximoff, "Vsevolod Mikhailovich Eikhenbaum (Volin)," *Delo Truda-Probuzhdenie*, January 1946; and Rudolf Rocker, preface to Volin, *The Unknown Revolution, 1917-1921* (Detroit and Chicago, 1974), pp. 9-15.

4. See his poem, "Vision," written in St. Petersburg prison in 1907. *An Anthology of Revolutionary Poetry*, ed. Marcus Graham (New York, 1929), pp. 336-337.

5. *Delo Truda-Probuzhdenie*, July 1963.

6. Volin, *Revoliutsiia i anarkhizm* (Kharkov, 1919).

7. Quoted in Daniel and Gabriel Cohn-Bendit, *Obsolete Communism: The Left-Wing Alternative* (New York, 1968), pp. 218-19.

8. Ibid., p. 127.

9. *Pervaia konferentsiia anarkhistskikh organizatsii Ukrainy "Nabat": Deklaratsiia i rezoliutsii* (Buenos Aires, 1922).

10. Interview with Mark E. Clevans (Mratchny), New York, February 15, 1974. Emma Goldman, it might be noted, considered Volin "a highly cultured man, a gifted writer and lecturer." Goldman, *My Disillusionment in Russia* (London, 1925), p. 240.

11. See Paul Avrich, *The Russian Anarchists* (Princeton, 1967), pp. 205-208; and Anthony D'Agostino, *Marxism and the Russian Anarchists* (San Francisco, 1977), pp. 195-220.

12. Avrich, *The Russian Anarchists*, p. 136.

13. Emma Goldman, *Living My Life* (New York, 1931), pp. 786-87; G. P. Maximoff, *The Guillotine at Work* (Chicago, 1940), p. 121.

14. *Ni dieu, ni maître*, ed. Daniel Guérin, 4 vols. (Paris, 1970), IV, 113.

15. Rocker, preface to Volin's *Unknown Revolution*, p. 14.

16. P. A. Arshinov, *Istoriia makhnovskogo dvizheniia (1918-1921 gg.)* (Berlin, 1923).

17. *Encyclopédie Anarchiste*, ed. S. Faure, 4 vols. (Paris, 1934).

18. V. Eikhenbaum, *Stikhotvoreniia* (Paris, 1927).

19. Volin began his analysis of the revolution as an eyewitness and participant during 1917. His views, first evolved in *Golos Truda*, were elaborated in the early 1920s in *Anarkhicheskii Vestnik* and *La Revue Anarchiste* and afterwards in such essays as "La Révolution russe," in *La véritable révolution sociale*, ed. S. Faure (Paris, 1935), pp. 105-227; and Volin, *La Révolution en marche* (Nîmes, 1938).

20. *Organizatsionnaia platforma vseobshchego soiuza anarkhistov* (Paris, 1926).

21. *Otvet neskol'kikh russkikh anarkhistov na Organizatsionnuiu platformu* (Paris, 1927).

22. N. Makhno, *Pod udarami kontr-revoliutsii (aprel'-iiun' 1918 g.)* and *Ukrainskaia revoliutsiia (iiul'-dekabr' 1918 g.)* (Paris, 1936-1937). See also Volin's sympathetic obituary of Makhno, "Der shtendik-farfolgter," *Fraye Arbeter Shtime*, October 12, 1934.

23. Volin, *Le fascisme rouge* (Brussels, 1934).

24. Interview with Ernesto Bonomini, an Italian anarchist exiled in Paris, who attended Volin's classes, North Miami Beach, Florida, January 16, 1985; Alex-

ander Berkman to Michael A. Cohn Papers, April 11, 1927, YIVO Institute for Jewish Research, New York.

25. Emma Goldman, in a letter to a German comrade, described Volin as being "almost destitute." Goldman to Augustin Souchy, July 27, 1937, in *Vision on Fire: Emma Goldman on the Spanish Revolution*, ed. David Porter (New Paltz, N.Y., 1983), p. 43.

26. Quoted in Arthur Lehning, *From Buonarroti to Bakunin* (Leiden, 1970), p. 15.

27. George Woodcock, "The Anarchists in Russia," *Freedom*, May 8, 1954.

28. The original French version, *La Révolution inconnue (1917-1921)*, was published by the Friends of Volin in Paris in 1947, two years after its author's death. It has since appeared in Spanish, Italian, German, Japanese, and Korean translations. An incomplete English version, *The Unknown Revolution (1917-1921)*, was published in two volumes in 1954-1955, and a full edition, in one large volume of over 700 pages, restoring the omitted sections, was published in 1974.

29. *Politics*, February 1946.

30. Mollie Steimer to Paul Avrich, December 9, 1974, Avrich Collection, Library of Congress.

NINE : PROUDHON AND AMERICA

1. Eunice M. Schuster, *Native American Anarchism: A Study of Left-Wing American Individualism* (Northampton, Mass., 1932), pp. 127-28.

2. Charles A. Dana, *Proudhon and His "Bank of the People"* (New York, 1896), pp. 2-5, 15-18.

3. *Liberty*, January 16, 1892.

4. Ibid., February 1906. For an analysis of Greene's financial ideas, see James J. Martin, *Men against the State: The Expositors of Individualist Anarchism in America, 1827-1908*, rev. ed. (Colorado Springs, 1970), pp. 125-38.

5. Twenty years later, referring to the International Working Men's Association, of which he was a member, Greene wrote: "The title of the association is this, *L'Association Internationale des Travailleurs*; and the word *travailleurs* is false rendered, when it is translated working-*men*, instead of being translated, as it ought to be, 'toilers,' without distinction of sex. Working-*women* are 'toilers,' or working-*people*." William B. Greene, *Socialistic, Communistic, Mutualistic, and Financial Fragments* (Boston, 1875), p. 239.

6. For Greene's description of Proudhon, see *The Word*, January 1874.

7. *Liberty*, December 24, 1892.

8. *The Collected Works of Ezra H. Heywood*, ed. Martin Blatt (Weston, Mass., 1985), p. 65.

9. *Liberty*, January 16, 1892.

10. *The Word*, August 1872, January 1874. "You will perceive," wrote Greene to Heywood, "that Proudhon and our dear friend, Josiah Warren, smite on substantially the same anvil." Warren, however, disavowed any connection with Proudhon, whom he associated with the French Revolution and the Jacobin tradition of centralization and compulsion. Ibid., March 1874.

11. "The Life of Benjamin R. Tucker, Described by Himself in the Principality of Monaco at the Age of 74," manuscript, pp. 69, 85-87, Tucker Papers, New York Public Library; Tucker to Ewing C. Baskette, October 11, 1935, Baskette Collec-

tion, University of Illinois; Pearl Johnson Tucker to Joseph Ishill, December 4, 1938, Ishill Collection, Harvard University.

12. *Liberty*, January 5, 1889; Pearl Johnson Tucker to Agnes Inglis, May 27, 1942, Labadie Collection, University of Michigan. Cf. Tucker to Baskette, n.d. [1930s], Baskette Collection: "Greene was one of the finest men that I ever knew. I owe him my appreciation of the giant Proudhon, with whom Greene was personally acquainted."

13. *Liberty*, January 7, 1882.

14. Ibid., May 13, 1883, January 14, 1888. As an interpreter of Proudhon, according to a well-informed anarchist writer, Tucker was "probably unequalled." W. C. Owen, "Tucker and Proudhon," *Freedom*, April-May 1926.

15. P. J. Proudhon, *The General Idea of the Revolution in the Nineteenth Century* (London, 1923), p. 294. Tucker, however, was of two minds regarding the translation. See Tucker to W.C. Owen, June 22, 1927, Ishill Collection; and Tucker to Baskette, March 28, 1935, Baskette Collection.

16. J. B. Robinson, *Economics of Liberty* (Minneapolis, 1916).

17. C. L. Swartz, *What Is Mutualism?* (New York, 1927), p. 51.

18. *The Letters of Sacco and Vanzetti*, ed. Marion Denman Frankfurter and Gardner Jackson (New York, 1928), pp. 155, 288. The manuscript is preserved in the Felicani Collection of the Boston Public Library.

19. *Liberty*, August 22, 1896.

20. Cohen in *Proudhon's Solution of the Social Problem* (New York, 1927), p. 3.

21. Ibid., p. ix.

22. Tucker to C. L. Swartz, July 22, 1930, in *Free Vistas: An Anthology of Life and Letters*, ed. Joseph Ishill, 2 vols. (Berkeley Heights, N.J., 1933-1937), II, 300-301.

TEN : BENJAMIN TUCKER AND HIS DAUGHTER

1. Joseph Ishill to Pearl Johnson Tucker, September 7, 1938, Tucker Papers, New York Public Library.

2. *Liberty*, January 1897.

3. Laurance Labadie to Joseph Ishill, May 7, 1935, Ishill Collection, Harvard University.

4. H. L. Mencken to Joseph Ishill, May 18, 1935, in *The Oriole Press: A Bibliography*, ed. Joseph Ishill (Berkeley Heights, N.J., 1953), p. 332.

5. Henry Appleton, in *The Truth Seeker*, April 2, 1887.

6. *Free Vistas: An Anthology of Life and Letters*, ed. Joseph Ishill, 2 vols. (Berkeley Heights, N.J., 1933-1937), II, 281.

7. See Joseph Ishill to Pearl Johnson Tucker, December 26, 1938, Ishill Collection.

8. Foreword to *Individual Liberty: Selections from the Writings of Benjamin R. Tucker*, ed. C. L. Swartz (New York, 1926), p. v.

9. *Liberty*, June 27, 1896.

10. Andrews to Tucker, May 7, 1876, Tucker Papers.

11. William W. Gordak to George Schumm, July 31, 1898, Labadie Collection, University of Michigan.

12. Voltairine de Cleyre, *Selected Works* (New York, 1914), pp. 115-16; *Liberty*, July 26, 1890.

13. *Freedom*, June 1927; Tucker to Owen, June 22, 1927, Ishill Collection.

14. Emma Goldman, *Living My Life* (New York, 1931), p. 232; Goldman to Agnes Inglis, April 11, 1930, Labadie Collection.

15. Tucker to Joseph Ishill, October 27, 1934, Ishill Collection.

16. Ishill, ed., *Free Vistas*, II, 280-81, 298. Cf. George Schumm's remark that Tucker was "one of the pleasantest of men, without, however, being what we call a 'good fellow.' " Schumm, "Benj. R. Tucker: A Brief Sketch of His Life and Work," *The Freethinkers' Magazine*, July 1893.

17. Bertha F. Johnson to Agnes Inglis, February 12, 1936, Labadie Collection.

18. J. William Lloyd, in *Free Vistas*, ed. Ishill, II, 280.

19. Benjamin R. Tucker to Joseph A. Labadie, August 12, 1888, Labadie Collection.

20. Benjamin R. Tucker to Charles Almy, March 15, 1925, Tucker Papers.

21. Victor S. Yarros, "Philosophical Anarchism: Its Rise, Decline, and Eclipse," *American Journal of Sociology* 41 (January 1936): 471. Yarros, during the late 1880s and early 1890s, was associate editor of *Liberty* and one of its most prolific contributors.

22. Benjamin R. Tucker to editor of *American Journal of Sociology*, April 11, 1936, Tucker Papers.

23. The description is J. William Lloyd's, *Free Vistas*, ed. Ishill, II, 282-83.

24. Benjamin R. Tucker to George Schumm, June 28, 1937, Tucker Papers.

25. Alexis Ferm, the anarchist educator, noted Tucker's "simple delight in all that pertains to the child, and if there is any relationship between man and woman that is more dignified than that of yourself and Pearl, we have yet to meet it." Ferm to Tucker, December 18, 1908, Tucker Papers.

26. Tucker to Almy, March 15, 1925, Tucker Papers. "I know of no man," wrote C. L. Swartz of Tucker, "who has come nearer to living his life according to his philosophy and to his desires than he." Ishill, ed., *Free Vistas*, II, 300.

27. Bool was a British-born furniture dealer in Ithaca, New York, who supported Tucker's publishing ventures. He returned to his boyhood home at Montecute, Somerset, where he died in 1922.

28. Mackay, a half-Scottish, half-German anarchist of the individualist school, was a contributor to *Liberty* and a friend of Tucker's until his death in 1933. His remarkable novel, *Die Anarchisten*, was published by Tucker in an English translation in 1891.

29. Hopkins, a libertarian socialist, had run an experimental school in Santa Barbara, California, from 1912 to 1918. In 1926 he started another school near Paris, which continued for several years, and it was during the late 1920s or early 1930s that he visited Tucker at Monaco.

30. Tucker's only book, *Instead of a Book: By a Man Too Busy to Write One* (New York, 1893), was actually a selection of his writings in *Liberty*.

31. According to W. C. Owen, Tucker had "always been removed from life," and his work "smacks too much of the fine abstractions philosophers have written from time immemorial." Owen to Joseph A. Labadie, December 5, 1913, Labadie Collection. In a similar vein, George Bernard Shaw observed: "Tucker is a very decent fellow; but he persists, like most intellectuals, in dictating conditions to a world which has to organise itself in obedience to the laws of life which he doesn't understand any more than you or I." Shaw to James Gibbons Huneker, April 6, 1904, in Shaw's *Collected Letters, 1898-1910*, ed. Dan H. Laurence (New York, 1972), pp. 415-16.

32. Macdonald was a former Tuckerite and longtime editor of *The Truth Seeker,* a leading free-thought publication.

ELEVEN : C. W. MOWBRAY: A BRITISH ANARCHIST IN AMERICA

1. Paul Avrich, *The Modern School Movement: Anarchism and Education in the United States* (Princeton, 1980), p. 213.

2. Hermia Oliver, *The International Anarchist Movement in Late Victorian London* (London, 1983), p. 162; Nicolas Walter, introduction to Charlotte M. Wilson, *Three Essays on Anarchism* (Sanday, Orkney, 1979).

3. William Morris to Jane Morris, September 22, 1885, *The Letters of William Morris to His Family and Friends* (London, 1950), p. 239; May Morris, *William Morris: Artist, Writer, Socialist,* 2 vols. (Oxford, 1936), II, 223-25.

4. C. W. Mowbray to William Morris, October 4, 1886, Socialist League Archive, International Institute of Social History, Amsterdam.

5. J. W. Mackail, *The Life of William Morris,* 2 vols. (London, 1899), II, 170-71. See also C. W. Mowbray, "Prison Life in England," *The Commonweal,* November 12, 1887 ff.

6. *The Commonweal,* November 24, 1888.

7. Ibid., November 28, 1890, November 21, 1891; John Quail, *The Slow Burning Fuse* (London, 1978), p. 92.

8. *The Commonweal,* April 9, 1892.

9. F. S. Merlino, "The Zurich Congress," *Solidarity,* August 26, 1893.

10. C. W. Mowbray, "Strikes, Organized Labor and the Militia," *Solidarity,* February 1, 1895; *L'Ami des Ouvriers,* September 1894; Oliver, *The International Anarchist Movement,* p. 55. See also *El Esclavo,* September 9, 1894.

11. "A Letter from Comrade Mowbray," *Solidarity,* January 1, 1895; Voltairine de Cleyre, *The Past and Present of the Ladies' Liberal League* (Philadelphia, 1895), p. 6, and "Mowbray's Arrest," *Solidarity,* January 15, 1895: *L'Ami des Ouvriers,* January 1895.

12. C. W. Mowbray to Josef Peukert, March 5, 1895, Peukert Archive, International Institute of Social History; Mowbray to Max Metzkow, April 28, 1895.

13. *Solidarity,* April 1, 1895; *The Firebrand,* August 18, 1895; *The Rebel,* October 20, 1895; C. W. Mowbray to Josef Peukert, November 11, 1895, Peukert Archive.

14. Harry Kelly, "Roll Back the Years," unpublished autobiography, ch. 4, p. 2, Avrich Collection, Library of Congress; Emma Goldman, *Living My Life* (New York, 1931), p. 178.

15. Harry Kelly, "An Anarchist in the Making," *Mother Earth,* April 1913.

16. *The Star* (London), December 14, 1910. According to Harry Kelly, Mowbray drank himself to death.

TWELVE : SACCO AND VANZETTI: THE ITALIAN ANARCHIST
BACKGROUND

1. *The Sacco-Vanzetti Case: Transcript of the Record of the Trial of Nicola Sacco and Bartolomeo Vanzetti in the Courts of Massachusetts and Subsequent Proceedings, 1920-7,* 6 vols. (New York, 1928-1929), V, 5065. [Hereafter cited as *The Sacco-Vanzetti Case.*]

2. Herbert B. Ehrmann, *The Untried Case: The Sacco-Vanzetti Case and the Morelli Gang* (New York, 1933).

3. *The Sacco-Vanzetti Case*, V, 5378l.

4. *The Nation*, November 23, 1921.

5. *Sacco-Vanzetti: Developments and Reconsiderations—1979* (Boston, 1982), p. 4.

6. *The Letters of Sacco and Vanzetti*, ed. Marion Denman Frankfurter and Gardner Jackson (New York, 1928), p. 274; Bartolomeo Vanzetti, *The Story of a Proletarian Life* (Boston, 1923), p. 20.

7. Peter Kropotkin, *Memoirs of a Revolutionist* (Boston, 1899), p. 394.

8. Max Nettlau, *Saverio Merlino* (Montevideo, 1948).

9. Carlo Molaschi, *Pietro Gori* (Milan, 1959), p. 15, gives a figure of three hundred meetings.

10. See Ugo Fedeli, *Giuseppe Ciancabilla* (Imola, 1965).

11. On Malatesta's sojourn in America, see Max Nettlau, *Errico Malatesta: Vita e pensieri* (New York, n.d.), pp. 255-56; Armando Borghi, *Errico Malatesta* (Milan, 1947), pp. 135-39; and Luigi Fabbri, *Malatesta* (Buenos Aires, 1945), pp. 113-15.

12. William O. Reichert, *Partisans of Freedom: A Study in American Anarchism* (Bowling Green, Ohio, 1976).

13. Luigi Galleani, *The End of Anarchism?*, tr. Max Sartin and Robert D'Attilio (Sanday, Orkney, 1982).

14. For this account of Galleani's career, I have drawn on Ugo Fedeli, *Luigi Galleani: Quarant'anni di lotte rivoluzionarie (1891-1931)* (Cesena, 1956); "Luigi Galleani: Note biografiche," *L'Adunata dei Refrattari*, December 19, 1931; "Luigi Galleani non è più," *L'Emancipazione*, December 15, 1931; and "Luigi Galleani: 12 agosto 1861-4 novembre 1931," *Studi Sociali* (Montevideo), January 10, 1932.

15. Paul Ghio, *L'Anarchisme aux Etats-Unis* (Paris, 1903), p. 140.

16. *Freedom*, June 1907.

17. Galleani, *The End of Anarchism?*, p. 5.

18. *Pensiero e Volontà*, June 1, 1926, in Vernon Richards, ed. *Errico Malatesta: His Life and Ideas* (London, 1965), p. 34. See also Max Nettlau, "Luigi Galleani (1861-1931)," *Die Internationale*, January 1932.

19. Fedeli, *Luigi Galleani*, pp. 189-90; Nettlau, "Luigi Galleani."

20. *Free Society*, September 24, 1899.

21. See Robert D'Attilio, "La Salute è in Voi: The Anarchist Dimension," in *Sacco-Vanzetti: Developments and Reconsiderations*, pp. 75-89.

22. Interestingly, as Robert D'Attilio has shown, the phrase itself, attributed to Vanzetti before his execution, was in fact invented by the reporter who interviewed him in his cell. *Journal of American History* 69 (December 1982): 793-96.

23. Errico Malatesta, *A Talk Between Two Workers* (Oakland, 1933), p. iii.

THIRTEEN : JEWISH ANARCHISM IN THE UNITED STATES

1. Anarchism, as one devotee remarked, does "not wipe out nationality." Interview with Israel Ostroff, Bronx, N.Y., September 28, 1972. The history of Jewish anarchism in eastern Europe and other areas lies outside the scope of this study, which limits itself to the United States.

2. In her memoirs, Emma Goldman calls them "young men of ability and promise." Goldman, *Living My Life* (New York, 1951), p. 55.

3. Joseph Jaffa, "Di arbeter-bavegung in Niu-York," *Varhayt*, March 1, 1889.

4. *Der gezetslekher mord in Shikago fun 11 November 1887*, ed. Roman Lewis (New York, 1889), with a poem by David Edelstadt. The death sentences of two of the seven Haymarket defendants were commuted to life imprisonment, and a third defendant committed suicide in his cell. On the impact of Haymarket on the Jewish radicals in New York, see also S. Yanovsky, *Ershte yorn fun yidishn frayhaytlekhn sotsializm* (New York, 1948), p. 413.

5. Marcus Graham, "Anarchists: Chaim Weinberg," *Man!*, April 1933; Abraham Cahan, *The Education of Abraham Cahan* (Philadelphia, 1969), p. 413.

6. Morris Hillquit, *Loose Leaves from a Busy Life* (New York, 1934), p. 5.

7. I. Kopeloff, *Amol in Amerike* (Warsaw, 1928), pp. 113-14; E. Tcherikower, *The Early Jewish Labor Movement in the United States* (New York, 1961), pp. 220-21.

8. L. Lipotkin [Lazarev], "Russkoe anarkhicheskoe dvizhenie v Severnoi Amerike," manuscript, pp. 112-15, International Institute of Social History, Amsterdam.

9. See Lloyd P. Gartner, *The Jewish Immigrant in England, 1870-1914* (Detroit, 1960), pp. 100-37; and William J. Fishman, *East End Jewish Radicals, 1878-1914* (London, 1975).

10. *The Alarm*, January 19, 1889.

11. H. Burgin, *Di geshikhte fun der yidisher arbeter bavegung in Amerike, Rusland un England* (New York, 1915), pp. 49 ff.; Rudolf Rocker, *The London Years* (London, 1956), p. 125; Tcherikower, *Early Jewish Labor Movement*, p. 226. See also Jaffa to the Council of the Socialist League, September 19, 1887, Socialist League Archive, International Institute of Social History.

12. On the *Varhayt* and its history, see Elias Schulman, "Di 'Varhayt,' " in *Zamlbukh lekoved dem tsvey hundert un utsiken yoyvl fun der yidisher prese, 1686-1936*, ed. Jacob Shatsky (New York, 1937), pp. 197-211.

13. *Tfileh Zakeh*, nos. 1-5, New York, 1889-1893. The contributors included Edelstadt, Solotaroff, and Maryson.

14. Tcherikower, *Early Jewish Labor Movement*, pp. 259-60. It was the anarchists of Whitechapel who, in 1888, started the custom of holding a ball on Yom Kippur.

15. *New York Sun*, September 24, 1890. See also Tcherikower, *Early Jewish Labor Movement*, p. 261; and Moses Rischin, *The Promised City: New York's Jews, 1870-1914* (Cambridge, Mass., 1962), p. 155.

16. *Fraye Arbeter Shtime*, October 10, 1890; Tcherikower, *Early Jewish Labor Movement*, p. 264.

17. *Tfileh Zakeh*, no. 3, 1891; *Fraye Arbeter Shtime*, October 16, 23, 30, 1891; Tcherikower, *Early Jewish Labor Movement*, pp. 264-65.

18. *Fraye Arbeter Shtime*, August 8, 1890.

19. J. Most, "Der nayer yetsies mitsraim," *Varhayt*, February 15, 1889.

20. Hillquit, *Loose Leaves*, p. 5.

21. Such as "Political action vs. propaganda by the deed" and "Is it necessary for the workers to agitate for an eight-hour day?" *Fraye Arbeter Shtime*, October 10, 1890; Melech Epstein, *Jewish Labor in U.S.A.*, 2 vols. in 1 (New York, 1969), I 199; J. A. Maryson, "Der ershter period fun der anarkhistisher bavegung," *Moyshe Katz Zamlbukh*, ed. A. Frumkin and Chaim Feinman (Philadelphia, 1925), p. 31; Kopeloff, *Amol in Amerike*, pp. 230-31; Tcherikower, *Early Jewish Labor Movement*, p. 224.

22. *Di Konventsion: An di yidishe arbeter fun Amerike* (New York, 1889); *New*

York Sun, December 26, 1889. See also Kopeloff's letter in the *Arbeter Fraynd*, January 24, 1890; A. Cahan, *Bleter fun mayn lebn*, 2 vols. (New York, 1926), II 13-15; and B. Weinstein, *Fertsik yor in der yidisher arbeter-bavegung* (New York, 1924), p. 118.

23. Among the other prominent anarchists in attendance were Max Girzdansky of New York, S. Garson of Baltimore, and Max Staller, Chaim Weinberg, and Isidore Prenner of Philadelphia.

24. Cahan, *Bleter*, II, 15; Epstein, *Jewish Labor*, I, 205. See also the reports in the *Arbeter Fraynd* by Michael Cohn (January 17, 1890), Louis Miller (February 21, 1890), and Roman Lewis (February 28, 1890).

25. On the character and history of the *Fraye Arbeter Shtime*, see H. Frank, "60 yor 'Fraye Arbeter Shtime,' " *Fraye Arbeter Shtime*, February 16, 1951; Shelby Shapiro, "Freie Arbeter Shtime," *Cienfuegos Press Anarchist Review*, no. 5 (1981): 60; and P. Constan [Ahrne Thorne], "Oldest Anarchist Journal Suspends Publication," *C.I.R.A. Bulletin*, no. 35 (Summer 1978): 8-10.

26. *Fraye Arbeter Shtime*, January 1, 1891, February 16, 1951; Epstein, *Jewish Labor*, I, 43. Lewis committed suicide in 1918.

27. For the early editors of the *Fraye Arbeter Shtime*, see Joseph J. Cohen to Agnes Inglis, April 19, 1945, Labadie Collection, University of Michigan.

28. Emma Goldman to Thelma Koldofsky, February 1, 1936, Nettlau Archive, International Institute of Social History.

29. Goldman, *Living My Life*, p. 55.

30. On Edelstadt's life and work, see *Dovid Edelstadt Gedenk-Bukh* (New York, 1953); D. Edelstadt, *Shriften* (London, 1910); and Kalman Marmor, *Dovid Edelstadt* (New York, 1950).

31. Sonia Edelstadt Keene to Paul Avrich, December 9, 1974, Avrich Collection, Library of Congress. In 1948, it might be noted, a *Kropotkin Zamlbukh*, edited by J. Sigal, was published by the Edelstadt Group of Buenos Aires.

32. See "M. Katzes tetikayt in der anarkhistisher un sotsial-revolutsionerer bavegung." in *Moyshe Katz Zamlbukh*, ed. Frumkin and Feinman.

33. *Fraye Arbeter Shtime*, January 1, 1891, January 1, 1892.

34. I. Rudash [Rudashevsky], "An Evening with Elisée Reclus," *Man!*, April 1938. During an earlier trip to New York, in 1889, Reclus had called on Johann Most in the offices of the *Freiheit*.

35. Joseph J. Cohen, *Di yidish-anarkhistishe bavegung in Amerike* (Philadelphia, 1945), p. 194.

36. *Tfileh Zakeh*, the Yom Kippur annual of the Pioneers of Liberty, ceased to appear after the 1893 issue, also a victim of the depression.

37. See, for example, *The Firebrand*, October 4, 1896.

38. On *Di Fraye Gezelshaft* see A. Frumkin, *In friling fun yidishn sotsializm* (New York, 1940), pp. 79-85. Leontieff served also as a consultant in the construction of the George Washington Bridge, which bears a bronze plaque in his honor.

39. Interview with Sophia Janoff [Yanovsky], Bronx, N.Y., June 1, 1972.

40. Yanovsky, *Ershte yorn*, pp. 95-101.

41. Rocker, *London Years*, p. 128.

42. Ibid., pp. 129-30. Yanovsky's oratorical style, in the description of his biographer, was "witty, sharp, volcanic, explosive." Abba Gordin, *S. Yanovsky: Zayn lebn, kemfn un shafn, 1864-1939* (Los Angeles, 1957), p. 129.

43. Lucy Robins Lang, *Tomorrow Is Beautiful* (New York, 1948), p. 112; interview with Israel Ostroff, September 28, 1972.

44. Cohen, *Di yidish-anarkhistishe bavegung*, p. 92.

45. Emma Goldman to Dear Comrade, April 16, 1929, Goldman Archive, International Institute of Social History; Alexander Berkman to Minna Lowensohn, February 2, n.y. [1930?], Avrich Collection; interview with Bessie Zoglin, New York, February 3, 1977. See also Berkman to Michael Cohn, December 16, 1930, Berkman Archive, International Institute of Social History.

46. See Paul Avrich, *An American Anarchist: The Life of Voltairine de Cleyre* (Princeton, 1978).

47. Pressed for time, Yanovsky could dictate a whole column directly to the printer, who "set it up as he talked." Interview with Morris Ganberg, Bronx, N.Y., February 2, 1974.

48. Epstein, *Jewish Labor*, I 207. Cf. Charles A. Madison, *Yiddish Literature* (New York, 1968), p. 138.

49. Radio interview with P. Constan [Ahrne Thorne], WBAI, New York, June 18, 1976; Constan, "Oldest Anarchist Journal," p. 9.

50. S. Yanovsky, "Kropotkin kakim ia ego znal," in *P. A. Kropotkin i ego uchenie*, ed. G. P. Maximoff (Chicago, 1931), p. 219.

51. Interview with Israel Ostroff, September 28, 1972.

52. *Fraye Arbeter Shtime*, January 7, 1911.

53. Ibid., September 20, 1901; Rischin, *Promised City*, p. 161.

54. *Free Society*, September 18, 1904. Cf. the announcement of a Yom Kippur ball, held on September 28, 1906, sponsored by the Edelstadt Group of Chicago, Michael A. Cohn Papers, YIVO Institute for Jewish Research, New York.

55. Kopeloff, *Amol in Amerike*, p. 458, quoted in Nora Levin, *While Messiah Tarried: Jewish Socialist Movements, 1871-1917* (New York, 1977), p. 172.

56. Maximoff, ed., *P. A. Kropotkin i ego uchenie*, p. 332.

57. Rocker, *London Years*, p. 80.

58. On the Workmen's Circle see J. S. Hertz, *Fuftsik yor arbeter ring in yidishn lebn* (New York, 1950); and Judah J. Shapiro, *The Friendly Society: A History of the Workmen's Circle* (New York, 1970).

59. *Man!*, April 1933; Avrich, *An American Anarchist*, p. 133; interview with Morris Beresin, Philadelphia, November 28, 1971.

60. Ferrer's execution in 1909, mourned in bold headlines in the *Fraye Arbeter Shtime* (October 16, 1909), inspired the founding of more than twenty such schools in the United States. See Paul Avrich, *The Modern School Movement: Anarchism and Education in the United States* (Princeton, 1980).

61. The Anarkhie Group, the Likht Group, the International Group, the Fraye Arbeter Shtime Group, the Broyt un Frayhayt Group, the Germinal Group, the Jewish Self-Education Group, the Shturm Group, the Frayhayt Group, and the Friends of Art and Education Group.

62. Delegates attended from New York, Philadelphia, Boston, Baltimore, Paterson, Chicago, Winnipeg, and other cities. *Fraye Arbeter Shtime*, January 7, 1911; *The Agitator*, January 15, 1911. The Federated Anarchist Groups was succeeded in 1914 by the Anarchist Federation of America, which itself disbanded two years later.

63. See Paul Avrich, *The Russian Anarchists* (Princeton, 1967), pp. 66-67.

64. Quoted in Rischin, *Promised City*, p. 199.

65. See S. Linder, "Max N. Maisel," *Fraye Arbeter Shtime*, November 1, 1959.

66. Yanovsky, "Kropotkin kakim ia ego znal," p. 216.

67. *Di Abend Tsaytung*, March 11, 21, 30, and April 11, 1906; *Fraye Arbeter Shtime*, December 29, 1906.

68. Boris Yelensky, *In the Struggle for Equality: The Story of the Anarchist Red Cross* (Chicago, 1958); Avrich, *The Russian Anarchists*, pp. 113-14; *Fraye Arbeter Shtime*, February 10, 1956; interview with Morris Ganberg, Bronx, N.Y., February 2, 1974.

69. Maryson himself did some of the most difficult translations, including Stirner and Marx. According to one estimate, the Kropotkin Literary Society had three thousand members at its peak. *Fraye Arbeter Shtime*, January 1970.

70. *Mother Earth*, May 1915.

71. *Fraye Arbeter Shtime*, December 26, 1914. Other Jewish anarchists, including Michael Cohn, took a strongly pro-German view. Ibid., November 21, 1914; *Mother Earth*, December 1914.

72. *Fraye Arbeter Shtime*, April 17, 1917, cited in Z. Szajkowski, *Jews, Wars, and Communism*, 4 vols. (New York, 1972-1977), I, 72.

73. Emma Goldman, *The Truth about the Boylsheviki* [sic] (New York, 1918), pp. 5, 10; Lang, *Tomorrow Is Beautiful*, p. 112.

74. Louis Levine, *The Women's Garment Workers* (New York, 1924), p. 494.

75. *Di yidish-anarkhistishe bavegung* (see note 35 above).

76. Alexander Berkman to Michael Cohn, November 7, 1930, Berkman Archive; Berkman to Minna Lowensohn, February 2, n.y. [1930?], Avrich Collection. Cf. Abraham Blecher, "Problems of Theory and Practice," *The Road to Freedom*, August 1 and 15, September 1, 1926.

77. For example, *Yubiley Zaml-Bukh, 1899-1929* (New York, 1929), in honor of the thirtieth anniversary of the revival of the paper under Yanovsky.

78. The English page, titled the "Voice of Youth," was "not really a youth organ," recalled one young anarchist of the period, "but old-fashioned and outdated, almost a translation of the Yiddish into English." Interview with Louis Slater, Long Beach, N.Y., October 27, 1972.

79. Other works published under the imprint of the *Fraye Arbeter Shtime* or of the Jewish Anarchist Federation were Armando Borghi's *Mussolini, Red and Black* (1938) and two pamphlets by Rudolf Rocker on the Spanish Civil War: *The Truth about Spain* (1936) and *The Tragedy of Spain* (1937).

80. On March 23, 1925, both Yanovsky and Cohen spoke at a dinner in New York to raise funds for the museum. *The Road to Freedom*, March 1925. A letter to Cohen from Kropotkin's widow Sophie, dated January 19, 1926, acknowledges receipt of $150. Cohen Papers, Bund Archives of the Jewish Labor Movement, New York.

81. Benjamin Axler, secretary of the Jewish Anarchist Federation, to Max Nettlau, July 11, 1929, Nettlau Archive.

82. *Der Yunyon Arbeter*, December 4 and 21, 1925, November 8, 15, and 22, 1926. See also Abraham Blecher, "The War in the International Ladies' Garment Workers' Union," *The Road to Freedom*, August 1925; Simon Farber, "Di frayhaytlekhe sotsialistn un di treyd-yunyon bavegung," *Fraye Arbeter Shtime*, February 16, 1951; and "An Important Declaration," leaflet of the Anarchist Workers' Group, 1925, Labadie Collection.

83. The Anarchist Red Cross, it might be noted, was revived in 1924 and issued an appeal "To the Workers of America: Save Your Brothers Tortured in the Prisons of Russia." *Behind the Bars*, January 1924.

84. Rudolf Rocker to Ben Capes, April 16, 1941, Cohen Papers, Bund Archives;

Rocker, *London Years*, p. 34. From the moment of his arrival, Rocker became a force within the Jewish anarchist movement in America, lecturing from coast to coast, writing for the *Fraye Arbeter Shtime*, and producing a series of books that made a permanent contribution to anarchist philosophy and history.

85. See Joseph J. Cohen, "The Sunrise Co-operative Farm Community," *Freedom* (New York), June 1933; and Cohen, *In Quest of Heaven: The Story of the Sunrise Co-operative Farm Community* (New York, 1957).

86. Interview with Mark E. Clevans [Mratchny], New York, February 15, 1974. On Mratchny see Rudolf Rocker, *Revolutsie un regresie*, 2 vols. (Buenos Aires, 1963), I, 251-52; Avrich, *The Russian Anarchists*, pp. 206, 222, 232-35; and P. Constan [Ahrne Thorne], "Tsu di shloyshim nokh unzer gutn khaver Mark Mratchny," *Fraye Arbeter Shtime*, May-June 1975.

87. Michael Cohn to Alexander Berkman, December 29, 1930, Berkman Archive.

88. Thomas H. Bell to the *Fraye Arbeter Shtime*, May 13, 1940, Labadie Collection.

89. Isidore Wisotsky, "Such a Life," manuscript, Labadie Collection, p. 322. See also Wisotsky's recollections in *New York Times Magazine*, October 12, 1958.

90. *New York Times*, June 5, 1977.

91. A one-hour documentary. "The Free Voice of Labor: The Jewish Anarchists," was made by Pacific Street Films in 1980 and shown in theaters and on television throughout the United States and in several foreign countries. Ahrne Thorne, the paper's last editor and a key figure in the film, died on December 13, 1985, just short of his eighty-first birthday.

FOURTEEN : ALEXANDER BERKMAN: A SKETCH

1. Alexander Berkman, *Prison Memoirs of an Anarchist* (New York, 1912); *Now and After: The ABC of Communist Anarchism* (New York, 1929); *The Bolshevik Myth (Diary 1920-1922)* (New York, 1925).

2. Alexander Berkman to Ben Capes, April 25, 1927, Berkman Archive, International Institute of Social History, Amsterdam.

3. Victor Serge, *Memoirs of a Revolutionary, 1901-1941* (London, 1963), p. 154.

4. *New York World*, April 26, 1925.

5. Berkman, *Prison Memoirs of an Anarchist*, p. 86.

6. Berkman to Hudson Hawley, June 12, 1932, Berkman Archive.

7. Berkman, *Prison Memoirs of an Anarchist*, p. 16.

8. Modest Aronstam (later Modest Stein), the "Feyda" of Berkman's and Goldman's memoirs.

9. Berkman, *Prison Memoirs of an Anarchist*, p. 415.

10. Ibid., p. 508.

11. Emma Goldman, *Living My Life* (New York, 1931), p. 398.

12. Richard H. Frost, *The Mooney Case* (Stanford, 1968).

13. *Bulletin of the Relief Fund of the International Working Men's Association*, March 1927; *Fraye Arbeter Shtime*, December 1, 1971.

14, Goldman, *Living My Life*, p. 698.

15. Ibid., p. 709.

16. Alexander Berkman, *The "Anti-Climax": The Concluding Chapter of My Russian Diary "The Bolshevik Myth"* (Berlin, 1925).

17. Berkman to Hudson Hawley, June 12, 1932, Berkman Archive.

18. Berkman, *The Bolshevik Myth*, p. 319.

19. Berkman to Ben Capes, August 25, 1924, Berkman Archive.

20. Emma Goldman, preface to Berkman's *Now and After*, 2d ed. (New York, 1937).

21. Berkman to Max Nettlau, June 28, 1927, Berkman Archive.

22. *New York World*, April 26, 1925.

23. Berkman, *Now and After*, p. 223.

24. Goldman, preface to Berkman, *Now and After*.

25. Berkman, *Prison Memoirs of an Anarchist*, pp. 7-8.

26. *Vanguard*, August-September 1936.

FIFTEEN : RICARDO FLORES MAGÓN IN PRISON

1. See James D. Cockroft, *Intellectual Precursors of the Mexican Revolution, 1903-1913* (Austin, 1968); and John M. Hart, *Anarchism and the Mexican Working Class, 1860-1931* (Austin, 1978).

2. W. C. Owen, "Death of Ricardo Flores Magón," *Freedom*, December 1922.

3. Voltairine de Cleyre, "Written-in-Red (To Our Living Dead in Mexico's Struggle)," *Regeneración*, December 16, 1911.

4. *Regeneración*, February 11, 1911.

5. *The Blast*, March 15, 1916.

6. *Regeneración*, March 16, 1918, English translation in *Land and Liberty: Anarchist Influences in the Mexican Revolution*, ed. David Poole (Sanday, Orkney, 1977), pp. 104-105.

7. Ricardo Flores Magón to Gus Teltsch, December 15, 1920, *Epistolario revolucionario e íntimo*, 3 vols. in 1 (Mexico City, 1925), I, 30.

8. Ralph Chaplin, *Wobbly: The Rough-and-Tumble Story of an American Radical* (Chicago, 1948), pp. 255, 278. The warden at Leavenworth described Flores Magón as a "well educated, cunning Mexican." Quoted in Dirk Raat, *Revoltosos: Mexico's Rebels in the United States, 1903-1923* (College Station, Texas, 1981), p. 273.

9. Lilly Raymond, *Miscellaneous Poems* (Stelton, N.J., 1971). For further information about the Raymonds see *Vicisitudes de la Lucha* (Calgary, Alberta), no. 8 (1975).

10. Flores Magón, *Epistolario revolucionario e íntimo*, reprinted by the Ediciones Antorcha of Mexico City in 1975. One letter from Flores Magón to Lilly Sarnoff, dated March 27, 1922, is preserved in the Weinberger Papers, Yale University.

11. *Ricardo Flores Magón: Su vida, su obra y 42 cartas escritas en ingles durante los dos ultimos años de su prision y de su vida*, tr. Proudhon Carbó (Mexico City, 1976). The most important of the letters have been reprinted as "Prison Letters of Ricardo Flores Magón to Lilly Sarnoff," ed. Paul Avrich, *International Review of Social History* 22 (1977): 379-422.

12. "Prison Letters of Ricardo Flores Magón," pp. 386, 394, 404.

13. Owen, "Death."

14. Vanzetti, it might be noted, was familiar with the case of Flores Magón. See *The Letters of Sacco and Vanzetti*, ed. Marion Denman Frankfurter and Gardner Jackson (New York, 1928), p. 169.

15. Harry M. Daugherty to Harry Weinberger, April 18, 1921, in *Land and Liberty*, ed. Poole, pp. 106-107.

16. Ricardo Flores Magón to Nicolás T. Bernal, December 6, 1920, *Epistolario revolucionario e íntimo*, I, 24.

17. Chaplin, *Wobbly*, p. 310.

18. Alexander Berkman to Michael A. Cohn, December 14, 1922, Michael A. Cohn Papers, YIVO Institute for Jewish Research, New York.

19. *Freedom*, December 1922.

20. Lowell L. Blaisdell, *The Desert Revolution: Baja California 1911* (Madison, 1962), p. 204.

SIXTEEN : MOLLIE STEIMER: AN ANARCHIST LIFE

1. *J. Abrams-Bukh* (Mexico City, 1956), pp. 9-19.

2. Zechariah Chafee, *Free Speech in the United States* (Cambridge, Mass., 1942), pp. 109-110; Zosa Szajkowski, "Double Jeopardy—The Abrams Case of 1919," *American Jewish Archives* 23 (April 1971): 6-32.

3. B. Aurin, "The 'Third Degree,'" *Freedom* (New York), January 15, 1919.

4. For an excellent and comprehensive treatment of the case, see Richard Polenberg, *Fighting Faiths: The Abrams Case, the Supreme Court, and Free Speech* (New York, 1987).

5. *New York Times*, October 18, 1918. See also Richard Polenberg, "Progressivism and Anarchism: Judge Henry D. Clayton and the Abrams Trial," *Law and History Review* 3 (Fall 1985): 397-408.

6. *New York Times*, October 28, 1918; Szajkowski, "Double-Jeopardy," p. 22.

7. *Sentenced to Twenty Years Prison* (New York, 1919), p. 20.

8. Chafee, *Free Speech*, p. 127.

9. Ibid., p. 237.

10. Agnes Inglis to Harry Weinberger, February 9, 1920, Weinberger Papers, Yale University.

11. Emma Goldman, *Living My Life* (New York, 1931), p. 705.

12. Ibid., pp. 701-702.

13. Mollie Steimer, "To My Comrades," *Freedom* (New York), October-November 1919.

14. *Is Opinion a Crime?* (New York, 1920), p. 2.

15. Szajkowski, "Double-Jeopardy," pp. 25-26.

16. Jacob Abrams to Harry Weinberger, March 3, 1920, Weinberger Papers.

17. *Free Society* (New York), October-November 1921.

18. Mollie Steimer to Harry Weinberger, November 19, 1921, Weinberger Papers.

19. *Fraye Arbeter Shtime*, November 26, 1921.

20. Mollie Steimer to Harry Weinberger, December 20, 1921, Weinberger Papers.

21. *Nabat* (Kharkov), March 23, 1919.

22. *Letters from Russian Prisons*, ed. Alexander Berkman (New York, 1925), pp. 92-111.

23. Mollie Steimer, "On Leaving Russia," *Freedom*, January 1924, reprinted in leaflet form as *A Worker's Experience in Russia* (Los Angeles, 1924).

24. Mollie Steimer to Comrade Ginev, November 30, 1927, Fleshin Archive, International Institute of Social History, Amsterdam. See also *Fighters for Anarchism*, ed. Abe Bluestein (New York, 1983), pp. 50-62.

25. Harry Kelly, "Roll Back the Years: Odyssey of a Libertarian," manuscript, Avrich Collection, Library of Congress, ch. 39, p. 4; Emma Goldman to Alexander

Berkman, February 29, 1932, Berkman Archive, International Institute of Social History; Goldman to Michael Cohn, August 12, 1931, Goldman Archive, International Institute of Social History.

26. Mollie Steimer to Paul Avrich, April 18, 1975, Avrich Collection; interview with Clara Larsen, New York, May 21, 1974.

27. Mollie Steimer to Rudolf and Milly Rocker, December 5, 1942, Rocker Archive, International Institute of Social History.

28. Interview with Clara Larsen, May 21, 1974. See also Augustin Souchy, "Zum Gedächtnis Jakob Abrams," *Die Freie Gesellschaft* (Darmstadt), no. 42, 1953, pp. 31-32.

SEVENTEEN : THE PARIS COMMUNE AND ITS LEGACY

1. Engels, quoted in Frank Jellinek, *The Paris Commune, 1871* (London, 1937), p. 176; Marx to Ludwig Kugelmann, April 12, 1871. All other quotations by Marx are from *The Civil War in France* (London, 1871).

2. This and other quotations by Bakunin are from *The Paris Commune and the Idea of the State*, ed. Nicolas Walter (Lausanne, 1971).

3. Guillaume, quoted in Jacques Rougerie, ed., *Procès des Communards* (Paris, 1964), p. 14. All Kropotkin quotations are from his essay *The Commune of Paris*, included in *Freedom Pamphlet* No. 8, ed. Nicolas Walter (London, 1971).

4. Eugene Schulkind, ed., *The Paris Commune of 1871: The View from the Left* (London, 1972), p. 39.

5. Stewart Edwards, ed., *The Communards of Paris, 1871* (London, 1973), p. 135.

6. George Woodcock, *Pierre-Joseph Proudhon* (London, 1956), pp. 276-77.

7. Schulkind, *The Paris Commune*, p. 33.

8. See also Nicolas Walter, "The Paris Commune and the Anarchist Movement," in *Freedom Pamphlet* No. 8, ed. Walter.

9. Alistair Horne, *The Fall of Paris: The Siege and the Commune, 1870-1871* (Garden City, N.Y., 1967), p. 472.

10. Jellinek, *The Paris Commune*, p. 320.

11. Voltairine de Cleyre, *Selected Works* (New York, 1914), p. 246.

12. Schulkind, *The Paris Commune*, p. 27.

13. See Jeanne Gaillard, *Communes de province, Commune de Paris, 1870-1871* (Paris, 1971).

14. Schulkind, *The Paris Commune*, p. 74.

15. *Revolution and Reaction: The Paris Commune of 1871*, ed. John Hicks and Robert Tucker (Amherst, Mass., 1973), p. 113.

16. Schulkind, *The Paris Commune*, p. 294.

17. Paul Avrich, *The Russian Anarchists* (Princeton, 1967), pp. 48, 126.

18. Alexander Berkman, *The Bolshevik Myth (Diary 1920-1922)* (New York, 1925), p. 303.

19. Stewart Edwards, *The Paris Commune, 1871* (London, 1971), preface.

EIGHTEEN : PAUL BROUSSE: THE POSSIBILIST ANARCHIST

1. James Guillaume, *L'Internationale: Documents et souvenirs (1864-1878)*, 4 vols. (Paris, 1905-1910), III, 90-91.

2. Quoted in David Stafford, *From Anarchism to Reformism* (London, 1971), p. 37.

3. Kropotkin, *Memoirs of a Revolutionist* (Boston, 1899), pp. 393-94.

4. Max Nettlau, *Anarchisten und Sozialrevolutionäre* (Berlin, 1931), pp. 131-32; Andrew Carlson, *Anarchism in Germany* (Metuchen, N.J., 1972), pp. 83-84, 401-402.

5. *Arbeiter-Zeitung*, July 15, 1876, quoted in Carlson, *Anarchism in Germany*, p. 84.

6. Propaganda by the deed, wrote Brousse later that year, was "a powerful means of awakening the popular consciousness." *Bulletin de la Fédération Jurassienne*, August 5, 1877, quoted in Jean Maitron, *Le mouvement anarchiste en France*, 2 vols. (Paris, 1975), I, 76-77.

7. J. Langhard, *Die anarchistische Bewegung in der Schweiz* (Berlin, 1903), p. 95; George Woodcock, *Anarchism: A History of Libertarian Ideas and Movements* (Cleveland, 1962), p. 293.

8. Quoted in Theodore Zeldin, *France, 1848-1945*, 2 vols. (Oxford, 1973-1977), I, 753.

9. Stafford, *From Anarchism to Reformism*, pp. 44, 183-84, 246-50.

10. Ibid., pp. 143, 163.

11. Aaron Noland, *The Founding of the French Socialist Party (1893-1905)* (Cambridge, Mass., 1956), pp. 22, 93.

NINETEEN : THE MARTYRDOM OF GUSTAV LANDAUER

1. Max Nettlau, "La vida de Gustav Landauer segun su correspondencia," *La Protesta*, supplement, July 31, 1929, reprinted in *Incitación al socialismo* (Buenos Aires, 1947), pp. 187-325.

2. Wolf Kalz, *Gustav Landauer: Kultursozialist und Anarchist* (Meisenheim am Glan, 1967); Charles B. Maurer, *Call to Revolution: The Mystical Anarchism of Gustav Landauer* (Detroit, 1971); Eugene Lunn, *Prophet of Community: The Romantic Socialism of Gustav Landauer* (Berkeley, 1973); Ruth Link-Salinger (Hyman), *Gustav Landauer: Philosopher of Utopia* (Indianapolis, 1977).

3. Most notably, *Zwang und Befreiung*, ed. Heinz-Joachim Heydorn (Cologne, 1968); *Gustav Landauer und die Revolutionszeit, 1918/19*, ed. Ulrich Linse (Berlin, 1974); and *Erkenntnis und Befreiung*, ed. Ruth Link-Salinger (Hyman) (Frankfurt, 1976).

4. Gustav Landauer, *Shakespeare*, 2 vols. (Frankfurt, 1920), reprinted in 1962: *Briefe aus der französischen Revolution*, 2 vols. (Frankfurt, 1918), reprinted in 1961.

5. Gustav Landauer, *For Socialism* (St. Louis, 1978); *Anarchy*, August 1965; *Social Democracy in Germany* (London, 1896).

6. Rudolf Rocker, *The London Years* (London, 1956), p. 90.

7. Maurer, *Call to Revolution*, p. 47.

8. Next to his marriage, according to Buber's biographer, his friendship with Landauer was the most "decisive relationship of his adult life." Maurice Friedman, *Martin Buber's Life and Work: The Early Years, 1878-1923* (New York, 1981), p. 77.

9. *Der Sozialist*, July 15, 1911, quoted in Lunn, *Prophet of Community*, p. 200.

10. Landauer, *Social Democracy in Germany*, p. 8.

11. Martin Buber, *Paths in Utopia* (Boston, 1958), p. 53; Lunn, *Prophet of Community*, p. 184.

12. James Joll, *The Second International, 1889-1914* (London, 1955), p. 72.

13. Gustav Landauer, *Aufruf zum Sozialismus*, ed. Heinz-Joachim Heydorn (Frankfurt, 1967), p. 93; Landauer, *For Socialism*, p. 60.

14. Max Nettlau, *Michael Bakunin* (Berlin, 1901), pp. 56-58.

15. *Der Sozialist*, January 1, 1910.

16. Quoted in Buber, *Paths in Utopia*, p. 56.

17. Etienne de la Boétie, *A Discourse of Voluntary Servitude*, translated into German by Landauer in *Der Sozialist*, September 1, 1910-January 1, 1911.

18. Quoted in Buber, *Paths in Utopia*, p. 46.

19. Rocker, *The London Years*, p. 90.

20. Quoted in Lunn, *Prophet of Community*, p. 242.

21. Ibid., p. 254.

22. Landauer to Georg Springer, November 27, 1918, quoted in Maurer, *Call to Revolution*, p. 188.

23. See Will Wyatt, *The Man Who Was B. Traven* (London, 1980).

24. *Gustav Landauer: Sein Lebensgang in Briefen*, ed. Martin Buber, 2 vols. (Frankfurt, 1929), II, 424; Lunn, *Prophet of Community*, p. 342.

25. *Gustav Landauer*, II, 421-24; Lunn, *Prophet of Community*, pp. 338-40. Buber described Landauer's murder as a death in which "the inhumanity of our time has been delineated and portrayed." Friedman, *Martin Buber's Life and Work*, p. 256.

TWENTY : BRAZILIAN ANARCHISTS

1. Eric A. Gordon, "Anarchism in Brazil: Theory and Practice, 1890-1920" (Ph.D. diss., Tulane University, 1978), pp. 67-68.

2. See Giovanni Rossi, *Utopie und Experiment* (Zurich, 1897); Afonso Schmidt, *Colônia Cecília* (São Paulo, 1942); and Newton Stadler de Souza, *O anarquismo da colônia Cecília* (Rio de Janeiro, 1970).

3. Quoted in John W. F. Dulles, *Anarchists and Communists in Brazil, 1900-1935* (Austin, 1973), p. 8. On Damiani and Brazilian anarchism in general, see also Edgar Rodrigues, *Socialismo e sindicalismo no Brasil, 1675-1913* (Rio de Janiero, 1969) and *Nacionalismo e cultura social, 1913-1922* (Rio de Janiero, 1972).

4. Quoted in Dulles, *Anarchists and Communists in Brazil*, p. 8.

5. Ibid., p. 15.

6. Sheldon L. Maram, "Anarchists, Immigrants, and the Brazilian Labor Movement, 1890-1920" (Ph.D. diss., University of California, Santa Barbara, 1972), p. 106.

7. Dulles, *Anarchists and Communists in Brazil*, p. 328.

8. Quoted in Gordon, "Anarchism in Brazil," pp. 168-69.

TWENTY-ONE : AN AUSTRALIAN ANARCHIST: J. W. FLEMING

1. Emma Goldman, *Living My Life* (New York, 1931), p. 436.

2. Jim Garvey, "Chummy Fleming, 1863?-1950: A Memoir," Avrich Collection, Library of Congress. I am grateful to John Arrowsmith of Carlton, Victoria, for providing me with a copy of this manuscript.

3. From Fleming's own statements it is unclear whether he was born in 1863 or

1864, but K. J. Kenafick, in his dedication to *Marxism, Freedom and the State* (London, n.d.), gives the year as 1864.

4. *The Tocsin* (Melbourne), October 17, 1901; Sam Merrifield, "John William (Chummy) Fleming," *Recorder: Melbourne Branch, Australian Society for the Study of Labour History*, July 1964, pp. 3-5.

5. Bob James, "Fleming, John William," *Australian Dictionary of Biography*, and *Chummy Fleming: A Brief Biography* (Melbourne, 1986).

6. *The Tocsin*, October 17, 1901.

7. Sam Merrifield, "The Melbourne Anarchist Club, 1886-1891," *Labour History* (Melbourne), no. 3, pp. 32-43.

8. *Freedom*, January 1911.

9. James, "Fleming, John William"; *Freedom*, June 16, 1979.

10. Sam Merrifield to Paul Avrich, September 30, 1977; *100th Australian Anarchist Centenary Celebrations*, leaflet (Melbourne, 1986), Avrich Collection.

11. *The Age*, June 25, 1902.

12. Garvey, "Chummy Fleming."

13. Ibid.; David Stephens to Paul Avrich, September 5, 1977, Avrich Collection.

14. *The Syndicalist*, September 1-15, 1913.

15. *The Age*, April 4, 1904.

16. Quoted in *Freedom*, June 16, 1979. Fleming was echoing the courtroom speech of the French anarchist Emile Henry, delivered in 1894: "You have hanged men in Chicago, cut off their heads in Germany, strangled them in Jerez, shot them in Barcelona, guillotined them in Montbrison and Paris, but what you will never destroy is anarchism." Quoted in James Joll, *The Anarchists* (London, 1964), p. 138.

17. *Freedom*, June 1904.

18. Ibid., August 1911.

19. Ibid., June 1904.

20. Ibid., August 1913.

21. Ibid., January 1911.

22. Goldman, *Living My Life*, pp. 436, 449; *Mother Earth*, March and April 1909.

23. *The Herald of Revolt*, August 1912.

24. Fleming to Emma Goldman, November 12, 1914, in *Mother Earth*, February 1915.

25. *The Labour Call*, July 8, 1915; Bertha Walker, *Solidarity Forever!* (Melbourne, 1972), p. 104.

26. Stuart Christie, introduction to *Man! An Anthology of Anarchist Ideas, Essays, Poetry and Commentaries*, ed. Marcus Graham (London, 1974), p. ii.

27. Garvey, "Chummy Fleming."

28. Fleming to Emma Goldman, January 18, 1933, in *Freedom* (New York), March 18, 1933.

29. Ibid.; *Man!*, November 1938.

30. *Man!*, January 1940.

31. Garvey, "Chummy Fleming."

32. *Melbourne Herald*, June 7, 1947.

33. Walker, *Solidarity Forever!*, p. 271.

Index

303